The New Office Professional's Handbook

FOURTH EDITION

HOUGHTON MIFFLIN COMPANY

Boston New York

Material in Chapter 14 having to do with the accounting process and bank reconciliation is based on information found in *Introduction to Financial Accounting* by Kirkland A. Wilcox and Joseph G. San Miguel. Copyright © 1984 by Harper & Row, Publishers, Inc. Reprinted by permission of HarperCollins Publishers Inc.

Visit our website: www.houghtonmifflinbooks.com

Library of Congress Cataloging-in-Publication Data

The new office professional's handbook. — 4th ed.
    p. cm.
    Rev. ed. of: The professional secretary's handbook. 3rd ed. c1995.
    Includes index.
    ISBN 0-618-03608-3
    1. Office practice—Automation. 2. Secretaries. 3. Secretaries — Vocational guidance.
  I. Title: Professional secretary's handbook.

HF5547.5 .P7 2001
651.3'741 — dc21   2001016911

Manufactured in the United States of America

Book design by Melodie Wertelet

ACKNOWLEDGMENTS

Amtrak is a registered trademark of National Railroad Passenger Corp. Anadex is a registered trademark of Anadex Instruments, Inc. Bufferin is a registered trademark of Bristol-Meyers Products, a division of Bristol-Meyers Squibb Company. Coke is a registered trademark of The Coca-Cola Company.

Dacron is a registered trademark of E. I. DuPont de Nemours & Co. Express mail is a registered trademark of the U.S. Postal Service. Kleenex is a registered trademark of Kimberly-Clark Corporation. Lotus and 1-2-3 are registered trademarks of Lotus Development Corporation.

MasterCard is a registered trademark of MasterCard International, Inc. Microsoft and Word are registered trademarks of Microsoft Corporation. Pepsi is a registered trademark of the Pepsi-Cola Co. Ping-Pong is a registered trademark of Parker Brothers.

Standard & Poor is a registered trademark of Standard & Poor's Corporation. Visa is a registered trademark of Visa International Service Association. Xerox is a registered trademark of Xerox Corporation.

Contents

MAIL PROCESSING   98

DOCUMENT CREATION   119

BUSINESS STYLE GUIDE   156

BUSINESS ENGLISH   207

CORRESPONDENCE   262

INFORMATION MANAGEMENT   308

MEETINGS AND CONFERENCES   332

Preface

For a long time, office professionals have been taking positive steps to enhance their skills and increase their worth to employers. Unexpectedly, this effort got a big boost from late twentieth-century technologies. Instead of being replaced by the new devices and processes, as some had predicted, they were transformed by the emerging technologies into essential administrators and middle managers. They had become indispensable professionals in fact, not just in name or desire. It's at this point that the fourth edition of *The New Office Professional's Handbook* begins — in the rapidly evolving twenty-first-century workplace.

This fourth edition describes the key practices and procedures in today's online office. However, it doesn't neglect the traditional topics, such as business English and career development. Those topics will be with us as long as people talk and write to each other and as long as they look for jobs and pursue careers. This symbiotic mix of new technologies and traditional practices is presented in 14 chapters:

Chapter 1, "The Online Office" profiles a modern office, including the associated technologies. Foremost among them is the personal computer, which has dramatically changed the way that businesses operate. However, the chapter also reviews other key technologies, such as the copier, fax machine, scanner, desk telephone, cell phone, multifunction machine, and miscellaneous other devices, such as the personal digital assistant (PDA). In addition, it describes the way that the Internet and the World Wide Web work and concludes with predictions about the workplace of the future.

Chapter 2, "Professional Career Development" considers how you should prepare yourself for a successful career. It outlines important duties and responsibilities, suggests the necessary education and training to handle them, and concludes with both traditional and new ways to find a job, including how to behave on an interview and how to use the Internet in a job search. The chapter also describes other important avenues of career development, such as networking and professional certification, and tells you how to measure your personal qualities and job skills.

Chapter 3, "Human Relations" deals with the all-important subject of personal interaction in the workplace — how to get along with others. It answers common questions, such as how to introduce an important visitor and how to work with a telecommuter. The chapter also provides tips on working for more than one person and working with assistants and coworkers, including what to do if sexual harassment occurs. It concludes with numerous suggestions for managing your time better in a hectic office atmosphere.

Chapter 4, "Telecommunications" guides you through the world of telephone-related technologies and procedures, including voice mail, domestic and international calling, options in telephone services, and telephone etiquette. This is one of several chapters that unites the new and the old as it blends traditional topics, such as common telephone systems, with new-technology topics, such as cellular and satellite communication.

Chapter 5, "Mail Processing" describes common duties and procedures associated with the main types of electronic and paper mail. It details the necessary steps in handling incoming and outgoing fax mail, e-mail, postal mail, and private-courier mail. The chapter takes an in-depth look at the various transmissions and deliveries and provides practical tips ranging from preparing and sending e-mail to handling hate mail to printing e-postage with your PC.

Chapter 6, "Document Creation" examines the various stages of document preparation from research to duplication, with special attention to in-house word processing and desktop publishing but also including outside photocomposition and printing services. To help you put together an actual document, such as a report, it describes key parts, such as the table of contents (with examples and models), and tells you how to format and write basic elements, such as footnotes and figure captions.

Chapter 7, "Business Style Guide" is a detailed treatment of the points of style that you must know to prepare an intelligent, consistent work. The chapter has extensive do's and don'ts about punctuation, capitalization, spelling, word division, and the use of numbers and symbols. For those who deal with technical matter, it concludes with special sections about preparing mathematical and chemical material and working with the metric system.

Chapter 8, "Business English" is a traditional subject that has as much impact in the twenty-first-century office as it had in any previous office. Since businesspeople must still communicate properly and speak and write correctly, the chapter gives a refresher course in the basics of English grammar, followed by a concise guide to usage. This guide is an extensive list of troublesome, easily confused, and commonly misused words, all with explanations and examples of correct and incorrect usage.

Chapter 9, "Correspondence" gives up-to-date rules and guidelines that apply to writing e-mails and traditional memos and letters, with examples of style and models of common formats. The chapter also provides a collection of sample business messages, such as complaints and introductions. Since one of the most difficult aspects of message composition is knowing how to address someone, such as what title to use, the chapter has a long list of correct forms of address for everyone from a businessperson to a government official to a college professor.

Chapter 10, "Information Management" discusses a vital subject in business — how to control the vast amount of electronic and paper material coming into an office and being generated within an office. The chapter explains the basic procedures in processing material for storage, including the main types of electronic and paper filing systems; how and where the material can be safely stored; and how to control the excessive proliferation of certain material, such as business reports.

Chapter 11, "Meetings and Conferences" deals with a familiar subject in most business environments — meetings held in person, by phone, by computer, and by video transmission. The chapter describes the different types of business meetings, how to arrange and conduct them, what type of seating arrangements to use, and how to prepare common meeting documents, such as agendas and minutes. For those who have not had experience with more formal meetings, the chapter also has a brief primer on parliamentary procedure, including the main types of motions.

Chapter 12, "International and Domestic Travel" describes the steps to follow in collecting travel information and working with a travel agent or using the Internet to make arrangements, with a host of additional tips about international travel. A collection of country profiles concludes the chapter. In a global business environment, office professionals need to know certain basic facts about other countries, and the profiles give such information. They include the main languages spoken and currency used, as well as each country's embassy address and website, when available, for those who want to learn more.

Chapter 13, "Accounting" is both a practical and a legal requirement in business, and those who work in an office should be familiar with the fundamentals of modern accounting. This chapter therefore discusses the basic accounting principles and describes the main financial reports, such as the income statement, including a realistic model of each report. It also describes common office activities, such as replenishing the petty cash fund, and some procedures that may not be so common, such as maintaining a record of interest and dividend income.

Chapter 14, "Business Law" is another subject that office professionals should know something about, and this chapter introduces important legal topics, such as contracts, agency, and corporate law. It describes a valid contract and provides important insights into the matter of agency, such as the fact that an employee is an agent of the employer, and his or her actions may thus have potential consequences for the firm. The chapter also explains the Universal Commercial Code governing commercial transactions and the various laws that regulate business activities.

To help you visualize the material described in these 14 chapters, the book includes hundreds of in-text examples as well as dozens of models and other illustrations. The table of contents provides a summary of main topics in each chapter, and the detailed index at the end of the book directs you to specific subjects. [In addition, cross-references within a chapter will lead you to further information within the same chapter or in another chapter.]

The various topics throughout the book are intended to be beneficial to both beginners and career professionals in all types and sizes of organizations. Especially, the fourth edition carries a message of change, something that office professionals learned about firsthand as they went from taking dictation to taking charge.

Other changes are certain to follow, especially as ever newer technologies cross the office threshold. Among the most important of these changes will be a better-informed workforce, and office professionals will be taking advantage of every opportunity to train themselves to assume greater responsibility and be more competitive in the current and future workplace. *The New Office Professional's Handbook* is one of many resources available to these new administrators and managers, and the previous edition was revised not only to make it current but also to accommodate more fully the needs of today's rising office professional.

The Online Office

The office as we know it — a place where business is handled — has existed for a little more than a century. However the important technologies that power today's office didn't exist in 1900. The term *online office* didn't exist then either and wouldn't be coined until many decades later.

The technology that has contributed the most to productivity in modern business is, indisputably, the computer. Not only has it revolutionized the way that businesses operate, but it has also propelled the evolution of advanced technologies such as computer voice recognition. Nevertheless, the online office, like its predecessor, is still a place where information is received, processed, transmitted, and stored.

To the office professional, the computer has dramatically changed the way that work is performed. For example, as executives began to use their own desktop, notebook, and laptop computers for e-mail and other communications, their assistants had more time to handle additional administrative and supervisory duties.

Although the proliferation of PCs in business is of relatively recent origin, the computer itself is not a recent phenomenon. A massive twentieth-century forerunner, the Electronic Numeric Integrator And Calculator (ENIAC), was built in the 1940s. The personal computer (PC), however, didn't make an appearance until the 1980s, and it deserves most of the credit for revolutionizing office practices and procedures, with a computer on every desk.

AN OFFICE PROFILE

Much of the transition in office duties that was spurred by the PC took place during the last two decades of the twentieth century. To many, though, it seemed to happen overnight, along with the approach of the twenty-first century. A new, more egalitarian office had suddenly arisen from the vanishing corporate hierarchy.

The On-Site Office

Two types of office were evident in the later decades of the previous century: the on-site office and the virtual (remote) office. The on-site office of the twenty-first century is, functionally, a computerized system. This type of office is designed around a PC, copier, fax machine, telephone, and other equipment and technologies, all of which are becoming increasingly integrated.

You may start the day in your office by keying in your personal access code at a computer terminal and calling up (bringing on screen) the information you need to begin work. At the push of a key or click of a mouse, for example, your e-mail in box will appear on screen, listing its contents. Perhaps you'll immediately deal with the urgent messages and quickly route some of the messages or attachments to others in the organization.

Next, you may call up your e-calendar to confirm the time of a meeting you're expected to attend. Shortly, you'll call up files for the projects you're coordinating or managing and work on them in between phone calls, the arrival of visitors, package deliveries, and other daily fare.

The Virtual Office

An on-site office terminal may be connected to various remote terminals located in someone's home, in a hotel room in another state or country, or in someone else's office. As cell phones, fax machines, computers, copiers, and other equipment have become smaller and more affordable, virtual offices that rival the capabilities of on-site offices have been created.

In many companies, telecommuting (also called *telework*) has become a realistic and economically attractive alternative to working on-site in the company's main facilities. This option has enabled more people to work from their homes or from other remote locations apart from the company's regular business offices. As a result, assistants to telecommuting executives often assume more managerial and decision-making responsibilities at the on-site facility.

Like their supervisors, assistants may also work from a virtual office. In other cases, they may use their on-site computers to communicate with virtual offices or remote facilities. For example, instead of researching the company's paper files or visiting a traditional library, they may use their computers to access an electronic library or database in another city or state.

In many ways, the virtual office has become a semi-independent, practical alternative to the on-site office. However, the same computer technology and, by extension, the electronic network that makes a virtual office possible also provide an essential lifeline to the main, on-site office.

Basic Office Arrangements

Company size and information volume. Two factors — company size and information volume — significantly affect the way that offices, departments, and activity centers are set up. In large companies requiring a huge volume of information processing, work is often organized by task and function. Large information-processing centers may be established, although a more diversified pattern may be common too.

Smaller satellite centers, for example, may also exist for more specialized or urgent work in certain departments, in addition to the individual PCs and terminals located throughout the organization. Medium-size companies, however, often have only one or two fairly small information-processing centers.

Companies with a relatively small central office staff are less likely to use task organization. Equipment is often installed on an ad hoc basis and is gradually integrated with other equipment and upgraded as specific needs are identified over time.

Type of information work. The systems that are required in an office are in large part influenced by the type of information processing that is performed:

- Offices in a law firm, a company involved in technical research, or a public relations firm may need a very sophisticated information-processing system, whereas those in a company processing vast amounts of similar information, such as an insurance company or a bank, will need something simpler but more powerful.

- In some offices, the emphasis may be on routing information where it's needed as fast as possible, such as to remote offices or to senior corporate executives. In this type of setting, the communications components, such as local area networks (LANs) or intranets, are vital. For more about networks, see the discussion in The Internet.

- In other offices, the emphasis may be on effective record keeping, such as in a medical research facility or a library. There, the systems will be geared toward software with good database-management capabilities and related systems so that information can be rapidly retrieved through a keyword search. See Keyword retrieval in Chapter 10, "Information Management."

- Still other offices may need computer graphics capability that will enable the user to display graphic information quickly and dramatically. Combining graphics with photocomposition or desktop publishing (see Photocomposition and Desktop publishing in Chapter 6, "Document Creation") enables companies to do more in-house publishing.

The workstation. Managing your workstation properly and efficiently will help you work effectively with your coworkers, assist your supervisors competently, and perform your duties faster and more easily. Arranging the equipment and furniture conveniently, for example, and keeping your workstation neat and well organized will yield benefits day after day.

The system of document creation (see Chapter 6, "Document Creation") that you use should allow you to receive information or data at a moment's notice, promptly produce an error-free document, and immediately transmit or deliver it. This type of capability and efficiency comes from having properly and regularly maintained and serviced equipment and developing the skills needed to operate it.

Furniture. Desks should be functional, compact, versatile, and (one hopes) attractive. Space in an office is often limited, and ideally, almost everything you need during the day will be no more than three to five feet from the focal point of your workstation.

From a seated position on a swivel chair, you should therefore be able to swing around from left to right without any barriers or difficult maneuvering. Equipment and other items on the top of your desk should be organized for maximum efficiency.

Supplies. Basic supplies are always needed to handle a variety of work. They should include specific items required for a particular project, as well as miscellaneous items used in daily activities. The miscellaneous items should include a stapler and staple remover, paper clips, rubber bands, pens, pencils, highlighters, erasers, cellophane tape, and diskettes.

You'll need an employee manual, current equipment and operator instruction manuals, an office handbook, and a recent edition of a collegiate-level dictionary or one geared especially to your profession (in addition to your computer spell-checker). As well as making use of online resources, you should also keep paper copies of office supply catalogs and telephone books within easy reach.

Ergonomics. The term *ergonomics* refers to the design and arrangement of things that people use so that the users can interact safely and efficiently with them. For example, an ergonomically designed business system will be comfortable for the operator to use and will not cause eyestrain, hand fatigue, backache, or any other discomfort.

A typical computer terminal, therefore, should be designed for user comfort, be quiet, have a detachable keyboard, and not produce unnecessary screen glare. It should also allow the user to adjust the monitor to a variety of positions and require only minimal physical effort to operate.

An effective design is essential for a high-performance workplace, whereas an ineffective design is uncomfortable, hinders worker productivity, and is usually counterproductive.

Health concerns. The concentration of a person's time in a single location results in various forms of stress — especially neck, back, and hand strain, as well as eye fatigue — and in a variety of other health problems caused by noise pollution, air pollution, and toxic chemicals. A system that successfully addresses health concerns must be designed with comfort and modularity in mind. These two factors allow users to modify and reconfigure the furniture and hardware as needed.

Computer display problems. Many health problems have been linked to computer displays (monitor screens), including cataracts, birth defects and miscarriages, blurred vision, headaches, backaches, and neck and shoulder pain. Sometimes a unit must be replaced, such as when the unit generating an image on a computer screen is faulty, causing a flicker that induces headaches and eye fatigue.

Manufacturers are making progress, however, in preventing certain problems. Computer terminals, for example, now produce radiation levels *below* government standards for safety. The designs also allow users to sit back from the screen through the use of detached keyboards and movable keyboard trays, further reducing radiation exposure and eye fatigue.

Furniture problems. Eyestrain is a general health problem linked not only to computer screens but also to other parts of the physical work environment. Remedies frequently involve a change in furniture or accessories. When the desk or other lighting is not right, for example, an adjustable lamp may be helpful.

Other common problems such as back and neck strain may be remedied by adjustable chairs. If the seat of a chair isn't set at the right height, it won't provide sufficient back support and may cause wrist and elbow strain while the user is keyboarding.

Repetitive-motion injuries. Common injuries such as elbow tendinitis (similar to tennis elbow) and carpal tunnel syndrome are serious disorders. The latter originates in the upper arm and spreads to the wrists and hands, causing pain and weakness in that region. Preventive measures include the following adjustments in workstation layout and use:

- The chair's seat and back slant and height, its arm height, and the keyboard height and distance must all be adjusted so that your elbows are comfortably bent at a 90 degree angle while keyboarding.

- The keyboard tilt must be adjusted so that your wrists remain nearly horizontally straight while keyboarding.

- Wrist rests should be placed in front of the keyboard to help support your wrists.
- Other tools, such as adjustable copyholders, may be used as needed to ease strain.
- Periodic rest and stretch breaks should be built into all keyboarding sessions.

Office Security

The equipment and technologies used in an online office require more than routine maintenance and proper handling. Security has become a mounting concern. Whereas companies once worried about the physical break-in and theft of materials and equipment from offices, they now must be alert to cybertheft and abuse.

Office professionals may help to prevent security breaches by observing these guidelines for the online office:

- Read and learn as much as possible about potential threats and preventive measures, including information provided in employee manuals and other internal documents.
- Be wary of unusual or suspicious telephone, e-mail, and other requests for information about your equipment, software, work habits, and so on.
- Select systems and devices that have built-in forms of security.
- Use *passwords* (private access codes), *encryption* (coded or scrambled messages), *firewalls* (software that prevents intruders from accessing private company material), and other protective measures that stop outsiders from gaining access.
- Use regularly updated antivirus software to prevent the manipulation or destruction of material in your computer.
- Avoid trading disks or accepting them from unfamiliar sources, and avoid opening e-mail attachments without first filing them on your hard disk where your antivirus software can scan them.
- Make frequent backups of important computer material, and store them in a secure place.
- Use physical locks on diskette, tape, and other storage containers.
- Disconnect from the Internet, intranet, other networks, your e-mail program, and so on if you leave your terminal, even briefly.

- Use encryption or other protective measures that are available when you must purchase by credit card over the Internet, and when possible, use sites that are secure.

BASIC TECHNOLOGIES

The online office of the early twenty-first century primarily owes its character to the PC, copier, and fax machine. However, office technologies have extended far beyond the reach of those three key players. When they're combined with the older technology of the telephone, the results include e-mail, voice mail, and perhaps the most important recent technology — the Internet. (See The Internet and the discussions Using Voice Mail in Chapter 4, "Telecommunications," and Electronic Mail in Chapter 5, "Mail Processing.") All have had a profound effect on business communications. In addition, they continue to spawn other technologies, such as wireless Internet access and audio e-mail.

One of the most significant developments, or trends, is the integration of technologies. Computer technology, for example, is not distinctly separate from telecommunications technology. Rather, the technologies are melding, and the integrated office directly links computers, copiers, fax machines, telephones, and other equipment. In addition, manufacturers are combining different machines, such as the copier, fax machine, scanner, and printer, into a single multifunction unit, as described in The Multifunction Machine.

Businesses no longer operate as entities isolated by time and distance. The technologies described in the other chapters of this book have made communication nearly instantaneous, and vast electronic networks have connected people and businesses around the globe.

The Computer

Nothing has enhanced the processing of information more than the computer, which is available in a variety of sizes, from tiny, hand-held mobile units with built-in phones and Internet capability to huge, powerful mainframes or supercomputers that power vast networks. The term generally refers to *any* machine that can accept structured information or data (input), manipulate and process it, and provide results (output).

Digital computers represent values by discrete signals based on the **binary digits** (*bits*) 0 and 1 (or on and off). Although a single bit represents very little information, a group of 8 bits makes up a *byte*, which may represent a letter, decimal digit, or other character.

Binary numbers therefore have a base of 2, unlike decimal numbers, which have a base of 10. Notice the difference in the following list:

Decimal	Binary	Decimal	Binary
0	000	6	110
1	001	7	111
2	010	8	1000
3	011	9	1001
4	100	10	1010
5	101		

Although manufacturers regularly upgrade specific computer systems, the type of components included generally remains the same from year to year. In their office workstations, users commonly have either a *self-contained PC* that has all the components required for it to function alone or a *dumb terminal* that has only a monitor and keyboard connected to a large central processor (CPU), printer, and so on, which are shared by others in the company.

A self-contained, stand-alone system has a CPU, with built-in storage device (hard disk); monitor; keyboard; printer; internal or external modem; mouse; and possibly other peripherals, such as a scanner.

Those who travel often additionally have small, portable computers, referred to as notebooks or laptops, as well as other portable devices, such as cell phones and small printers and fax machines.

Memory. The two basic types of memory in a computer are ROM (read-only memory) and RAM (random-access memory). ROM is permanent memory that you *can't* alter, such as the instructions that make a computer's operating system run. RAM is temporary memory that you *can* alter, such as the text of a report that you're preparing.

Information may be stored on a built-in magnetic hard disk (and possibly an additional add-on hard disk) and on removable magnetic disks and tapes or optical disks and tapes. Magnetic and optical storage devices, including CD-ROMs, are described in Magnetic storage and Optical storage in Chapter 10.

The amount of RAM and ROM that a computer has — how much information the computer can hold at any time — is expressed in *kilobytes (KB):* 1,024 bytes; *megabytes (MB):* 1,048,576 bytes; or *gigabytes (GB):* 1,073,741,824 bytes.

Monitor. Traditionally called *cathode-ray tubes (CRTs)* or *displays,* monitors are frequently classified by their diagonal screen sizes, such as 14, 17, or

20 inches, although other factors, such as resolution, affect the quality of images. Specialized businesses or those involved in global trade may have special monitor requirements, such as a foreign-language display.

Printer. Printers vary in terms of print quality, speed, and features such as the availability of color printing. Two common types of printer are the *ink-jet printer,* which sprays ink to form characters and graphics on paper, and the *laser printer,* which forms an image on a photosensitive drum that attracts toner and fuses it to the paper. Although laser technology is usually considered superior to other printer technologies, some ink-jet machines rival the laser units in print quality. An older, lower-quality technology, the *impact printer,* forms marks on paper by striking a ribbon similar to a typewriter ribbon.

Printers, like copiers, are usually compared according to speed and volume handled per month. Both speed and volume will vary within a category, depending on the specific model or unit. In most cases, color printers run at slower speeds when in the color mode. The following examples refer to black-and-white printing:

- *Low-volume laser printers* run at speeds below 30 pages a minute and may handle up to 20,000 pages a month (usually less).
- *Midvolume laser printers* usually run at speeds of 20 to 50 pages per minute and may handle 50,000 to 300,000 pages a month.
- *High-volume laser printers* vary the most but may run at speeds of 50 to 135 pages a minute and may handle up to 1 million pages a month.

The high-end printers are used for both long- and short-run work, including *print-on-demand publishing*—the production of books and other large documents in very small quantities, even a single copy. See Print-on-Demand Publishing in Chapter 6, "Document Creation."

Refer to other chapters for information about the preparation of various types of material by computer, such as message preparation and transmission (Chapters 5, "Mail Processing," and 9, "Correspondence") and report preparation and desktop publishing (Chapter 6, "Document Creation"), as well as the use of the computer for other tasks, such as teleconferencing (Chapter 11, "Meetings and Conferences).

The Multifunction Machine

Some machines, such as the combined copier printer scanner-fax machine or the pager-cell phone-personal digital assistant (PDA) device, are designed to handle two or even numerous functions. These units are becoming more popular because of the convenience of having several machines combined in one unit and the space-saving advantage they offer. For more about single-function devices, refer to discussions of each item, such as the PDA described in Integration at the end of this chapter.

Multifunction machines vary considerably in sophistication and cost. Those with print capability, for example, range from an inexpensive, low-volume ink-jet unit to a high-volume laser device. Speeds may vary from 20 to 80 pages (or more) per minute, with a volume range of 5,000 to 100,000 pages a month.

The Copier

Few offices could survive without a copier. Companies select a copier according to the volume of copies it can handle per month and the number of pages per minute that it can copy. In each case, the range that a company requires depends on the amount of information processing it does.

Medium-size and large companies often need large, high-volume copiers that can be shared by two or more offices. Even when a high-volume copier is shared in a company, individual offices may have a small desktop model for limited in-office work. Some copiers may also include laser-printing, scanning, or fax capability (multifunction units).

The speed and number of copies that a copier can handle depends on the specific model or unit. However, in general, manufacturers classify copiers as follows:

- *Low-volume copiers* run at below 20 pages per minute and may handle monthly workloads of up to 10,000 copies.
- *Midvolume copiers* run at speeds of 20 to 50 pages per minute and may handle monthly workloads of 10,000 to 35,000 copies.
- *High-volume copiers,* the most sophisticated and also the most expensive models, run at speeds of 50 to over 100 pages a minute and may handle monthly workloads of 35,000 to 500,000 copies a month.

Color copiers vary from those that let you add a single or highlighted color to those that will reproduce a full-color original. Color copiers don't handle black-and-white work very well, however, so offices that need a color copier for special photographic or other reproduction work will also need a regular black-and-white unit for routine copying.

The Scanner

Scanning pages of text and graphics into an electronic format is a form of document imaging. (See Microstorage and Electronic Files in Chapter 10,

"Information Management.") The process has various uses. For example, scanning an already prepared text into a word processing program will save the time and effort of rekeying the document. Scanning a photograph into a newsletter being prepared by computer will enhance the presentation. Scanning inactive file material into electronic form will save substantial storage space.

Scanners are therefore becoming more common either as stand-alone units or as one of the functions in a multifunction machine. In either case, the devices will scan a page and digitize the images for storage or for further use in electronic form. Depending on the specific model, it may be able to handle color, black and white, or gray scale (for photographs). The higher the resolution of the scanner, the better will be the image that is reproduced.

Speed and other features and capabilities vary depending on the specific model. Some, for example, have sheet feeders that automatically feed a certain number of pages through the unit.

Special scanning software is needed to scan material into a computer. Usually, the software has a correction feature that allows you to correct errors introduced by the scanning process, such as when a speck of dust or blemish on the page is erroneously scanned as a comma or period.

The Fax Machine

Independent (stand-alone) fax machines or computers with a PC fax board (see Methods of fax transmission in Chapter 5, "Mail Processing") are standard features in the online office:

- An *independent fax machine* is a transmission device that operates by scanning pages and converting the text and graphics into signals that will travel over the telephone lines to a destination machine. There, the signals are converted again, and the receiving machine prints a duplicate of the faxed material.

- A *PC fax board,* installed in a computer, enables the computer to transmit both text and graphics, the same as a stand-alone machine. When a separate fax machine is used, the material must be prepared elsewhere and physically moved to the fax machine for transmission. With a PC fax board, the material can both be prepared on and transmitted from the computer.

- An *Internet-enabled fax machine* is a fax machine modified to send faxes via the Internet. Some machines are specifically manufactured to do this. In both cases, you can bypass the Public Switch Telephone Network and avoid long-distance fax charges. The user pays a monthly Internet service provider fee, which also provides for e-mail transmissions and Internet usage. Internet faxes may be sent to either an independent fax machine or an e-mail address. In either case, an Internet transmission will be slower than a regular fax transmission.

Like other devices, fax machines vary in speed, print quality, and special features such as color printing, multiple transmissions (*broadcast*), and *polling* (contacting remote machines, one after another, such as to collect sales figures from field offices). Fax capability may also be included in the multifunction machines described earlier.

The Telephone

The telephone and other telecommunications devices (see Telephone Technology in Chapter 4, "Telecommunications") share the spotlight with the computer in an online office. Together, they provide virtually instant communication around the globe via the Internet and other networks. For more about the use of networks, see The Internet.

Key systems. Most offices have a key (pushbutton) telephone system or an exchange system. Although the distinction between the two is disappearing, a *key system* traditionally consists of interconnected telephones with various buttons, or keys, each of which represents a telephone line. To answer a call, you must push the button that is lit. With a key system, anyone can use any telephone to answer calls.

Exchange systems. An *exchange* consists of equipment that switches calls among various telephone extensions. Most exchanges are broadly referred to as *PBX* (private branch exchange) systems. *PABX* refers to a private automatic branch exchange, *CBX* refers to a computerized branch exchange, and *PC-PBX* refers to a PBX system operated by a desktop PC.

Other Telecommunications Devices

Companies often have various other equipment and systems, such as cell phones, voice mail, and automated-attendant systems (see Cellular facilities and Using Voice Mail in Chapter 4, "Telecommunications"); and audio-, video-, and computer-conferencing systems (see Teleconferences in Chapter 11, "Meetings and Conferences").

For further information about office technologies, including machines, software, and other devices and supplies, refer to the individual chapters discussing the specific topics in which you're interested. Also, refer to the predictions in The Future.

THE INTERNET

The *Internet,* or *Net,* is a vast worldwide collection of interlinked networks and a low-cost communications tool that connects computer users across a distance. It represents a large pool of information that can be readily accessed, retrieved, used, transmitted, and stored. This process of transmitting and receiving information takes place in a computer-generated environment popularly referred to as *cyberspace.*

Development of the Internet

The Internet was created by the U.S. Department of Defense in the 1960s. It then expanded to include educational and research organizations and eventually individuals and businesses. Computers on the various interlinked networks are connected by telephone lines or some other means of transmission. Information is sent over the Internet from one computer to another through the use of a universal electronic language that each machine understands.

For a monthly fee, an *Internet service provider (ISP)* or an *online service,* such as America Online (AOL), will connect users to the Internet. An ISP allows users to dial in to use its Internet connection. An online service also offers dial-in access to the Internet and additionally provides access to other resources, such as encyclopedias and specialty information normally available only by fee or subscription.

An upgraded Internet, known as *Internet 2,* or the *Next Generation Internet,* will eventually allow very high speed Internet access to all users.

Transmission Protocols

Information is routed from one place to another over the Internet via the *Transmission Control Protocol (TCP)* and the *Internet Protocol (IP).* The TCP divides information, such as an e-mail message, into packets that can be transmitted from one computer to another. The IP makes certain that the information goes to the correct destination.

A *gateway* at each network through which the message must pass reconstructs the message into a format that the next network uses. At the destination, the TCP reconstructs the packets into the form of the original message. The TCP also ensures the integrity of a transmission. Together, the TCP/IP makes it possible for all computers on all networks worldwide to share or exchange information.

During transmission, information is sent to a *domain name,* such as *bensonco.com* (for Benson Company). A central Internet computer, called a *domain name server,* translates the domain name to an *Internet Protocol address* and back to the domain name at the destination. The IP address consists of a four-part number, such as *273.19.4.2.*

Online Chats

The Internet makes it possible for computer users in different locations to have keyboard chats. One method is the *bulletin board system (BBS),* in which participants may publicly post and pick up electronic messages. A *chat-room connection,* such as Internet Relay Chat (IRC), enables two or more people to have keyboard discussions on selected topics, which are available over different channels.

Another discussion forum to which computer users may subscribe is the *mailing list,* or *maillist.* In moderated lists, an administrator screens messages for appropriateness. In unmoderated lists, all mail is distributed unscreened. A *listserv* manages lists, processes subscriptions, and distributes messages.

A *newsgroup* is another type of public Internet discussion group, available with Usenet software. Newsgroups also are devoted to a particular subject, and computer users may subscribe (or unsubscribe) on screen, the same as with a *maillist.* Groups also may be moderated or unmoderated.

Intranets

An *intranet* is a private, internal network that employees in an organization use in the same way that they would use the Internet. Through their company intranet, they may exchange and share information, software, e-mail messages, keyboard chats, and other resources, such as a printer. See also Electronic Mail in Chapter 5, "Mail Processing."

If the intranet is connected to the larger Internet, customers and others who have passwords may be able to visit certain company sites. However, to keep the outsiders from seeing private files on its intranet, a company usually installs *firewall* software that will block outside access to designated information. This type of limited-access intranet is also called an *extranet.*

The World Wide Web

The *World Wide Web (WWW),* or *the Web,* is the most widely used part of the Internet. Today, it is a place where every imaginable type of information is stored, but its beginning was more limited. It was created in the 1990s when consultants in a Swiss research facility developed a *Web browser* program that allowed researchers in various locations to share data.

Browsing software. Later, graphical browser software called *Mosaic* provided widespread access to the Web. After that, *Netscape Navigator* and then *Microsoft Internet Explorer* were developed to enable PC users everywhere to find and use information stored on the Web in places called *websites*. Users who repeatedly want to return to the same site can add its name to a "favorites" list or add a "bookmark" for it. Thereafter, they can click on the listed name and immediately go to that site.

Recent word processing programs, such as Microsoft Word, enable users to create Web documents, further expanding Web activity. Users who require sophisticated sites may also hire Web designers to construct a site for them.

Webpage format. The documents that you see on the Web are formatted with a code known as the *Hypertext Markup Language (HTML)*. Each HTML-formatted page, therefore, not only has the text that you read but also has hidden tags that tell your browser things such as which words to display in bold and where to put the graphics.

HTML also tells your browser which words or graphics are *hypertext links* to other documents — places to which you can jump by clicking on the words or graphics that are highlighted or in some other way designated as the hyperlinks. These links point to a Web address, also known as a *universal resource locator (URL)*.

A website consists of one or more *webpages*. Users may view all pages, one after another, or jump here and there to different pages within a site by clicking on the hypertext links. The first, or startup, page of a particular site — an introductory page called the *home page* — usually has all the necessary links to other parts or pages in a site. Some may also have links to entirely different sites.

Document transfer. Users who navigate the Web may find certain pages or complete sites that they want to *download* (receive on their computers and print out). The method used to transfer the documents from a *host computer*, or *server*, where the Web documents are stored, to a user's Web browser program is called the *Hypertext Transfer Protocol (HTTP)*.

When a Web document is HTTP-compatible, the first letters in the Web address are *http://*. Each request made of a Web server to see a page or document is called a *hit*. For example, if a user reaches a page with text and two graphics, it means that three requests were made of the server or that there were three hits. Therefore, if a page has a hundred hits an hour, it refers to the number of text and graphics requests made of the server for that page but does not necessarily mean that a hundred people visited it.

A newer standard, *HTTP-NG* (next generation), will offer additional features, such as added security, along with file delivery. In addition, a more versatile version of HTTP — *eXtensible Markup Language (XML)* — is available, and a newer protocol nicknamed *Blocks* is designed to move XML documents more smoothly and quickly.

Web information. An endless array of information is stored on the Web, ranging from headline news to scientific data to merchandise for sale. Although it's not always clear whether information is current or reliable, such a massive collection of data makes the Web a useful tool for research, as well as for online shopping.

Users who don't have the address of a particular site containing information or merchandise that they're seeking may use a *search engine.* To do this, they would enter *keywords,* such as *stock transactions,* on the home page of their browser program or on the opening page of one of the dozens of *search engines* available on the Web. The selected search engine, which continually indexes information on the Web, will then display possible sites where the requested information may be found. However, only a portion of the Web has been indexed, and any queries that you make will therefore be limited to the sites included by the search engines.

A *metasearch site* is a multiple-search site that accesses various search engines and directories when you make a query. However, because it explores numerous search engines, it may take longer to find something through a metasearch site.

For information about the practical use of the Internet and the World Wide Web, refer to the discussions in the forthcoming chapters. For example, refer to the information about sending e-mail messages (see E-Mail Transmission in Chapter 5, "Mail Processing"), conducting electronic research (see Research in Chapter 6, "Document Creation"), and making online travel reservations (see Reservations in Chapter 12, "International and Domestic Travel").

THE FUTURE

Although the global emergence of the Internet (see The Internet) caught many people by surprise, the first part of the twenty-first century may be more predictable. Businesspeople have become increasingly comfortable with technological advances and look forward to them.

The Work Force

We expect to see more women move into middle-management positions (although 95 percent of senior management positions were still filled by men at the turn of the century). We also expect to see more telecommuters at all professional levels and the adoption of more flexible working hours (flex time) as management relaxes its former adherence to the traditional workweek.

Moreover, as employees throughout companies become more familiar with the new technologies, productivity levels will increase, and a more efficient workforce in general will emerge.

The Office Layout

Businesses will continue to modify the physical office to accommodate the new technologies and to respond to concerns about ergonomics, such as those described in Ergonomics.

As information is more easily processed and exchanged, the expanding flow will necessitate a more open workspace, and a corresponding change in furniture designs will accompany this movement. The overall trend toward a free-flowing, open work area may in turn contribute to the demise of the familiar twentieth-century cubicle. Telecommuters will increasingly use time-share office space equipped with a computer and a telephone and one lockable file drawer for each user.

E-terminology

We can easily predict that the ubiquitous *e-* prefix will be attached to more and more items and processes in the early twenty-first century. Terms such as *e-books* (publishing) and *e-tickets* (travel) were already familiar in the late twentieth century, and technology enthusiasts then were beginning to tack an *e-* onto everything from shredders to writing pens.

This tendency is likely to continue until a particular subject, such as *e-tickets,* is the only alternative. When paper tickets are no longer issued, for example, language authorities may decide that the *e-* prefix is no longer needed to distinguish electronic from paper tickets — they will all be electronic.

Integration

We expect devices to become smaller and be more fully integrated in the coming years. Also, more devices will be manufactured as multifunction machines (see The Multifunction Machine), such as the copier-printer-scanner-fax machine and the pager-cell phone-personal digital assistant (PDA) device. The versatile PDAs, which are really miniature computers, are designed to do everything from check your e-mail to maintain your calendar to hold the full text of a book. Most keyboard-based PDAs allow you to exchange information with your desktop PC.

Newer technologies, such as Internet access through cell phones or through portable PCs and hand-held PDAs, will become more widespread and further enhance the mobility of users. In addition, automatic speech-to-text transcription with mobile digital voice recorders will unite the dictation-transcription process with PC voice recognition. Meanwhile, television and the Internet will become a single, fused technology.

Wireless Technology

The big news at the turn of the century was wireless technology. In fact, it emerged well before the twenty-first century. In the last decade of the twentieth century, we saw the widespread use of cordless and cell phones at home, on the road, and even on the street. Along with the emergence of wireless Internet access, we also saw executives using miscellaneous portable devices — from notebook computers to personal digital assistants (PDAs) to cell phones — in airports, in hotels, and, in general, everywhere they went.

Although the convergence of voice and data is a significant development in itself, it becomes even more important in relation to wireless technology. The union of the two over a wireless network is certain to simplify and enhance communications and shrink the world business community even further.

The Paperless Office

With technology moving at an accelerated pace in the twenty-first century, will anything be left from yesterday's office? Yes, at least one thing: paper. The much anticipated paperless office did not materialize by the year 2000, as once predicted, and manufacturers and others no longer expect the demise of paper anytime soon. Although devices and technologies such as the personal digital assistant (PDA) have provided serious competition for paper-based procedures, manufacturers readily acknowledge that people still like to see and read paper copies of messages and documents.

Nevertheless, we're already using much more nonpaper *storage,* especially in the archival stage, a trend prompted by lack of physical space. Therefore, rather than seeing a significant increase in bulky cabinets and shelves for paper files, we'll see more small magnetic and optical disk and tape containers.

Information Management

In general, with higher transmission speeds, increasing storage capacity, and easier-to-use universal interfaces, the focus will likely shift in the twenty-first century from accessing information to managing it. Access will be so fast and easy that it won't require much thought. Therefore, it won't matter whether you print e-mail from your desk telephone, cell phone, television, PC, personal digital assistant (PDA), or other device.

The main concern will be how to manage the flow of e-mail and other information, especially since the flow is certain to increase as it becomes easier to generate more information. The pressure created by an increasing flow of information will lead to better information- and document-management techniques, including new software and devices for this purpose.

Professional Career Development

DUTIES AND RESPONSIBILITIES

The technologies described in Chapter 1, "The Online Office," have changed traditional office positions and duties, just as they have changed the way that offices operate. In addition to handling traditional office duties, such as greeting visitors and processing incoming mail, office professionals also must manage the new technologies and direct the flow of information in and out of the office. To handle their greater responsibilities, they must be able to work independently and make more decisions within the scope of their individual responsibilities.

Some office professionals are specialists and concentrate largely on a particular function, such as word processing or telecommunications. Others are generalists and do a little of everything in the office. The particular duties are always defined by the organization and the office in which the professional works. However, the following are common duties and responsibilities in many offices:

- Place, answer, and route internal and external telephone calls
- Process electronic, postal, and voice mail
- Answer and initiate electronic and postal correspondence
- Establish standards, and handle other quality-control functions
- Interview, hire, train, and supervise assistants and other support personnel
- Conduct job evaluations, and handle merit (performance) ratings
- Schedule appointments, and handle follow-ups and reminders
- Schedule, arrange, and attend meetings and conferences
- Prepare the minutes of meetings

- Make travel arrangements, and plan itineraries
- Operate computers and other office equipment
- Use word processing, spreadsheet, and other software programs
- Use the Internet for research, purchasing, networking, and other purposes
- Purchase supplies, equipment, and furniture for the office
- Process maintenance contracts and leases
- Set up and maintain electronic and traditional filing systems
- Set up and use online databases
- Develop and manage special projects
- Coordinate office functions with telecommuters, other offices and departments, and external organizations
- Maintain various books, records, and schedules
- Prepare budgets, financial statements, and other reports
- Conduct online and traditional research
- Make arrangements for or handle desktop publishing of office/ company documents
- Make arrangements for in-house or outside printing of office/ company documents

Job Titles

Office professionals work at many levels of responsibility, ranging from following instructions to managing office activities. It's important to recognize the various levels and the diverse functions that can be channeled into more specialized careers and to formalize them into an occupational standard.

The specific titles assigned to office professionals depend on the duties involved and vary from one organization to another. In general, a decline in the use of the title *secretary* has been accompanied by an increase in titles such as *administrative assistant* and *executive assistant,* as well as the traditional titles of *office manager, supervisor,* and *receptionist.* Where the title *secretary* is still used, it may vary from *secretary* alone to *executive secretary* or *administrative secretary.*

Job Descriptions

For convenience, you might group the positions available to office professionals in two general categories: entry-level positions and advanced (second-tier) positions.

Entry-level positions. Entry-level positions in most companies require only basic communications skills and keyboarding ability. Usually, no substantive responsibilities are included in such positions. However, entry-level jobs represent the first step toward an administrative or managerial career in business.

Some office professionals begin their careers in word processing pools, in file centers, or by handling other single-task activities. They also may start by handling a variety of duties for executives who have no personal assistant. The range of duties and the challenge of preparing material for different executives usually prove to be excellent training for advancement.

Advanced positions. Certain basic competencies are required for any office position, particularly one with administrative or managerial responsibilities. Computer literacy, keyboarding speed and accuracy, a thorough command of business English, and leadership skills are all important. The specific level of the position may be defined by the complexity of tasks that the office professional must perform without supervision. Refer to the list at the beginning of this chapter for other common duties.

Some office positions are specialized, such as legal, medical, or accounting office positions. Although the required training for specialized positions is very specific, many other positions rely just as much on experience in the field as they do on specialization, such as a position in a human resources department.

Some jobs require extensive experience in a particular field, and the employers equate such experience with a certain number of years in a business school or college. The following examples illustrate variations in the required experience and education for different specialties:

- A *human resources assistant/administrator* should have prior experience with personnel record-keeping systems and should be able to work under rules of strict confidentiality.

- A *sales assistant/administrator* should be familiar with active lead follow-up and sales record keeping, as well as with customer files and correspondence. Other important tasks include performing math operations, interacting positively with members of the sales team, and planning sales meetings.

- A *publishing assistant/administrator* should have an excellent command of English, good writing skills, proofreading and copyediting experience, and word processing or desktop publishing experience.

- An *advertising assistant/administrator* should be able to work under intense pressure and meet demanding deadlines. Excellence in communication is essential to be able to assist in preparing ad copy and press releases. The ability to project a highly professional image through person-to-person contact is also requisite.

As you can see from the preceding examples, a specialty requires particular abilities that can be improved and enhanced as you gain more experience in the workplace.

Although the titles may differ, depending on the precise duties and the particular company, two common positions held by office professionals are that of executive assistant and administrative assistant. Since companies may differ in their definitions of the various positions, it's important to understand and evaluate a help-wanted ad or job description in relation to the employer and to investigate the opportunities for advancement in each organization offering employment.

Executive assistant. The position of assistant to a top executive often requires a high degree of confidentiality and formality. It may involve scheduling meetings, preparing minutes of board meetings, doing public relations work, composing correspondence, handling instructions without supervision, and performing miscellaneous other tasks, such as screening calls and visitors and evaluating the incoming mail. Interpersonal skills are essential in any such highly visible position, and the assistant must be honest, mature, sophisticated, and diplomatic at all times.

Administrative assistant. In many cases, this title refers to an administrative support job performed with little or no supervision. For example, an administrative assistant may handle the dissemination of contract information or work with the chief financial officer of a company in preparing important corporate reports. The position usually involves supervising others and may require a college degree. Office professionals are typically promoted to administrative assistant when an executive decides to delegate additional responsibilities requiring more intensive effort.

Specialized positions. The specialized positions, particularly those in a technical field, require very specific skills and abilities. This becomes clear when you examine the differences between the requirements for a medical assistant/administrator and a legal assistant/administrator.

- A *medical assistant/administrator* requires training in medical terminology, medical office ethics and practices, and medical keyboarding and transcription. The person may be required to manage the entire office and must have a sound knowledge of accounting procedures, financial record keeping, and computerized data processing. He or she must also understand and be able to process complex health insurance forms and must have excellent human relations skills.

- A *legal assistant/administrator* requires highly specialized training with a knowledge of legal and court procedures, familiarity with myriad forms and legal documents, and the ability to work with software programs used to process the forms and documents. Often, the person serves as office manager as well. If an office professional wants to achieve a higher level of specialization in the legal field, he or she may decide to become a paralegal aide, a position requiring further specialized education.

Career Paths

When businesses were small and run by rule of thumb, support personnel were usually generalists — office managers, administrators, executive assistants, correspondence assistants, and so on. Promotion into management wasn't guaranteed, but it happened often enough to establish general office work as a premanagement training ground.

Today, when businesses are infinitely more complex and almost of necessity run by technical experts on productivity and scientific management, office professionals have more opportunities to pursue different career paths. One route — a horizontal path — might lead to repetitive work as a computer operator in data or word processing. Another route — a vertical path — might lead to a career in office management, information management, or some other information segment of the workforce. The gateway to the latter route involves at least two things: specialization and personal initiative. Examples of areas of specialization are computer graphics, systems analysis, and database management.

Although information work is wide ranging, much of it fits in one of three general categories, with each type also being a stepping-stone to a more advanced computer-assisted information position:

- Information administration and management
- Information formatting and packaging
- Information research and dissemination

A career path leading to administration and management would be appropriate for those with strong organizational and leadership skills. A career path leading to information formatting and packaging might appeal to someone with artistic talent and could lead to work in companies specializing in providing computer-based information goods and services. A career path leading to information research and dissemination would be attractive to those who enjoy dealing with facts and details. As the number of commercially available databases increases, so does the need for information research and dissemination increase.

Information administration and management. Although office work involves many activities, information administration and management are two of the most important. The health and success of an organization depend on its success in these areas. Capable administrators and managers know how to interact productively with sources of information and how to direct the flow of information through an organization and its systems with efficiency and tact.

Database management. As technology advances, more information will be stored electronically, and, eventually, there will be less paper and fewer people to manage. Instead, electronic bits of information will be routed through hardware and software components. As a result, one possibility in developing a career path in this area is database management.

The computer languages and systems specifically designed for this application have existed for some time and are regularly updated and improved. However, besides having a general knowledge of how organizations work and how information flows through them — knowledge that most office professionals acquire intuitively on the job — it would be helpful to study referencing and indexing systems. For example, one might begin by studying those used by search engines on the Internet (see The Internet in Chapter 1, "The Online Office") and those used by large libraries that must continually organize, store, and retrieve massive amounts of information.

The difference between operating an ordinary office filing system and managing a library or other large system is mostly a matter of degree. The larger systems require more formal systematized procedures for categorizing and cross-referencing information. Database management systems (DBMSs) are similarly formal and systematic. You might begin a career path here, therefore, by helping a technical expert set up an electronic filing system or a corporate database.

The next step might involve working with the database — sorting and updating its files. Although many commercial DBMSs are flexible enough to make it unnecessary for you to change the associated computer program, it would be helpful to know something about the programming languages used to set up such a system. This knowledge would make it easier for you to assist a technician who is modifying database software according to your office's needs. It would also be helpful should you eventually want to move into more technical areas, such as program analysis, systems design, and systems analysis.

General management. To aim for more generalized management, it would be helpful to take courses in business and office administration, accounting, and computers. An office professional with a thorough understanding of how an electronic office works might begin by finding employment as an assistant to a systems analyst or a computer programmer and work on a new office-systems design that would improve the organization's work-flow, operating style, and various procedures.

After taking some computer courses, such as introduction to computer systems, the principles of programming, and programming in a specific language, an assistant could advance to a position as office-systems administrator. This position in turn might lead to a middle-management opportunity.

Middle management has become more technical and more technology oriented. Although its human-resource aspect still exists, the technical aspect requires that managers be able to control the technological resources of an electronic office. This responsibility includes putting the resources to use both cost effectively and flexibly according to the changing needs of the professional and executive personnel.

Moving into middle management, however, doesn't mean that you have to become a computer scientist or an electrical engineer. It does mean that you must be aware of technological developments and changes in office automation, be comfortable working with computer systems and technical experts, and have a solid knowledge of business administration and the systems theory associated with computer technology. Although occupational titles vary, a middle manager today is in many ways a systems administrator.

Information formatting and packaging. This career path picks up where ordinary word processing leaves off. It involves the use of creative talent in conjunction with computer graphics and the color and typographical features associated with computer printers. It might lead to paraprofessional and professional information work within a company, such as in a public relations or human resources department. It might also lead to a position in a company that is expanding the horizons of the information sector. In this sector, employment involves creating and marketing new information goods and services.

Word processing and desktop publishing. The path to a career in information formatting and packaging might lie in word processing or desktop publishing (see Chapter 6, "Document Creation"). In either case, you should acquire a working knowledge of word processing and desktop publishing systems and their software and then find opportunities in which to apply that knowledge and the related skills. For example, you should be proficient in using document-production and presentation-graphics software with which you not only can create text but also can do other things such as set up columns and charts, draw pictures and graphs, and color or shade selected areas of a page.

Opportunities for using such software are available in public relations, for example, where the goal is to communicate information and a particular corporate image at the same time. Human resources departments offer possibilities, too, since employee manuals and instructional materials are prepared in electronic as well as paper form for display on employees' computer terminals at home or in the office.

To augment your basic word processing and information-display skills, therefore, you might take courses in graphic arts and computer graphics. It would also be helpful to study public relations and advertising if you're interested in the media or to study education and organization behavior patterns if you're interested in preparing training materials or in handling other aspects of human resources work.

Video-based opportunities and the Internet. In addition to providing organizational structures and occupations, video-based information industries offer a variety of opportunities. Through Internet or television shopping, for example, catalog-type items are relayed directly to the consumer's computer terminal or television set. Designing and creating webpages and editing electronically displayed material requires good organizational skills, an ability to relate material to an intended audience, and a sense of effective communications, as well as the technical skills associated with display setup and management.

In a bank, for example, that wants to prepare packages of financial information and how-to advice for customers doing their banking by computer, an editor might help to design an overall package and sketch the information to be contained on each display. Some companies also use this process for in-house training programs. Office professionals employed by such companies might move into this type of information field without ever having to leave their current place of employment.

Information research and dissemination. A third example of a possible career path involves information usage as well as buying and selling or collecting and disseminating information. It might lead all the way to the executive ranks. From simply collecting information according to given specifications, one might demonstrate additional research initiative and, from there, move into information analysis and decision making. This work would appeal to those who are curious, want to find answers, and like solving problems and seeing the results — all essential qualities for success as an executive.

Entry-level research. At the beginning level, the work would not differ substantially from other basic office activities, such as finding information in the files. For example, one might dial up a database and relay the specifications provided by a chemical engineer who is designing a new product and needs the latest data on the properties of a particular chemical or material.

Advanced-level research. At a higher level, an information researcher would be responsible for formulating keyword searches — providing the word or words that the computer can use to locate information in a database — and relaying the information to a client company. It takes learning and experience to become proficient at formulating keyword search commands, and hands-on practice is essential. (See Keyword retrieval in Chapter 10, "Information Management.") One might begin by using Internet search engines (see The Internet in Chapter 1, "The Online Office") to locate information. It's also important to take appropriate in-house or outside courses in information management and computer information-processing systems.

A middle manager would be responsible for keeping up with developments in the field of commercial databases, computer-assisted research, and Internet resources. The middle manager should be prepared to advise senior management on the most useful databases to subscribe to on a regular basis and should be able to prepare budgets for the company's research needs. Although research and information dissemination could become a rewarding career in itself, the option of moving beyond research into analysis also exists in areas such as production planning, financial analysis, and marketing.

EDUCATION AND TRAINING

Many office positions require a college background, as well as certain technical skills. Continuing education is therefore essential for those aspiring to a higher professional level. To encourage career advancement, some companies have made tuition assistance available for office employees or offer on-site or computer-based company programs.

Education

When Canadian philosopher Marshall McLuhan coined the phrase "learning a living" in the 1960s, few people knew what he meant. Today, however, people realize that ongoing technological change has made continuous adult education a necessary component of their working lives. Office professionals must stay informed about new developments in their area of specialization: information management, electronic and voice messaging, financial spreadsheets, and various other computer applications.

Basic education. A basic education is the foundation on which you can continue to learn more easily. All forms of communication and information skills must be stressed: effective writing, listening, graphics, and other skills. For example, in addition to learning professional writing techniques, one must learn the techniques of preparing computer graphics, slides, transparencies, and computer-assisted oral presentations. In addition to knowing general math, one must develop polished reasoning skills. Such skills might range from the discipline of thinking systematically and being able to break down complex problems or projects into a logical series of discrete steps to the methodologies associated with higher math and computer programming.

Recommended courses. Office professionals interested in an information-management career should take courses in business administration and computer-systems theory. Those interested in information packaging should take courses in graphic arts and computer graphics. Those interested in information research and dissemination should take courses in research and reference systems and database management systems.

In general, the education and training should focus on language skills, data processing, word processing, organizational skills, office technologies, and business management. The courses may be part of a company-sponsored, in-house training program (seminars, workshops, and so on) or may be part of the curriculum of a nearby college or university offering both on-site programs and broadcast or Internet programs.

Language skills. An office professional must be able to write effectively, clearly, and accurately for both a domestic and a foreign audience. Since most business communications are read by a number of people inside and outside the organization, the content of any outgoing correspondence (see Chapter 9, "Correspondence") or other document must be grammatically correct (see Chapter 8, "Business English"), concise, and easy to understand.

Many guides designed to help you enhance your writing ability are available. Along with a basic writing guide, you should also have a current dictionary, a business style manual (see Chapter 7, "Business Style Guide"), and a thesaurus. In many ways, business writing is like newspaper reporting. If you follow the "who, what, where, when, and why" formula used by reporters, you'll be able to cover the essential aspects of a communication. If you still have trouble with writing, consider taking one of the many college, home-study, and other courses that are available, some of which are geared specifically to the communications needs of office professionals.

Business math, accounting, and data processing. Knowing basic math and how to use an electronic calculator, as well as accounting and spreadsheet software, are essential in a business environment. Many executives depend on the ability of administrative personnel to compile routine financial reports and handle some or all of the financial record keeping. In many cases, knowledge of basic accounting techniques can mean the difference in job status between an entry-level assistant and an administrative or executive assistant. Chapter 13, "Accounting," describes the main principles of business accounting.

Word processing. Keyboarding speed and accuracy are prerequisites for many office positions, and knowledge of word processing software and computer operations is essential. A familiarity with desktop publishing software will further enhance one's qualifications in this area. General skills should include formatting and editing capabilities, as well as an understanding of the additional features of a program, such as graphics capabilities, templates, and mail merge features. For more about word processing and desktop publishing, refer to Chapter 6, "Document Creation."

Planning and organization. Planning and organization skills are solid ingredients for success in any administrative position. The ability to schedule work, set priorities, coordinate projects, and handle several tasks at once is necessary to direct an efficient workflow. As office professionals assume more responsibilities, the need for better organizational ability increases. You become more valuable to an employer to the extent that you can plan and organize not only routine tasks but also special projects. Initiative, independent judgment, and leadership qualities are key assets. For more about organization, see Time Management in Chapter 3, "Human Relations."

Office technology. A working familiarity with the current office technologies (described in Chapter 1, "The Online Office") is important to ensure success in an online office. Office professionals should understand the purpose and general operations of the various electronic and telecommunications systems, as well as know how to use the associated equipment, such as computers, fax machines, scanners, copiers, and postal equipment. They should understand office procedures that depend on the latest technologies, such as how to access an online database and how to use the Internet for conducting research, tracking parcels, purchasing supplies, and other matters.

For further information on practices and procedures in using the various systems and technologies, refer to other discussions in this book: message transmission (Chapter 4, "Telecommunications"), mail processing (Chapter 5, "Mail Processing"), document creation (Chapter 6, "Document Creation"), correspondence (Chapter 9, "Correspondence"), information management (Chapter 10, "Information Management"), meetings and conferences (Chapter 11, "Meetings and Conferences"), and travel (Chapter 12, "International and Domestic Travel").

Business management. To work effectively and confidently in a business environment, it's necessary to be familiar with the principles and terminology associated with the various disciplines that affect business management and operations. Independent reading, seminars, and college-level courses in subjects such as accounting, law, economics, and business management are useful in providing an appropriate background. Most companies can supply information to employees about online study; continuing-education workshops, seminars, and academic courses; and other career-development programs.

Other Forms of Education and Training

Although it's essential to keep up with technological developments and continue to learn and grow in your work, this doesn't mean that you must spend the rest of your life in night school or in front of your computer or television screen. With earning and learning so closely intertwined, a host of educational options are available for continuing your education on informal as well as formal levels.

Formal education. On a formal level, many colleges, business schools, and home-study schools offer courses to people in their homes or places of work. Often, the traditional classroom instructor is replaced or augmented by an audio- or videotape, a computer disk, or a CD-ROM.

Networking. You can also enhance your learning through a variety of information channels, such as networking, whereby you exchange practical information on a computer network or by mail, telephone, or personal meetings. In addition, you can read books or subscribe to journals specializing in computer applications in your own area of work, and you can join associations that support your occupational or professional activity. Aside from general associations, such as the International Association of Administrative Professionals, various technical associations have been formed to focus on law, medicine, information processing, database management, systems administration, and other fields. Check the Internet or a print directory of associations for names, numbers, and addresses where you can request information.

Associations usually have information on networking opportunities and publish newsletters and magazines with information useful in advancing your career. They often sponsor educational programs or at least can counsel members on the best local educational opportunities available. They hold annual or monthly meetings devoted to continuing education and self-improvement, and you can contribute, as well as learn, by volunteering to organize meetings, prepare and give a talk, and so on. Having such credentials listed on your resume will impress prospective employers with your talents, intellectual flexibility, and initiative.

Ongoing career development. Once you've found a comfortable niche in a company, it may be difficult to stay interested in further professional development. People often settle for job situations that are less than satisfactory because comfort and convenience have become a habit. Involvement in associations and networks, however, will help you continue to focus on educational opportunities and ongoing career development. With the strong impact of technology on the business world, your networking activities, continuing education, and intellectual flexibility will be crucial in any long-term efforts to make use of the new technologies and the career opportunities generated by them.

Professional Certification

Your professional development should involve the regular learning of new skills and the sharpening of those already acquired. This is the only way to survive and progress in a fast-paced, high-technology business world.

One way to enhance your professional status is by achieving certification through some of the examinations administered for office professionals. Certification is a worthwhile goal for a career-oriented individual. The International Association of Administrative Professionals, for example, offers the Certified Professional Secretary (CPS) certification, and various specialized groups offer certification in areas such as law and medicine. Check the Internet or a print directory of associations for current names, numbers, and addresses where you can request information on application requirements and subjects covered in the qualifying exam.

Performance Measures

Companies usually have some means of measuring an employee's performance. They may use a standard commercial program, such as Management by Objectives (MBO), or design their own performance-rating system. The purpose of any such program is to compare and evaluate employee performance in regard to productivity, goal achievement, and standard of excellence. Evaluation, which may occur at different times during the year according to company policy, is often linked to salary reviews and budgetary considerations.

If your company has a performance-rating system, you may want to conduct your own self-evaluation in advance of each periodic company review or according to some other schedule that's convenient to you and will provide the information you need. To do this, create a list of performance factors and a set of performance measures. Ideally, you'll use the same factors and measures that your company uses. If this information isn't available to you, however, develop lists of performance factors and measures applicable to your job.

To begin, use your computer to set up and print a columnar-style, fill-in sheet, or purchase a columnar accounting pad. List the *performance factors* that you've chosen in the left column. Head the next several columns with the *performance measures* used by your company or those that you've selected, ranging from *well above average* to *well below average:*

PERFORMANCE FACTORS	WELL ABOVE AVERAGE	ABOVE AVERAGE	AVERAGE	BELOW AVERAGE	WELL BELOW AVERAGE

The performance factors that you list in the first column will depend on your position and the associated duties. For many office professionals, however, the list will include the following factors (for convenience, listed alphabetically):

Personal Qualities and Abilities
Accuracy — concern with
Businesslike appearance
Decision-making ability
Detail — attention to
Initiative
Interpersonal relations — success in
Leadership ability
Listening ability
Organizational ability
Personality — appeal of
Quality — concern with
Reading comprehension
Retention ability (memory)
Speaking ability
Supervisory ability
Temperament — stability of, control of
Trustworthiness

Job Skills and Abilities
Accounting/record-keeping knowledge
Administrative ability
Clerical skills
Computer literacy
Database usage
Equipment operation — copier
Equipment operation — fax
Equipment operation — telecommunications
Equipment operation — other
Filing skills — electronic
Filing skills — paper
Formatting ability
Grammar — knowledge of
Internet — proficiency in use of
Keyboarding skills — accuracy
Keyboarding skills — speed
Math and reasoning abilities
Punctuation skill
Second-language knowledge
Special-field [e.g., advertising] knowledge
Technical-subject [e.g., physics] knowledge
Writing skill — correspondence
Writing skill — other

To rate yourself, put an *X* or a check mark in one of the performance-measure columns. For instance, is your *computer literacy* well above average, above average, average, below average, or well below average? Be ruthlessly objective and honest. No one will see your ratings. They're meant only to help you develop a self-portrait so that you can easily see what weaknesses you have, which qualities or skills need improvement, and what type of additional education and training you need — *before* your company rates your performance. Keep in mind, though, that your employer will also be considering questions such as how much satisfactory work you produce on a timely, regular basis; how well you work under pressure; and how well you adapt to new job requirements and emergencies. See Chapter 3, "Human Relations" for more about such factors.

INTERPERSONAL RELATIONS

Communication

Communication is the exchange of information, thoughts, or messages by some means, such as writing, speech, physical signals, or behavior. Communications skills are needed in any profession, but they are especially important to office professionals, since a major responsibility involves handling numerous daily communications, both oral and written. In addition to written-communication skills and the need to be clearly understood when executing a well-crafted document, the additional skills and qualities of speaking and listening, body language, and appearance are also important components in interpersonal communications. Refer to Chapter 3, "Human Relations," for more about interpersonal interaction in the office.

Speaking and Listening

You may have good ideas to contribute, but if you can't articulate them effectively, they'll be lost. Speaking well requires a thorough command of English, clear enunciation, and self-confidence. To be able to respond properly and absorb the contributions of others, it's also important to be attentive and patient when others are speaking (be a good listener).

If you're shy and have little or no experience speaking in front of a group, you may benefit from a course in public speaking that will help you overcome your fear of addressing a group. Other students will be there for the same reason and will understand your difficulty. If you expect to advance to a position as supervisor or trainer, you'll probably have to speak regularly in front of at least one or a few persons, and the more you speak publicly, the easier it will become.

Body Language

The physical mannerisms that people use and the signals that they send in communications are known as *body language.* Your posture and gestures convey a number of attitudes and emotions. If you're nervous, for example, you'll appear uncertain or insecure. Office professionals must therefore try to be aware of their habits without becoming self-conscious.

During a conversation, a smile or nod tends to assure the other person that you agree with or understand what he or she is trying to convey. If you want to send a self-assured, confident signal, look directly into the eyes of the person who is talking with you. When you're dealing with an international audience, however, keep in mind that gestures and other body language sometimes have different meanings in other countries. In some cultures, for example, direct eye contact may suggest a pushy, disrespectful attitude rather than attentiveness or interest in what the other person is saying.

Analyze some of the gestures and nuances of your nonverbal communication style, and try to determine what kind of message you're conveying. It's easy to develop bad habits in conversation and in the gestures used to support our speech. If you become aware of what you're doing, however, it will be easier to correct any bad habits that you've developed.

Table 2.1 Body Language and Messages Conveyed

NEGATIVE MANNERISM OR POSTURE	POSSIBLE IMPRESSION CONVEYED
Arms folded across chest	Insecurity; defensiveness; dissatisfaction
Fiddling with rings, necktie, lapels, buttons	Nervousness; stress
Biting of fingernails	Deviousness and deceit; nervousness and general insecurity
Lack of eye contact with the other person (in the United States and some other countries)	Disinterest in the other person, the conversation, or instructions being given to you; deviousness
Slouching while standing or sitting	Boredom; laziness; lack of interest in job or conversation
Holding hand over mouth while talking	Fear; self-consciousness

POSITIVE MANNERISM OR POSTURE	POSSIBLE IMPRESSION CONVEYED
Arms folded across lower body	Relaxation; receptiveness
Hands held loosely at sides or behind back	Ease; confidence; relaxation; openness with others
Steady eye contact with other person (in the United States and some other countries)	Interest in other person, the conversation, or instructions being given to you; straightforwardness, candor, and honesty
Erect yet relaxed posture while standing, walking, or sitting	Energy; control; self-confidence

Table 2.1 gives a few examples of familiar negative and positive body language. Mannerisms must be studied carefully, however, to be certain which impression is really being conveyed. To be safe, one should not reach a hasty conclusion. For example, arms folded tightly across a person's chest may signal dissatisfaction, but it also may simply mean that the person is cold.

Appearance

The way that you look — cleanliness, hairstyle, fingernails, cosmetics, jewelry, and style of dress — is as important as your posture and gestures in nonverbal communication. Although vast differences in dress codes exist from one office to another, career-motivated professionals pay special

Table 2.2 Dressing for Success: Questions and Answers

QUESTIONS	ANSWER
Do most companies have formal, written dress codes?	No, but they do have unwritten rules or standards. Some simply state in their handbooks that employee dress should be appropriate for a business office. Observe the style of executives and their assistants to determine the general company style.
In what type of environment would corporate style be considered important?	A traditional dress code might be followed in a television network, a law firm, a bank, or a government office (where the general public, clients, and public figures are received and image is considered very important).
Who sets the dress style in a company?	The chief executive and operating officers usually set the general style, and it is then reflected in the dress of office personnel at all other levels. Since no national standard exists, it may range from very formal to very informal, with something in between being most common.
What dress would be *generally* acceptable in a business setting?	Tailored suits or dresses, with mixed and matched separates (coats, skirts, and trousers). Jewelry, shoes, hairstyles, and so on should be businesslike. (Some companies have casual Fridays, when employees may dress casually-no ties, nice jeans, sensible shoes, and so on). Each company must be considered individually in determining appropriate office attire. (When in doubt, ask.)

attention to appearance in all cases. To dress for the position you *want to have,* not merely the one you already have, strictly follow your company's code for employees, and imitate the style of the firm's executives or those who have positions to which you aspire. A neat, clean, professional, businesslike appearance is always an appropriate choice. You should, therefore, look as though you're dressed for an important business meeting, not for a nightclub or a camping trip. Table 2.2 answers a few questions commonly asked about an appropriate business dress style.

THE JOB SEARCH

Occupational Outlook

Before beginning your job search, examine your own marketability and your position in the marketplace. A vast array of information on available positions, prospective employers, business trends, and other factors is available. Consult the Internet, newspapers and journals, public and private libraries, employment agencies, and the organizations that are hiring.

For example, if you have access to the Internet at home, you can locate a wealth of domestic and foreign job opportunities and related information, ranging from who is hiring to resume-preparation tips to interview guidelines to salary-benefits negotiation suggestions. You'll also find a variety of labor statistics, such as wage surveys and average vacation days. For more about job information sources, see the forthcoming discussion of the Internet in Job Information Sources.

Opportunities in other countries. If you'd like to live and work in another country, pay special attention to governmental and private organizations that have international interests. The Department of State, for example, offers positions in countries around the world to those who meet the criteria for foreign service. You must pass a security check and be willing to work anywhere. If you pass the investigation, you'll be assigned to the Foreign Service Institute for orientation and further training before receiving an assignment.

Large multinational corporations also recruit employees in the United States for assignment in other countries. Foreign job opportunities are advertised over the Internet and in various publications, including the major newspapers.

Self-evaluation. Before you apply for a job, assess your overall proficiency so that you can accurately match your skills level with the available positions. A realistic, objective assessment of your own qualifications (including your weak points) will help you to avoid disappointments and failed expectations during your job search. Use the same type of self-rating system described in Performance Measures.

Professional assistance. If you're career oriented and upwardly mobile, it's important to establish the right connections with people who can help you further your career. (According to one study, the most significant factor in being hired and advancing is *who you know,* although *what you know* is always an essential ingredient.) You may have a relationship with a professional person whom you consider to be a role model. A mentor has the kind of professional wisdom gained through experience that is invaluable to another person who wants to improve his or her job status. When you want to make a career change, for instance, this person can advise you about the positive and negative aspects of the move.

Having made a connection with such a person, you should nurture the relationship. Counseling and guidance from an experienced person based on trust and mutual admiration is one of the most valuable elements for success in business. Connections often make the difference between a mediocre career and success in reaching your professional goals.

Your First Job

If you have recently graduated from college or business school or have a certificate for business training, you'll already know something about your performance level in the most basic areas, such as written communication and word processing. If you have little or no job experience, however, it may be difficult to decide what kind of job will suit your abilities and personality. Ask yourself the following questions:

- Am I a people-oriented person? If so, would I enjoy a position where I'll be dealing regularly with the public, such as in a sales or customer-service department?
- Would I rather work in a large, midsize, or small company?
- Is there a profession or business that I find particularly fascinating?
- What are my salary requirements? If you're a recent graduate, your placement office may have information on salary levels that you should pursue. Employment agencies may also have salary surveys and job classifications to help you assess opportunities.
- Where do I want to work: in the city? The suburbs? Another country?

If you have no idea of the kind of job you want or where to start, a *temporary* employment agency may be the answer. With basic office skills, you can usually find work through a temporary agency. Contract work, whereby you're hired for a specific period or a specific project, is another option. Both alternatives are becoming more common in companies of all sizes and are excellent ways of trying different jobs in different companies without making a commitment until you're ready for a permanent position.

In addition to helping you become familiar with contemporary practices in the business world, temporary employment or contract work may help you develop some recent work history that you can include on your resume. For some, it will also help build self-confidence after a long absence from the workforce. See Returning to the Workforce.

Companies need temporary help or contract work when they have an overload of work, when they want to reduce their full-time, regular staff and payroll, or when someone has left the company unexpectedly or is away for a while. If you're filling in for someone and you make a favorable impression, you may be offered a permanent position in the company.

Temporary agencies usually charge a fee to an employer who hires a temporary worker on a permanent basis. Since the fee is often less than the ones charged by most permanent placement agencies, some companies hire temporaries with the prospect of offering permanent jobs if the people do well. Use of temporary employment services gives the employer a chance to observe candidates in action and to see if the people fit in well with the company.

Returning to the Workforce

Some people want to return to the workforce after being out of work for an extended period. This may be necessary to provide extra income, or someone may simply want to be active in the workforce again. If you're returning to the workforce after considerable time has passed, the first step is to renew your skills through independent reading and study. A computer course or a course in basic word processing is a must. If you don't have a good idea of the kind of job you want from your previous experience, you also may want to try temporary work, described in the previous section.

The Job Change

If you're presently working at a job and believe it's time for a change, consider several things before looking elsewhere:

- What condition do you expect to improve or change by moving to another job?
- Have you been at your present position long enough to have exhausted all possibilities of increased responsibilities or promotion?
- Have you considered seeking employment in another part of the company?
- Does your company encourage career pathing? (See the introductory sections in this chapter.) If so, have you talked with your supervisor or with the human resources office to determine what your next step for advancement would be?

If you've done all of these things and still believe that you need a change, set some goals to achieve the kind of change that will be beneficial to your career. When you already have a job, you have the financial security and time needed to search out another position.

The Resume

Your resume should be used as a marketing tool to sell yourself to a prospective employer. Before preparing it, however, take an inventory of your present abilities and the responsibilities you've had in your present and previous positions. After completing the inventory, decide which tasks you like the most and which you like the least. By doing this, you'll have a basis for comparing what you want to do with what is available to you when looking for your new job. It will also help you to avoid getting into a pattern similar to the one causing you to seek a change. When you've completed an accurate ability and task analysis, you'll be ready to prepare your work history.

Since you'll have limited page space on which to present everything relevant about your work history, you must be concise, well organized, and clear in your presentation and format. Many people are looking for jobs, and all of them have resumes. An employer may have to look through a hundred or more resumes for the same job before selecting people to be interviewed. Therefore, your resume must be written so that someone scanning it can immediately pick out your best assets and work experience.

The first step is to take the abilities and tasks you've listed on your inventory and put them into categories similar to the ones in the following list:

Planning and organization

Project coordination and management

Writing and editing

Supervision

Training

Purchasing

Record keeping

Word processing

If you have a definite career objective, state it on your resume. (See Format and the opening "objective" summaries in the sample resumes.) However, if you state a specific job title, such as *executive assistant*, you may be limiting yourself to a particular job market. There may be another job available that can combine all your skills with a title that doesn't even resemble that of *executive assistant*. On the other hand, you may have determined in your research that you definitely want the particular type of job atmosphere associated with the title *executive assistant*.

Preparation. It's possible to use identical information but change the emphasis in different resumes, thereby presenting a different image in each case. The resume format that you choose will depend on the way that you want to focus attention on your proficiencies and how you plan to submit the resume, such as electronically or by traditional mail.

The appearance of your resume is almost as important as its content, because it's a reflection of your professionalism. To project a professional, businesslike image, follow these general guidelines:

- Use quality, 20-pound, white or off-white paper for copies submitted by traditional mail.

- Use a high-quality copying process, such as offset printing or laser printer. Use a photocopier only if it produces copies of exceptional quality.

- Don't include personal information other than your name, residence/mailing address, telephone and fax numbers, and e-mail address. Employers don't need to know your marital status, height, weight, or sex and can't legally require you to provide extensive personal data.

- Include a heading (name, address, telephone and fax numbers, e-mail address, website) followed by your job objective (optional), work experience, educational background, and any pertinent information you want to list about other matters, such as club memberships or awards.

- Use action words (*developed, managed,* and so on) and the active voice (*I did,* not *it was done*), and avoid illogical changes in verb tenses (*arrange/arranged*) throughout the resume.

- Emphasize nouns (*telecommunications, records management,* and so on) in your resume since some employers use computers to scan resumes for keywords that match their job requirements.

- Try to keep the format open, uncluttered, and easy to read (see the sample resumes in Format), and avoid overuse of all-capital letters or italic type.

- Spell out names of organizations and titles.

- List educational and work experience in reverse order (most recent first).
- Use different headings for different categories of work or activities, such as *Student Teaching Experience, Community Volunteer Work,* and *Special Skills.*
- Be truthful, and don't overstate your skills or experience or provide other inaccurate or misleading information.
- Spell-check and manually proofread your resume carefully, several times, and have someone else also proofread it a final time.

Check the Internet for e-resume preparation and submission tips, including resume banks where you can post your resume, and make note of available writing services in case you need help in preparation. Various sites explain the formatting requirements and the various steps you should follow in sending your resume by e-mail, in posting it directly to a resume databank on an e-form, or in submitting a scannable paper resume (follow the instructions precisely).

The resume sites also have a wealth of other information, such as how to do an online job search, how to find job networking opportunities, and how to create a webpage advertising your skills and services to prospective employers. Many sites also have sample resumes and cover letters along with writing tips.

Although e-resumes have certain advantages (for example, they show an employer that you know how to use such technologies), it's important to be aware of the pitfalls too. Assess the resume banks you're considering, and choose those that selectively target employers instead of broadcasting resumes.

Also, be aware that your current employer may discover your resume on a job-seekers' site. Some agencies unethically take resumes from a site and post them elsewhere. To avoid this, include a statement when you file your resume saying that it may not be posted elsewhere by others. As a further precaution, file your resume *without your name.* Instead, have replies sent to an anonymous e-mail account. Or don't post your resume at all; rather, register with an online job agent service that will e-mail appropriate want ads directly to you.

Format. The general format that you use for a resume depends in part on the information you want to emphasize and the type of job you're seeking. It also depends on whether you intend to submit it as a traditional paper resume, a scannable paper resume, an e-mail attachment, or an e-form resume to be posted in a job databank. If you send an electronic version,

LINDA LEE WEBB
19 Monroe Drive
Cambridge, MA 02140

Phone 617.555.0000 *Fax* 617.555.0001 *E-mail* llwebb@freenet.com

OBJECTIVE   An administrative position offering responsibility, growth, and public contact

SUMMARY OF QUALIFICATIONS

Twelve years' successful experience in positions requiring extensive public contact.

College and business-school graduate, with numerous business, office, and computer courses.

Excellent oral and written communication skills.

Proven organization and planning abilities.

Practical experience as supervisor and team builder, with tested ability to train and motivate others.

RELEVANT ACCOMPLISHMENTS

1997-   DATATRONICS, INC., Burlington, MA
present *Executive Secretary to Vice President, Human Resources*

   Assisted in selecting, purchasing, and managing new office technologies.

   Managed all office activities in vice president's absence.

Chronological Resume

you should ask the recipients in your accompanying e-mail message if they would like a printed copy for their records.

Unless you're having your resume prepared by a resume writing service, you should not only check the information available on the Internet but also review a current book on resumes and cover letters. Books explaining how to use the Internet for job searches are also available.

LINDA LEE WEBB   **Page 2**

Scheduled executive committee meetings and recorded minutes for distribution to committee members.

Disseminated confidential personnel information to regional branch offices.

Supervised an assistant and periodic temporary help.

Prepared and scheduled newspaper and Internet ads for corporate job openings.

1993–
1997
DUNN AND TAYLOR ADVERTISING, INC., Medford, MA
Account Secretary

Organized and maintained electronic and paper client files for three executives.

Scheduled layout, design, and launch meetings with freelance designers and staff writers.

Corresponded with clients about scheduled advertising activity.

Arranged travel and planned itineraries for account executives.

EDUCATION AND TRAINING

1990–
1991
BUSINESS TRAINING PROGRAM
New England School of Business
Boston, MA

1989
B.A., ENGLISH
University of Massachusetts
Amherst, MA

Chronological Resume (continued)

Two popular types of resume for emphasizing either employment history or skills are the chronological resume (employment) and the functional resume (skills). A *chronological resume* (see the model Chronological Resume) is intended to emphasize previous types and places of employment. It's easy to follow and focuses on your job history or career development.

GEORGE F. WARD
119 Oakley Boulevard
Chicago, IL 60606

Phone **312.555.1324**   *Fax* **312.555.1325**   *E-mail* **gfward@proworld.com**

OBJECTIVE

Position as executive assistant to corporate officer or top executive, with opportunity to use strong communications skills

SUMMARY OF QUALIFICATIONS

- Eleven years' successful experience in administration and oral and written communication.

- Highly computer literate and skilled in electronic communications, document creation, information management, and new office technologies.

- Strong leadership qualities, with flexibility to work alone, as team member, or as a supervisor.

PROFESSIONAL SKILLS

ADMINISTRATION

- Standardized electronic and paper contract filing systems for sales department.

- Developed schedules and agendas for national sales staff.

- Created a new lead follow-up system for sales staff.

Functional Resume

If you want to emphasize your skills and abilities, as opposed to the positions held, you should use a *functional resume* (see the model Functional Resume). This type of resume details your skills and abilities under the specific function areas that you choose to highlight. If you've had too few or too many jobs, or if your experience looks scattered, a functional resume is desirable because it focuses on your marketable skills and avoids

---

GEORGE F. WARD   **Page 2**

- Maintained department's human resources records.

- Planned and coordinated activities for exhibits and trade shows.

COMMUNICATIONS

- Corresponded with customers about shipments and product information, and handled customer mail and telephone complaints.

- Instructed staff in the use of new telecommunications system.

- Wrote and published sales newsletter with desktop publishing software.

- Served as company representative, greeting public at trade shows.

TECHNICAL SKILLS

- Skilled in use of telecommunications equipment, computer, fax, scanner, voice mail, copier, and other equipment, systems, and technologies.

- Familiar with desktop publishing, word processing, and database software.

EMPLOYMENT HISTORY

1991-present: Administrative assistant to national sales manager, Parker-Hill Chemical Company, Chicago, IL

1989-1991: Customer relations assistant, Bona Labs, Inc., Chicago, IL

EDUCATION

1989: B.A., English, University of Chicago, Chicago, IL

Functional Resume (continued)

giving the impression that you haven't been around enough or have made too many moves.

Cover letter. When you write to a prospective employer, you should always send a cover letter with your resume or an e-mail with your resume attachment (unless an ad to which you're replying asks you not to do this).

Your message should be brief and businesslike while sparking the interest of the prospective employer. It should convey that you've researched the company and have related your skills to the company's needs. Since your letter may be scanned by computer, along with your resume, it's important to use keywords (nouns), as described previously.

Refer to the sample Cover Letter for Resume, and also study the models of winning cover letters provided on the Internet and in published resume books. Consider having the letter, as well as your resume, prepared by a professional resume-writing service if you have any doubts about your skill in doing it yourself.

Job Information Sources

The Internet. Thousands of company profiles and help-wanted sites are available for job searches on the Internet. Published books are also available in bookstores and libraries for those who aren't familiar with electronic career exploration and job hunting. Some of the books provide navigation tips and list dozens or even hundreds of websites and databanks containing regional, national, and international job listings. The available jobs are often organized by subject, such as broadcasting, education, and retail.

If you have access to the Internet at home, you can search online job databanks by industry, function, company name, geographic location, salary level, and various other factors. Therefore, before you write your resume or meet someone for a job interview, you can learn something about the company (also check the company's home page), find out the name of the company's recruiter, and study the requirements of the available position.

Since it's unlikely that a single list or site will have all the information you need, you should be prepared to take advantage of all available resources. These resources include electronic discussion groups used in networking, such as Internet mailing lists and newsgroups; help-wanted ads in electronic journals and newspapers; and other Internet services and resources, such as labor statistics.

Newspapers. Most job seekers check print or electronic newspapers before anything else. In fact, according to one study, responses to help-wanted ads in Sunday newspapers — not online help-wanted ads — result in most job hires. The classified sections often break down job opportunities by general categories of professional help, such as medical, business, and sales. Most office jobs are advertised in the business section of the classifieds, but specialized positions (medical, law, and so on) may appear under a different heading.

100 School Street
Framingham, MA 01701
508-555-0505

February 11, 2001

Ms. Valerie Kaishian
Human Resources Manager
Trademark Publications
50 Broad Street
Boston, MA 02110

Dear Ms. Kaishian:

I'd like to apply for the position of editorial assistant advertised in the February 10 edition of the *Boston Globe*. I believe this position would give me an excellent opportunity to apply my six years of experience in publishing and to use my strong educational background in English and written communication. My resume is enclosed for your review.

I greatly enjoyed my work in the editorial departments of two other publishing companies. In addition to handling the manuscript-review process, I communicated regularly with outside authors concerning deadlines and production schedules.

It would be a challenge and a privilege to work with the writers and editors at Trademark Publications, a company well known for its quality books and journals, and I'd like to tell you about my qualifications and how they match your requirements. I look forward to hearing from you about the possibility of a personal interview.

Thanks very much, Ms. Kaishian.

Sincerely,

Elizabeth Simms

Enc.: Resume

Cover Letter for Resume

If you're responding to numerous ads, keep a file of the ones you've answered so that you don't accidentally answer the same ad twice. If the ad requests a resume, promptly send one with a cover letter, but don't call companies unless they request it.

If possible, avoid blind ads that give only a box number instead of the employer's name. Companies placing blind ads often use box numbers because they don't want to reply to all of the applicants. If an ad sounds appealing, however, apply anyway, but don't expect a quick answer or even any answer. Companies usually do not acknowledge a letter or resume even when it's sent directly to them unless they want to schedule an interview. If you reply to an employment agency's newspaper ad, call first to find out if the job is still available. Agencies commonly run tantalizing ads or ads for jobs that have already been filled just to lure in job seekers.

Trade and specialty publication ads. If you're looking for a job in a specialized industry, check the ads in professional trade journals. If you want a job in advertising, for example, check the publications devoted to that subject.

Employment agencies. If you want to use an employment agency, look for one specializing in office jobs. You'll be able to tell from your yellow pages or from newspaper ads which agencies are best suited to your needs and qualifications. Since the agencies screen and test job candidates before sending them on interviews, you should treat an agency interview like an interview with a prospective employer, and prepare yourself accordingly.

Companies requiring confidentiality and wanting prescreened candidates often use employment agencies. If the hiring company has experienced success with employee placements from a particular agency, the employment counselor at that agency may be able to lead you to a good job. Avoid high-pressure agencies, however, whose walls are adorned with high-performance plaques for best placement records. Such agencies are more interested in the fee paid by the hiring company than in helping you find a job that fits your abilities.

When an agency is ready to send you on an interview, it will do all the communication and negotiation with the prospective employer before and after the interview. Therefore, you shouldn't call the company where you've been interviewed until you hear from your agency counselor.

If a job has been advertised as "fee paid," the hiring company may pay for the placement services. However, since some agencies charge placement fees to new hires, ask what the fees are before signing an employment contract.

School placement services. If you're a recent college or business school graduate, you should register with the school's placement office, which may conduct an electronic search for you. Companies often list job openings with school registrars. Be prepared to give the placement office full information on your background and job interests, the same as you would do with an employment agency. Some schools sponsor job fairs at which job recruiters and job seekers can meet.

The Interview

Interviewing is stressful, and everyone who has been on a job interview recognizes that uncomfortable feeling of being put on the spot. You must prepare yourself psychologically for the interview so that you can take control. Think of it as an opportunity to emphasize all of your positive professional qualities. At the same time, you must be aware of your weaknesses and know how to defend them or put them in a more positive perspective. In any case, being positive and enthusiastic is crucial to a successful interview.

Multimedia interview. Most interviews are held face to face, but some are initially conducted by telephone or by video. You can record a video for prospective employers by entering your electronic profile in a network database (check the Internet for database sites). You'll be asked to respond to questions such as "What is your most noteworthy achievement?" "What are your key strengths?" and "How did you solve a recent problem you encountered?"

If you're not happy with your answers, you can rerecord them. After you've finished, the network will match your skills with company requirements, and companies that have the network's software can access your prerecorded video and observe your performance. If a company is impressed, it may contact you to set up a traditional, face-to-face interview.

Image. Regardless of the type of interview — telephone, face-to-face, or video — you should consider your image. For face-to-face and on-site interviews, dress conservatively and professionally. Avoid too much jewelry or makeup, unruly hair, and unbusinesslike habits. All interviewees should follow the same rule used by employed persons: Look as though you're going to a business meeting rather than to a nightclub or on a camping trip.

In addition to considering your appearance, you need to be alert to other things that affect your image. Other factors to consider include your body language, voice tone and quality, command of the English language, and attentiveness and listening skills.

Pre-interview research. Use the Internet, your local library, and other available sources to find out as much as possible about the company before you go to the interview. If you're dealing with an employment agency, you may be able to collect some of this information from the employment counselor. Allow plenty of time to get to the interview, and if you're unsure of the location, call and ask the receptionist or operator for directions.

If you're leaving your present job for a negative reason, don't discuss it with the interviewer. In fact, don't discuss former jobs in any context other than explaining your responsibilities, skills, and overall work experience. Speak confidently, and try not to appear nervous or jittery when answering questions.

Salary. If the salary range was not stated by the employment agency or in the company's ads, wait for the interviewer to introduce the topic. If you use an employment agency, it will handle the salary negotiations. Find out what the salary range for the position is *before* you answer any questions about your requirements. Keep in mind that you should aim for an increase in salary when you make a job change. The Internet and many published books on interviews, careers, and job searches have tips on such negotiations.

Ask questions about the benefits package, overtime policy, and the salary and performance review process. If you're going to be reviewed within six months for a salary increase, you may be willing to start at a lower rate than if you will not be reviewed for a year from your starting date with the company.

Interview questions. Prepare yourself in advance for some of the more difficult questions an interviewer might ask:

- Give me an example of how you exercised leadership in a recent work situation.
- How did you organize one of your recent projects and manage your time?
- Tell me about a recent decision you made and the process you used to arrive at the decision.
- How did you go about solving some problem you recently had to deal with?
- Have you ever been criticized about some aspect of your work, and if so, how did you respond to the criticism?

- What type of communications skills do you have, and how have you put them to use?
- Have you worked as a team player recently, and if so, how did you perform?
- Give me an example of how you've had to use persuasion and whether it worked.
- Did you have to deal with a lot of pressure in a previous job, and if so, how did you cope with it?

Try to anticipate as many questions as you can — including traditional ones such as "What are your goals?" "Why do you want this position?" and "Why should we hire you?" — and prepare yourself with sound answers in advance. For example, if someone asks you why the company should hire you, you might respond in this way:

> You've said that you need a person with state-of-the-art technology skills, the ability to communicate effectively, and strong organizational abilities. I've had practical experience in all of those areas and have been successful in each one.

The key to a successful interview is being able to respond to questions with intelligent, confident, honest answers — answers that sound like a personal response, not a memorized cliche.

In addition to preparing answers to potential questions, also prepare a list of questions that you want to ask the interviewer, such as the following examples:

- How important is this job to the company?
- Why did the last person leave?
- What would a typical workday be like?
- What training programs are available?
- Does the company have any plans to expand or retract its operations [or other, specific activity]?

When you meet the interviewer, stand up if you're seated somewhere, shake hands, and say something such as "I appreciate your [or thanks for] seeing me today." (Do and say something similar when you leave.) During the interview, make eye contact, sit straight and still, keep your hands in your lap, and avoid fidgeting. If the interviewer doesn't ask you to use his or her first name, use a title such as *Dr., Mr.,* or *Ms.*

100 School Street
Framingham, MA 01701
508-555-0505

February 27, 2001

Mr. Lee C. Costa
Editorial Director
Trademark Publications
50 Broad Street
Boston, MA 02110

Dear Mr. Costa:

EDITORIAL ASSISTANT POSITION

Thank you for the opportunity to discuss the editorial assistant position at Trademark Publications. I'm very excited about the work that you described during my interview yesterday. It sounds challenging, and I know that the activities involved in the position would motivate me to pursue an editorial career with great enthusiasm.

I want to reiterate my strong interest in this position, and I also want to thank you for taking time to show me around the company and explain in detail the nature of its publications. I look forward to further discussions with you.

Thanks very much, Mr. Costa.

Sincerely,

Elizabeth Simms

Follow-up Thank You Letter

Interview follow-up. Always send a thank you letter to your interviewer. This professional courtesy may be the touch that gets you the job over another equally qualified applicant who neglects to do this. Refer to the Follow-up Thank You Letter for an example of a brief, but thoughtful, message.

Human Relations

PERSONAL INTERACTION

Although e-mail and other technologies may have reduced the amount of telephone and in-person contact for some, getting along with other people is a daily requirement for those who work in an office, regardless of the type of exchange. Within an office, there's still a substantial degree of interaction with coworkers, executives, customers, clients, and the general public.

Inevitably, you won't like everyone you meet or work with, but you don't have to like someone to foster a good working relationship. If you present an even-tempered, positive image to others, most will respond to you in the same way. This ability to interact successfully with many different personalities will play a major role in your career development.

It's a challenge to deal with difficult persons, and you'll likely encounter it many times. Nevertheless, to thrive, as well as survive, in a business environment, you must be objective and aware of the ways in which you interact with all types of people. Most people have prejudices or predetermined ideas about others that affect their ability to communicate positively. It's necessary to avoid stereotyping and approach everyone and every situation with an open mind. To deal with people effectively, even difficult people, you must be perceptive and understanding. Stereotyping builds an immediate barrier against open communication — a barrier that will thwart sensitive interactions with others.

It's just as important to evaluate the way that you interact with other people as it is to evaluate how they interact with you. If you have an innate understanding of why people project certain images, it will be much easier for you to respond appropriately and interact positively with employers, coworkers, customers, and clients.

Companies expect their employees to be pleasant and businesslike with visitors, servicepersons, and customers. People tend to associate a business with the person from that organization with whom they've had direct contact. Therefore, you're "the company" to someone from the outside who meets or talks with you, and the corporate image that you project should be above reproach at all times.

Image

Your *image* is the portrait that you present to others with whom you interact, and the more professional and knowledgeable that you appear to be, the more favorably others will view you and respond to you. Among the most prominent factors that affect image are appearance (grooming, style of dress, neatness, and so on), manner of communication (correct grammar, tone, enunciation, and so on), attitude, ethical standards, cooperativeness, level of self-confidence, intelligence, and work skills and abilities. Such factors singly and together create the image that you project and determine whether others will view you — and, in turn, your company — favorably or unfavorably.

Disposition. Certain characteristics are so important that they influence most of the other factors affecting your image. Disposition is such a factor. For example, it's necessary to be even-tempered and good-natured to maintain a pleasant working atmosphere. A moody or irritable employee can adversely affect the morale of the entire office. Also, a good sense of humor can help you through many stressful situations.

You may be asked to do a rush job that will involve overtime, or you may be asked to perform a task in an unreasonably short time. If you allow such situations to upset you emotionally or make you lose your temper, you'll be displaying an immaturity that will haunt you when later you want to make a career move. People remember unpleasant situations and the way that people respond to them.

Stability. Another crucial factor in image is stability. You may be well dressed and highly skilled in specific tasks, but if your responses to problems are emotional and ineffective, your image will suffer, and your good qualities will be overshadowed. A well-integrated personality stands out among others. If you're able to remain calm when an upsetting situation develops, you'll soon be known as a stable employee.

Problem solving is part of an office professional's job. A clear and logical approach to a problem is to identify it, break it down into components, and then determine a workable solution. Much valuable time and energy can be wasted by overreacting to a situation instead of calmly trying to devise a sensible way to change it for the better. The more responsibility you assume, the more problems you'll encounter. However, if you deal with problematic situations as they occur in a rational, step-by-step fashion, your self-confidence in assuming more responsibility will be enhanced.

Flexibility. Image is directly and significantly affected by a person's flexibility. Business environments can change rapidly as a result of growth, changes in the management, fluctuating economy, and many other factors. To maintain a position in a business that's going through such changes, you must be able to adapt easily to new situations and be flexible enough to accept changes in personnel, your duties, and office practices and procedures.

Effective Listening

How well you listen to others can profoundly affect your business relations with them. Psychologists believe that we *hear* only 20 percent of what's being said and *listen* to only 10 percent of what we hear. To follow instructions and successfully handle many of the tasks you're asked to do in an office, your listening ability must be markedly above those percentages. Actively listening is also important when disagreements exist so that others will believe you've been fair in hearing them and trying to understand their position.

To learn how to listen actively, try to clear your mind of all other thoughts and concentrate only on what is actually being said. Take notes, and avoid interrupting the speaker until his or her thought has been completed. Try not to analyze what you're listening to until you've heard the complete message. If you don't take time to listen carefully, you may reach the wrong conclusion, or you may have to redo your work.

Sometimes a speaker doesn't convey a thought clearly enough for you to be able to follow directions. But if you've taken notes, you should at least be able to ask the right questions to clarify the instructions. It's very irritating to a busy executive when an assistant continually returns with numerous questions, the answers to which were already provided in previous instructions.

Office Etiquette

A certain protocol must be followed in a business or professional office. Even though some practices, such as the use of first names, may vary from one office to another, basic courtesy should be an integral part of your work habits. If you share an open space with others, for example, you need to avoid doing things that might disturb them, such as playing music, humming or singing, or speaking too loudly.

Some rules of etiquette are obvious to anyone qualified to work in an office. You shouldn't, for example, attend to grooming in public areas or at your desk (use the restroom). But other rules of etiquette may not be as obvious, such as whose name you should mention first in making introductions.

This chapter describes some of the important rules of etiquette that affect one's interaction with other employees and with callers or visitors in the office. Chapter 4, "Telecommunications," Telephone Etiquette and Voice mail etiquette, and Chapter 5, "Mail Processing," E-mail etiquette, describe the rules that apply in various telecommunications contacts.

Interaction with coworkers and visitors. Office professionals regularly have contacts with assistants, coworkers, executives, and visitors. The trend today is toward informality in the office, particularly in small companies. Nevertheless, you should follow the established pattern in your office and company. In most cases, you should wait to be asked before addressing supervisors and executives by their first names. Even if an executive asks you to do this, you should generally use the person's last name and title, such as *Dr., Mr.,* or *Ms.,* in the presence of strangers: *Dr. Shaw will be out of the office until Monday.*

Maintaining the proper degree of formality and respect with visitors doesn't mean that you need to sound stiff and cold. It's possible to show respect and be friendly at the same time, and office professionals should aim to do no less. A voice-with-a-smile approach is mandatory, whether you're talking on the telephone, recording a voice-mail greeting or leaving a message, or greeting a visitor entering the office.

Visitors must never be ignored. If they have questions, be as helpful as possible, referring them to another person or office if appropriate. When they must wait in your office, offer them a chair and reading material. If they need to make a telephone call, direct them to a telephone, preferably one where they'll have some privacy.

Making introductions. You'll probably have to announce or introduce visitors from time to time, and your office may have a specific procedure that you should follow. For example, you may be required to announce visitors over an intercom or step into the executive's office and explain who is waiting and why. Even with such a policy, however, there may be certain people, such as the president of the company, who usually should be told to go right in without any inquiry about the purpose of the visit. In some offices, however, executives may not be willing to see visitors who don't have an appointment, and you'll then have to schedule the visit for a later time and day.

When you need to introduce a visitor, the rule is simple. In most cases, mention the name of the higher-ranking person first. However, if you're introducing a client or very important visitor, mention the other person's name first, regardless of rank:

> Dr. Samuels [*executive*], this is Wendy Baker from the Word Processing Department.
>
> Ms. Brewster [*client*], this is Dr. Samuels.
>
> Ms. Nielson [*executive*], this is Joel Inman, Bob Watt's assistant. He has a question about the new formula that we released last week.

To introduce yourself to an unannounced visitor, mention both your name (first and last or first only, as is customary or required in your office) and your supervisor's name, and ask if you may be of help. However, some believe the use of first names only stereotypes the person as a low-ranking employee and that office professionals should include their last names, the same as executives and other higher-ranking individuals do:

> Good morning. I'm Carla [*or* Carla Williams], Mr. McDermitt's assistant. How may I help you?
>
> Good afternoon, Ms. Whitman. I'm David [*or* David Ferguson], Mr. Winslow's assistant. He just left for a meeting, but is there anything I might help you with?

If you and the visitor know each other, the introduction is obviously unnecessary, but it's always polite to ask if you may be of help:

> Good morning, Tom. What can we do for you today?

Gift giving. Executives may give holiday or birthday gifts to their assistants, but the assistants are not required to give gifts to their employers. However, you may be expected to keep an address list and a record of all employees, customers or clients, and others to whom an executive sends cards or gifts throughout the year. If you maintain the information by computer, it can be quickly and easily revised. The list should identify the gift and the amount spent each year. This information is useful in future years and will help to ensure that an executive doesn't unintentionally give someone the same gift the next time.

For gifts to persons in foreign countries, consult a guidebook on the particular region. Protocol for gift giving varies in different countries, and it's important to determine the practices in the particular country to avoid offending someone. A clock, for example, has a morbid connotation in China, and handkerchiefs suggest the breaking of a relationship in the

Middle East. White flowers in Japan are associated with death, and red roses in Germany signal a romantic interest.

Office Politics

The term *office politics* often has a negative connotation, although it shouldn't. It's true that getting involved in office politics in terms of gossip and deceitful behavior is negative. However, to do your work, you'll find it necessary to understand the overall political structure of your office and your place within it. Whether your office is large or small, there's always a political structure based on power and decision making. People striving for advancement in business regularly develop and apply new strategies to enhance their positions within the corporate political structure.

Someone who doesn't have a keen political sense can easily be caught in the middle of difficult situations. To avoid this, you need to be observant and aware of other people's positions in the organization. Determine who gets certain jobs done and who makes the really important decisions. Treat those people accordingly. Read the company's organization chart and determine the structure of your office and that of the corporation in general. This kind of knowledge will help you in dealing with other departments and disseminating information outside your office. Few things are more embarrassing than making political blunders because of your ignorance about someone else's position.

Beneficial office politics. Those who accept the fact that office politics exists can use it as a beneficial tool rather than a hindrance. For example, instead of waiting for things to happen and simply responding to situations and conditions, you could actively develop your own program:

- Regularly demonstrate a commitment to your employer in terms of interest, appreciation, and loyalty.
- Absorb as much information as you can — every day — about your job and the company.
- Develop as many contacts as possible in your own office, in other offices, and outside the company.
- Show a willingness to take on additional responsibilities.
- Treat both company personnel and outsiders with consideration and respect at all times.
- Cultivate a reputation for being cooperative and helpful.
- Offer praise when it's due, and never criticize assistants or coworkers in the presence of others.

- Ignore gossip, and don't participate in spreading rumors.

- Document your progress and achievements, and periodically provide a brief status report to your supervisor. This will help counteract any effort by others to claim credit for your work.

- Always use honest, legitimate, and ethical strategies to advance your position.

- Refute unfair or inaccurate claims against you immediately with clear and accurate facts, but don't lose your temper or get involved in an emotional argument.

- Never reveal confidential information or give others reason to doubt your trustworthiness.

- Don't hesitate to accept honest offers of assistance that will advance your career, but beware of offers that have undesirable conditions placed on you.

Assertiveness. Often a fine line exists between being assertive and aggressive. Aggressive behavior is usually counterproductive, but assertiveness can be beneficial. You can stand up for your rights at work without being hostile. For example, you should be able to deal with those who may be rude or trying to take advantage of you without becoming emotionally upset, intimidated, or overaggressive in response. Assertiveness training teaches you to express your opinions and feelings candidly and freely, without putting others down. One way to do this is by using the pronoun *we* when problems arise: *We* have a problem. What should *we* do about it?

Avoid continual emphasis on *I* (not *I* think; *I* want; *I* need) to the extent that you sound demanding and self-centered. Giving the impression that "we're all in this together" and "we all want what's best for the company" will help ensure that your assertiveness is not mistaken for hostility or aggressiveness.

Study a book or tape on assertiveness training if you want to know more about the subject. In today's highly competitive business environment, recognition of an assertive personality, a nonassertive personality, and an aggressive/hostile personality is essential to enjoyment of your work as well as to survival in the workplace.

Human Relations Problems

The types of human relations problems that develop in a company are as varied as the people who work there. The problems that an office professional must deal with may be different from those that an executive must handle. It's not usually an assistant's responsibility to deal with absenteeism, for example, unless the person's overall responsibility includes supervising someone who is often absent or late. Then it's necessary to discuss the problem with the one who's not performing properly, monitor the situation, and report it to the executive in charge if dismissal appears necessary.

Sexual harassment. One of the most serious problems that an office professional may face is sexual harassment. Although specific guidelines are available from the Equal Employment Opportunity Commission (EEOC), the manner in which individuals define *sexual harassment* is not always the same.

According to the EEOC, sexual harassment includes any unwelcome attention that focuses on an employee's sex rather than his or her status as an employee. It may include leering, offensive remarks, unwanted touching, or demands for sexual favors. Therefore, using sexual references or gestures that create a hostile or intimidating environment is illegal, and receiving sexual favors may not be made a condition of employment or advancement in a company.

Companies may be held legally responsible for acts of sexual harassment by their employees and are required to take steps to prevent this occurrence. For example, they should publish for their employees a description of the sanctions that will be imposed on harassers and explain what an employee should do if sexual harassment occurs. If it does, employers should take immediate steps to end it and discipline the harasser. It's also important to protect the victim from retaliation or further harassment.

If you feel intimidated, pressured, or uncomfortable and believe you are the object of sexual harassment, take the following action:

- Firmly state to the person doing the harassing that the behavior disturbs you and that you want it to stop immediately. Hesitation or delay may cause the harasser to believe that you're willing to tolerate the behavior.

- Document the behavior. Write down all dates, times, places, circumstances, and types of improper and unwanted behavior, including your attempts to discourage it.

- If the actions persist, write to the harasser (if you feel comfortable doing this), explaining that the behavior is disturbing and again state that you want it to stop. Tell the person what steps you will take if the harassment doesn't stop. Be certain to keep a copy of your letter where it cannot be found and destroyed by the harasser.

- Keep copies of other evidence that you find, such as offensive jokes or drawings posted on a bulletin board.

- Collect written comments or other evidence indicating that you're a skilled, successful employee whose good work and proper behavior will dispel any suggestions by the harasser to the contrary.

- If your letter doesn't end the problem, discuss it with your supervisor or the person specified in your company's complaint guidelines.

- If that also fails to end the harassment, file a formal complaint with the nearest EEOC office (employers may not legally demote or fire you for filing a complaint).

- Consult a reliable attorney if you have questions about bringing a lawsuit against the offender.

Substance abuse. Alcoholism and other forms of substance abuse cost companies millions of dollars in lost productivity, inferior-quality work, and absenteeism. If someone has such a problem and it affects *your* work, you have no choice but to respond to it. However, it's unwise to play doctor or psychologist. Rather, if you're asked for help, recommend that the person seek professional assistance, and, if possible, provide names and addresses where such help can be found.

Injuries and illnesses. Accidents and illnesses are a part of life and must be handled in the workplace as well as at home. Most companies have standard procedures for handling emergencies and minor problems. Usually, the proper steps are described in the employee handbook.

In large companies, a doctor or nurse may be on the premises and should be contacted immediately in case of emergency. If a coworker is ill or injured but can report to a nursing station without help, offer to take the person's telephone calls, and notify the person's supervisor of his or her absence. If in-house medical help does not exist, telephone the paramedics or hospital emergency room if an employee is severely ill or injured. If the problem is minor, offer to call a taxi, or find someone to drive the person to a doctor. In general, be as helpful as possible, and make the person's health and well being the major consideration.

Troublemakers. Some people thrive on disruptive behavior, but office professionals know that a cooperative, harmonious environment is essential for them to perform effectively. Although it's often best to ignore disruptive behavior, unresolved conflicts divert energy from the job and may escalate into violence. If unpleasant behavior doesn't dissipate from lack of attention (most troublemakers are fueled by attention), it will be necessary to deal with it.

Hostile employees create stress and tension in the office for everyone. Sometimes, however, it's possible to defuse a situation by agreeing without really agreeing:

> *Hostile employee:* I'm sick of this stupid company and all the stupid people in it. All I ever do is work, work, work.
>
> *Response:* Now and then we all need to get away from everything and everyone. I can appreciate your frustration if you haven't had a break for a while. Why don't you ask Mr. Brown for a little time off?

If someone is angry with you, keep a comfortable distance between you and the irate individual. Either stand and face the person or invite the person to sit down. Make eye contact, use your listening skills, and show concern by nodding or asking questions. If you've made an error, admit it, and express your strong interest in rectifying matters. If you haven't made an error, express appreciation for the person's concern, and calmly explain the true facts.

If the situation escalates, state that you don't want to disturb others in the office, and suggest talking in another place or at another time. However, never agree to meet an irrational or aggressive person in a place where others are not available to help you, should you need assistance. Instead, you might suggest that the two of you meet with your supervisor (or other authority figure) to resolve the matter.

Above all, don't allow yourself to be goaded into a shouting match or violent argument. If you believe that you're in danger, immediately buzz or call security, step into your supervisor's (or other) office, or ask any other nearby person for help.

Ethics in the Office

Many companies have a written code of ethical conduct, often included in their employee handbooks. It usually describes professional standards that all employees are expected to meet, including the proper procedures for safeguarding confidential information and protecting the privacy of sensitive company decisions and actions. The discussion also should state the consequences of unethical behavior.

Companies have a right to expect their employees to conduct themselves ethically and appropriately and to demonstrate their loyalty to the company when their behavior is put to the test. However, companies don't have a right to ask employees to break the law or commit some questionable, dishonest act on their behalf. Employees can and should refuse to commit a crime or behave improperly, unethically, or immorally.

In the absence of written rules or guidelines, employees should, on their own initiative, conduct themselves properly. To ensure that you're within the bounds of ethical behavior, do *not* do any of the following:

- Discuss with outsiders your employer's private business affairs or any dealings with clients or customers
- Participate in conversations or actions designed to injure the reputation of or compete unfairly against another person
- Take credit for another employee's accomplishments
- Allow another employee to be blamed for your errors or failures
- Take company supplies for personal use
- Use company equipment (fax, computer, copier, telephone, and so on) for personal purposes
- Leave private company files, diskettes, or other confidential material in an unprotected or unsecured area
- Leave drawers, files, storage areas, and other rooms or containers unlocked overnight or at other times when you're away
- Allow visitors to wait in your supervisor's office while he or she is away
- Leave sensitive material on your desk uncovered and in full view for anyone to read
- Discard sensitive documents without shredding them (but follow state and federal laws and company policy regarding the disposition of documents)
- Copy paper or electronic documents illegally (observe the copyright statement on the material)

WORKING WITH EXECUTIVES AND COWORKERS

Successful office professionals know not only how to work *for* someone but how to work *with* someone. They understand the goals of their supervisors and the overall objectives of their companies. By exercising initiative, using common sense, and accepting responsibility, they're able to work effectively as team players.

Working as a Team Player

Team players respect the contributions and value of other participants in an office. They show this respect by being concerned about their welfare and being happy and enthusiastic about their accomplishments. The following are examples of steps that you can take to become a better team player:

- Replace *I* and *me* whenever possible with *we, us, the company,* and other team words.
- Accept responsibility for your own mistakes, and never blame others for your failings.
- Be willing to admit your weaknesses and take steps to overcome them, and be willing to help others overcome their weaknesses, thereby helping the team in both cases to function more effectively.
- Translate individual successes and failures in terms of team successes and failures, and have discussions about both with others.
- Focus on company needs and priorities, and cooperate with others who are pursuing objectives that satisfy such needs and priorities.
- Meet daily or at least regularly with others to plan work and set up cooperative individual schedules and deadlines that will preclude time-wasting conflicts.
- Communicate changes in your own plans or schedules regularly to others so that they can make any necessary or helpful adjustments in their plans and schedules.
- Offer to help others when they're absent or overloaded with work, and accept their help when you have the same problem.
- Avoid gossip, but maintain confidences when someone reveals something to you and needs your support and loyalty.
- Develop a networking philosophy in which you share (both give and receive) thoughts, questions, ideas, skills, and so on.
- Find a mentor if you're a newcomer, and encourage other new members to do the same.
- Develop a sensitive tone, whether you're a team leader or member, when you must offer corrective advice.
- Set standards, if you're a team leader, and clearly communicate and enforce them (always in terms of group objectives and the organization's overall goals).

Increasing Your Worth in the Office

In an office, your ability to accept responsibility and be accountable for your tasks is judged daily. If you're conscientious and well organized, you should be able to perform those tasks efficiently. Especially, your willingness to assume additional responsibility will be looked on as an asset when your supervisor evaluates your performance.

One way to increase your worth is to assist your supervisor actively in managing the flow of information and projects in the office. To effect true teamwork, you should meet with the executive in charge at least once a day, preferably early in the day, to set priorities for the day's activities, including matters such as appointments, anticipated telephone calls, correspondence keyboarding, and incoming and outgoing mail.

Try to avoid crises by knowing the executive's daily plans in advance. Then you can at least try to expedite the inflow and outflow of people and paper. For example, be certain that the executive's appointment book and electronic and paper calendar entries match yours, and take the initiative to call expected visitors if you know that the executive is running behind schedule.

Try to remember what took place the day before (consult your calendar or appointment book) so that you can, if possible, anticipate tomorrow's events. If your supervisor travels a lot, know where he or she can be reached at all times, and find out what's required of you during the absence.

Working with an Executive

Getting along with your supervisor, who will have a major impact on your future, is essential. Many qualified office professionals have lost chances for advancement because of personality conflicts or other situations that resulted in poor recommendations.

Learning to control your temper and emotions in business is therefore essential to your professional development. If you take criticism personally, for example, and harbor resentment about it, you probably won't be able to handle your job very well. It helps to evaluate a situation before taking oral or written action. Usually, criticism from an executive is warranted, and it's meant only to help you improve your work, not to hurt your feelings or embarrass you.

Sometimes, however, you may have to work with an extremely difficult person. Even though you may make every effort to get along with an executive, it just won't work. In such a case, you may believe it's best to ask the human resources office for a transfer or to look for another job in a different company.

Trust is another factor in a successful relationship with an executive. Many persons are under a great deal of pressure and will use you as a sounding board for confidential matters, particularly if you display good judgment. Absolute loyalty to your supervisor is therefore essential and can mean the difference between working *with* someone instead of simply *for* someone. If you're able to look on your working relationship as a *team* effort, you'll be considered capable of assuming as much responsibility as your supervisor is willing to delegate.

Working for One Person

Most office professionals work for just one person, but the job similarity ends there. An office professional's duties and relationship with an executive will depend on the type of activities handled by the executive and the type of person he or she is — an easygoing individual, a workaholic, someone who likes delegating responsibility, someone who dislikes delegating work, and so on. Regardless of any difference in personalities and duties from one office to another, a few general guidelines apply in most cases:

- Use open and regular communication with your supervisor to contribute to a more successful and enjoyable relationship.
- Do everything possible to encourage a spirit of teamwork and cooperation.
- Respect your supervisor, and show appreciation for the demands and pressures of his or her position.
- Support the executive's policies and practices in and out of the office, whether or not you have other preferences or opinions.
- Learn how to accept criticism, and use it as a learning experience to improve your skills and abilities.
- Use tact and diplomacy in pointing out serious errors made by the executive (correct minor errors yourself without mentioning them).
- Don't let annoying personal traits in your supervisor weaken the relationship (you may have annoying habits as well).
- Regularly demonstrate a willingness to learn and perform new and difficult tasks that will help the person and will increase your value to the executive.

Working for More Than One Person

An office professional who works for more than one person has to be especially adaptable and flexible. Some people are able to handle the special demands of this type of work better than others. Since the personalities and types of work may vary, you'll need to make abrupt shifts during the day to adjust to each person's needs and workload. The same guidelines just mentioned about working for only one person apply here, too, with a few additional tips:

- Don't let any personal preferences for one executive or for one type of work over another show. Rather, treat everyone as part of the team, pursuing the same overall objectives for the benefit of the company.

- Don't criticize or find fault with a more demanding executive. Adjust your own work habits to fit each situation and each person.

- If problems in scheduling occur, discuss them with each executive so that they can work out a priority schedule that's agreeable to everyone. Keep all of them informed about your workload so that they don't develop unreasonable expectations.

- Study time-management guidelines (see Time Management), and implement suggestions that will help you handle an unpredictable and, at times, complex schedule of work.

Working with Travelers and Telecommuters

If your supervisor travels or often works in a remote location, such as another business office or a home office, you'll have to handle many functions in a different way. The executive is no longer immediately available to solve unexpected problems, meet visitors, sign letters or documents, and do all of the things an on-site executive normally does. Nevertheless, many of the guidelines described in the previous two sections not only apply but also become more critical, and a few new requirements come into play when an executive works by telecommuting:

- Be prepared to work independently, without supervision, most of the time.

- Be prepared to assume greater responsibility, since you may have to take over some duties and decision making usually handled by an on-site executive.

- Develop clear guidelines with your supervisor concerning the limits of your authority during the person's absence.

- Develop clear guidelines with your supervisor concerning the proper procedures for handling specific tasks (make a list of such duties, and ask your supervisor to comment on each one).

- Make full use of e-mail, fax machines, voice messaging, and other communication devices and processes to overcome the distance between you and the remote office.

- Ask your supervisor whom you should contact in his or her absence in case an emergency arises that you can't handle.

- If you're the one who is telecommuting, clarify the procedures you're expected to follow and other requirements, as well as hours of work, the schedule for attending on-site meetings, and so on.

WORKING WITH ASSISTANTS

Most office professionals will work with a temporary or permanent assistant at some time during their careers. They may be responsible for recommending or hiring the assistant and training and supervising the person. In some cases, they may also be responsible for firing an assistant who doesn't work out.

Assistants may be hired to perform one task, such as keyboarding, but usually are needed for miscellaneous work, such as making copies, filing paper documents, opening the postal mail, processing correspondence and other material, and delivering or picking up various items. The more of such work that an assistant does, the more time that you'll have for higher-level assignments.

Delegating Guidelines

The only way that an assistant can help you cope with a work overload is if you delegate the extra work. Although you may be able to solicit additional help from coworkers or persuade your supervisor that he or she must handle certain tasks when you're seriously behind schedule, the best solution is often a temporary or permanent assistant.

To delegate effectively to this person, you need to know something about him or her so that you don't have to redo work that really wasn't appropriate for the assistant:

- What educational level and skills does the assistant have?
- Is the assistant known to be accurate and capable?
- How much time should you spend in training the assistant?

Be certain that the assistant can do the work that you want to delegate, and make your expectations fit the person and the situation. Give very clear, precise instructions. Write them down if necessary, and ask questions to be certain that the assistant understands you. Especially, be willing to give up some of your duties, even if you would rather do the work yourself, and give the assistant a chance.

Training and Supervising an Assistant

Most assistants will need orientation, training, and ongoing supervision. Presumably, they will know how to use basic office machines and common software, such as word processing, and will have learned the fundamentals of filing and processing routine information. However, they'll need to learn the specific practices and procedures used in your office, and they'll need to be briefed on the activities of your company. Certain traits and strategies will help both you and the assistant develop an effective working relationship:

- Welcome the newcomer, and show him or her around the office and the company. Invite the assistant to join you and other coworkers for lunch.

- Conduct an orientation session that covers office ethics and etiquette, the use and care of all office equipment and software, the use of the Internet, and how to handle various practices and procedures, such as filing and answering the telephone.

- Give the assistant a copy of the company's employee handbook and a directory of officers and department heads or of all employees, if available.

- Assure the person that it's not necessary to absorb everything at once. You'll answer questions and provide more detailed assistance later.

- Be patient, and adjust your training to the learning rate of the assistant.

- Use your sense of humor to alleviate tension and help the newcomer relax.

- Set up a routine, such as a morning conference to introduce new work and review the previous day's work.

- Explain all new tasks slowly and carefully, including very basic information that you may take for granted.

- Be alert to special skills and abilities that the assistant may have but never mentioned.

- Regularly test the assistant's level of understanding by asking him or her to demonstrate some task.

- Regularly encourage questions, and give the assistant time to ask them.

- Try a different approach if your initial instructions appear to fail, but don't show boredom or impatience.

- Discourage any tendency of the assistant to use office time discussing personal matters.

- Make all criticism positive ("only two errors this time — soon you'll be doing error-free work") to build up, rather than tear down, the person's confidence and self-esteem.

- Include instruction with your criticism when appropriate, such as how to improve spelling, punctuation, and grammar.

- Compliment the assistant whenever praise is due, and offer any other comments or suggestions that will motivate the person to work harder and better.

- Monitor the assistant's progress, and discuss all problems and solutions with the assistant as soon as possible.

- Discuss with your supervisor the need to replace an assistant who is clearly the wrong person for the job, and, if possible and appropriate, direct the assistant to a more suitable position.

A properly trained assistant will be very helpful to a busy office professional and the executive in charge. Although the task of training may seem time consuming in the beginning, it should save time in the end if the assistant successfully adjusts to the work and becomes a useful member of the office team.

TIME MANAGEMENT

Time management is a crucial factor in a successful career. Someone who is highly skilled in planning and scheduling tasks for optimum productivity and is adept at controlling distractions and interruptions has a head start. For most office professionals, time management must take into account the extent to which one must deal with and schedule work in cooperation with others — executives, coworkers, customers, and others outside the company.

Planning and Scheduling

Planning each workday and scheduling daily tasks and meetings with others are routine procedures for most office professionals. It's virtually impossible to handle a heavy workload, combining short- and long-term projects and high- and low-priority tasks, without some degree of planning and scheduling. To plan and schedule effectively, however, you need to know other factors, such as how much time certain tasks usually take and what times during the day you have the fewest interruptions.

Analyzing the workday. Time-management experts recommend that you analyze your workload over a two- to three-week period. To do this, you need to list all categories of work associated with your job and, each day, record both the total time spent on each category and the time of day when the work is done. You may use your computer to set up and print a columnar-style, fill-in record sheet, or you may purchase a columnar accounting pad or sheet.

In either case, start with the left column, listing the time of day in 15-minute increments from the time you begin work until the time you leave: *8:00–8:15 a.m., 8:15–8:30 a.m.,* and so on. Across the top of the page, head each of the other columns with a job category pertinent to your position: *mail processing, filing, telephoning,* and so on.

After the job categories are listed, make copies of this master sheet, one for each day of your analysis period. Throughout each day, put an *X* in, or check off, every time slot that applies to a particular task:

	TASKS			
TIME	Mail processing	Filing	Telephoning	Etc.
8:00-8:15 a.m.	X		X	
8:15-8:30 a.m.	X		X	
8:30-8:45 a.m.		X		
8:45-9:00 a.m.		X	X	
Etc.				

At the end of your record-keeping period, carefully analyze the results, and put your findings in writing:

- Is a pattern evident?
- Did you do each job at the best possible time?
- Were long jobs requiring a lot of concentration handled during periods of few interruptions?
- Should some similar tasks scattered throughout the day be combined at one time for greater efficiency?

Ask yourself as many questions as desired, and, as the record suggests, make any necessary adjustments in your future planning and scheduling.

Using to-do lists. After you have a better idea of how you should group activities and in which time slot you should schedule them, you'll be ready to begin each day with an orderly, intelligent plan. Start each morning by preparing a daily to-do list on which you write every known task that you'll likely handle that day. Also, at the beginning of each week and each month, make up weekly and monthly to-do lists for long-term projects. Incorporate pertinent daily tasks from these lists onto the daily lists that you compile each morning.

After you've prepared a list, assign to each task an appropriate time to do it. If your daily desk calendar has 15-minute time slots, you may want to copy the to-do list onto the calendar. If you have calendar or reminder software, key in the to-do list and print your schedule for the day, week, or month.

Controlling Interruptions

Your supervisor's work habits and the nature of business in your organization will affect the kind and frequency of interruptions that you experience. Even the office layout — open or closed — and the location of your desk may invite or discourage interruptions. Your daily schedule should take into account the normal pattern of interruptions. If the period 10 a.m. until noon usually consists of endless interruptions, for example, don't schedule work that requires uninterrupted concentration during those hours.

Some interruptions, however, can be avoided. Although office professionals are expected to respond to their supervisor's needs and schedules as events occur, through better time management you may be able at least to reduce the number of other, nonessential, time-wasting interruptions. If necessary, make a conscious effort to change your work habits:

- Use electronic or paper planners, schedules, and calendars regularly. Software often has alarms, or reminders, to alert you to approaching deadlines.

- Develop goals, set deadlines for important tasks, form the habit of putting your goals in writing, keeping them in a visible location.

- Arrange all tasks in order of priority. Schedule low-priority work after all rush jobs and high-priority tasks are completed.

- Be receptive to new timesaving procedures, and develop your own ideas on ways to streamline your work to save steps and, in turn, save time. Keep assistants and coworkers informed about any such changes that affect them.

- Avoid overdoing tasks, such as handling papers more times than necessary.

- Be prepared with tools, supplies, reference materials, and so on before you start a job. Having to stop in the middle of a job to find something you forgot wastes time and increases the possibility of introducing errors in your work.

- Use all available timesaving devices and technologies — even if you must take time initially to learn how to use a new system, feature, or procedure — and let your software or equipment do the work for you. Watch for newer versions that will increase your productivity.

- Store often-used standard messages, clauses, and so on in a computer forms file for later use to avoid repetitive rekeying.

- Use available software templates, and set up style sheets to facilitate future document formatting.
- Create macros for repetitive keystrokes to save steps and time in keyboarding.
- Use whichever is faster — a mouse or the keyboard — when preparing material by computer.
- Schedule difficult jobs during periods when you're feeling fresh and have a reservoir of energy. You'll be less likely to make mistakes and have to redo a job.
- Work at a steady pace, rather than a rushed pace, so that you'll do the work right the first time. It will only take more time if you have to redo it.
- Include stretch breaks throughout the day and other available break-time activities to reduce tension and refresh and energize yourself for further work.
- Learn to say no when you reach your full work capacity and cannot effectively or realistically handle additional tasks, and discuss the matter with your supervisor. Request an assistant when your work-load warrants it.
- Delegate lower-priority or other appropriate tasks to an assistant to make more time available for your more important responsibilities.
- Group similar activities, such as ordering supplies and renewing subscriptions, for maximum efficiency, and check your schedule for the rest of the week to see which upcoming tasks could be more efficiently grouped and rescheduled.
- Find ways to deal with procrastination, such as starting work with something you enjoy doing. Sometimes it helps to start with a short, easy task.
- Don't make personal visits or engage in social conversations during business hours. If others tend to waste your working hours with such discussions, suggest that they call you after work to chat about personal matters.
- Be very specific and clear in your instructions and communications with assistants and coworkers to avoid time-wasting errors, confusion, and misunderstandings. Likewise, if you don't understand instructions that you received, ask for clarification so that you don't waste time doing something the wrong way.
- Avoid time-wasting, energy-draining disputes and personal confrontations. Save your energy for your job and the tasks you must complete.

- Learn to use downtime, such as when a telephone call is on hold or while you're waiting for a repairperson, to think about and plan future work. If the delay will be long enough, find a short task on your schedule to complete while waiting.

- Return phone calls during slower, quieter periods and when you believe the recipient will likely be available, to avoid repeatedly having to redial.

- Develop your power of concentration so that you can shut out noise and other distractions. Try various strategies, such as quietly reading your work out loud to drown out noise (if your desk is in a location where others won't see or hear you do this).

- Keep up with your daily work, and reduce clutter and unfiled material that causes you to spend more time searching for things. When work has piled up, it takes more time to handle it.

- Make your paper files (filenames, type of filing system, and so on) consistent with your electronic files to make it easier to locate material in either place.

- Develop an efficient, ergonomic office layout (furniture, equipment, files, supplies, and so on) that saves physical steps and strain and provides for easy access to the things you use regularly.

Telecommunications

Telecommunications generally refers to some form of communication, or exchange, between two or more people or machines at different locations. Specifically, it involves the transmission and reception of data, images, signals, and sound by wire, radio, and other media. The process may involve traditional telephone communication, e-mail, voice mail, or any other such exchange. Usually, the exchange is facilitated by telephones and other telecommunications devices that are connected to the telephone lines or linked by another means, such as by satellites.

As offices become more integrated and voice and data technologies merge, telecommunications assumes a prominent place among the new technologies. Computers, fax machines, and copiers, for example, are all linked in modern telecommunications systems. Some are even manufactured as multifunction devices, as described in Chapter 1, "The Online Office" (The Multifunction Machine). This chapter focuses on voice communications, and Chapter 5, "Mail Processing," describes the written forms, such as e-mail and fax transmission.

THE TELEPHONE INDUSTRY

Common Carriers

Telephone companies that provide voice, data, and other telecommunications services are generally referred to as *common carriers*. Those that provide long-distance service are sometimes referred to as *interexchange carriers*. More and more companies have become long-distance carriers since the Regional Bell Operating Companies (RBOCs) that existed following the breakup of AT&T in the 1980s were allowed to offer long-distance as well as local service. The non-RBOCs that offer long-distance service are sometimes called *other common carriers* (OCCs) or *specialized common carriers* (SCCs).

All of these carriers are regulated by local, state, or federal agencies and sometimes by all three. The Common Carrier Bureau (CCB) administers the policies of the Federal Communications Commission (FCC) pertaining to the carriers of local and long-distance telephone services.

Transmission Facilities

A ten-digit telephone number, such as 311-555-6611, is standard in the United States and Canada. In this example, the first three digits (311) designate the *area code,* the next three (555) designate the *exchange,* or central office, to which the line is connected, and the last four (6611) designate the particular *line.*

Traditional facilities. In a business office, telephones are commonly connected to the central facility of a local or long-distance carrier where the process of *switching* calls takes place. Calls between numbers having the same prefix are handled within a telephone company's central facility. Calls to numbers with a different prefix must be routed over interoffice trunk lines. For more about telephone technology, refer to Telephone Systems, Telephone Features, and Telephone Services.

Cellular facilities. Calls placed with a cell phone are transmitted through geographic cells that are connected to a series of transmission towers. These towers switch calls to a nearby central telephone office that in turn routes them to another office and so on, as often as is necessary to reach the desired destination. Thus a person driving in a car from one geographic area to another (*roaming*) can place calls and speak to someone without interruption. Outside the area covered by a caller's cellular service company, however, the cost of the call becomes higher.

The International Telecommunications Union has taken steps to unify wireless standards worldwide. Once common standards exist in all countries, users will be able to roam from country to country without ever having to change cell phones.

Most cell phones in use at the beginning of the twenty-first century were digital, as opposed to the traditional analog devices. Like computers, *digital phones* encode input or output as discrete (separate) pulses. *Analog phones* encode input or output as continuously changing variables, such as that which is common in electric current or voltage. Digital networks provide superior voice quality and greater privacy features.

Cell phones have features similar to those of a typical office telephone, including special features such as voice recognition (for placing hands-free calls in a vehicle), outputs for other portable equipment, e-mail and fax messaging capability, and Internet access. For other examples, refer to the list in Telephone Features.

Satellite facilities. Satellites orbiting the earth enable callers to transmit data, video, voice, and other signals to and from distant earth stations. When a satellite is equipped with the proper antennae to receive radio signals, it can accept and resend the signals to as many other earth stations or other orbiting satellites as is necessary to reach the destination.

This high-speed bouncing process provides for rapid communication between countries and continents. Although the process is nearly instantaneous, each signal between an earth station and a satellite is delayed about 275 milliseconds. This creates a very brief delayed response, such as that which you see when a television reporter is interviewing someone in another country.

Hand-held satellite phones, similar to cell phones, are available for use with orbiting satellites. These devices can be used anywhere since they don't require the use of cellular-type transmission towers spaced a certain distance apart. Although charges for satellite phone usage currently exceed those for cellular communication, costs are expected to moderate and eventually rival those of cell phones.

TELEPHONE TECHNOLOGY

A substantial amount of any modern organization's business is conducted over the telephone. Effective use of the telephone depends on an understanding of the functioning and capabilities of the hardware and an awareness of proper telephone techniques. Refer to the second part of this chapter for information about telephoning procedures and proper etiquette.

Most pushbutton telephones have a tone type of dialing mechanism. These telephones send musical tones to the switching system. A pulse-dialing telephone may be designed in a pushbutton style but produce the same dialing pulses, rather than tones, as those of an old-style rotary telephone.

Telephone Systems

Telephone systems are designed for offices of all sizes. Traditionally, small and medium-size offices have used *multiline pushbutton systems,* also known as *key systems,* whereas larger offices have used *exchanges.* As the technology has evolved, however, the distinction has become blurred, and new systems borrow features from both types of systems. Most office telephones, or a variation or combination thereof (*hybrids*), fall within the following basic categories:

- *Single-line system.* Very small offices may use only one or sometimes two outside lines, with two to three telephones plugged into wall jacks. When making or answering a call, you commonly first press a key to select the line.

- *Multiline system.* The most popular system for small to medium-size offices is the pushbutton, or key, system. It may service as few as 5 or as many as 50 people. With this type of system, anyone may answer or place calls directly at his or her extension.

- *Exchange system.* Traditionally, exchanges have been used for organizations with more than 50 people. With this type of system, all incoming calls go to a central mechanism that generally requires one or more attendants to route each call to the right extension. However, individual users can still place their own calls.

An exchange system is usually more complicated than a pushbutton, or key, system. For example, it requires either a live or an automated operator-attendant to receive and route calls inside and outside an organization. The following are the principal types of exchanges:

- A simple *private branch exchange (PBX)* is a manual switching system operated by an attendant.

- A *private automatic branch exchange (PABX)* may or may not use a live attendant.

- A *computerized branch exchange (CBX)* is an electronic PBX that switches calls electronically.

- A *personal computer-private branch exchange (PC-PBX),* also known as a *telecommunications,* or *communications, server,* is a desktop PC with software that enables it to function like a regular PBX.

- A *central office exchange service (CENTREX)* is an off-site exchange service in which a telephone company assigns part of its central office to switch calls at a user's facility. The user thereby has the use of a large switching facility without having to install an in-house switching operation with attendant.

Telephone Features

As new telephone systems are developed, the traditional features may change, and new ones may be added. The fact that features once applied only to a pushbutton system or to an exchange may now apply to both is particularly evident in the case of hybrid systems. The following are examples of common telephone features, or a variation of them, that may be used with some or all types of telephone systems:

- *Answering machines.* These devices, common in homes as well as offices, answer the telephone with a recorded greeting and then record, store, and play back messages left by callers. Some units can receive and forward voice messages, faxes, and e-mail messages. Others can broadcast messages to hundreds of pagers in various remote locations.

- *Automatic attendant.* With this feature, a digitally recorded message and list of options greets callers and allows them to select a desired extension or voice mailbox by pressing certain numbers.

- *Automatic call distribution.* Organizations that have numerous incoming calls may set up a department of call takers served by an automatic call distributor (ACD). It distributes incoming calls to available call takers. If all representatives are busy, callers hear a reassuring message and are put on hold.

- *Automatic speed dialing.* This feature allows you to program a list of telephone numbers (intercom or outside) into your desk, portable, or cell phone. Depending on the system, you may be able to reach a programmed number either by pushing a button or dialing a code.

- *Beeper.* This is a small pocket device with a tiny display screen used to contact people who are away from their telephones. When someone calls the beeper's number, the device vibrates or emits a sound and displays the caller's number and sometimes a brief message.

- *Buzzer.* This feature enables you to push a single key or button on a telephone to signal the recipient to pick up the receiver.

- *Call accounting.* Through a feature sometimes called *station message detail recording (SMDR),* you receive a printout of every number called from each extension. Some SMDRs provide detailed management reports that analyze telephone traffic.

- *Call block.* Through your telephone company, you can arrange to prevent your name and telephone number from appearing on other people's caller ID displays when you call them. However, some organizations will ask you to press certain keys to unblock your call before they will accept it.

- *Call forwarding.* With call forwarding, or routing, you can program your system so that calls will be routed to another extension or telephone if no one answers after a certain number of rings or if the line is busy.

- *Call sequencing.* This feature lets you know which is the next call in line. It processes unanswered calls after a certain number of rings and monitors the volume of incoming telephone traffic.

- *Call transferring.* This feature allows you to transfer a call to another telephone number either by dialing a special code or by momentarily depressing the switch hook and then dialing the new number.

- *Call waiting.* With this feature, you'll see or hear a signal while you're on the line if someone else is trying to reach you. You then have the option of putting the present call on hold while you take the new call.

- *Caller ID.* Through arrangements with your local telephone company, you can use a small device with a display attached to or built into your telephone that will let you see the telephone number of an incoming call, and sometimes the caller's name, provided that the caller does not have a call block, described previously.

- *Conference calls.* With call conferencing, or three-way calling, you can be connected to several outside lines at once. All parties can talk and hear each other.

- *Continuous redial.* With this feature, the telephone will continue to dial a number, without your reentering it, leaving you free to do other things.

- *Dial safeguards.* A dial-restriction device can be used to prevent unauthorized people from dialing restricted outside numbers, exchanges, area codes, long-distance numbers, or any other designated numbers.

- *Direct inward dialing (DID).* This feature allows a caller to reach telephone numbers within a company by dialing them directly from the outside, even though outgoing calls must go through a company's exchange or other system.

- *Direct inward system access.* With this feature, you can call into a system from outside as though you were in the building that houses the system. A person at home can therefore access the company's system and place a long-distance call through it, provided that other restrictions don't exist.

- *Hold.* This feature allows you to put a call on hold by pressing the hold button. Options include a periodic tone (so that the caller will not think that the line has gone dead), music, or a taped message.

- *Last-call return.* This feature enables you to redial the last call that you made by pressing only one key.

- *LCD display.* Telephones may have LCD displays that show which features you activated, which number you dialed, the identification of an incoming call, and other information.

- *Least-cost routing.* With this feature, the system tries to find the least expensive way of placing a long-distance call. This may require waiting a preset period for a discount transmission facility to become available. If none becomes available, your call will be placed via regular direct-distance dialing (DDD).

- *Line status indicator.* Telephones often have buttons that light up to show whether a line is busy, on hold, or free.

- *Message waiting.* A special light or tone on a telephone is activated with message waiting to show that the receptionist or attendant has a message for you. Some companies have message centers to which all calls are routed if they're not answered after three rings.

- *Messaging.* This feature enables you to call another extension and leave a short message that is converted into words on the person's small telephone display. You can also input a brief message that people calling you will read on their displays if they call while you're away.

- *Music on hold.* A tape or radio station can be connected to your system so that callers will hear music or comments when they're placed on hold.

- *Paging.* With this feature, you can broadcast announcements through speakerphones or loudspeakers or send a message to someone who is in another location, away from his or her telephone.

- *Picturephone.* This feature enables you to see the person with whom you're speaking on a tiny screen built into the telephone.

- *Priority call.* With this feature, calls from certain people have a distinctive ring.

- *Privacy.* This feature prevents other people from accessing a line already in use. *A priority override feature,* however, may be used to break in when warranted.

- *Remote station answering.* With this feature, you can answer someone else's telephone from your own telephone by dialing a special code or pushing a specific button.

- *Speakerphone.* This device enables you to both talk to and listen to someone over the telephone without picking up the receiver. This feature should not be confused with *on-hook dialing,* which allows you only to dial, not speak with, someone without lifting the receiver.

- *Toll restriction.* This feature allows you to restrict the types of calls that can be made from certain extensions. For example, you may not be able to make 900 calls or international calls from those extensions.

- *Voice mail.* Voice mail involves the automated delivery of telephone messages through computerized processing of the speaker's voice. A voice mail system may be attached to an office telephone system in the user's facilities, or a voice mail service may be provided by an outside organization. See also the guidelines in Voice mail etiquette.

- *Cordless phone.* A cordless phone has a detached receiver that you can carry with you up to a certain distance, free of wires and cords.

- *PC cordless phone.* With a PC connection, you can plug the cordless phone into a PC so that it can function like a personal assistant, receiving and routing voice mail, e-mail, faxes, and so on to another phone or PC, even to a cell phone.

Telephone Cost Control

Call abuse. When firms make no effort to control telephone costs, a substantial portion of the telephone bill may result from call abuse, especially from employees using the office telephones to make personal long-distance calls. The best tool in combating call abuse may be simple psychology—reminding everyone that charging personal calls to the company is not a salary perk and announcing that a campaign has been launched against telephone abusers. The company should also publish the consequences of telephone abuse in its employee handbook.

Some companies post the telephone bill on a company bulletin board or circulate a copy of it and require that each person read and sign it. The prospect of having one's misuse revealed may discourage the practice in the future. Call accounting software may also help to identify call abusers, although none of these options will be entirely effective if management does not demonstrate a resolve to take action against the abusers.

Cost-control measures. Proper training in cost control is important, especially since one way of making a call may be much more expensive than another way. Therefore, companies must warn employees against needlessly making person-to-person calls and repeatedly remind them that WATS calls are not free to the company. It's also helpful to check the inventory periodically to confirm that all lines and equipment for which you're being billed have in fact been installed. In large organizations undergoing constant change, an expensive mistake is not uncommon.

Telephone-system management is a broad subject requiring specialized knowledge, especially in times of increasing competition among telephone companies. Organizations intending to change or upgrade their equipment should contact several vendors for recommendations and estimates and compare the cost of purchasing with that of leasing.

TELEPHONE COMPANY SERVICES

Depending on the telephone company that you're using, some or all of the following services may be available:

- *Cellular service.* This service, usually available for a monthly fee, enables you to use cell phones to place and receive calls in moving vehicles. See the description in Cellular facilities.

- *CENTREX.* (Also written as *Centrex.*) Local telephone companies provide this central office exchange service, which is similar to that of an in-house PBX system. The telephone company will assign a number of lines to your company and provide the necessary central switching mechanism. CENTREX-compatible key systems are also available. See the description of exchanges and key systems in Telephone Systems.

- *Calling cards.* Telephone companies provide *telephone calling cards* that enable you to place calls from other telephones and have the cost charged to your office telephone. They also may allow you to use VISA and MasterCard as calling cards. *Prepaid phone cards* are purchased in advance and allow you to place calls up to the amount of the card's value. *International calling cards,* available from long-distance carriers, are similar to regular calling cards but often have additional features, such as language translation. *Call-back cards* enable you to route a call through a computer network, just as you would route an e-mail message through the network.

- *Direct-distance dialing.* Direct-distance dialing (DDD) involves ordinary long-distance calls that you dial yourself. International direct-distance dialing (IDDD) is available from certain cities in the United States to many other countries.

- *Foreign-exchange and tie lines.* If your office makes numerous calls to a specific city, you can get a direct *foreign exchange (FX) line* to that city. FX lines are provided by common carriers, usually through a monthly lease for the line. A *tie line* is a similar leased line between two PBX systems in different locations.

- *Wide area telephone service (WATS).* Inbound WATS lines use an 800 or 888 area code and are toll-free to the caller. A company may also subscribe to outbound WATS lines if employees regularly place numerous calls to outside destinations. Enhancements include *customized call routing,* whereby calls from different areas of the country are routed to different offices, and *variable call routing,* whereby after-hours calls are routed to a separate office.

- *TTY (teletypewriter) service.* This service, where available, makes it possible for people with hearing, speech, or vision problems to communicate over the telephone lines with other TTY users. (A *TDD* device — telecommunications device for the deaf — is designed for use especially by hearing-impaired persons.)

See also the description of common features, such as *call forwarding,* in Telephone Features.

TELEPHONE TECHNIQUES

Projecting a positive company image is an important goal in every office. The role of an office professional is especially significant because his or her voice is often the first one that a caller hears.

Telephone Etiquette

Answering calls. You can help create a positive image for your company by observing proper telephone etiquette. (See also the tips in Voice mail etiquette.) For example, any incoming call should be answered on the second ring, if possible. Answering on the first ring tends to startle some people. Waiting to answer on the fourth ring or later tends to irritate some people or make them uneasy.

How you greet a caller may depend on the preference of your supervisor. If you work with just one person, you might answer by using his or her name, adding your own at the end:

> Good morning, Mr. London's office. This is Janet [*or* Janet Pearson] speaking.

If your work is more general, such as for a department rather than for a particular person, you might answer by identifying the department only:

> Good afternoon, Payroll.

The way in which you answer indicates your attitude toward the caller and your job. For example, callers are most impressed with a low, professional voice, with jargon-free language and clear enunciation. If you speak with a smile, it will affect your voice and prompt a friendlier tone. (See also the suggestions in Language.) In general, a friendly, helpful attitude will help project goodwill for you and your company.

If loud music or other distracting noise is in the background, briefly excuse yourself and reduce the volume (if possible). Be sensitive to the caller's needs and feelings, and adopt an understanding tone and attitude, particularly if the caller is unhappy. However, don't tolerate serious abuse or threats. In such cases, quietly state that you must hang up and do so immediately. Then promptly report the call to your supervisor. In routine situations, use a polite response to end a conversation:

> Excuse me, Mr. Wylie. I'm sorry to cut this short, but someone just came into the office. May I call you back?

Most people in a meeting want to be interrupted only if a call is urgent. For other calls, take messages, and give them to the intended recipient immediately after the meeting. If a caller has an accent that makes it difficult to understand the message, ask him or her to repeat it or spell out anything about which you're uncertain. However, before taking a message, give the caller as much information as possible yourself without revealing unnecessary facts:

> Mr. Wilson won't be available until later today [not *because he's working on a contract dispute*]. May I be of help, or is there someone else you'd like to speak with?

Be especially careful about using names and providing private information over a cell phone or public telephone where privacy may not be guaranteed. For more tips on handling calls, see Techniques for Incoming Calls and Techniques for Outgoing Calls.

Placing calls. If you're calling someone, immediately identify yourself:

> Good afternoon. This is Carol Stevens, Ms. Shandler's assistant.

Return calls during business hours and within 48 hours of receiving a message. In general, use the least-cost method for placing calls, such as a WATS line, as indicated in the employee handbook or according to office policy.

When you place the call, it's always thoughtful to ask someone if it's convenient to talk. Even if it is, you shouldn't assume that the other person is issuing an invitation to carry on a lengthy conversation. It's also important to avoid calling people at home about business matters, unless it's an emergency or you've been asked to do so.

Try to have all material that you'll need for reference in front of you, and quickly get to the point of your call. If you must put someone on hold, first ask permission. For more about hold procedures, see Placing a call on hold.

During the conversation, use courteous remarks and responses with words and phrases such as *please* and *thank you.* (See the tips in Language.) To close the conversation, make a polite comment such as "Thanks for the information, Don. Good-bye." Again, omit the use of names if you're using a public or cell phone. When you're finished, let the caller hang up first (in most cases). If you hang up first, replace the receiver gently.

If you often call listings in other cities, consider purchasing regular directories for those cities from your telephone company. Some directories are also available online, though you will probably also want print directories in the office. In-state directories may be free, but out-of-state directories are usually sold. Toll-free 800 and 888 numbers are published in separate directories.

Language. Your choice of language tells the other person a great deal about you and your company. A courteous person avoids crude expressions and replies distinctly with "yes," rather than "yeah" or "uh-huh." You can easily show respect with simple comments and responses such as "I beg your pardon," "Thank you," "I appreciate your help," and "Please." Also, avoid responding with noises or nonwords, such as "ah" or "ummm."

Office professionals should practice the art of conversation over the telephone as well as in face-to-face conversations. For example, one should never speak with a mouth full of food or while chewing on an eraser. A caller can easily hear such noises and the changes they produce in one's speaking voice. Also, listening is a key ingredient in all communication, and it's rude to interrupt a caller, rush the person, or finish his or her sentences. One of the most common mistakes, however, is speaking too fast and not enunciating clearly enough. The same guidelines apply to voice messages. See the suggestions in Using Voice Mail.

Techniques for Incoming Calls

Placing a call on hold. Always ask a caller's permission or preference before placing a call on hold. After you put the call on hold, check in about every 40 seconds. When you periodically return to the line, ask if the person wants to continue holding, and indicate how long the delay will be. If it may be extensive, offer to call the person back:

> I'm sorry, but it looks like Mr. Benson may be on the other line for another five or ten minutes. May I have him call you back?

You might also offer to transfer the call to someone else who could help the caller. (For more about this, see Transferring calls.) If you must immediately place a call on hold, you might say:

Mr. Rukeyser's office. Will you please hold a moment?

As soon as possible, return to the call, apologize for making the person wait, and proceed as usual.

Answering another telephone. A ringing telephone should never go unanswered. Whether you're assigned to answer someone else's telephone or just happen to walk by another, unattended telephone that's ringing, you should be as helpful as possible. If it's company policy to answer unattended phones, explain to the caller that this is not your office. However, rather than saying "I don't know" or "I can't help you," you might say:

No one in this office is available right now. May I take a message?

When taking a message, get all the pertinent data — time; caller's name, title, company, telephone or other number (including extension); and message. In some offices, you have to make arrangements in advance for someone to answer your telephone while you're away from the office. Sometimes employees who answer each other's phones keep a list of the various extensions next to their telephones.

If you must ask a coworker to answer your telephone, keep a pad and pencil on your desk, and indicate where you can be reached and how long you'll be gone. Usually, it's your responsibility to explain how the telephone in your office should be answered, what calls are expected by the executive, where the executive may be reached if necessary, and other pertinent information.

Alert your coworkers if the executive is expecting a particular call or does not want to accept certain calls. Explain how the executive prefers to have the telephone answered. For example, although you may call the person by a nickname when no one else is around, he or she may not want that name used over the telephone or in the presence of visitors to the office.

Transferring calls. If it's necessary to transfer a call, explain to the caller what you'll be doing rather than simply say, "Hold on." Follow the correct procedure with your system (ask others in the office if you're a newcomer). In some cases, for example, you may have to depress the switch hook and, as soon as you hear a dial tone, dial the desired extension. In that case, when the person at the extension answers, you might announce the call and hang up. With some systems, you would not hear the other person answer and would have to trust that the call was successfully transferred.

If a call comes in on the wrong line and you want to transfer it, give the caller the correct extension in case the call is cut off during the transfer and the person must call back later:

> Ms. Davis is at extension 5551, but if you'll hold a moment, I'd be
> happy to transfer your call.

If an executive temporarily needs to take calls on another extension, you
might say:

> Mr. Johnson is in another office right now, but I know he'd like to
> speak with you. If you'll hold, I'll transfer you to 6006.

Stay on the line, if your system allows this, and when someone answers
the other extension, explain that you're transferring a call and give the executive's name.

Screening calls. Executives differ about the way that incoming calls should
be handled. Many prefer to answer their own extensions. Others want an
assistant to answer and put through all calls without asking who's calling.
Some higher-level executives, however, expect their assistants to find out
who's calling and put through only certain calls. The assistant then must
screen all calls, handle some personally, transfer some to others in the organization, and put through only selected calls.

If you must do this, avoid giving the impression that you're screening
calls. For example, if you ask who's calling *before* stating that an executive is
or isn't available, it may sound as though you'll decide what to say depending on who's calling. To avoid offending a caller, you might say something
such as this:

> *Assistant:* Ms. Peterson's office. This is Max McCoy.
> *Caller:* Hello, may I speak to Ms. Peterson?
> *Assistant:* Yes, may I tell her who's calling?

If it's someone the executive won't want to speak with, you can then
say that apparently someone else is in the office or that the executive is on
another line. After that, you can follow up with the usual procedure for
offering to help, transfer the call elsewhere, or take a message. If you already know that Ms. Peterson will not want to speak with most callers,
you might handle the situation by first stating that she isn't available.
Then ask who's calling. If it's someone she'll likely want to speak with, say
that you'll check to see if she can be interrupted. Otherwise, as usual, ask
if you can help, offer to take a message, or offer to transfer the call to
someone else:

> *Assistant:* Ms. Peterson's office. This is Max McCoy.
> *Caller:* Hello, is Ms. Peterson in?
> *Assistant:* I believe she's on another line now. May I ask who's calling?
> *Caller:* Joe Ferguson in the mail room.

Assistant: Oh, yes, Joe. How are you? I'm not sure when she'll be free.
   Could I help in the meantime?
Caller: I don't know. I wanted to talk about a problem with the new
   bulk-mail imprint.
Assistant: I think Sally Beloit is working on that. Why don't I transfer
   your call to her. She's at extension 2222.
Caller: Sure. That'll be fine.

Handling annoying calls. Office professionals know that not every caller is pleasant and considerate. Although it may be tempting to respond in a similar tone, it's important to resist the temptation and maintain a pleasant, cooperative attitude. Sometimes a concerned, calm, understanding tone will defuse a loud, angry caller. If it doesn't, do the same thing that you would do for anyone else — offer to help if you can, and if you can't, offer to transfer the call to someone who can.

If a caller continues to be abusive, apologize for being unable to provide a solution, thank the caller for taking time to call, say good-bye, and hang up. If you believe the caller will persist, you might suggest that he or she write a letter to the company. However, follow company policy in regard to giving out the names of executives to abusive callers and in regard to the preferred procedure for handling such calls (your employee manual may cover this).

Terminating a call. Some callers ramble on as though you and others in the office have nothing else to do. These calls can be time-consuming and difficult to terminate. An executive may ask you to interrupt overly long conversations. For example, the executive may privately buzz you on the intercom as a signal to you that you should interrupt the call on some pretext such as interjecting that there's an incoming international call or a meeting about to begin.

If you're also bothered by someone who likes to use office hours for personal telephone visits, do the same thing — interrupt when you can, and pretend that an office visitor has arrived or that there's an incoming call on another line. If possible, use an excuse that not only will end the call but also will leave the impression that you're very busy in the office. However, avoid insulting the caller since it's always important to leave someone feeling good about you and the company.

Message-taking procedures. A wide variety of message forms are available in office-supply stores and catalogs. It may be up to you to select a useful form, or your office may have a standard company form that everyone uses. Most forms have room to write certain key facts:

Date

Time of the call

Caller's name

Caller's title and company

Caller's telephone number

Reason for the call

When taking a message, repeat the person's telephone or other number, such as a fax number or e-mail address. After finding out the reason for the call, consider whether someone else might be able to help the caller. In that case, offer to transfer the call to another extension.

Techniques for Outgoing Calls

Placing a call. When placing a telephone call, be certain that you know not only the name of the person you're calling but also how to pronounce it correctly. Check a time zone map before placing long-distance calls. (See the time zone map in Placing long-distance calls.) For information about placing international calls, refer to the guidelines in International dialing.

If you place a call for someone else, be certain that the person is still in the office when you make the call. An executive may ask you to place a call but then will step out briefly or will become involved in an impromptu meeting. If an unavoidable delay occurs after you've placed the call, stay on the line (don't put the call on hold), and explain the situation.

Give someone being called up to ten rings (about 45 seconds) to answer. Avoid beginning other work while waiting so that you'll be prepared to speak as soon as the person does answer. Use a pleasant voice, and follow the rules of telephone etiquette described previously.

If an assistant to the person being called answers, you might say:

> Good morning. Mr. Nash from ZBC is calling and would like to speak with Ms. Jenson. Is she available?

Wait for the assistant to notify Ms. Jenson. Then as soon as she comes on the line, buzz Mr. Nash and say simply:

> Ms. Jenson is on the line.

If Ms. Jenson, rather than her assistant, answers when you place the call, you might say:

> Good morning, Ms. Jenson. This is Ann Beale from ZBC calling. Mr. Nash would like to speak with you. May I put him on?

If Ms. Jenson says yes, buzz the executive, tell him that you have Ms. Jenson on the line, and immediately say to her:

Here he is [*or* Here's Mr. Nash].

When placing calls for someone else, try to avoid keeping either person waiting for more than a second or two. If the person being called isn't in, find out when he or she will be back. You may have the person return the executive's call, or you may have the executive call the person, depending on the schedule of each one. If the executive prefers to call later, find out what time would be best for both parties to avoid "telephone tag" in which one of the parties is always unavailable.

Placing long-distance calls. When you make a long-distance call by dialing direct, you simply dial the full number of the person you're calling, including the area code or international dialing codes in the case of international calls. Whereas faxes, e-mail, and voice mail messages can be sent at any time, day or night, telephone calls must be made during office hours.

Because communication occurs so rapidly, particularly with e-mail, it's important to check time changes in other areas before placing calls. (See the Domestic Time Zone Map, United States and Canada, for time changes.) It's also necessary to update your area code list throughout the year since new area codes are continually being added because of expanding telecommunications activity. Directories usually give the proper procedure for placing long-distance calls, including information about area codes and international dialing codes. For further information, contact your local company or long-distance carrier. See also the forthcoming discussions International dialing and International time.

If you need to speak with a particular person, dial the operator and give the person's name and number. Person-to-person calls are more expensive, however, and usually are used only if someone is seldom available and you need to avoid the cost of making numerous station-to-station calls.

If you accidentally call a wrong number or if there's a poor connection, immediately dial the operator. Report the error, and ask to have the charge removed from your monthly bill.

To place a long-distance call to a ship, plane, or train, you need to know its telephone number and, in the case of ships at sea, the appropriate international access code. Check with your long-distance carrier for details. Major airlines offer in flight telephone service, and certain Amtrak routes provide a similar service for rail passengers. For further information, check with the particular airline or Amtrak, or contact a travel agent.

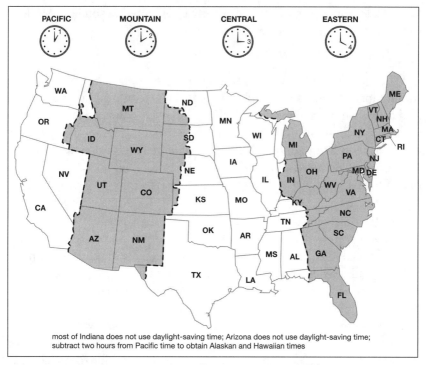

most of Indiana does not use daylight-saving time; Arizona does not use daylight-saving time; subtract two hours from Pacific time to obtain Alaskan and Hawaiian times

Domestic Time Zone Map, United States and Canada

International dialing. To call most countries, you usually must dial the international access code provided by your carrier followed by the country code, city code, and local number. (Depending on your telephone system, you may first have to dial 9 or another digit to get an outside line.) To reach the local number 555-6262 in Vitoria, Brazil, for example, you might dial 00-55-27-555-6262. You can reach some places, such as the Dominican Republic and the Virgin Islands, by dialing 1 plus the city code followed by the local number.

Since codes may change at any time, it's important to double-check them periodically throughout the year. Various websites for international dialing codes have relatively recent lists. Also, telephone directories usually publish updated lists annually, and AT&T publishes a revised edition of the *Area Code Handbook* each year. It contains U.S. and Canadian area codes as well as international country and city codes. If you need further information or instructions, contact your long-distance carrier.

International time. The world is divided into 24 time zones, each 15 degrees longitude wide. The starting point for measuring degrees is the *prime*

meridian, which passes through Greenwich, England. The standard time of this meridian, traditionally known as *Greenwich mean time,* is now referred to as *coordinated universal time* (both terms are sometimes capitalized).

Halfway around the globe from the prime meridian is the 180th meridian, known as the *International Date Line.* To the east of this line, the date is advanced one day; to the west, the date is set back one day.

Worldwide time differences must be considered when placing a call. Some of the websites that have international dialing codes also have a list of time differences you can consult before placing a call.

Placing calling card calls. Telephone companies issue calling cards for placing long-distance calls from another telephone away from your office. Some credit card issuers, such as MasterCard and VISA, may also allow their cards to be used for this purpose.

Follow the instructions provided by the issuer of the calling card or credit card, as well as any instructions posted by a pay telephone. Keep in mind that rates for pay phone calls may vary, depending on the carrier. (Look for the carrier's name on the phone.) As a security precaution when you use a public telephone, always shield from the view of others both your card and the number you're dialing. If you need further instruction in using a card, review the procedures usually outlined in the front of telephone directories. For examples of the types of calling cards that are available, refer to the descriptions in Telephone Company Services.

Using Voice Mail

A voice mail system stores and transfers voice messages electronically. Different types of systems are available, and businesses may purchase a voice mail system or rent a voice mailbox from a service provider or telephone company.

Sophisticated systems that are programmed to respond to voice commands are often described as *virtual assistants.* These systems use an advanced electronic technology to dial and screen calls and to locate users who are away from their telephones. A voice-response message system provides for conversations between people and computers. With this technology, you can speak to the system and receive a voice response.

Voice mail features. The following are examples of features that a typical voice mail system might have:

- *Automated attendant.* This feature provides a recorded greeting that includes a menu of choices from which you can select a department or office by pressing a single button.

- *Call forwarding.* With this feature, the system will route calls to other locations, such as to pagers or cell phones.
- *Call screening.* This feature includes a display that shows or announces a caller's name and phone number.
- *Fax on demand.* With this feature, callers can follow voice prompts to select information they want and have it faxed to them.
- *Remote access.* This feature lets you call in from another telephone to check your messages, record a different greeting, and use the system in other ways.
- *Unified messaging.* With this feature, the system will convert information from other media. For example, you can respond in voice to a print message.

Voice mail etiquette. Users should follow certain rules of etiquette in recording voice mail greetings and leaving voice mail messages. Many of the same requirements described earlier in Telephone Etiquette apply to voice messages. For example, your choice of language and tone of voice may leave a lasting impression on others, just as it would in a regular call. To be certain that your voice mail greetings are clear and courteous, follow these guidelines:

- Speak slowly and clearly in a low, professional voice.
- Give your name, title, department, or other pertinent information in your greeting.
- Change your greeting as appropriate throughout the day: "It's Monday, May 2, and I'll be in a meeting until 2 p.m., Central daylight time. If you'll leave your name, number, and message, I'll return your call by 5 p.m. You may start after the tone and leave a message up to ten minutes. Thanks for calling."
- Check your mailbox for messages throughout the day, such as every couple hours when possible.
- If the caller could talk to someone else in the meantime, include those instructions: "Press star 6 if you'd like to speak to someone else in the Sales Office."
- In an automated system, offer callers no more than four choices, and avoid sending them on to menu after menu.

If you're leaving a message on someone else's system, follow these guidelines:

- Even if you're given up to 10, 20, or more minutes of speaking time, try to limit your messages to 30 seconds.

- Speak slowly and clearly in a low, professional tone, the same as you would do if you were recording a greeting.

- Begin by identifying yourself: name, title, department, company, telephone number, date and time of your call, or any other pertinent information. Spell out any words that might be misunderstood or unfamiliar.

- Make your comments interesting, when possible, to arouse the person's curiosity and encourage him or her to call back right away: "I've got good news about your proposal."

- Give a date and time when the recipient may call you back: "I'll be here until 5 p.m. today, Tuesday, June 21, and all day tomorrow. If you'd rather talk another time, let me know when it would be convenient for me to call you back."

Voice mail, like e-mail, has made business communications more convenient and less intrusive. If someone is away and you don't need to converse with the individual personally, you can simply leave a message. However, neither e-mail nor voice mail should be used as an excuse to avoid personal interaction and personal conversations with others. It's most useful as an additional tool to supplement personal contact and as a substitute when personal contact is impossible or impractical. See the next chapter for more about the use of e-mail, including e-mail etiquette.

Mail Processing

Processing the incoming and outgoing mail is an important responsibility for office professionals. In most offices, the mail consists of both traditional paper mail and various forms of electronic communication, such as fax or e-mail. Regardless of the type of mail, messages must be handled carefully and expeditiously. When they're not handled properly, the company's image is affected adversely, and the company may lose clients or customers as a result.

ELECTRONIC MAIL

Fax mail and e-mail are the two principal forms of electronic mail in the United States. Certain other countries use some form of the older technology of Telex (Teleprinter Exchange Service). Telex, which requires specialized equipment, such as teleprinters, remains an important international communications tool. Therefore, most online services (see Service providers) in the United States also allow you to send and receive Telex messages.

Fax Transmission

A *fax,* which is short for *facsimile,* is an electronically transmitted copy of text or graphics that is usually sent over telephone lines. Fax transmission became common before e-mail was widely used and before the Internet became available to households and businesses alike. Today, both are heavily used forms of transmission in the United States, with e-mail more common for correspondence, although many businesses in other countries do not use e-mail.

Methods of fax transmission. In one method of fax transmission, the sender dials the recipient's fax number, and the fax machine scans the paper document that is fed into it. The machine then converts the images from digital (binary) signals to analog signals that can travel over the telephone lines. At the destination, the receiving fax machine converts the signals back from analog to digital form, and its printing mechanism produces a hard (paper) copy of the original document. With this method, the document must be prepared elsewhere and physically carried to the fax machine for transmission.

In another method of fax transmission, a computer that is equipped with a *PC fax board* can send and receive fax documents. In this case, the document may be prepared on or scanned into the computer and also sent directly from it. The document may be sent either to another properly equipped computer (with a browsing program, such as Microsoft Internet Explorer or Netscape Navigator) or to a separate, independent fax machine. See also Internet faxing.

Stand-alone fax machines may have a variety of features, such as copying or color-printing capability, *polling* (automatically contacting other remote machines to collect data), and *broadcasting* (sending the same message to numerous other fax numbers or e-mail addresses).

Integrated systems. Integrated message-transmission systems may have additional capabilities. For example, with the proper software, one system that combines voice, fax, and e-mail allows you to send fax and voice mail to an e-mail address where it is saved as a file attachment.

Internet faxing. Some systems are referred to as *Internet-enabled systems.* They may be manufactured to allow Internet faxing, or traditional, stand-alone fax machines may be converted for this purpose. In either case, a fax may be sent over the Internet to another fax machine or to an e-mail address. As with an e-mail transmission, the fax transmission then bypasses the Public Switch Telephone Network and may be sent anywhere in the world without the long-distance charges that would apply to a long-distance telephone call.

Wireless fax devices are also available for use while one is traveling. Unlike a traditional office fax machine, this type of portable fax usually has a keyboard so that messages can be both prepared on and sent from it.

Processing fax mail. The procedures followed in processing fax mail depend on the type of transmission. If a fax is sent to an office fax machine, the printing mechanism of the receiving machine will print a paper copy that is most often treated the same as postal mail. (See the guidelines for handling incoming Postal Mail.) However, a fax may be more urgent than routine postal mail and should then be processed immediately, rather than held until the postal mail is processed.

If a fax is sent to a receiving computer rather than to a fax number, it's usually treated the same as an incoming e-mail. Therefore, you may read and acknowledge it on screen, without printing out a paper copy, and file it electronically. Or you may print out a paper copy, acknowledge it, and file it the same as you would do with other paper mail. See the procedures described in E-Mail Transmission and Postal Mail.

E-Mail Transmission

E-mail is a computer-generated form of message transmission in which you send a message from your computer to another computer user's e-mail address or to someone's fax or Telex number. When someone doesn't have an e-mail address, you can sometimes send an e-mail message to a receiving computer in a post office or courier service office near the recipient. There it will be printed out and delivered to the recipient's physical office or residence address as a postal or courier message.

Service providers. An *Internet service provider (ISP)* is a service organization that connects a user's computer to the Internet but usually doesn't provide other services. An *online service,* such as America Online (AOL), is a service organization that not only connects a user's computer to the Internet but also provides access to other resources, such as large databases, discussion groups, and news reports.

Most e-mail is routed by a service provider that provides Internet access to users for a monthly fee. The provider's large host computer collects and holds a sender's e-mail message until the addressee's PC or other computer is turned on and ready to accept it.

Intranets and extranets. Smaller company networks, such as a private, in-house *intranet,* function like the worldwide Internet, offering information exchange, including in-house e-mail, among employees. Usually, an intranet is connected to the larger Internet and thereby also offers e-mail transmission outside the company. An *extranet* is a limited-access company intranet that also uses Internet technology to exchange public information. The exact configuration and range of capabilities depend on the particular type of in-house network system that a company selects.

With most types of in-house networks, a *firewall* (software that blocks outside access to private company files) is often used to protect confidential company material while allowing communication exchange with customers and others outside the company. Outsiders normally can access the company's network with a password that the company provides for them.

Intranet or extranet e-mail is generally prepared and sent the same as regular Internet e-mail. However, businesses have the option of installing special e-mail software. This type of commercial software usually has more editing features than free Web e-mail and the e-mail programs provided with some Internet browsing programs. If the commercial program can be used only within a company's limited network, Internet e-mail may be preferable because it can be accessed from any computer and exchanged with anyone else worldwide who also has a computer and an Internet connection. In addition, hotels and other places in many countries provide public access to the Internet.

The process of routing e-mail messages and other material over the Internet is described in Transmission Protocols in Chapter 1, "The Online Office."

Integrated systems. Like fax machines, an e-mail system may be integrated with other technologies. Voice mail, fax, and e-mail, for example, are commonly combined. In such cases, fax and voice mail may be sent to e-mail addresses, as described in Fax Transmission. With another innovation, *e-mail by phone,* users can access their e-mail messages from any location worldwide. Usually, if you dial a personalized number, the e-mail messages stored in your computer will be read *in voice* over the telephone. You may then respond to the messages in voice as well.

E-mail preparation. E-mail is prepared in a memo format, and your software will provide the necessary instructions (where to put information in the heading, where to begin the body, and so on). In addition, follow these general guidelines:

- Observe your company's e-mail policy (what you may and may not do or send via e-mail, legal implications, use of passwords and coded messages [*encryption*], required record keeping, and so on).

- Compose messages off-line, or leave the fill-in addressee field blank until you're certain that your message is ready for transmission (to avoid accidentally sending something unsuitable or incomplete).

- Fill in the required information in the e-mail template when your message is ready for transmission. This information should include the recipient's name and e-mail address (which you can store in an electronic address book so that the computer will automatically insert it in the future), the subject line, and the names and e-mail addresses of others who should receive copies of the message.

- Add as many other fill-in guidewords to the template as desired (purchase order number and so on).

- Compose the body the same as any other memo body. (See Chapter 9, "Correspondence," Memo and E-mail Formats.) See also the sample message in that chapter.

- Use brief, single-subject messages (send separate messages if you have other topics to discuss).

- Send lengthy comments or other supplementary material as a separate attachment (follow the instructions of your program for attaching a separate file).

- Consider sending very large attachments by postal mail or private delivery service if it would be time-consuming for the recipient to *download* (copy into his or her computer) an electronic version.

- Select the "Reply to Sender/Author" option rather than the "Compose New Message" option when you're responding to an incoming message. The sender's original message(s) and any other replies to that message will then be included along with your current message.

- Use the *unsend* feature immediately, if it's available on your software, when you want to take back a message that you sent accidentally or prematurely.

- Consider attaching a signature block at the end of your messages if it would be helpful to recipients. (Your program may allow you to prepare a signature file that will be automatically attached in each message you send.) Include facts such as your name, job title, company and department, physical company address (the computer automatically inserts your e-mail address and the date and time), telephone and fax numbers, and Web site.

- Use the word *Test* in your subject line when you're only testing your e-mail but have no message for the recipient.

- Follow the tips on composition in E-mail etiquette and in Chapter 9, "Correspondence," and refer to Other considerations for further guidelines about handling e-mail.

Other considerations. Some concerns in using e-mail involve matters other than message preparation. For example, security, privacy, procedures for handling incoming messages, and how to avoid unwanted messages are all important considerations. Follow these guidelines in dealing with such concerns:

- Check your e-mail several times throughout the day, and respond to all incoming messages within 24 hours (if you can't respond in full, send a brief note saying when you will respond).

- Program your computer, when and if necessary, to scan your mailbox at selected intervals and make an audible sound or display a notice when you have mail waiting.

- Immediately forward incoming messages sent to you by mistake to the intended recipient or back to the sender (include a message saying that you received the other person's mail in error).

- Follow company requirements for keeping a *message history* (what happens to the messages you send), filing or deleting messages, and requesting a receipt for something you send (if this feature is available on your software).

- Don't leave incoming or outgoing e-mail messages on screen when you leave your desk, and turn your monitor so that others who visit your office while you're there can't easily read your screen.

- Keep in mind that sophisticated programs and devices for breaking into company files may be used by curious or malicious parties, business competitors, and others. Such programs and devices may allow others to read your incoming or outgoing e-mail from their computers, even when you've taken ordinary precautions.

- Consider using filtering software to categorize messages and to block or delete unwanted mail.

- Use a filter rather than send a personal response or try to unsubscribe to junk e-mail. *Spammers* (those who send to every possible e-mail address) often use such messages to confirm and reuse or sell your e-mail address.

- Add the universal resource locator (URL) of spammers to your list of those that you want to delete in the future or to which you want to deny access through a filter. (An example of a URL is *http://www.widget.com.*)

- Delete any *cookies* (bits of data) that are stored on your computer's hardware when you visit a website. (Cookies include your name, password, and other facts enabling you quickly to revisit a site. However, they may contain viruses and also reveal facts about you to the site, which may result in unwanted e-mail.) Check whether your software prevents cookies from being stored on your disk, automatically deletes them, or stores them in a cache folder.

- Delete your *history file* (websites you recently visited) regularly since some marketers may break into it and begin spamming you.

- Check to be certain that messages you've deleted aren't backed up somewhere and therefore still in existence.

- Copy attachments that you receive onto a disk, before opening them to read, where your antiviral software can scan them.

E-mail etiquette. Some people believe that because of the informal format, brevity, and instantaneous nature of e-mail, the traditional rules of correspondence etiquette don't apply. This is a serious misconception that costs companies billions of dollars every year in lost business. Therefore, one of management's key objectives is to help employees understand that people are just as offended by rudeness and terseness in e-mail as they would be in postal or voice mail or in live conversations.

Although time is a valuable commodity in business and employees are often pressured to work faster, it's usually a mistake to set aside common sense. It costs a company less for someone to take time to compose a thoughtful, sensitive message than it costs to lose a customer or public confidence in the company because people feel mistreated and insulted when the messages they receive sound abrupt and cold. Although e-mail messages should be succinct, *brevity* and *rudeness* are not synonyms.

In some respects, courtesy is even more crucial in e-mail than it is in traditional mail. The informal format of e-mail — no greeting, such as *Dear Tom,* and (sometimes) the lack of a warm complimentary close, such as *Best regards* — make it very important that writers compensate by being especially thoughtful and courteous in their comments. (See Chapter 9, "Correspondence," for further tips on message composition.) In addition, the following general guidelines apply especially to e-mail messages (see also tips in E-mail preparation and Other considerations):

- Don't use e-mail for sensitive matters, such as firing someone or sending a sympathy message. Use a personal visit, telephone call, or sealed postal letter.

- Don't send formal invitations, such as a formal invitation to a dinner party, by e-mail. Send a traditional printed invitation or traditional postal letter. However, e-mail is acceptable for informal invitations, such as a query whether an associate is free for lunch or whether someone would like to serve on a committee.

- Don't use conversational abbreviations, such as *BTW* (by the way), in business e-mail.

- Don't use *emoticons* (symbols designating emotions), such as :(for frowning, in business e-mail.
- Don't use all capital letters, which give the appearance of shouting, in e-mail.
- Don't include comments that would embarrass you, the recipient, or a third party if the e-mail were accidentally sent to or retrieved by the wrong person. (Say nothing that you wouldn't want published in a newspaper.)
- Don't send nonessential material unless you're certain that the person wants to receive it (if it's impersonal, consider posting it on an electronic bulletin board where the person can read it when he or she has time).
- Don't compose messages when you're angry. When you're ready, compose such messages off-line so that you can reconsider and revise them before transmitting them.
- Don't send a hostile message (*flame*) to someone who appears to have committed a breach of computer etiquette.
- Don't reply angrily to someone who criticizes you for such a breach (send a polite acknowledgment or apology).

POSTAL MAIL

Many businesses have discovered that electronic transmission has often replaced telephone calls as well as postal and private delivery mail. Although the situation varies depending on the company and the type of business conducted in it, postal delivery nevertheless remains an important means of delivery and the preferred form for certain material, such as legal documents.

Industry experts no longer predict that paper-based mail will disappear in the near future. Many now expect that it will continue to be a significant form of message and document delivery for many years. They add that people still look forward to receiving the paper mail each day and that most people still feel more confident about security and privacy with paper sent or received in a sealed envelope. Also, a majority of U.S. consumers still prefer to buy something after receiving a *printed* mail advertisement, as opposed to receiving a phone call or e-mail. Therefore, until newer technologies (and societal acceptance of them) render this evaluation obsolete, office professionals need to remain informed about the proper practices and procedures in handling traditional mail.

Incoming Mail

Whereas private delivery mail, e-mail, fax mail, and other forms of communication may arrive throughout the day or night, postal mail arrives about the same time each day. The time when it's handled, as well as how it's handled, may therefore differ from that with other types of mail. See the previous discussions of fax mail and e-mail.

Practices for presenting pertinent pieces of postal mail to an executive may also differ from office to office. In some offices, you may be expected to deliver all incoming mail, paper or electronic, as it arrives throughout the day. In other offices, you may be expected to print out the electronic transmissions, add them along with fax copies to the incoming postal mail, and deliver everything to the executive at one time each day. Only urgent messages would be presented as they arrive. Since practices differ, you should follow the requirements in your office.

Preliminary sorting of paper mail. Some office functions cannot be relegated to automation. Opening the paper mail and sorting messages, as well as reading, annotating, and evaluating the contents, are examples of routine manual procedures. In regard to sorting procedures, you may do an initial sort before opening the envelopes and a final sort after opening them and removing the contents.

First, separate letters from periodicals and packages. With the envelopes still unopened, sort the letters into stacks containing personal correspondence and business correspondence, including First Class Mail, bills and statements, and mass mailings (also known as *direct mail*). The categories may vary, depending on the nature of your business, but if you follow this procedure every day, a pattern will soon emerge. Eventually, you may prefer to do an initial sort and open the envelopes at the same time.

Opening the mail. You'll probably use a hand-held, knifelike letter opener or, if you have a large volume of paper mail, an automatic opener. As you empty the contents, attach large enclosures in back of the letters and small ones in front. If enclosures are missing, promptly call or write to the sender. If anything was sent to you in error, write "Not at This Address," and add the material to your outgoing mail. If your office requires that mail be stamped and dated, take care of this step as soon as you've removed the contents from the envelopes.

If any letters or packages don't have sufficient return addresses, attach the envelopes or address labels to the contents. Otherwise, discard envelopes unless you need them for the postmark date. However, first double-check that nothing confidential was opened in error. One should never open mail marked "Personal" or "Confidential," but if this accidentally happens, reseal the envelope and make a note on it that it was opened in error.

Final sorting of the mail. After all pieces of incoming mail have been opened, all printouts of e-mail collected, and so on, divide the opened mail into final categories suitable for your business. General categories might include the following:

Correspondence

Bills and statements

Newspapers and periodicals

Direct mail advertising

Other material

Unless the mail is voluminous, set up a paper file folder for each category, and keep the items in the respective folders until they're presented to the executive or otherwise disposed of. If all pieces are taken care of promptly, the same folders can be emptied and reused the following day.

Follow the practice in your office for disposing of direct mail pieces (so-called junk mail). Executives often like to read about new products, seminars, and other material that's advertised or sold by mail. But if your supervisor doesn't want to receive mail from certain organizations, ask if you should have his or her name removed from the mailing lists, and then write to the senders with this request.

Forward any items that your office doesn't handle to the appropriate person or department. Bills and statements, for example, might go to an accounting department. Certain periodicals or other incoming material may have been ordered for another office. If your office has a mail-room pickup, put the item in an interoffice envelope for the next pickup, or attach a routing slip with the appropriate person's name and department on it, and put it in your out box. Otherwise, deliver it yourself as soon as you're able to leave your desk.

Correspondence often requires additional sorting into at least three subcategories:

Correspondence for the executive

Correspondence for others

Correspondence for you

As you become familiar with the activities in your office, you'll learn who should handle the various items. For mail to be presented to your supervisor, separate personal and business letters, and place priority items requiring immediate attention on top or in a separate color-coded priority folder. In addition to putting priority letters on top of other letters, arrange all mail by category for presentation, with the most important category (usually priority correspondence) on top of other categories, such as newspapers.

If it will be helpful to the executive in replying to a letter to know more about a situation, attach the pertinent material, such as a report or file folder. Try to anticipate what will be needed, and include it when you present the mail, rather than wait for your supervisor to request additional information.

Handling hate mail. Hate mail often has the same effect on readers as pathological or obscene telephone calls have on listeners. If you feel endangered by the contents of a particular letter or parcel, don't hesitate to call your company's security office, the police, or the Postal Inspection Service. There are laws against such abuse of the mail system, just as other statutes forbid obscene and obnoxious telephone calls. Simple letters of disagreement, however, should be treated the same as any other correspondence.

Reading and annotating the mail. Occasionally, executives want their assistants to read letters and memos and add pertinent comments on paper copies that will help them answer the correspondence. Some may want to have the gist of the letter summarized in the margin, to have questions answered, or to have key points underlined or highlighted with a yellow marking pen. Often, though, it's against company policy to write anything on a letter except the time and date of receipt. In that case, the key points can be noted on removable self-sticking notes. If comments are lengthy, prepare them on a memo and attach it to the letter.

The same procedure should be followed in reading and annotating articles, reports, and other incoming material. In all cases, though, follow the requirements and practices in your office.

Maintaining a mail record. For legal or other reasons, your office may require that you keep a daily record of all important pieces of mail received. Some offices need a record only of mail routed to others outside the office for action. You can make up and print out a fill-in form, similar to a columnar accounting pad, for this purpose. Your record may have ten or more columns, with headings such as this:

Date received

Time received

Date on item

Name and affiliation of sender

Name and department of recipient

Description of mail (such as an invitation to speak at a
banquet)

Type of mail (such as a fax message)

To whom forwarded for action

Type of action required

Follow-up date (if any)

You can hand-write the facts in the columns and, if required, prepare a computer copy later. This type of record is useful to traveling executives who need to have a summary of activity in the office while they're away. In other cases, an executive may believe that keeping such a record is too time consuming and that you should simply tell him about each day's activity.

Submitting the mail. Follow the executive's preference in submitting pertinent pieces of mail for his or her review and action. The practice in your office may include some or all of the following:

- Collecting incoming paper and electronic mail and submitting it to your supervisor one or more times a day, according to office requirements

- Organizing the mail according to category and priority, as described previously, before submitting it

- Using colored folders or labels to separate categories or designate priority

- Attaching routing slips or using interoffice envelopes for items to be circulated among persons outside the office

- Photocopying important material when appropriate and routing the photocopy, keeping the original in the files

- Forwarding mail to absent executives and other individuals by fax, express mail, or other means, as preferred by the absent person

- Using action-requested slips for mail forwarded to others on which you can check off action requested, such as ( ) For Your Information, ( ) For Your Action, ( ) For Your Approval, ( ) For Your Comments, ( ) Please Forward, ( ) Please Return, ( ) Please Review with Me, and ( ) Please File.

- Making printouts of waiting e-mail messages for submission (if paper copies are preferred by the executive)
- Annotating and highlighting the mail, as described earlier, before submitting it
- Attaching files and other pertinent material that will help the executive compose a reply

Outgoing Mail

After you've prepared a traditional or electronic message, as described in Chapter 9, "Correspondence," you'll need to follow the proper procedure in preparing each piece for mailing. Certain practices may differ from one office to another, but other steps are standard in all offices. Some small offices, for example, don't have enough mail volume to warrant the use of a postage meter and hence apply stamps manually to all postal envelopes. Other offices may send primarily faxes and e-mail messages or may have sophisticated electronic mailing equipment. Some may have the software needed to print postage with their PC printers. (See also Stamping the mail.) Although such matters differ from office to office, other practices, such as carefully proofreading a message, should be mandatory in all offices and for all types of mail.

Proofreading outgoing mail. An office professional should scrutinize outgoing correspondence for everything from format to style to spelling to syntax. (For further guidelines, see Chapters 7, "Business Style Guide," 8, "Business English," and 9, "Correspondence.") Spell-checkers will relieve you of part of the burden of proofreading, but they can't detect a missing sentence or a different word that you intended to use. Some errors are likely to be found only if the material is read or checked against an original draft. Since sloppy work, inaccuracies, and other errors may cause companies to lose clients and customers, and thus future or present income, the proofreading function should be handled with care, and nothing less than 100 percent accuracy is acceptable.

Getting signatures. Letters, contracts, checks, or forms in need of signing may be submitted to an executive in several ways. You might place all such paperwork in a file folder labeled simply "To Be Signed," indicate on complex pieces where the signature and date are to appear (use a self-sticking note if it will be helpful), and submit the folder with items for signing at the executive's convenience.

It's preferable to submit a stack of documents all at one time, when practical, rather than one at a time throughout the day. However, a letter, contract, or other document sometimes needs to be processed quickly, and you'll not be able to wait until you've accumulated numerous documents. In some cases, a clipboard is useful. It enables someone to sign a letter in the absence of desk space, such as while sitting at a computer terminal or in a reading chair. Ask your supervisor if he or she prefers receiving postal documents to be signed with or without envelopes attached. If you sign letters on an executive's behalf, follow the instructions given in Chapter 9, "Correspondence," Signature.

Before folding and inserting postal or private delivery mail in the envelopes, check them one more time to be certain that the executive did not forget to sign a letter. Sending unsigned material does not create a good impression, and certain material, such as an agreement, would be invalid without a signature.

Handling enclosures. Before sealing the outgoing envelopes, double-check that all required enclosures have been included. During the preparation phase, an enclosure notation should have been added at the bottom of a letter or memo. (See the examples in Chapter 9, "Correspondence," Enclosure notation.) The advantage of specifying *what* is enclosed, such as *Enc.: Schedule,* is that you can glance at the enclosure notation before sealing the letter to be certain that nothing was omitted. If you didn't specify what is enclosed, check the enclosures against your original instructions.

Small enclosures are usually attached in front of a letter and large enclosures behind it. Loose items, such as coins, should first be inserted in a small envelope or taped to a card. However, because paper clips can damage mailing equipment, many office professionals prefer to fold enclosures and tuck them inside the fold of the letter, rather than clip them to the letter. Enclosures too large to fold are usually placed flat and unattached behind the cover letter.

Handling file copies. Before a letter is mailed, the required number of file copies should be made. In the case of electronic filing, the document should be given the appropriate filename and saved. In the case of paper filing, copies of the document should be filed in the appropriate alphabetical, numerical, or other system. Refer to Chapter 10, "Information Management," for a description of the various filing systems and procedures.

Maintaining a follow-up record. Outgoing mail records are less common than incoming mail records. However, if an outgoing record is required in your office for legal reasons or as a follow-up guide, use a columnar format and include the following headings:

Date sent

Name and address of recipient

Description of material sent

Method of mail or transmission

Follow-up date

More common than a follow-up record, however, is the follow-up file or reminder system described in Chapter 10, "Information Management," Follow-up Files.

Preparing envelopes. Envelopes prepared for postal or private delivery should be addressed according to the format and style requirements given in Chapter 9, "Correspondence," Envelope Formats. Labels may be provided for private delivery packages, although some services provide their own envelopes and print out the labels on their own equipment. You simply give them the name and address to enter in their computer.

If you do prepare a label, however, follow the same style of addressing used for postal mail. Check that the degree of color contrast between the envelope or mailing label and the printed address is sharp enough to be detected by optical character scanners.

Folding and inserting letters. Postal letters should be folded and inserted according to the kind of envelope selected. Standard sizes are given in Chapter 9, "Correspondence," Envelope Formats, and the illustration in this chapter indicates the traditional way of folding and inserting material in standard envelopes.

If you're mailing multiple sheets, arrange them so that when the envelope is opened and the letter is unfolded, the text will be right side up. However, if you use clips to attach the pages, insert the pages in the envelope so that the clip falls at the bottom of the envelope, where it is less likely to damage mailing equipment.

When including a letter with a larger item, you can fold and insert the letter into a matching envelope and pack it with the enclosure in a larger mailer. Or you can put both letter and enclosure into a single large envelope. If you choose to use a large envelope and send them unfolded, add a piece of cardboard to help prevent damage in transit. Offices sending a lot of international postal mail may use overseas airmail envelopes that are lighter than standard office envelopes.

Use padded mailers or boxes for books, small manuscripts, press kits, files, and similar materials, and use diskette mailers for floppy disks and photo mailers for photographs. Other special mailers are available for rolled material such as blueprints and various fragile or sensitive material.

Number 6³/₄ Envelope

 1 2 3  4

1. Fold the bottom half of the stationery to within ¹/₂" of the top edge. Crease it.
2. Fold the stationery from right to left, a bit more than one third of the width. Crease it.
3. Fold from left to right, allowing a ¹/₂" margin at the right. Crease it.
4. Insert the last folded side into the envelope first.

Number 10 Envelope

 1   2   3

1. Fold the lower third of the stationery. Crease it.
2. Fold the stationery from the top down, allowing a ¹/₂" margin from the edge of the first fold. Crease it again.
3. Insert the last folded side into the envelope first.

Window Envelope

1   2   3

1. Fold the bottom third of the letter. Crease it.
2. Fan-fold the upper section of the letter back to the edge of the first fold so that the inside address will be on the outside and not on the inside. Crease it.
3. Insert the stationery so that the inside address is clearly visible through the window (¹/₄" margins needed).

Note: Some printed letterhead intended exclusively for window applications is marked to indicate placement of the inside address. Printed fold lines are often included.

Folding and Inserting Stationery into Envelopes

Using window envelopes. Window envelopes, often used in mass mailings, require careful insertion of letters. If the recipient's name and address don't appear through the window, the time you've saved by not addressing the envelope separately will have been lost. Generally, the procedure is to fold the sheet in thirds, with the inside address outside on the top. Allow about a fourth to an eighth inch between the edge of the window and the address to prevent blocking part of the address.

Sealing envelopes. Some small offices don't have electronic equipment that seals as well as meters postal mail, and all offices occasionally mail odd-sized material that requires manual attention. There are several ways to seal an envelope or mailing container, such as by mouth, sponge, or mailing tape. (Health practitioners warn that if you lick envelopes and stamps, you may be consuming toxic chemicals and bacteria.) Very large, heavy packages may have to be banded or reinforced in some other way. Consult your local post office for current requirements.

Stamping the mail. You have several options for stamping outgoing postal mail, including using postage meters, e-postage, imprints, and manual methods. If you don't have a mail room, you should keep an accurate postage scale in your office and a list of the current postage rates applicable to the classes of mail service that your office uses. If you do a substantial amount of postal mailing, consider subscribing to the domestic and international postal manuals described in Types of Postal Mail.

Stamps and meters. Traditional postage stamps (most are now self-adhesive) can be purchased at a postal facility, and e-stamps can be purchased over the Internet by signing up with one of the vendors. Through such services you can download up to a certain amount of U.S. Postal Service postage and print it as needed with your PC. However, some accounting departments object to having individual users print stamps as needed with their PCs because it's difficult to control such usage and allocate the postage used to the various accounts for accounting purposes.

Another alternative is to purchase or lease from a commercial vendor a metering device that can be set for the amount of postage that you purchase. It will then print out tapes up to that amount. The Postal Service also offers a thermal printer that connects to your PC and does essentially the same thing. Since new technologies and new hardware and software are continually being introduced, check the Internet periodically for recent innovations.

Permit imprints. With a permit imprint, you can have postage printed directly onto a supply of envelopes or postcards. This is a common procedure for large mailings. In fact, postage for presorted mail must be paid by permit imprint, meter, or other such precanceled method. To use imprints, you must first obtain a permit and then purchase the required amount of postage before or at the time of mailing. Imprints may be used on labels, wrappers, envelopes, and other containers. Contact your local post office for further information and the regulations concerning *indicia* (the postal markings imprinted on envelopes and labels).

Types of Postal Mail

The U.S. Postal Service mail accounts for a substantial portion of all paper mail, and office professionals therefore need to be aware of the principal domestic and international classes of mail and the associated postal services.

Information sources. Subscriptions to the *Domestic Mail Manual* and the *International Mail Manual* are available from the Superintendent of Documents in Washington, D.C. The *Postal Explorer,* which includes both manuals as well as related publications, is available on the Internet at the U.S. Postal Service website. A CD-ROM version includes a rate calculator that lets you compute and print rates for all classes and discount options. Other information and copies of forms can also be downloaded from the Postal Service site.

Miscellaneous brochures and pamphlets are available at no charge from local post offices. Commercial zip code directories are sold in bookstores, and the *National ZIP Code Directory* is available from The National Information Data Center in Washington, D.C. All of these publications are helpful to those who regularly handle outgoing traditional mail.

Domestic mail. Domestic mail consists of four major classifications: Express Mail, First Class Mail, periodicals, and standard mail. Since extensive rules and regulations apply to each one and since information frequently changes, you should consult your local post office or one of the information sources just mentioned for current details. The Postal Service describes the four main classes of domestic mail as follows:

- *Express Mail* provides expedited delivery for Next Day/Second Day Service, Same Day Airport Service, Custom Designed Service, and Military Service.

- *First Class Mail* is any mailable matter that is wholly or partially in handwriting or type, including postcards, letters and sealed parcels, and priority mail.

- *Periodicals* refers to mail in the form of magazines, newspapers, and publications formed of printed sheets and issued at least four times a year at regular intervals from a known office of publication.

- *Standard mail* is that which weighs over 16 ounces and up to 70 pounds. Subclass A includes circulars, printed matter, catalogs, pamphlets, newsletters, direct mail, and merchandise. Subclass B includes bound printed matter, library mail, parcel post, and special standard mail.

The Postal Service also offers a variety of services, including the following: registered mail, certified mail, insured mail, certificate of mailing, return receipt, restricted delivery, return receipt for merchandise, collect on delivery (COD), business reply mail, merchandise return service, and bulk parcel return service. Check one of the postal information sources mentioned earlier for details and recent changes and for information about bulk-mailing discounts, ZIP + 4 addressing charges, and other instructions for mailers.

International mail. International mail consists of three major classifications: Postal Union mail, Parcel post, and Express Mail International Service. As is the case with domestic mail, extensive rules and regulations apply to international mail, with country by country variations, and changes occur frequently. For current information, consult your local post office or one of the information sources mentioned previously. The Postal Service describes the three main classes of international mail as follows:

- *Postal Union mail* is governed by the regulations of the Universal Postal Union. Categories include *LC (letters and cards) mail* (letters, letter packages, post and postal cards, and aerogrammes) and *AO (other articles) mail* (regular printed matter, books and sheet music, publishers' periodicals, matter for the blind, and small packets).

- *Parcel post,* sometimes referred to as *CP mail (colis postaux,* or postal parcels), includes only one category that is equivalent to domestic standard mail (B): zone-rated parcel post.

- *Express Mail International Service* is an expedited service exchanged with certain other countries. The two categories that are provided are Custom Designed Service and On Demand Service.

A variety of services similar to those offered for domestic mail are also available to international mailers (check the sources mentioned previously for details and recent changes): insurance, registered mail, return receipt, restricted delivery, recall/change of address, special delivery, special handling, postal money orders, international reply coupons, and international business reply service.

Barcoding. One of the more significant developments in the mailing industry is the use of bar codes to identify addresses, track documents and packages, and speed the movement of mail from sender to receiver. A *bar code,* which you see on products everywhere, from grocery stores to office supply stores, is a pattern of ink on paper. It consists of parallel bars and spaces representing various data that can be read by electronically scanning a light across the bars. Using bar codes involves three steps:

- Printing the codes for use in identifying items or tasks
- Capturing, or retrieving, the information contained in a code
- Converting the data for computer analysis or storage

Preparing and printing the codes requires the right software and hardware. The codes are best printed by specialized thermal printers but can also be printed with laser, ink jet, or even dot matrix printers. To learn more about the use of bar codes and handling address changes, contact your local post office, or check the information provided by the National Customer Support Center at the U.S. Postal Service website.

PRIVATE DELIVERY SERVICES

Private delivery services, once known primarily for package delivery, handle a variety of mail, from one-page letters to large packages. Some also provide Internet services, such as electronic document delivery, as described in the final section of this chapter.

Although practices in handling private delivery mail are similar to those for handling postal mail, deliveries may arrive at irregular times or more than once during the day. Unless a document is urgent, however, it may be added to and processed along with the incoming postal mail.

Physical Transport

Private shipping, delivery, and courier companies offer services that rival those of the U.S. Postal Service. In some instances, these operations feature services that a post office may not provide. For example, some companies will set up an account providing for monthly billing.

Since each delivery service has its own regulations, rates, and delivery schedule, it's necessary to contact each one for comparisons. Large organizations offer both national and international services, and some bus lines, taxi companies, and other organizations also offer package delivery as a secondary service. For further information, look at company websites, or look in the yellow pages of your local telephone directory for names and telephone numbers. Telephone directories commonly list such companies under "Air Freight and Package Express Services," "Delivery Services," "Courier Services," or "Messenger Services."

Although next-day and second-day delivery is a prominent service offered by the major companies, mailers need to consider whether the extra cost for overnight service is warranted. For example, it serves no useful purpose to send a package by overnight service on Friday if no one will be available at the destination on Saturday to receive and act on it.

Delivery services usually provide both pickup and delivery. You can also visit a nearby office of the service or take your material to a local mail service that acts as an agent of the company. However, such mail services add their own handling charge to the transport charge of the delivery company.

Electronic Delivery

In addition to providing physical transport, some companies offer electronic document delivery. If you inquire about this, ask whether the service includes maximum encryption (coding for security) levels, receiver authentication, and proof of delivery. You usually need only a PC and an Internet connection to use an electronic delivery service. Websites may provide all the information you need and also enable you to track packages sent by physical transport and find out a wealth of other information.

Document Creation

Creating documents is one of the most important functions in the electronic office. The term *document creation* is often used interchangeably with *word processing* to refer to the use of a computer and word processing software to create, format, edit, print, and store documents. In a broader sense, the term refers to the creation of any type of document, regardless of the particular equipment or software that is used.

In some businesses, for example, correspondence, reports, newsletters, and a variety of other material may be prepared only by computer and, occasionally, by electronic typewriter. In other organizations, particularly those that produce sophisticated in-house documents, such as a book or magazine, desktop publishing or other typesetting equipment may be used.

The duplication of routine company messages and documents is often handled in-house by a computer printer or copier. The printing of more elaborate material may be handled by a small offset press or, less commonly, by a larger printing press.

The generation of documents is an important and highly visible means of communication and presentation for executives and their staffs. Teamwork is an essential ingredient, for without the refined skills of office professionals in collecting information, assimilating it, and producing effective, accurate documents, business would come to a debilitating and expensive halt.

WORD PROCESSING SKILLS

Office professionals commonly follow these basic steps in creating a document with word processing software: format, input, edit, save, proofread (screen), print, proofread (paper), correct, save, print, and store. However, not everyone follows all steps in precisely this order. Highly skilled computer operators, for example, usually make so few errors that the errors can often be corrected during the initial on-screen machine proofreading, including the spell-check and grammar-check. This eliminates the need for a final correction step (but not the final proofreading of hard copy). Nevertheless, the series of steps generally suggests the basic skills that one should have to create the many types of documents required for the daily conduct of business.

Even though a current word processing program has numerous features, one must still be a fast and accurate computer operator. In addition to having good keyboarding skills, an operator must know how to format correctly and attractively. Especially, one must have excellent language skills, with high competency in spelling, punctuation, grammar, word choice, and general composition, such as sentence and paragraph development. See Chapters 7, "Business Style Guide," and 8, "Business English," for more about these subjects.

One of the most important but sometimes neglected skills is proofreading. No person or machine automatically does perfect work. A spell-check program, for example, may accept the word *lose* as correct even if you really mean *loose*. Careful proofreading of printouts, in addition to on-screen checking, will compensate for such machine or keyboarding deficiencies and will enable you to produce error-free documents.

COMPUTER PRODUCTION

Document preparation by computer is the most common method of processing text and graphics. Those who are familiar with their employers' equipment and word processing program can prepare and print out as many originals as desired, make revisions without having to rekey entire documents, combine two or more documents with only a few keystrokes, merge a letter with a list of various addresses, and automatically and quickly search through hundreds of documents to locate the one needed. The list of capabilities is increasing every day as ever more powerful programs are developed.

Computer Capabilities

Input. The input function corresponds to traditional activities such as note taking or listening activities in which information is recorded or taken in. In office information systems, the most common input devices are the computer keyboard and the mouse, although other input devices, such as light pens, scanners, and voice, are also used. Once the information has passed through an input device to become digitized (made electronic in form), it can be automatically processed, moved, stored, and printed as text, graphs, drawings, and so on.

Processing. A processing unit, the brains of a computer, manipulates the information that is input according to instructions given to it through software. It may, for example, automatically combine numbers or shift paragraphs in a letter, store material in files locally or in remote office locations, justify text, and check for spelling errors before printing.

Output. The output function is the usable and legible form in which the information is produced. It corresponds to the end product of office work, such as the final text of a speech, report, or letter. The most common output devices are the printer and the computer screen. Offices that produce substantial printed information may also have desktop publishing or photocomposition units to transform text prepared with word processing software into final copy.

Storage. A storage unit files information in the computer's memory or outside on disks or tapes. Whereas in traditional offices storage areas consisted of filing cabinets, libraries, ring binders, desk drawers, and so on, in electronic offices this array is replaced or at least supplemented by electronic storage at different levels of accessibility and related cost. If information is stored within a computer terminal, it's said to be stored *online,* one of the most accessible forms of storage. It may also be stored on removable disks or tapes. Micrographic devices (see Chapter 10, "Information Management," Microstorage) that transfer information from computer memory onto microfilm for storage are usually found more often in libraries and offices with large volumes of fixed information (not needing further modification), such as personnel files and general ledgers.

Communications. The information generated with word processing software must be communicated in some way. Traditionally, communication has been the action binding offices together, making the information flow from decision to outcome and back again. In the electronic office, communication devices link computers to other computer terminals around the company or, through the Internet (see Chapter 1, "The Online Office," The Internet), to other computer terminals around the world and, through them, to endless databases or electronic files.

The media used in communication may take many forms, from the traditional telephone and the cell phone to the two-way coaxial cable to the more advanced fiber optics. Information may also be moved via satellite around the world and through switching mechanisms, such as computerized telephone exchanges. (See Chapter 4, "Telecommunications," Telephone Systems.) Exchanges route voice and data messages through a maze of transmission lines and operating systems to a variety of destinations — workstations, computers, fax machines, and so on.

Software Capabilities

To create a document with word processing software, you must understand how to select options and give commands. The specific steps differ from one program to another, so you should follow the instructions that accompany the word processing program in your office. (Save the manuals. Once they're lost, it's often impossible to replace them.) For example, you may be using menus, icons, the older command languages, or a combination of them.

- A *menu* in a word processing program is a list of the options that are available. It enables you to give the system commands and open and close the doors to avenues of travel within the various levels of the software. A menu may appear on the screen as a vertical list of items with a small check-off box next to each one; as a bar across the top, bottom, or side of the screen, with options printed on the bar; or in some other format. Often both menus and icons are available in a program.

- An *icon*-based interface uses pictures or images to represent system functions. Icon-based systems may feature touch-sensitive screens or involve the use of a mouse to select options. An electronic mail application, for example, may be represented by a small picture of a mailbox on the screen. By touching the on-screen mailbox or by positioning the cursor on it (via a mouse) and selecting it, you'll be able to open the mailbox and read the messages that are waiting there.

- An older system, *command languages* do not rely on a menu to receive instructions. A command language enables you to give the system direct keyboard instructions in the form of a system code or keyword. Each code or keyword invokes a specific action by the system. Although command code language enables you to combine several steps at once, it's not user friendly in a word processing environment. This type of user interface can be very complicated and requires that you memorize numerous commands or repeatedly refer to tables and charts listing the desired function and their associated commands.

Editing features. When you prepare text by computer, you use the capabilities of the word processing software to manipulate the data on screen. These capabilities include important features such as on-screen *Help* (to answer questions) and special features such as *Merge* (to combine items such as an address list with a standard message). Most programs also offer a wide variety of functions, such as the following examples, to help you create and edit your documents:

- *Vertical and horizontal scrolling:* The *vertical scroll* function moves the text up automatically as additional text is entered. The *horizontal scroll* function allows you to have lines of text wider than the actual width of the screen. The screen slides the text to the left as additional text is added to a line on the right.

- *Insert:* The insert function lets you pick a particular place in the text and enter new words there. The system automatically adjusts the rest of the text to accommodate the new entry without requiring that the page be rekeyed.

- *Delete:* The delete function works on the same principle as insert. Through it, you can select text to be removed from the document. Afterward, the remaining text is automatically adjusted to reflect the change.

- *Copy:* The copy function lets you select any text in a document, copy it, and insert (paste) the copy in another part of the same document or in a different document.

- *Indent:* The indent function lets you indent an entire block of text from the left or right margins (or both). It can be used to alter an existing document or, during text input, to create an indented block, such as an extract.

- *Search:* With the search function, the computer automatically searches for words, punctuation, spaces, or some other aspect of a document that you specify.

- *Replace:* The replace function lets you select text or other material for deletion in an existing document and replace it with something else. The search and replace features may be used together in most programs.

- *Decimal alignment:* The decimal alignment function lines up numbers on their decimal points to provide numeric columns. Each number in the column will have its decimal point positioned below the one above it.

Formatting. The more powerful your word processing program is, the more formatting options you'll have. If you prepare numerous tables or text with multiple columns, lists, and other special material, you'll want a program that enables quick and easy setup of each item. Programs with such capability have provisions for saving a document as a template, or standard format, that can be used with future documents. In addition, certain basic formatting options, such as the following examples, are common in most programs:

- *Autoformat:* The autoformat feature applies a consistent style to the various parts of a document, such as headings, body text, and lists.

- *Reformatting:* To reformat a document, you simply change the format settings of an existing document to a new configuration of tab spaces, line length, line spacing, and so on. The system will automatically modify the text associated with the change to your revised format specifications.

- *Justification:* Text justification is the system's ability to modify the arrangement of the characters on each line to make both left- and right-hand margins even. This capability makes some documents, such as a book or newsletter, look more professional.

- *Spacing and alignment:* The system's spacing and alignment capabilities let you change the appearance of a document by adjusting the paragraph alignment, indention, line spacing, space between paragraphs, and so on.

- *Character format:* Numerous character format options are available for any text that you select, including bold, italics, all capital letters, small capital letters, and color.

- *Tables:* Most software will let you choose different styles of tables and will automatically align and format the information you provide.

- *Font:* The font option lets you select any style of type that your software and printer provide. You can also specify the size of type that you want for any part of your document.

- *Graphics:* Most word processing programs offer clip art, symbols, boxes and shaded backgrounds, and other graphics features that you can use to enhance a document.

- *Headers and footers:* Most programs also allow you to specify lines, numbers, and so on that will be automatically repeated on each page. A *header,* or *running head,* is a text entry to be repeated in the top margin of all pages in a document. A *footer,* such as a page number, is similar to the page header, except that it is positioned at the bottom instead of the top of the page.

In addition to providing basic editing and formatting capabilities, most large word processing programs have special features, such as sorting, index generating, and math calculation. Also, they may enable you to use the word processing program to create webpages and establish *hyperlinks* for your files — colored or underlined text or graphics that you can click on with a mouse to jump to another file or another location in the same file. See Chapter 1, "The Online Office," Webpage format, for a description of the Hypertext Markup Language (HTML) used to format a webpage.

Desktop Publishing

Desktop publishing (DTP) is a computerized application with which you can prepare complex documents using a broad range of typefaces and incorporating graphics, borders, and other special page-makeup features. With DTP you can produce brochures, newsletters, magazines, annual reports, letterheads, and other material in-house. A major advantage of DTP is that you can view each finished page on your computer screen exactly as it will appear when printed.

Although the quality of the output may be inferior to that of other methods of composition, such as Photocomposition, which uses a high-resolution photographic technology, the similarity to other word processing activities makes DTP a logical extension in many companies. Keyboard operators can apply the same skills to both DTP and basic word processing. The DTP operator, however, often must possess a better understanding of graphics, scanning processes, and publishing terminology.

DTP terminology. In addition to understanding general computer and word processing terms, such as *format* and *input,* those who are involved in DTP activities should be familiar with the basic publishing terminology, including the following terms:

- *Font:* A particular size and style of type. A font includes all the capital, lowercase, and small capital letters, punctuation marks, and math or other symbols associated with the particular type family.

- *Graphics:* Any type of pictorial image, such as a chart or graph; also, a software program that lets you create, insert, or merge pictures, tables, maps, charts, graphs, and so on into other documents.

- *Justified type:* Type that is set with an even right margin; that is, the last words of each line of type are aligned. The type in this book is justified.

- *Leading:* (Pronounced "leding," not "leeding") The space between lines of type, usually measured in points (described below). Publishers commonly add one or two additional points of space between lines (10/12 means that the type is 10 points and the leading is 12 points). This book has a leading of 13 pts.

- *Lowercase:* A reference to small letters; often written in abbreviated form as *lc* by typesetters.

- *Page proof:* A copy of each full page of material prepared by DTP, presented to the person responsible for proofreading.

- *Pica:* A unit of measure used to indicate the length of a line (6 picas = 1 inch, and 12 points = 1 pica). Most lines of type in this book are 26p6 picas wide. In reference to type size, 10 spaces of pica type equal 1 inch, whereas 12 spaces of elite type equal 1 inch.

- *Point:* A unit of measure used to indicate the size of type (72 points = 1 inch). This book is set in 10.75 point type.

- *Ragged right:* A reference to an uneven right margin; that is, the last words of each line of type are not aligned, and each line may be a different length from the others. Business letters and memos are usually typed ragged right.

- *Roman type:* A style of type with upright characters and serifs (described below) and vertical lines thicker than horizontal lines, unlike italic, which has oblique letters. This book is set in a roman typeface.

- *Sans serif:* A style of type in which there are no serifs (described below) that finish off the main strokes of a letter; also called gothic. This sentence is set in sans serif type.

- *Serif:* A fine line that finishes off the main strokes of a letter. This book, for example, has a typeface with serifs.

- *Typeface:* The style of printed characters, identified by the name that is given to it. This book, for example, is set in Minion type.

- *Uppercase:* A reference to all capital letters; often written in abbreviated form as *uc* by typesetters.

- *WYSIWYG:* (Pronounced *wiz-ee-wig*) An acronym for "What you see is what you get" in reference to being able to view pages on screen in DTP in the way that they will appear when printed.

Advantages and disadvantages of DTP. Organizations use DTP for various reasons. Without this capability, certain complex material would have to be sent to an outside typesetter, often at higher cost than that incurred by using in-house DTP. Some organizations therefore consider it more cost-effective to purchase DTP software, train one or more word processing operators for DTP, and produce most, if not all, complex material in-house.

DTP is less desirable when company personnel don't have the time or skills to handle DTP and when an organization is already overburdened with other work. Also, if exceptional quality material is required, other forms of composition (see Photocomposition) may be preferred. In addition, the cost savings from using in-house DTP may be less significant if an organization must also purchase scanning equipment and graphics programs to supplement the DTP equipment and software. Each organization must conduct its own analysis and weigh the pros and cons in terms of its own situation.

Using DTP. When manuscripts presented to the DTP department are first prepared by computer using a word processing program, the disk copy of the material must be prepared according to the instructions (if any) from the DTP department. Although instructions will vary depending on the type of DTP software that is used, the DTP operator may need a disk containing a single-spaced, *unformatted* document. Headlines, for example, should then be in a regular typeface, without bold, italic, or other styling (such matters will be up to the designer). Everything should be positioned flush left (no paragraph indentions), with no extra space between lines or around heads and only one character space between sentences, after colons, and so on. Also, depending on the DTP program, you may be expected to code each special element, such as lists, subheads, and footnotes, in a specific way. See Tagged Document for an example.

TAGGED DOCUMENT

@CN:Chapter 4
@CT:Word Processing
@H1:Word Processing Skills
@NORMAL:The basic steps in word processing point to the skills that are needed to create any type of document.
@UNL:Format
@UNL:Input
@UNL:Edit
@UNL:Print
@H2:Basic Computer Capabilities
@H3:Input
@NORMAL:In the electronic office, the input function corresponds to traditional activities such as taking notes or dictation, typing, and listening — activities whereby information is recorded or taken in.

Tagged Document

However, even if the disk you submit to the DTP department contains an unformatted document, your manuscript printout should be formatted and double-spaced. This is necessary for ease in editing and will make it clearer and easier for the proofreader to use after the copy has been set in the DTP department.

Creating Documents. The specific steps to follow in creating a document with DTP will vary. A brochure with photographs or drawings will require additional design and graphics considerations compared to an announcement of a company picnic that consists of text only. Depending on the publication you're producing, you may be concerned with some or all of these steps:

- Using a standard word processing program to write and edit your manuscript

- Using a computer graphics program to create your illustrations or a scanner to input already prepared illustrations

- Developing a format using the master-page feature of your DTP program (selecting column width, boxes, headers, and so on)

- Bringing the text from your word processing disk, graphics from your graphics program or from scanned input, and other material into the DTP program where on-screen DTP prompts will help you position the material within the format you developed

- Viewing each completed page on screen and making final adjustments as desired

- Printing a master copy with your laser printer or, for higher-quality output, sending your disk to a service bureau with compatible high-resolution equipment

Refer to Report Preparation and to Chapters 7, "Business Style Guide," and 9, "Correspondence," for details about the preparation of different kinds of business documents.

Photocomposition

Companies that don't have in-house desktop publishing equipment may send material to be set to an outside typesetter. Various computerized and mechanical photocomposition, or phototypesetting, methods that produce high-quality material are available. Generally, text is entered with a keyboard; edited, stored, and retrieved by computer; and transferred by a typesetter mechanism to photosensitive paper or film. The exact procedure, however, depends on the specific equipment being used. Broadly, *photocomposition* refers to one of three processes:

- *Photomechanical composition* (the oldest process) by machines that generate images by flashing light through film matrices onto a light-sensitive medium
- *CRT composition* by computers that create images digitally on the surface of a cathode-ray tube
- *Laser composition* by machines that project images on paper with a laser beam

E-books

Traditionally, computer-generated material has been printed by one of the Duplication Processes described in the next section. E-books, however, are digitally stored copies of book-length documents that are read on screen rather than in printed form. Although some e-books are also published on paper, those that are produced only in electronic format eliminate the costs of print production, warehousing, and shipping. (Compare with Print-on-Demand Publishing.) They may be ordered from a publisher or through an e-book distribution system. There, a master version is installed on a central database, and electronic copies are created for customers when ordered.

An electronic copy can be downloaded from a vendor or purchased as a CD-ROM and read on a computer screen. However, e-books are primarily being promoted for use with small reading devices, such as the personal digital assistant (PDA), described in Chapter 1, "The Online Office," Integration.

Portable, battery-operated readers may have a variety of features. Usually, you can browse, mark text, and link passages, just as you might do on a website. Some operate at high speed, so you can download an e-book of several hundred pages in only a few minutes. Readers also may enable you to download other material, such as business files or reports. Some are available with voice synthesis, so you can listen to as well as read a document. As the technology has improved, on-screen print quality has also improved, making the device more palatable to many users who otherwise would find it difficult to read lengthy documents entirely on screen.

DUPLICATION PROCESSES

Documents that are created by computer or desktop publishing software usually have to be duplicated, whether only one file copy is needed or whether hundreds or even thousands of copies are needed. Three common duplication processes are photocopying, computer printing, and offset printing. A more recent innovation, known as Print-on-Demand Publishing, eliminates the initial print run traditionally associated with publishing books and other large documents.

Photocopying

Since the introduction of the copier at midcentury, photocopying has been a useful means of making paper copies and transparencies (for use with overhead projectors) directly from original letters, memos, and other documents. Although transparencies are being replaced by computerized projection in many firms, paper copies are still required, sometimes even more than before as modern copiers make it easy to generate quality duplicates in an instant.

In most businesses and even small home offices, therefore, the copier remains an essential reproduction machine. Although it is most often used for limited-volume copying, high-speed, high-volume copiers can handle thousands of copies a month. Refer to Chapter 1, "The Online Office," The Copier, for a description of copier speed, copy volume, and other capabilities.

Centralized reproduction department. In a large organization with many departments and high copy volumes, there may be a centralized reproduction department (CRD), with various satellite reproduction centers for high-volume work and individual office copiers for midvolume or low-volume use. The CRD may have both high-volume copy equipment and offset presses, as well as machines for various support and finishing operations such as offset platemaking, collating, folding, and binding.

The high-speed copy machines in a CRD are likely to have many special features, such as a computer forms feeder, automatic document handler, collator, automatic two-sided copying, color copying, and variable enlargement and reduction. If your equipment has a wide range of reduction selections, refer to Table 6.1 for selected standard settings and Table 6.2 for selected variable settings.

Decentralized copiers. Decentralized copy machines are individual units located in work areas for walk-up use. In a large company, they may be midvolume copiers used by departmental staffs for general administrative work or low-volume desktop units located in executive suites.

Computer Printing

Printers print the images they receive in digital form from a nearby or remote computer or terminal. No conventional hard-copy original or master is needed, although an outside document may be scanned into a computer for editing and printout. Chapter 1, "The Online Office," Printer, describes the major types of printers (laser, ink jet, and dot matrix) and scanning equipment.

Table 6.1 Standard Reduction Percentages

ORIGINAL SIZE	REPRODUCE ON 8½ × 11 INCH	REPRODUCE ON 8½ × 14 INCH
8½ × 11 inch	100%	100%
8½ × 14 inch	77%	100%
11 × 15 inch	74%	77%
11 × 17 inch	65%	77%
8½ × 11 inch with a narrow margin	98%	98%

Table 6.2 Determining Variable Reduction Percentages

% Reduction Chart

Original Dimension in Inches	5	5.5	6	6.5	7	7.5	8	8.5	9	9.5	10	10.5	11	11.5	12	12.5	13	13.5	14
17												62	65	68	71	74	76	79	82
16.5												64	67	70	73	76	79	82	85
16											62	65	69	72	75	78	81	84	87
15.5											65	68	71	74	77	81	84	87	90
15										63	67	70	73	77	80	83	87	90	93
14.5									62	65	69	72	76	79	83	86	90	93	96
14									64	68	71	75	79	82	86	89	93	96	100
13.5								63	67	70	74	78	81	85	89	93	96	100	
13							61	65	69	73	77	81	85	88	92	96	100		
12.5							64	68	72	76	80	84	88	92	96	100			
12						62	67	71	75	79	83	87	92	96	100				
11.5						65	69	74	78	83	87	91	96	100					
11					64	68	73	77	82	86	91	95	100						
10.5					67	71	76	81	85	90	95	100							
10				65	70	75	80	85	90	95	100								
9.5			63	68	74	79	84	90	95	100									
9			67	72	78	83	89	94	100										
8.5		65	71	76	82	88	94	100											
8	62	69	75	81	87	93	100												

Copy Paper Dimension in Inches

Since printer speed, number of fonts, and the quality of output vary, businesses may have more than one type of printer. For example, there may be some older high-speed, low-quality dot matrix printers for drafts and other work where type quality is unimportant and newer laser or ink-jet printers for correspondence and other work requiring higher-quality output and a variety of fonts. Some high-quality printers that have the features of both copiers and printers combine microprocessor, laser, and photocopier technology in one unit and can print a hundred or more pages a minute. Other printers are part of a multifunction unit that combines copying, printing, scanning, and faxing. See The Multifunction Machine in Chapter 1, "The Online Office."

Printer operations. Like copiers, computer printers may be located in a central department or in individual offices or workstations. The specific steps required to initiate printing depend on your software program and the type of printer. Older dot matrix printers commonly use continuous-form paper and are loaded differently than sheet-fed laser and ink-jet printers, which typically house paper in trays similar to a copier tray. Users should thoroughly study instruction manuals accompanying the printer and be prepared to train assistants on its use.

Program control. Printers are controlled by the program used to create the document to be printed. Your word processing program, for example, has certain formatting commands, and the program sends those commands to your printer, translating them into other commands that your printer can understand. A printer driver (PRD) file in your word processing program contains information that tells your program what your printer can do and how to instruct it to do it.

Depending on your equipment and word processing program, the printed version of your document may look different from the on-screen version. The special characters that you see on screen may not appear or may look different on the printed page. Use your printer's self-test feature, which displays all the characters your printer will print. If you have questions that aren't answered by your instruction manual, call the toll-free number of the software vendor, or check the vendor's website.

Offset Printing
The offset process. Offset printing is based on the principle that water and grease don't mix. It uses a grease-based ink that sticks to the dry image area on the offset master (also called the *plate*). The nonimage areas of the master are kept wet to repel the ink. After the impression on an offset

plate is inked, it's transferred to a rubber blanket, and the blanket — not the plate — comes in contact with the paper on which the images are printed.

Offset printing presses are high-speed machines that can create thousands of impressions of consistently excellent quality from an offset master. Small, sheet-fed presses commonly handle small to medium runs, and large web presses, which print on huge rolls of paper, are used for the very large runs. The offset process is used by commercial printers, publishers, and centralized corporate reproduction departments for long runs in which multiple colors or photographs are being printed and in cases where very high quality is desired. Offset is less economical for very short runs, however, because of the initial investment in equipment and the time and skill involved in creating masters, setting up the job, and cleaning up afterward.

Platemaking. Traditionally, you would photograph material to be printed, prepare a negative, and transfer the images to an offset plate. Now, electronic images may be transferred directly to a plate without the need for a negative. Since an offset master is a specially coated sheet, images can be created directly on it. Special electrostatic platemaking equipment can also be used to make masters quickly and inexpensively, and some copiers will copy a computer-generated or etched original image onto a direct-image master. Direct-image masters are economical, easy to create, and suitable for relatively short-run jobs. However, more durable and precise offset masters are created on sensitized metal plates.

Print-on-Demand Publishing

Print-on-demand publishing is a technology that makes it possible to store a large work electronically and print a single copy when requested. (Compare with E-books.) Generally, a print-on-demand service can scan a printed work into a digital library where it is stored until an order for it arrives. On request, the work is then printed, bound, and delivered.

With on-demand technology, a single copy consisting of several hundred pages can be printed in a minute or less and bound in the manner requested by the customer. Only the number of copies ordered are printed, thereby eliminating traditional warehousing and large-run printing costs. In other respects, the document is treated like a traditional book. For example, a book publisher (not the print-on-demand service) would create the initial version, pay royalties to the author, copyright the work, and so on. Like e-book technology, print-on-demand technology is expected to become more prevalent and more popular over time.

REPORT PREPARATION

One of the more complex documents produced in an office is the business report. Several kinds of reports may be generated, ranging from a short, informal letter, memo, or e-mail report to a long, complex, formal report. These documents may be directed to various readership levels inside and outside the company, including the staff, line management, top management, or outside clients, and they may be general or highly technical.

Reports serve many needs. For example, they may introduce and then analyze in detail a given market; discuss a particular business problem in depth and offer a solution; lay out an annual or multiyear strategic plan; delve into a highly complicated legal or financial question; provide impetus for the research, development, and the launching of a new product; or offer a stock or investment prospectus.

Office professionals usually organize the draft materials logically and consistently, producing a final product devoid of typographical and factual errors. Some staff members also help to produce tabular and graphic exhibits and help with online and manual research. In addition, the staff is usually responsible for proofreading, fact checking, copying or printing, collating, binding, and distribution.

Research

If you're asked to handle some of the research, be prepared to conduct an online search and, if necessary, to go outside your own office and internal library. Although company files and personnel represent a useful source of information, it may be necessary to visit the reference room of an outside library, call schools and other organizations listed in the yellow pages or another directory, visit websites, or access an online database through your company's internal network or over the Internet.

Whether you're using the Internet or accessing an internal database, it's important to be clear and specific in providing keywords for your computer search. Some databases instruct users how to limit searches and provide examples of both efficient and unwieldy searches. In any case, if you're vague, the computer either may be unable to provide what you want or may provide massive amounts of nonessential information. See Chapter 10, "Information Management," Keyword retrieval, for more about the use of keywords and Chapter 1, "The Online Office," The World Wide Web, for a description of the Web and the use of search engines.

Style and Format

Although shorter reports are often prepared as letters, memos, or e-mails, the longer ones are generally set up in the style of a book or booklet. In many cases, a long report represents the work of more than one person. One person may write the summary in a new product report, and another, such as the sales director, may prepare the sales forecast. A manufacturing manager may work out the manufacturing cost estimates and production schedule, and a business manager or accountant may prepare other financial data. An advertising manager or outside agency may develop the advertising or promotion strategy.

Multiauthor reports often have a large number of stylistic, spelling, and factual inconsistencies. Therefore, before entering the information into the computer, it's important to read the entire document from beginning to end and note all inconsistencies, errors, and unclear points. Flag them with self-sticking notes, and query the author(s). Check all major and subsidiary headings in the text to ensure consistency of style. Find out where the displayed tables and graphics are to appear. Will they be scattered throughout the text, or will they all be collected at the end or in a separate appendix? After keying the report into your program, store it for final editing and correction, and save the format you use as a template for future documents.

Informal Report

Short, one- to three-page reports intended for in-house distribution are usually formatted the same as a letter, memo, or e-mail message, although other elements, such as subheads and lists, may be added to make it easier for the reader to scan the information and see at a glance what is covered. Letter reports are usually set up in a full-block format. (See the Full-Block Format illustration in Chapter 9, "Correspondence.") If a report is intended for numerous recipients, however, it may be more convenient to use a memo format with a distribution list at the end.

Instead of a report title, as would be used in a long, formal report, a subject line is used in a letter, memo, or e-mail report. A variety of styles should be developed for the headings to distinguish one level from another. Two or three levels are adequate for most small reports. More than this could be counterproductive and might clutter rather than clarify the brief text. For examples of headings, refer to the Letter Report Format illustration in this chapter and to the discussion of the subject line in Chapter 9, "Correspondence," (Subject).

Proposal Report

Like regular business reports, proposals may be either long or short and formal or informal. Although brief, informal proposals are prepared in a letter, memo, or e-mail format, longer formal proposals should be styled

---

COMPANY LETTERHEAD

December 31, 2001

Mr. Arthur R. Lacey
Lacey, Middleton & White
123 Beacon Street
City, ST 98765

Dear Mr. Lacey:

REPORT HEADINGS

This is a model letter report format in which the title is written as a subject line in all capital letters.

I. FIRST-LEVEL HEAD

The first-level head is often centered and may be written in all capital letters or with the main words capitalized.

II. Second-Level Head

The second-level head may be centered or flush left and often is written in uppercase and lowercase letters.

III. Third-Level Head

The third-level head may be positioned flush left and is often written in uppercase and lowercase letters.

IV. Fourth-Level Head. The fourth-level head is most often run in with the paragraph text to which it relates. It may be written in uppercase and lowercase letters or with an initial capital only.

Letter Report Format

and formatted the same as any other long, formal report (see the next section). Some proposals must be prepared on fill-in forms provided by the requesting department or organization.

An example of a company proposal is a technical job proposal prepared for an outside client in which an organization or person proposes to do

Continuation-Page Letterhead

Arthur R. Lacey
December 31, 2001
page two

Notice that the headings are set in bold type (optional), and additional space is placed before and after the heads. Often, one or two spaces precede a head, and one space follows it (in the case of freestanding heads).

The four levels of heads illustrated in this letter are sufficient for most letter, memo, and e-mail reports. If additional levels are needed, some clear and logical variation of these styles can be devised. For example, you might have a run-in head written with an initial capital only. Or if the letter text has indented paragraphs, a lower-level head would also be indented like the paragraphs.

Sincerely,

Robin N. Brown
Word Processing Department

ARL.ltr

Letter Report Format (continued)

certain work for a specified fee or price. Model forms programs have samples that can be used for such purposes, and office-supply stores have standard forms commonly used for bids or brief quotations and cost estimates. If additional detail is required, you can modify one of the samples to suit your needs.

Proposal content and organization of material will vary depending on the subject and purpose. However, a detailed proposal might begin with an *introductory section* in which the problem to be solved is defined, the objectives of the study are set forth, the proposed solution to the problem is described in steps or work phases, the resultant benefits to the client are given, and the capabilities of the contracting company are delineated. This introduction might be followed by a *technical operations plan*— a detailed section explaining how the goals and objectives will be met and how the total program will be implemented, step-by-step. Next, a *management plan* might detail the project's organization — the number of personnel required, the ongoing documentation to be generated (such as progress reports), and the quality-control procedures to be maintained throughout the program. The report might conclude with a *financial section* outlining the forecast costs and fees. This basic format, however, should be modified as needed to fit the particular topic and purpose of a proposal.

Formal Report

A formal report may be distributed to an outside client or internally to other members of the writer's company. The following sections describe the principal parts of a formal report, although not all formal reports include every part. Some, for example, may have no cover or flyleaves. Others may omit the letter of authorization or the acknowledgments page. However, a long, complex formal report should always have a title page and a table of contents in addition to the body and any material associated with the text, such as a list or table.

Cover. If you use a cover, select one that will protect the report for a long time and one that is appropriate for the overall length of the report. A ring binder, for example, is appropriate for a five-year plan consisting of hundreds of pages. The cover should contain a label bearing the title and perhaps the writer's name or the name of the company. The printing on the label should be neat and clear.

Flyleaf. Formal reports often have a *flyleaf*— a blank page appearing after the cover at the very beginning. Sometimes a report may have two, one at the beginning and another at the end. Flyleaves protect the rest of the document and allow space for the reader to write comments.

Title page. If a report doesn't have a separate cover, the title page must serve that purpose. Usually, information on the title page is centered on the available space after calculating any room required for a side binding (if any). It may state the report title, to whom submitted, by whom submitted, and the date submitted. The submission information may include the writer's and receiver's departmental affiliation or job title.

Job numbers, purchase orders, or contract numbers may be included if required. If the report is a revision of an older work, that fact should be noted too. Sometimes keywords reflecting the main topics discussed in the body of the report are appended to the title page for use in subject-coded, computerized information-retrieval systems. Spell the keywords exactly as the author has written them.

Position the report title about a third of the way down the page, printed in uppercase and lowercase letters or in all capital letters. Place the "submitted to" information in approximately the center of the page, single-spaced, about midway between the title and the "submitted by" information:

Submitted to
Jason Van Vleet
Manager, Sales Department
A-Z Data Processing, Inc.
1111 West Avenue
City, ST 98765

Place the "submitted by" information and the date at the bottom of the page, single-spaced, with a blank space between the address and the date:

Submitted by
Lynda C. Colwell
Director, Market Research
The Research Company
2132 Parkway North
City, ST 98765

February 6, 2001

Letter of authorization or transmittal. If official, written authorization was given to do a study, the writer may include a copy of the authorization letter in the front matter of the report. A letter of transmittal summarizing the purpose, scope, and content of the study may also be included if the report has been commissioned by an outside source. The letter of transmittal replies to the letter of authorization and basically says, "Here's what you asked for." It should be prepared on company letterhead and signed by the writer or the person having overall responsibility for the project. Be certain that the left margin of the letter is wide enough to accommodate any side binding, and format the letter according to the guidelines for correspondence given in Chapter 9, "Correspondence."

Acknowledgments page. When other people or organizations have contributed to the report, a brief notation acknowledging their help, support, and work may be included. Acknowledgments of this type are included on a separate page, usually styled in one or two short, single-spaced paragraphs. The word *Acknowledgments* is stated in uppercase and lowercase letters or in all capital letters, the same as other chapter or division titles. Begin all titles the same distance from the top of the page. If the text paragraphs are single-spaced, double-space between them, and center and balance all of the material attractively on the page.

Table of contents. The table of contents is important in a long, complex report because it presents at a glance an outline of the major and subsidiary topics covered in the report and the appropriate page numbers. To compile the table of contents, use the major and subsidiary headings found in the body of the report. If the writer has used roman numerals and letters to introduce the headings, include them in the table of contents. If the writer has used an all-numeric system of signaling heads in the text, use these numbers in the table of contents. Word the headings in the table of contents exactly as they are worded in the text.

Center the table of contents on the page, leaving ample margins all around. (For an example, see the Table of Contents illustration.) Double-space between main headings and subheadings. Single-space runover lines within these headings. Align heading and page numbers horizontally and vertically, and also align numbers, letters, or other devices introducing heads.

Use a continuation sheet for a table of contents exceeding one page, and head the continuation sheet *Contents — continued* or some variation thereof. The heading on the first page — *Contents* — should be styled the same as other chapter or division titles and should begin on the same line as the titles of other chapters and divisions.

The use of leaders (a row of periods) connecting headings with their page numbers is optional. After the table of contents has been drafted, check all items and page numbers against the text subheads and page numbers.

Lists of figures and tables. If a report has more than a few illustrations, prepare either a combined list of illustrations or separate lists of figures (drawings, graphs, and so on) and tables (tabular matter). Common titles are "List of Illustrations," "List of Figures," "List of Graphics," and "List of Tables."

These lists should be formatted the same as the table of contents. If tables and graphics are combined in one list, add subheadings such as "Figures" and "Tables," and group the appropriate illustrations in proper order under these headings.

Foreword and preface. Although uncommon in a business report, a foreword or preface or both may be included. The *foreword* — written by someone other than the writer of the report — comments on the work, usually with words of praise or a statement about the importance of the work. The *preface* — written by the author of the report — is a short statement regarding the purpose, scope, and content of the study, often including a summary of the research and methodology that was used. These sections should be single- or double-spaced, the same as the body of the report. Style and position the foreword and preface titles the same as all other main titles in the report.

CONTENTS

vi

Table of Contents

Abstract or summary. An abstract or summary is more common than a preface in a business report. Styled and formatted the same as a preface, it also states the purpose, scope, and content of the report; summarizes the research and methodology; and briefly states the author's conclusions. Although an abstract might consist of dozens or even hundreds of pages in a very long report, it's more commonly presented in 200 words or less.

Body. The body, or text, of a business report typically includes an introduction, a methodology or background section, the main discussion or data analysis, and the final statement of conclusions and recommendations. The body may be single- or double-spaced, but it's usually single-spaced when the report is very long. Refer to the models First Text Page of Long Report and First Main Section of Long Report.

Complex business reports use different levels of headings in the body to present the information in a clear and orderly arrangement. Three or four levels are usually enough, but if a report is very complex, one or two additional levels may be used. Arabic numbers (1, 2, 3, 4, and so on), roman numerals (I, II, III, IV, and so on), or an alphabetical system (A, B, C, D, and so on) may be used with the heading titles. Some business reports, especially technical reports, are written using an outline system for headings:

```
1.0  FIRST MAIN SECTION
     1.1  First Main Subsection
     1.2  Second Main Subsection
     1.3  Third Main Subsection
          1.3.1  First subunit
          1.3.2  Second subunit
          1.3.3  Third subunit
2.0  SECOND MAIN SECTION
```

In this type of outline system, the decimals signal the heading level. (Notice that the decimals are aligned vertically within each level.) Another type of outline system consists of a combined numerical-alphabetical outline:

```
I. MAIN HEADING
   A. Subheading
      1. Sub-subheading
      2. Sub-subheading
   B. Subheading
      1. Sub-subheading
         (a) Most limited subcategory
         (b) Most limited subcategory
      2. Sub-subheading
II. MAIN HEADING
```

Carefully follow the writer's directions when using this format. Also, keep in mind that if you have a heading labeled A, 1, or (a), you must have at least one other heading in the same set, such as B, 2, or (b). A heading in one set should never stand alone.

Appendix. An appendix contains supplementary, or supporting, material, such as forms, tables, and charts, that are not inserted in the text. Usually, if more than one appendix is used, each is given a number or letter: *Appendix A: Trade Division Forecast, 2001.*

The appendix(es) are placed in the back matter immediately after the last text page of the report and before any notes, glossary, bibliography, or index. Style and format the opening page the same as the first page of a chapter or other division. Refer to the model Appendix Format.

Notes. Footnotes may be placed at the bottoms of the pages where they're referenced in the text, or collected in a notes section placed after the appendix. Sometimes, notes that represent sources of quoted material are collected in a notes section, and those that represent additional comments (expository or substantive footnotes) are placed at the bottoms of the appropriate pages. Often, then, the source notes are numbered and the expository notes lettered. In either case, numbering or lettering should be consecutive within chapters (if any) or throughout the entire report, as preferred. The text letters or numbers that correspond to the footnote letters or numbers should be set as superscripts (raised elements) just after the pertinent text passage: "The market that year was static."[4]

Style and format the title of the notes section the same as the titles of other chapters or divisions in the report. Prepare each note in paragraph style, indented or flush left, the same as the text paragraphs, and place the letter or number preceding each note on line, as illustrated in the forthcoming examples. Single- or double-space the notes the same as the body of the report.

The following notes are examples of an acceptable style for a business report. *Ibid.* is used in reference to the immediately preceding note, and a *short reference* (author's last name and shortened title) is used to refer to a previous note other than the one immediately preceding. Both city and state are listed in a note when the location may be unfamiliar to some readers. The city alone is sufficient for a well-known location such as Chicago. When the state is given, the traditional form of abbreviation (*Tex.*) should be used unless your employer requires the two letter postal form (*TX*). For additional examples, consult a comprehensive style book such as *The Chicago Manual of Style:*

Book (one author or editor):

1. Samuel T. Brownstein, ed., *How to Reduce Your Taxes* (Chicago: ABC Press, 1999), 78.

Journal (two or three authors or editors):

2. James A. Schultz and Harriet Whitney Schultz, "How You Can Profit from Gold," *Business Journal* 101, no. 2 (1998): 16–21.

Magazine (more than three authors or editors):

3. Adam A. Kline et al., "Investing in the Future: Key Growth Companies," *Industry Today,* 10 May 2000, 5.

Newspaper (regular department or feature):

4. Securities and You, *Holbrook Daily News,* 17 March 2001, 2.

Translated book:

5. Jennifer M. Flagg, *The Stenmark Files,* trans. Thomas P. Jones (New York: Jones & Associates, 1998), 100–101.

Later edition:

6. Jennifer M. Flagg, rev., *Labor Relations,* 2d ed. (Concord, N.H.: McCain-Lewis, 2001), 364.

Report (corporate author):

7. *Report of the Commission on Arbitration* (New York: American Council on Arbitration, 1997), 3.

Short reference to a prior note:

8. Kline et al., "Investing in the Future," 5–6.

Interview:

9. Nancy C. Redstone, interview by author, Peoria, Ill., 3 November 2000.

Public document:

10. U.S. Senate Committee on Banking, *Report of Activities,* 99th Cong., 1st sess., 12 October 1985.

Unpublished paper:

11. Andrew M. Ardmore, "The True Cost of Inflation" (paper presented at the annual meeting of the Business Society, Chicago, Ill., June 1996), 21–23.

Reference to previous note:

12. Ibid., 24.

Web document:

13. "Internet Businesses Decline," URL: http://www.nelson.org/newsletr/Dec27-01.html.

1.1. AVAILABLE INFORMATION

The corporation is subject to the informational requirements of the Securities Exchange Act of 1934 and in accordance files reports, proxy statements, and other information with the Securities and Exchange Commission. Such reports, proxy statements, and other information filed by the company can be inspected and copied at the public reference facilities maintained by the commission at Room 1024, 450 Fifth Street, N.W., Washington, D.C. 20549, and also at the commission's regional offices at Room 1028 in the Everett McKinley Dirkson Building, 219 South Dearborn Street, Chicago, Illinois 60604.

1.2. INCORPORATION OF DOCUMENTS

Each of the following four documents is incorporated by reference into this prospectus:

1. The corporation's Annual Report on Form 10-K for the year ended December 31, 2000, filed pursuant to Section 13 or 15(d) of the Securities Exchange Act.

2. The plan's Annual Report on Form 11-K for the year ended December 31, 2000, filed pursuant to Section 13 or 15(d) of the Securities Exchange Act.

3. All other reports filed pursuant to Section 13 or 15(d) of the Securities Exchange Act with respect to the corporation and the plan since the end of the fiscal year covered by the reports referred to in items 1 and 2.

4. The corporation's definitive Proxy Statement filed pursuant to Section 14 of the Securities Exchange Act in connection with the latest guidelines of

1

First Text Page of Long Report

SUMMARY OF THE PLAN

1. General

The XYZ Corporation Employees' Savings and Thrift Plan has been established to encourage retirement savings by participating employees of the corporation and of designated subsidiaries and affiliates of the corporation. Beginning January 1, 2001, such savings shall be effected by means of pretax salary-adjustment arrangements. The corporation will also make matching contributions to the plan in an amount based on certain savings by members.

All of the corporation's contributions will be invested in common stock of the corporation, and all or part of the members' savings may be so invested. All contributions and savings will be held in trust and invested by Bank of New England, N.A., trustee of the plan. An Employees' Savings and Thrift Plan Committee, appointed by the Board of Directors of the corporation, will supervise and administer the plan.

The plan will form part of the corporation's program for providing competitive benefits for its employees. The operation of the plan is expected to encourage employees to make added provision, through savings on a pretax basis, for their retirement income. It will also encourage them to participate in ownership of the corporation's common stock.

On June 6, 2000, the corporation publicly released the following statement:

> The Board of Directors believes that the plan will provide an additional incentive to employees to contribute to the continued success of the corporation and will be in the best interests of the corporation and its stockholders.

3

First Main Section of Long Report

APPENDIX A: PLAN STRUCTURE

1. CURRENT ADMINISTRATION

The present members of the Employees' Savings and Thrift Plan Committee are John M. Roe, Jane T. Smith, Martin I. Miller, Joseph L. Edge, Sally A. Harris, Leila B. Summers, and John T. Williams.

Harry B. Selkirk, director of the corporation, is also a director of the Bank of New England, Inc., parent company of Bank of New England, N.A., trustee of the plan.

2. MEMBERS OF THE PLAN

As of December 31, 2001, there were 999 employees participating in the plan, from a total number of approximately 1,600 employees eligible to participate. As of July 1, 2001, there were 981 employees participating out of 1,500 eligible.

3. INVESTMENT PERFORMANCE

The following table indicates values for shares of the corporation's common stock in Fund B as of the indicated dates, which are based on the quoted New York Stock Exchange closing prices.

Valuation Date	*Fund B: Price/Share, Common Stock**
December 31, 2000	$11.75
August 31, 2001	19.37
December 31, 2001	22.50

*Adjusted for 2-for-1 split on July 3, 2001

55

Appendix Format

Glossary. A glossary is placed after the notes section, before the bibliography or name-date reference list. It's an alphabetical list of special terms used in the document, sometimes including additional terms pertinent to the subject, along with the definitions.

A glossary should be formatted the same as other main divisions, with consistent spacing and margins. The style adopted for the entries may vary, although terms are usually set in an italic or a bold face type:

> *diode*　A device that permits electric current to pass in one direction but not the other.

Bibliography. A bibliography, which follows the glossary (if any), is an alphabetical list of books and other material consulted by the writer of the work in which the bibliography appears. If it includes only works referred to in the text or appearing in the notes section, it may be called "Works Cited" or "References." If it includes other works, it is usually called "Bibliography" or "Selected Bibliography."

The list is placed at the end of the book, report, or other document after the glossary or, if there is no glossary, after the notes section. A hanging-indent format (flush and hang) is used, with the first line flush left and runover lines indented about 1/2 to 1 inch, the same as a paragraph indent. A long dash is used for repeated authors' names in succeeding entries. Entries with authors precede those of editors, revisors, translators, and others. For example, "John Doe, *XYZ Book*," precedes "John Doe, ed., *ABC Book*."

The following entries are bibliography versions of the notes illustrated in the previous section. For additional examples, consult a comprehensive style book:

Ardmore, Andrew M. "The True Cost of Inflation." Paper presented at the annual meeting of the Business Society, Chicago, Ill., June 1996.

Brownstein, Samuel T., ed. *How to Reduce Your Taxes.* Chicago: ABC Press, 1999.

Flagg, Jennifer M. *The Stenmark Files.* Translated by Thomas P. Jones. New York: Jones & Associates, 1998.

_____, rev. *Labor Relations,* 2d ed. Concord, N.H.: McCain-Lewis, 2001.

"Internet Businesses Decline." URL: http://www.nelson.org/newsletr/Dec27-01.html.

Kline, Adam A., et al. "Investing in the Future: Key Growth Companies." *Industry Today,* 10 May 2000, 5–11.

Redstone, Nancy C. Interview by the author. Peoria, Ill., 3 November 2000.

Report of the Commission on Arbitration, New York: American Council on Arbitration, 1997.

Schultz, James A., and Harriet Whitney Schultz. "How You Can Profit from Gold." *Business Journal* 101, no. 2 (1998): 16–34.

Securities and You. *Holbrook Daily News,* 17 March 2001.

U.S. Senate Committee on Banking. *Report of Activities.* 99th Cong., 1st sess., 12 October 1985.

Reference list. Instead of using numbered notes for documentation, a writer may use author-date text citations and an accompanying reference list in place of a bibliography. This is a practical, easy-to-use system. Instead of placing a superscript number in the text corresponding to the note number, a writer places the author's last name and the year of the publication in parentheses after the quoted passage. No source footnotes or notes section for source notes is needed since a reader can locate the full data in the reference list.

If the same author has several works, all published in the same year, they can be differentiated by placing *a, b, c,* and so on after the appropriate year:

(Brown 1997a)
(Brown 1997b)

If two authors have the same last name, initials designating first names may be added:

(J. Brown 1997a)
(M. Brown 1994)

The abbreviation *et al.* (and others) is used in place of additional names when there are four or more authors.

(Davis, Hendricks, and Meirs 1996)
(Davis et al. 2000)

If page, table, or other numbers are included in successive listings, separate them with a semicolon:

(Brown 1997a, 421; Davis et al. 2000, Figure 2)

Since no notes section for source notes is needed, the list of references to which the text citations refer is placed after the glossary or, if there is no glossary, after the appendix or last text page. The list resembles a bibliography, except that the date is placed immediately after the author's name.

The following entries are reference-list versions of the notes and bibliography entries given in the preceding sections:

Ardmore, Andrew M. 1996. "The True Cost of Inflation." Paper presented at the annual meeting of the Business Society, Chicago, Ill., June.

Brownstein, Samuel T., ed. 1999. *How to Reduce Your Taxes.* Chicago: ABC Press.

Flagg, Jennifer M. 1998. *The Stenmark Files.* Translated by Thomas P. Jones. New York: Jones & Associates.

———, rev. 2001. *Labor Relations,* 2d ed. Concord, N.H.: McCain-Lewis.

"Internet Businesses Decline." 2001. URL: http://www.nelson.org/ newsletr/Dec27.html.

Kline, Adam A., et al. 2000. "Investing in the Future: Key Growth Companies." *Industry Today,* 10 May, 5–11.

Redstone, Nancy C. 2000. Interview by the author. Peoria, Ill., 3 November.

Report of the Commission on Arbitration. 1997. New York: American Council on Arbitration.

Schultz, James A., and Harriet Whitney Schultz. 1998. "How You Can Profit from Gold." *Business Journal* 101, no. 2: 16–34.

Securities and You. 2001. *Holbrook Daily News,* 17 March.

U.S. Senate Committee on Banking. 1985. *Report of Activities.* 99th Cong., 1st sess., 12 October.

Index. An index is often needed for a long, detailed report. Like the index at the back of this book, it will list alphabetically all major and subsidiary topics along with the applicable page numbers.

You can develop an index manually or by computer, or you may hire an outside professional indexer. With the appropriate indexing and sorting software, your computer will alphabetize and format the entries and check cross-references. If you don't use an indexing service, don't have indexing software, and want to prepare an index manually, you'll need a 3- by 5-inch index card file with alphabetical dividers.

Selecting the entries. Take a copy of the document (set of page proofs), and on each page underline words and phrases that will become main entries or subentries. Select nouns, such as *budget,* rather than adjectives or other parts of speech, such as *excessive.*

Most indexes to business documents have a combination of main entries and one level of subentries:

```
input systems
    for computers, 22, 53-63
    optical character recognition for, 16
input-output units, 53-63
```

In the preceding example, *input systems* and *input-output units* are main entries. The first word of an entry is often written with a small (lowercase) letter, unless it's a proper noun. Main entries are arranged alphabetically by the first keyword.

Like main entries, subentries, which represent topics of secondary importance, are composed of headings and page numbers. Place the subentries under the main entries with which they're associated. Arrange them alphabetically by the first keyword, and indent them an additional amount. Also, lowercase all subentries, unless they contain proper nouns. In the previous example, *for computers* and *optical character recognition for* are subentries.

Some indexers devise a system to distinguish entries and subentries while underlining keywords on page proofs during the initial step. They may, for example, check any underlined item that they believe will be a main entry. Whether you prefer to make such decisions while underlining keywords or later, it's important initially to write only one item on a 3- by 5-inch card.

Combining items. After you've underlined all appropriate items on the page proofs, transfer each underlined word to a separate index card, and after the word, write the page number where it appears. Eventually, you may have several cards for a single item or word, each with a different page number. After all underlined items have been recorded on cards, combine on a single card the page numbers from all cards that list the same item or word.

Arrange the cards by subject before you alphabetize them. For example, collect all cards pertaining to "input systems" together. If the decision about which item is a main entry was not made during the underlining step, make that decision now, and group the items that will become subentries *behind* the card for the main entry. Then arrange all main entry cards in alphabetical order, and arrange all subentry cards in alphabetical order behind each main entry.

Editing. Once you have the cards organized alphabetically, you can begin editing and polishing. For example, the subentry card behind the main entry *input systems* may say only *computers,* and you may decide to add the word *for* in front of *computers:*

> Input systems
>   for computers, 22, 53-63

If you haven't already combined the various cards with pages numbered 22 and 53 to 63, do so now. Next, add any cross-references that are needed:

> Input, 35, 61. *See also* input systems.

Edit all main entries and subentries for consistency in capitalization and punctuation. When you're satisfied that the index is complete and accurate, enter it in the computer, using the same general spacing, margins, and so on used for the rest of the report.

Illustrations. Although your software program may provide automatic formatting for tables and certain types of figures, you may want to develop your own template (standard format). The following guidelines are widely accepted in business documents.

Numbering. Number tables and figures consecutively from beginning to end (1, 2, 3, and so on) or consecutively within a chapter (1.1, 1.2, 2.1, 2.2, and so on). Place the number after the word the writer has chosen for the document, as in *Table 2, Figure 4.7, Exhibit 6,* and *Illustration 21.*

Refer to *each* illustration at the appropriate place in the text, such as "See Table 7 and Figure 14." Ideally, you will place the appropriate table or figure in the text at or near this place of reference. In some business documents, though, illustrations are collected at the ends of chapters or at the end of the document after the appendix. In all cases, the numbers and titles that are used should be consistent with the numbers and titles appearing on the list(s) of illustrations in the front matter.

Titles. Make table titles and figure captions as short as possible. However, you can add a descriptive line as a table subtitle, a figure legend, or a general note immediately after the body of the table or figure:

> Table 12
> Policy Claims by Age Group, 18-65
>
> Figure 9
> A Basic Accounting Cycle

Place a table subtitle on a separate line below the table title or on the same line, as preferred, usually separated from the title by a colon:

> Table 2
> Career Paths: Occupational Titles and Work Functions for Various
> Office Positions

Also, place a figure *legend* (description or comment about the figure) on a separate line or on the same line, as preferred, separated from the *caption* (title of figure) by a period:

> Fig. 3. Chronological Resume. The chronological format starts with
> your latest job experience and works backward. Only inclusive years
> should be used, without months.

Footnotes. Format footnotes to a table or figure like text notes, described earlier, and place them immediately after the table or figure body. Like text footnotes, the notes to an illustration are often preceded by note numbers, letters, or sometimes symbols.

List a *source note* (introduced by the word *Source:*) stating the source (if any) of the information or illustration first, followed by any *general note* (introduced by the word *Note:*) that applies to the table or figure as a whole. However, don't place the word *Source* before a brief credit line for an illustration, such as *Courtesy J. R. Miller Co.*

List numbered or lettered notes after any general note, and place corresponding superscript numbers or letters at appropriate places in the body of the table or figure. However, don't place a note number or letter after a table or figure title. Instead, for comments about the title or the illustration as a whole, use a general note preceding the numbered or lettered notes.

Column headings. Make column headings in tables brief and descriptive. If necessary, include subheads, or use a two-tier "decked" head:

2001	
Country	No. of Delegates

Capitalize important words in column headings, and make them either singular or plural, as desired, except for the head above the stub (left-hand column). It should always be singular.

Body. Either single- or double-space the body of a table or figure. Usually, you should double-space the body of a very short table and single-space the body of a longer table. However, even when the body is double-spaced, single-space the notes beneath the body.

Copyright

Reports that are to be distributed outside an organization are frequently copyrighted to protect the material from appropriation by others. If a report isn't copyrighted, it's in the *public domain,* which means that the information may be used by anyone without permission of the writer or publisher.

Registration. Forms and information about registering various types of material are available from the Copyright Office, Library of Congress, Washington, D.C., and at its Web site.

Copyright notice. Although it's not required that a printed or online work carry a copyright notice for registration to be valid, placing such a notice in the work may discourage others from using the material without permission. The following are examples of copyright notices. The words *All rights reserved* are necessary for protection under the Buenos Aires Convention:

©1970 James Hill. All rights reserved.
©1970 by James Hill. ©renewed 1998 by James Hill. All rights reserved.
Copyright 2001 by Mary Jones. All rights reserved.
Copr. 2001 by Mary Jones. All rights reserved.

In a printed work, place the notice on a separate copyright page in the front matter, following the document's title page. See the copyright page in this book for an example of the notice used by a book publisher. On a website, place it at the bottom of the home page and at the end of each division in the site.

Period of protection. Most registered works created before January 1, 1978, are protected for 95 years. (Refer to information from the Copyright Office for exceptions.) Registered works published after January 1, 1978, are protected for the author's life plus 70 years. Jointly produced works are protected for 70 years from the death of the last living author. Online works are protected under the Digital Millennium Copyright Act. Refer to information from the Copyright Office for current information.

Permission. Those who want to quote or use original material from other registered copyright sources must get the permission of the copyright owner to use the material. If the material to be used is in the public domain, permission is not needed, although a writer should nevertheless credit the source of the material. When a copyright owner grants you permission to quote or use material in a registered work, include the exact wording for the permissions note supplied by the owner. Usually, position the credit as follows:

- Beneath a table or figure body as an unnumbered source note or credit line
- In a text footnote pertaining to certain information in the text
- At the bottom of the first page of a chapter, section, or other part as an unnumbered note crediting the source of, or basis for substantial information in, the part

Although the exact wording required by the copyright owner may vary in each case, the following are common examples:

Illustrations
Photograph courtesy of ABC Company.
Drawing by Nora Blakely.
Courtesy of XYZ Company, Inc.
Illustration by Jennifer Seale for Thomas Ulster, *Economic Heartbreak*
    (New York: Investors Unlimited, 1999).

Text
Reprinted by permission of the publisher.
Adapted from Harold Wynberg, *The Next Generation* (Dallas: The
    Research Institute, 1996), Table 5.

Reprinted from Benjamin J. Rogers, *Business Ethics* (Detroit: Kensing-
ton Printers, 2001).

Reprinted, by permission of the publisher, from Anne Ashton, "The
Insurance Debacle," *Pennington's Review* 4 (2000): 26.

For ongoing information about changes in copyright law, periodically request current information from the Copyright Office, or check its website.

Business Style Guide

Whether you're preparing a traditional or electronic document, the importance of using proper capitalization, punctuation, and other points of style can't be overemphasized. Improper or inconsistent use will result in unprofessional messages and documents that will detract not only from your company's image but from yours as well.

The key to excellence in business writing is impeccable use of the language and strict attention to presentation so that a document will be admired for its sound construction, attractive packaging, and appropriate, consistent style. Making certain that something is styled correctly and consistently is a task often delegated to office professionals. The following sections, therefore, contain composition and style guidelines to help you produce attractive, professional documents. For information about researching, formatting, and other aspects of document creation, refer to Chapter 6, "Document Creation."

The style recommended in this chapter is suitable for a variety of organizations and offices. If you work in an office that must follow a style intended for a particular profession, however, purchase a copy of a suitable style manual. Specialized style guides are available for various disciplines, such as physics, biology, chemistry, mathematics, and education. General guides, such as *The Chicago Manual of Style,* are suitable for a variety of professional activities. Or your company may have its own in-house manual. In all cases, follow the guide consistently.

If you're preparing material for outside periodical or book publishers, ask them for a copy of their house style and formatting and submission requirements. Many such organizations have specific guidelines for manuscript preparation and disk submission as well as for writing style.

GUIDE TO CAPITALIZATION AND PUNCTUATION

You should use an American style of capitalization and punctuation whether you're preparing a document for a domestic or foreign audience. In exact quotations, however, follow the style of the original writer. Also, in international correspondence, follow the style of your foreign contacts in writing their personal names, company names, and addresses.

Capitalization

The following guidelines apply to the capitalization of words, terms, and other expressions in most cases. But in matters of style, be alert to exceptions to the rule. Most software languages, for instance, are styled in all capitals (*BASIC*), but a few should have only an initial capital (*Pascal*).

Beginnings

1. Capitalize the first word of a single sentence. (See also the rule for numbers in Numbers, General guidelines.)

> Personal income increased 0.9 percent in December.

2. Capitalize the first word of a direct quotation. Lowercase the first word of the second part of a split quotation:

> "It's not a matter of what they want," commented the spokesperson, "but a question of timing and tactics."

3. Capitalize the first word in every line of traditional verse, unless the poet has intentionally lowercased it:

> The quiet mind is richer
>> than a crown. . . .
> A mind content both crown and
>> kingdom is.
> — Robert Greene, *Farewell to Folly*

Proper names

1. Capitalize proper names, such as the names of deities; people or words used in personification; corporations; organizations and their members; councils and congresses; and historical periods and events. Lowercase general references that don't include the proper names:

> God, Allah, the Messiah
> Death, the Grim Reaper
> Pope John Paul III, the pope
> United Airlines, the airline
> First Lutheran Church, the church

Republican Party, the party, a Republican
Civil Rights Commission, the commission
U.S. government, the federal government, the government
General Assembly of Illinois, Illinois legislature, the assembly
War on Poverty
Reconstruction

2. Capitalize the names of places, including structures, geographic divisions, districts, regions, and locales. Lowercase general references that stand alone or precede the proper name:

Wall Street
New York State, the state of New York, the state
North Pole
the South, southern, southerner (general), Southerner (Civil War context), south on I-17
George Washington Bridge, the bridge
the Sunbelt
China
New England
Division Street, the street

3. Capitalize the names of rivers, lakes, mountains, seas, and oceans. Lowercase general references to them:

Atlantic Ocean, the ocean
Mississippi River, the river
Arkansas and Mississippi rivers
Lake Superior, the lake
Blue Ridge Mountains, the mountains

4. Capitalize the names of ships, airplanes, and space vehicles. Lowercase general references to them:

USS *Enterprise,* the *Enterprise,* the spaceship
Sputnik II, the satellite
Voyager, the space shuttle
the Concorde, the airplane
a Boeing 727, an airplane

5. Capitalize the names of nationalities, races, tribes, and languages. Lowercase general references that aren't part of the proper name:

Americans, American English
Caucasians, whites
French, the French language
Spaniards, the Spanish language

African-Americans, blacks
Native Americans (American Indians)

6. Capitalize words derived from proper names when used in their primary sense. Lowercase most derivatives. (*Note:* Numerous exceptions apply to this guideline. Often, the choice is up to the writer.)

European cities
British royalty
arabic numerals (*or* Arabic numerals)
dutch oven (*or* Dutch oven)
moroccan leather (*or* Moroccan leather)
french fries (*or* French fries)
roman numerals (*or* Roman numerals)

Titles

1. Capitalize titles of people when they precede their names or when a title represents an epithet. Lowercase most titles when they follow the names or are used alone (but see exceptions):

Mr. Eldon Waterbury; Eldon Waterbury, Esq.
Professor Janice Croft; Janice Croft, professor of biological sciences; the professor
Secretary of State Warren Christopher; Mr. Secretary; Warren Christopher, the secretary of state; the secretary
General C. V. Roswell, General Roswell, the general (*General of the Army* and *Fleet Admiral* are both capitalized after a name to avoid confusion with other generals and admirals.)
Elizabeth II, queen of England; Her Majesty, Queen Elizabeth; the queen
The Great Emancipator
George Herman "Babe" Ruth

2. Capitalize the important words in titles of publications, awards, and artistic and musical works. Lowercase most general references to the type of publication or work (but see exceptions):

Office Science, the book
"How to Write Effective E-mail," the chapter
Office Systems, the magazine
Bible (specific religious book), biblical, the pharmacist's "bible" (an important book)
Scriptures, scriptural
Talmud, talmudic (*or* Talmudic)
Koran, Koranic
Nobel Prize in literature, Nobel Peace Prize

> *A Sidewalk Cafe at Night* (Van Gogh)
> *Gone With the Wind,* the movie
> *The Wall Street Journal,* the newspaper
> Adagio from the Fifth Symphony
> Piano Concerto no. 5

Education

1. Capitalize the names of institutions and their divisions. Lowercase general references to them:

> University of Hawaii, the university
> School of Medicine, the medical school
> Physical Education Department, phys. ed. department, the department

2. Capitalize the names of classes and the official names of programs or courses. Lowercase general references to members and other general descriptions:

> Senior Class
> a senior
> Economics 102, the economics course
> Administrative Business Program, the program

3. Capitalize educational degrees and honors when they follow a name. Lowercase general references to degrees:

> James V. Roulette, Doctor of Law; a doctor of law
> Victoria Johnson, M.D.
> Henry Snowden, Fellow of the Royal Academy; a fellow

Days and time

1. Capitalize the days of the week, months of the year, holidays, and holy days. Lowercase period designations, numerical periods that are not part of a proper name, and recent cultural periods:

Monday	Ramadan	nuclear age
March	twentieth century	space age
Fourth of July	Tenth Dynasty	colonial period
Labor Day	Middle Ages	antiquity, ancient Greece
Election Day	Iron Age	A.D., B.C. (*or* A.D., B.C.)
Passover	Victorian era	Age of Reason

2. Capitalize proper nouns in time zones. Lowercase the other words referring to time, time zones, and seasons:

> mountain standard time (mst)
> Pacific standard time (Pst)
> a.m., p.m. (*or* A.M., P.M.)

10 o'clock, ten o'clock
spring
winter solstice

Law

1. Capitalize the formal names of specific courts. Lowercase general references to a type of court or to any court except the U.S. Supreme Court (but see exceptions):

U.S. Supreme Court, the Court
Arizona Supreme Court, the court
the U.S. Court of Appeals for the Seventh Circuit, the court of appeals,
    the circuit court, the court
traffic court
New York Court of Appeals, the Court of Appeals (the highest state
    court, capitalized to distinguish it from the U.S. court of appeals,
    which is not the highest U.S. court)

2. Capitalize the important words in treaties, laws, and cases. Lowercase most general references to the document or event:

U.S. Constitution, the Constitution
Ohio Constitution, the constitution
Fifth Amendment, the amendment
Civil Rights Act of 1964
Social Security (*or* social security)
a drug-reform law
Labor Management Relations Act
Miranda v. Arizona, the *Miranda* case, the case
Franklin's case, Franklin's trial

Military service

1. Capitalize the names of military branches and organizations. Lowercase general references to them:

United States Air Force, the air force
United States Marine Corps, the Marine Corps, the marines
Second Battalion, the battalion
Joint Chiefs of Staff
armed forces
Allied forces, the Allies (world wars)

2. Capitalize the formal names of battles and wars. Lowercase general references to the involvement:

World War I, First World War, the war
Vietnam War, the war

Korean conflict
invasion of Kuwait

3. Capitalize military awards. Lowercase general references to an honor or award:

Purple Heart
Navy Cross
Croix de Guerre (*or* croix de guerre)
Distinguished Service Cross
military honor

Business

1. Capitalize the official names of equipment and software. Lowercase general references to equipment, programs, and procedures:

Rawlins Computer Systems
Microsoft Word, the software
MKDIR, the command
Lotus 1-2-3, the program
Pascal, the language
Filesaver, the database
format instructions

2. Capitalize trademark names. If desired, omit the circled symbol ® (registered product or service mark) or the symbol ™ (product trademark) or ᔆᴹ (service mark) after the name:

Xerox, copier
Bufferin, buffered aspirin
Kleenex, tissue
Ping-Pong, table tennis
Dacron, polyester

Science

1. Capitalize geologic time designations and words such as *Lower* that refer to a time within a period. Lowercase the word *period* in most cases, and lowercase most adjectives, such as *late,* that are used descriptively:

Paleozoic era
Quaternary period
Pliocene epoch
late Pliocene
Lower Jurassic
Middle Pliocene
Ice Age, an ice age
Piedmont Lowland, the lowland

2. Capitalize official names in astronomy. Lowercase general references to types of bodies and phenomena:

> Mars, the planet
> Earth (planet), earth (soil)
> North Star
> the Galaxy, a galaxy
> aurora borealis, northern lights

3. Capitalize the proper nouns in chemistry and physics theorems and laws, and capitalize the word *Law* in popular, fictitious names and laws. Lowercase the names of chemical elements and general references to laws and principles. (For the capitalization of chemical symbols, consult an appropriate chemistry handbook or style guide.)

> iron, Fe
> the Pythagorean theorem
> Einstein's theory of relativity
> Boyle's law
> Murphy's Law

4. Capitalize the proper nouns in the names of diseases, the brand names of drugs, and the genus names of infectious organisms. Lowercase generic names and general medical terms:

> Hodgkin's disease
> Fertinic (brand name), ferrous gluconate (generic name)
> chronic fatigue syndrome
> *Trichinella spiralis,* the disease trichinosis
> *Phthirus* (lice), *P. pubis*

5. Generally, capitalize family, order, and genus names and the proper nouns in common names. Lowercase species names:

> *Eschscholtzia californica, E. californica,* California poppy
> *Cervus elaphus, C. elaphus,* elk
> the family Mutillidae
> the order Mecoptera
> black-eyed Susan
> Canada thistle
> rainbow trout
> Cooper's hawk

Numbers. Capitalize names that contain numerical designations. Lowercase general references to the names and numbers:

> Thirteenth Precinct, the precinct
> Room 2020

Chapter 2 (*or* chapter 2)
Fifth Avenue, the avenue
line 16
size 10
four people

Abbreviations. Capitalize abbreviations of official names and personal or professional titles preceding names. Lowercase the abbreviations of common nouns (*admin.:* administration) and most initialisms (*rpm:* revolutions per minute) that don't refer to a proper noun:

Oct.
Tues.
Dr. Jones
1600 Pennsylvania Ave.
FBI
OPEC
mgr.
asap (as soon as possible)

Punctuation

The purpose of punctuation is to make what is written clearer and to avoid misinterpretation. Although the trend is toward less punctuation in some types of writing, such as in fiction and general nonfiction, business writers know that misunderstandings are costly and hence that punctuation should be used whenever it is correct to use it.

Those who deal with an international audience in particular should use punctuation wherever it is appropriate to guide foreign readers through each sentence. However, misplaced or overused punctuation can be just as confusing as too little punctuation. The following guidelines apply to the 14 basic marks of punctuation.

Apostrophe (')

1. Use an apostrophe to indicate the possessive case of singular and plural nouns, indefinite pronouns, and surnames combined with designations such as *Jr.* and *II:*

The superintendent's office is at the end of the hall.

That could be anyone's pen.

Donald Harris II's term on the board is almost over.

2. Use an apostrophe with the last of two or more nouns in a series to indicate joint possession:

Standard and Poor's data

Coke and Pepsi's competition
Jane and Bob's law firm

3. Use an apostrophe with each of two or more nouns in a series to indicate individual possession:

Tom's and Nancy's suggestions (two separate suggestions)
Smith's, Roe's, and Doe's reports (three separate reports)

4. Use an apostrophe to indicate the plurals of figures, letters, or words when this is not clear without the apostrophe:

poorly formed *a*'s and *e*'s, *6*'s and *7*'s
But: 1900s, 88s and 99s, MBAs

5. Use an apostrophe to indicate omission of letters in contractions:

isn't (is not)
it's (it is)
wouldn't (would not)

6. Use an apostrophe to indicate omission of figures in dates:

the class of '01
fiscal year '01-'02

Brackets [ ]
1. Use brackets to enclose words or passages in quotations to indicate insertion of material written by someone other than the original writer:

"Justice Potter did not think it [increasing the Court's membership to
ease the work load for each justice] would solve the problem."

2. Use brackets to enclose material inserted within matter that is already in parentheses:

(The return on equity [ROE] is 35 percent.)

Colon (:)
1. Use a colon to introduce words, phrases, or clauses that explain, amplify, or summarize something that has preceded them:

There are two choices: use temporary help, or use part-time help.

2. Use a colon to introduce a long quotation:

Said the chairman: "The deficit is our principal consideration. Business
is hesitant to expand when the country is burdened with run-away
inflation, and when there is no expansion, there is no increase in employment."

3. Use a colon to introduce a list:

> The report outlined results of the increase in trauma disorders, including the following:
>> a. More than 80 percent of the population suffers from back ailments.
>> b. The greatest risk of back strain, at home as well as at work, is between ages 35 and 55.
>> c. Repetitive actions are the major cause of back injuries.

4. Use a colon to separate chapter and verse numbers in references to biblical quotations:

> Romans 12:6
> Ecclesiastes 9:11

5. Use a colon to separate city from publisher and dates from page numbers in footnotes and bibliographies:

> Boston: Houghton Mifflin, 2000.
> *Atlantic,* 132, no. 3 (2001): 41-92.

6. Use a colon to separate hour and minute in time designations:

> 3:45 P.M.
> an 8:30 A.M. meeting

7. Use a colon after the salutation in a business letter:

> Ladies and Gentlemen:
> To whom it may concern:
> Dear Ms. Kane:

Comma (,)

1. Use a comma to separate the clauses of a compound sentence connected by a coordinating conjunction. The comma may be omitted in short compound sentences:

> The title of the department's forthcoming report has not been decided, and the release date has not been set.
>
> Jim agreed but Tom objected.

2. Use a comma to separate items in a series:

> The program explains how to overcome obstacles of worker resistance, resentment, and skepticism.

3. Use a comma to separate two or more adjectives modifying the same noun if the word *and* can be used between them:

> The company selected a bold, modern letterhead design.

4. Use a comma to set off a nonrestrictive clause or phrase (one that if eliminated would not affect the meaning of the sentence). Omit the comma when the clause is restrictive (essential to the meaning of the sentence):

> The classified section, which gets larger every year, has more than 200,000 business listings.

> The classified section that was published in December 2000 has more than 200,000 business listings.

5. Use a comma to set off words or phrases that are in apposition to (equivalent to) a noun or noun phrase. Do not use a comma if such words or phrases precede the noun they modify:

> Marilyn Stowe, former president of Stowe Industries, will be the keynote speaker.

> Former president of Stowe Industries Marilyn Stowe will be the keynote speaker.

6. Use a comma to set off transitional words and short expressions that require a pause in reading or speaking. Usually, however, the comma can be omitted after a short introductory word such as *thus* or *hence:*

> Consequently, the new product announcement will be delayed.

> Hence the new product announcement will be delayed.

7. Use a comma to set off words used to introduce a sentence (if the comma is needed for clarity):

> At best, the shipment will be ready by August 1.

8. Use a comma to set off a subordinate clause or a long phrase that precedes a principal clause:

> If we underestimate the competitive drive of the other members, we could lose our market share.

9. Use a comma to set off short quotations and sayings:

> "That's typical," said the mayor, responding to his opponent's charges.

10. Use a comma to indicate omission of a word or words:

> To err is human; to forgive, divine.

11. Use a comma to set off the year from the month in full dates. Omit the comma when only the month and the year are used:

> I began the study on February 6, 2000, after receiving the grant.

> I began the study in February 2000 after receiving the grant.

12. Use a comma to set off city and state in geographic names:

> The product was tested in Princeton, New Jersey, and other eastern locations.

13. Use a comma to separate series of four or more figures into thousands, millions, and so on:

> Every time bulk diesel fuel goes up a penny, it costs us $100,000.

14. Use a comma to set off words used in direct address:

> Mr. Stone, would you be able to open the meeting while Ms. McKenzie takes a long-distance call?

15. Use a comma to separate a question from the rest of the sentence:

> That's a remarkable improvement, isn't it?

16. Use a comma to set off any sentence elements that might be misunderstood if the comma were not used:

> When the report is in, the committee will vote on the resolution.

17. Use a comma after the salutation only in a personal letter but after the complimentary close in both a business and personal letter:

> Dear Lee, (personal letter)
> Dear Lee: (business letter)
> Sincerely, (personal or business)

18. Use a comma to set off some titles, degrees, and honorary designations from last names and from the rest of a sentence:

> Sandra Maynard, Esq.
> John Kennedy, Jr.
> Susan P. Green, M.D., who presented the case

Dash (—)

1. Use a dash to indicate a sudden break or change in continuity:

> Last year, the Hyatt Wonder World attracted more than 500,000 people — more than Thomas Jefferson's Monticello — at $14 a head for adults.

2. Use a dash to set apart a defining or emphatic phrase:

> Only one service — day care — improved in 2000.

3. Use a dash to set apart parenthetical material:

> The East Coast division's income from retail ads was three times as much as from other ads — $6 million versus $2 million.

4. Use a dash to mark an unfinished sentence:

> "I demand we take a vote on — ," the shareholder insisted before his
> microphone was shut off.

5. Use a dash to set off a summarizing phrase or clause:

> The real measure of employee satisfaction is intangible — it can't be
> counted in dollars and cents.

6. Use a dash to set off the name of an author or source, as at the end of a
quotation:

> The good of the people is the chief law.
> — Cicero

Ellipsis points (. . .)

1. Use three spaced periods to indicate the omission of words or sentences
within quoted matter:

> "It is . . . very hard to . . . please everybody." (Publilius Syrus)

2. Use four spaced periods to indicate the omission of words at the end of a
sentence:

> "Antisthenes used to say that envious people were devoured by their
> own disposition. . . . " (Diogenes Laertius)

3. Use three to five spaced periods centered on a line alone to indicate the
omission of one or more lines of poetry or one or more paragraphs:

> Vice itself lost half its evil by losing all its grossness.
>
> . . . . .
>
> Kings will be tyrants from policy, when subjects are rebels from principle.
> — Edmund Burke

4. Use three spaced periods to catch the reader's attention in certain types
of writing, such as in advertising copy:

> Your representative owes you the highest ethical standards . . . some-
> thing we at Variety Industries take very seriously.

Exclamation point (!)

1. Use an exclamation point after an emphatic or exclamatory sentence.
(But overuse will cause it to lose its effectiveness.)

> No, never! We will not yield a single microinch!

2. Use an exclamation point after an emphatic interjection.

> Great!

Hyphen (-)

1. Use a hyphen in word division to indicate that part of a word or more than one syllable has been carried over from one line to the next:

> Complex information isn't easily re-
> duced to outline form.

2. Use a hyphen to join the elements of certain compounds:

> cost-effectiveness
> jack-of-all-trades

3. Use a hyphen to join the elements of some compound modifiers preceding nouns:

> a cattle-feeding enterprise
> a heavy-duty press

4. Use a suspended hyphen to indicate that two or more compounds share a single base:

> three- and four-ton stamping machines
> eight- and ten-year-old foundries

5. Use a hyphen to separate the prefix and root in some combinations, such as a prefix preceding a proper noun, a prefix ending in a vowel when the root begins with the same vowel, and a prefix that must be hyphenated to indicate a different meaning or pronunciation:

> pro-Democrat
> anti-intelligence
> re-form (to form again)

6. Use a hyphen as a substitute for the word *to* between figures or words in tabular material:

> 1-2 years
> $25-$30

7. Use a hyphen to separate the parts of spelled-out compound numbers from *twenty-one* through *ninety-nine:*

> fifty-seven clients
> thirty-one messages

Parentheses ( )

1. Use parentheses to enclose material that is not an essential part of the sentence and that if not included would not alter its meaning:

> Kansas City television (KCTV-5) anchor Wendell Anschutz said that he
> would ask the source.

2. Use parentheses to enclose letters or figures to indicate subdivisions in some series:

> It seems that our choices are to (a) launch a counteroffensive marketing campaign, (b) get our new model out six months ahead of the competition, or (c) do nothing.

3. Use parentheses to enclose figures following and confirming written-out numbers, especially in legal documents:

> Cauldren, Inc., will provide service for the following three (3) machines.

4. Use parentheses to enclose abbreviations of written-out words when the abbreviations are used for the first time in a text and may be unfamiliar to the reader:

> According to Martin Costell, administrator of the National Office Organization (NOO), the new directory will sell for $45.

Period (.)

1. Use a period to end a complete declarative or mild imperative sentence:

> Hotline telephone numbers are becoming increasingly popular. (declarative)
>
> Please sign here. (imperative)

2. Use a period between the letters of or after some abbreviations. (*Note:* The trend is to omit periods in certain cases: after abbreviations that are forms of contractions [*nat'l*]; after most technical [*cos* for cosine] and metric [*mm*] abbreviations, unless the term spells another word such as cot. [*cot* = *bed*]; after and between letters of initialisms, such as *aka* [also known as]; and after and between the letters of acronyms, such as *BASIC* [computer language].)

> Inc.   etc.   Calif.
> Jan.   Ltd.   ave.

Since abbreviation style differs among businesses, follow the style preferred in your company, or consult a modern dictionary of abbreviations.

Question mark (?)

1. Use a question mark after a direct question, but use a period when the remark is really a statement:

> Are you going to the conference?
>
> Would you please take care of this. (Please take care of this.)

2. Use a question mark to indicate uncertainty or a query, such as a question to an author about something in his or her manuscript:

> Ferdinand Magellan (1480?-1521)
> OK?

Quotation marks ("/", '/')

1. Use double quotation marks to enclose direct quotations. Put commas and periods inside closing quotation marks; put semicolons and colons outside. Put other punctuation, such as exclamation points and question marks, inside the closing quotation marks only if it is part of the matter quoted:

> "I believe Plautus was right," he said, "that sometimes it's better to take a loss."
>
> Did he really say "It's a waste of time"?

2. Use double quotation marks to enclose words or phrases to clarify their meaning or to indicate that they are being used in a special way:

> The human "robots" in the pressroom point to boredom as their worst enemy.

3. Use double quotation marks to set off the translation or meaning of a term:

> The French word *oeuvre* means "work(s)," such as the work of an artist.

4. Use double quotation marks to enclose the titles of articles, chapters in books, essays and unpublished papers, short stories, television and radio episodes, songs and short musical pieces, and short poems:

> "Economic Courtship" (article)
> "Document Creation" (chapter)
> "The Structure of Datalinks" (thesis)
> "Maude and Her Prince" (short story)
> "Mark I" (television episode)
> "Forever" (song)
> "The Dancer" (short poem)

5. Use single quotation marks to enclose a quotation within a quotation. However, when quotations are set off as extracts, omit the opening and closing quotation marks, and change any single quotation marks within the quotation to double quotation marks:

> Mason often turned to Byron in his analysis: "I concede the motivation, but I also recognize the admonition of Lord Byron that 'fame is the thirst of youth.'"

Mason often turned to Byron in his analysis:

> I concede the motivation, but I also recognize the admonition of
> Lord Byron that "fame is the thirst of youth."

Semicolon (;)

1. Use a semicolon to separate the clauses of a compound sentence having
no coordinating conjunction:

> Some employees resigned in protest; others formed a grievance com-
> mittee to fight the new policy.

2. Use a semicolon to separate elements of a series in which the items already contain commas:

> According to the register, special meetings were held on December 6,
> 2000; March 17, 2001; and May 2, 2001.

3. Use a semicolon to separate the clauses of a compound sentence in
which the clauses contain other internal punctuation, even when the
clauses are joined by a conjunction:

> The toys are assembled in Kansas City, Missouri, and warehoused in
> Peoria, Illinois; and the company has at least a dozen field offices in the
> United States, Canada, and Great Britain.

4. Use a semicolon to separate the clauses of a compound sentence joined
by a conjunctive adverb, such as *nonetheless, however,* or *hence:*

> We will produce the product; however, it will cost $15, not $12.

Slash (/)

1. Use a slash (also called *diagonal* or *virgule*) to separate successive divisions in an extended date (but a hyphen is more common):

> the fiscal year 1998/99 (1998-99)
> the term 2000/2001 (2000-2001)

2. Use a slash to represent the word *per* in tabular material, invoices, and
similar copy:

> 6/doz.
> rev./sec.

3. Use a slash to mean *or* between the words *and* and *or* and sometimes between other words to indicate possible options or words of equal value:

> and/or
> owner/operator
> book/catalog

GUIDE TO COMPOSITION

Many office professionals compose their own messages and revise and refine the messages of their supervisors and others. The art of composition involves skills beyond the use of proper punctuation and capitalization. It involves the development of sentences and paragraphs; the proper use of alternative typefaces, particularly italics; the careful and consistent spelling of words and numbers; and the proper use of symbols and other technical expressions in both text and illustrations.

Those who prepare manuscripts for desktop publishing or other composition (see Chapter 6, "Document Creation," Desktop Publishing and Photocomposition) need to mark their manuscripts in a way that will be understood by editorial personnel and compositors. Table 7.1 lists the appropriate marks to use in preparing material for composition.

Sentence and Paragraph Development

Sentence style. There are two types of sentences — the periodic and the cumulative. The *periodic sentence* places the main idea at the end, and the previous matter serves as a buildup. The *cumulative sentence* puts the main point first, followed by supporting data or commentary:

> *Periodic:* The most interesting aspect of office administration has nothing to do with administrative tasks or skills *but is, very simply, a matter of diversity.*

> *Cumulative: Diversity is the most interesting aspect of office administration,* and this quality is not a prerequisite of, or a procedural guideline relative to, any individual task.

Problems in sentence development. There are four kinds of sentence structure — simple, compound, complex, and compound-complex. When the proper punctuation or the appropriate coordinating conjunction is omitted between independent clauses, the result is an incorrect, run-on sentence:

> The automobile had faulty brakes it was therefore recalled.

This problem can be corrected by restating the sentence in one of the following ways:

> The automobile had faulty brakes, and it was therefore recalled.
> The automobile had faulty brakes; therefore, it was recalled.
> Since the automobile had faulty brakes, it was recalled.
> The automobile, having faulty brakes, was recalled.

Another impediment to the proper development of a complete sentence with a subject and predicate is the comma fault. *A comma fault* occurs

Table 7.1 Examples of Selected Proofreader's Marks

MARK	INSTRUCTION
Copper is highly toxic *to* many aquatic organisms.	Insert indicated letter, word, phrase, or sentence.
Copper is highly toxic to many aquatic organisms.	Insert space.
Copper is highly toxic to many aquatic organisms⊙	Insert period.
Copper is highly toxic to many aquatic organisms and . . .	Insert punctuation (or subscript).
We have measured the mussels sensitivity to copper.	Insert apostrophe (or superscript).
Copper is highly toxic to many aquatic organisms.5	Raise to superscript.
Copper (29Cu) is highly toxic to many aquatic organisms.	Lower to subscript.
Copper is highly toxic to to many aquatic organisms.	Delete.
Copper is highly toxic to all aquatic organisms.	Delete and insert.
Copper is highly toxic to many aqua tic organisms.	Close space.
Copper is highly toxic to many aquatic organisms.	Delete and close.
Copper is highly toxic to many aquatic organisms.	Let it stand.
copper is highly toxic to many aquatic organisms.	Capitalized letter.
Copper is highly toxic to many aquatic Organisms.	Lowercase letter.
Copper is highly toxic to many AQUATIC organisms.	Lowercase word.

Table 7.1 (continued)

MARK	INSTRUCTION
Copper is highly toxic to many aqa̱tic organisms.	Transpose letters.
Copper is highly to toxic many aquatic organisms.	Transpose words.
¶ Copper is highly toxic to many aquatic organisms.	Begin new paragraph.
No ¶ Copper is highly toxic to many aquatic organisms.	No new paragraph.
Copper is highly toxic to many ⌐ aquatic organisms.	Move left as indicated.
Copper is highly toxic to many aquatic organisms. ⌐	Move right as indicated.
Copper is highly toxic to many aquatic organisms.	Raise as indicated.
Copper is highly toxic to many aquatic organisms.	Lower as indicated.
⌐APPENDIX A ⌐	Center.
Copper is highly toxic to many aquatic organisms.	Run in.
APPENDIX A	Italics or underscore.
APPENDIX A	Boldface.

when two independent clauses are separated by a comma instead of being linked by a coordinating conjunction, such as *and:*

> The chemical industry in the United States has contributed much to our economy, it should not be condemned on the basis of isolated instances of pollution.

The following sentences illustrate easy ways to eliminate the comma fault:

> The chemical industry in the United States has contributed much to our economy, *and* it should not be condemned on the basis of isolated instances of pollution.

The chemical industry in the United States has contributed much to our economy. It should not be condemned on the basis of isolated instances of pollution.

The chemical industry in the United States has contributed much to our economy; it should not be condemned on the basis of isolated instances of pollution.

The United States chemical industry, having contributed much to our economy, should not be condemned on the basis of isolated instances of pollution.

Once a sentence has been properly composed, it should be organized along with other sentences to form logical paragraphs that lead readers from beginning to end in an orderly, intelligent fashion.

Paragraph style. A paragraph is a distinct division of a written work that expresses a thought or point relevant to the whole but is complete in itself. It may consist of a single sentence or several sentences. When there are several sentences, the paragraph should contain a topic sentence that expresses the main thought. It in turn should be developed and supported by the other sentences of the paragraph.

Although it's possible for a topic sentence to be placed anywhere within a paragraph, it's most often found at the beginning as a statement that is expanded or amplified by the sentences that follow. A topic sentence at the end of a paragraph usually functions as a cohesive summation of the ideas and arguments in the sentences leading up to it. In all cases, the topic sentence is the cement that binds a paragraph together into a coherent whole.

Paragraphing can be easy if you follow a few simple guidelines:

- Keep your paragraphs unified, with every sentence related to the main topic. Avoid needless digressions from the main point that will destroy unity.

- Avoid overshort or overlong paragraphs. A short one may not cover a topic adequately, and a long one may be uninviting and difficult to assimilate.

- When preparing letters and business reports, split long paragraphs into shorter ones, and combine short paragraphs into a single longer one.

- Remember that transitional words and phrases, such as conjunctive adverbs, are an invaluable aid in guiding a reader from one sentence to another.

The following are topic sentences that begin a series of paragraphs arranged in a logical order, with one point smoothly moving to the next:

> In 2000 a series of mishaps led us to examine problems of customer dissatisfaction.
>
> The first step was to talk extensively with the people involved in direct customer contact.
>
> We learned that the most helpful ideas were coming from office professionals throughout the company.
>
> The next step was to develop a series of "what if" proposals.

Another way of achieving smooth transition is through the repetition of key words that serve as guides to the reader:

> You can apply the same principle to sentences that is applied to words: short is beautiful.

Keeping the vocabulary limited to a finite number of terms that are used over and over reinforces the message and enables the reader to understand the material more easily. However, you can develop your paragraphs in any number of ways to make them lucid and effective. You might, for example, start with a definition:

> The term *office automation* refers to the use of a computer in an office environment to facilitate normal operating procedures. The impact of office automation on workflow may be very small or very great, depending on the extent to which organizational structures are affected.

The first sentence defines *office automation*. The second sentence in the paragraph talks about the impact of office automation in the workplace. Here are several other ideas to employ in paragraph development:

- Using a technique such as comparison, contrast, or analogy, you can make two points and discuss first one and then the other.

- You can use cause and effect, whereby you describe the situation or state of affairs and then discuss the underlying causes that prompted the problem or condition.

- You can first describe the underlying causes and then build up to the result or consequence.

- You can include examples by way of support or illustration for an idea or point of view that you have already expressed.

- When categories are involved, you can set down classes or sets relating to a topic and define each one as a means of introducing the main topic to which the categories pertain.

No firm rule exists for the particular pattern(s) you choose. Your topic will suggest logical ways to move from one paragraph to another. The most important point is that the movement be smooth and understandable in a way that will help the reader gain as much as possible from the discussion.

Use of Italics

Regular text is traditionally set in a light or medium roman typeface. Certain words and phrases, however, such as a heading, may be set in boldface at the discretion of the writer, designer, or compositor. Other words and phrases may be set in an italic face, and certain guidelines apply to the use of italics in styling business material:

1. Use italics to indicate the titles of books, plays, and long poems:

> the book *Silent Spring*
> the play *Phantom of the Opera*
> the epic poem *Paradise Lost*

2. Use italics to indicate the titles of magazines and newspapers:

> *Time* magazine and *The Wall Street Journal* both carried the report.

3. Use italics to indicate the titles of motion pictures and radio and television series:

> the movie *The Lion King*
> the television series *Friends*

4. Use italics to indicate the titles of long musical compositions:

> Beethoven's *Emperor* Concerto
> *William Tell* Overture

5. Use italics to indicate the names of paintings and sculptures:

> the painting *American Gothic*
> the sculpture *The Thinker*

6. Use italics to indicate words, letters, or numbers that are referred to as such:

> the word *pueblo*
> the letter *A*
> the number *4*

7. Use italics to indicate unfamiliar foreign words and phrases:

> *bleich* (German: pale)
> *raiz* (Portuguese: root)

8. Use italics to indicate the names of plaintiff and defendant in legal citations (the *v.* or *vs.,* meaning "versus," may be either roman or italic):

> *Franklin* v. *Madison*
> *Miranda* vs. *Arizona*

9. Use italics to emphasize a word or phrase (but avoid overuse):

> Too many of those studies were *not* being implemented.

10. Use italics to indicate the Latin names of genus, species, subspecies, and varieties in botanical and zoological nomenclature. (Do not italicize phyla, classes, orders, or families.)

> the genus *Homo*
> the species *alba*
> the subspecies *macrothrix*
> the variety *hirta*

11. Use italics to indicate the names of ships and planes but not an abbreviation preceding the name:

> USS *Rover*
> *Apollo II*

12. Use italics for letter symbols in mathematical expressions:

> $(6n - m)\log a, \exp[(2x - y)/4]$
> $x^1 + x^2 + \cdots + x^9$

Spelling

Spelling errors and inconsistencies detract from the professional appearance and effectiveness of a message. Although a computer spell-checker will locate many such problems, it can't distinguish between correctly spelled, but misused, words such as *to* in place of *too,* and the spelling program may have a different style from that of your company. Perhaps your spell-checker selects *micro-unit* (hyphenated), whereas your company follows the modern trend to write most prefixes and base words closed *(microunit)* Also, your spelling program probably does not include all the terms that you use every day — hence the need for an up-to-date dictionary.

Although numerous spelling rules exist, they're so complex and so riddled with exceptions that many office professionals would rather double-check doubtful spellings in a reliable dictionary. Nevertheless, the following guidelines may be helpful:

Nouns

1. To make most singular nouns plural, add *s* or *es* without changing the original spelling of the singular part:

> offices
> boxes
> McCoys
> Harrises

2. For certain irregular nouns, you must change the spelling to make the singular form plural:

> alumnus, alumni
> child, children

3. In other cases, spell both singular and plural forms the same:

> corps, corps
> deer, deer

4. Some nouns ending in *s* are plural in form but may function as either singular or plural (or both) in number:

> Politics is always an issue/Their politics are misleading.
>
> Economics isn't the principal consideration/The economics are unsound.

Possessives

1. Add an apostrophe and *s* to a word if it already ends with an "s" sound and if using a possessive form creates a new syllable:

> the boss's office
> the witness's statement

2. If the possessive form is hard to pronounce with the newly created syllable, add only the apostrophe and omit the *s:*

> Mr. Phillips' proposal
> for appearance' sake
> Los Angeles' population

3. When the plural form of a noun has a different spelling from the singular form, add both an apostrophe and *s:*

> children's playground
> women's program

4. Otherwise, in most cases, add an apostrophe but omit the *s:*

> cars' features
> computers' memory

5. Add an apostrophe but omit the *s* when a word ending is pronounced as "eez":

> Yerkes' law
> Euripides' life

Compounds

1. Compounds are spelled in three ways: open (separate words without a hyphen), closed (one word without a hyphen), and hyphenated (words connected with a hyphen). Since no firm rule exists for most compounds, writers should consult a current dictionary when in doubt:

> Latin America
> paperwork
> know-how

2. Usually, you should hyphenate a compound adjective before a noun, except for very familiar, permanent compounds such as *public relations,* which are written open both before and after a noun:

> the well-written paper
> the paper that is well written
> the word processing program
> the program used for word processing

Prefixes. In contemporary writing, you should usually add a prefix to a base word without a hyphen. A few prefixes, however, such as *ex-*, meaning "former," are always hyphenated, and some, such as those creating a double vowel that is hard to read, are also hyphenated. Any prefix that precedes a capitalized word must also be hyphenated:

> counterproductive
> ex-senator
> semi-independent
> pro-American

Suffixes. In some cases, when a suffix is added to the end of a word, you should double the final consonant of the base word. In other cases, you should not double it. Since no general rule exists to account for all cases, consult a modern dictionary when in doubt:

> cancellation
> management

Foreign terms

1. The plural of many words of foreign origin is different from the regular English plural, and some terms have Anglicized plurals. Consult a modern

dictionary when in doubt. The following are examples of preferred English plurals:

appendix, appendixes
formula, formulas
focus, focuses

2. Some foreign words may require one of the nine principal diacritical marks:

acute	ó	grave	à
breve	ŭ	hacek	č
cedilla	ç	macron	ō
circumflex	â	tilde	ñ
dieresis	ö		

3. Unfamiliar foreign terms should be italicized, but those that have become Anglicized in business usage may be written without diacritical marks and without italics. Some style guides, such as the U.S. *Government Printing Office Style Manual,* do not use accents on or italicize familiar terms such as those in the following list, whereas other sources use accents on both familiar and unfamiliar foreign terms (follow the preferred style in your office):

Foreign Terms That May Be Written without Accents or Italic Type

abaca	cliche	decollete
aide memoire	cloisonne	dejeuner
a la carte	comedienne	denouement
a la king	comme ci comme ca	depot
a la mode	communique	dos-a-dos
angstrom	confrere	eclair
apertif	consomme	eclat
applique	cortege	ecru
apropos	coulee	elan
auto(s)-da-fe	coup de grace	elite
blase	coup d'etat	entree
boutonniere	coupe	etude
brassiere	crepe	facade
cabana	crepe de chine	faience
cafe	critique	fete
cafeteria	critiquing	fiance
caique	debacle	fiancee
canape	debris	frappe
cause celebre	debut	garcon
chateau	debutante	glace

Foreign Terms That May Be Written without Accents or Italic Type

grille	nee	risque
Gruyere	opera bouffe	role
habitue	opera comique	rotisserie
ingenue	papier mache	roue
jardiniere	piece de resistance	saute
litterateur	pleiade	seance
materiel	porte cochere	smorgasbord
matinee	porte lumiere	soiree
melange	portiere	souffle
melee	pousse cafe	suede
menage	premiere	table d'hote
mesalliance	protege	tete-a-tete
metier	puree	tragedienne
moire	rale	vicuna
naive	recherche	vis-a-vis
naivete	regime	

Word Division

When the right margin of a letter or document is so uneven that it's unattractive, you may decide to divide some very long words at the end of a line. The rules for word division at the end of a line are as complex as those for spelling and also have numerous exceptions. Spelling dictionaries and regular dictionaries indicate the division of words by syllables. In addition, the following guidelines apply to most types of business writing:

Words not to divide

1. Don't divide single-syllable words and words with fewer than five letters:

> stayed (*not* stay- / ed)
> into (*not* in- / to)

2. Don't separate a single letter from the beginning or end of the word or vowels that are pronounced together:

> abate (*not* a- / bate)
> ready (*not* read- / y)
> re-ceive (*not* rece- / ive)

Common divisions

1. If possible, divide a word after a single-letter syllable within the word:

> busi- / ness (*not* bus- / iness)
> posi- / tive (*not* pos- / itive)

2. When two vowels within a word are pronounced separately, divide between them when possible:

> experi- / ence (*not* exper- / ience)
> situ- / ation (*not* situa- / tion)

3. When there are two consonants between two vowels, divide the word between the consonants if it does not change the pronunciation:

> im- / por- / tant
> ad- / van- / tage

4. Keep at least two letters and the hyphen on the top line and at least three characters, one of which could be a punctuation mark, on the bottom line:

> re- (*top line*) new (*bottom line*)
> remind- (*top line*) er: (*bottom line*)

5. If possible, divide words with affixes *at* the prefix or suffix, and divide compounds *between* the principal parts:

> non- / essential
> trust- / worthy
> all- / important

6. Generally, divide gerunds and present participles *before* the -*ing* ending, but if you double the final consonant, divide *between* the double letters. If the base word already ends with a double consonant, divide *after* the two letters:

> learn- / ing
> control- / ling
> fill- / ing

7. When you pronounce an *le* syllable as "ul," divide the word before that syllable:

> cubi- / cle
> can- / dle

8. Don't divide an abbreviation unless it already has a hyphen:

> asap (*not* as- / ap)
> AFL- / CIO

9. If it's necessary to divide a name, divide between the first name or initial and the last name when possible:

> Jennifer C. / Brewster
> S. M. / Cantor

10. If a title precedes the name, divide after the title when possible:

> President / Aaron Beil
> Dr. / G. D. Shriner

11. If it's necessary to divide long numbers, divide only at a comma, with at least two digits before and after:

> 3,912,- / 076 people
> $209,- / 765

12. Divide dates between day and year:

> August 16, / 2000
> February 1, / 2001

13. Divide places between city and state or state and ZIP code:

> Mill Valley, / CA 94941
> Mill Valley, CA / 94941

14. Divide streets between words, not within words and not after the street number:

> 1927 Second / Street
> 421 Citrus / Grove Boulevard
> 421 Citrus Grove / Boulevard

15. Divide numbered or lettered items in a series before the number or letter:

> (1) pens, / (2) pencils, and (3) erasers
> (a) computers, (b) faxes, and / (c) copiers

Numbers

Principal styles. Two principal styles are used for writing numbers — a general, or nontechnical, style and a specialized, or technical, style.

1. In *general writing,* spell out numbers from *zero* through *ninety-nine* and large round numbers, such as *one thousand.* But if a sentence or paragraph has a large uneven number, such as *107,* use figures for all other numbers within the same category. (If your office has another style, however, follow it.)

> forty-seven applicants
> 371 tons of iron ore

> For the three shop positions, there were 75 women applicants and 121 men applicants.

2. In *scientific, technical, or other specialized writing,* spell out numbers from *zero* through *nine* or *ten,* and use figures if any other larger numbers are used within the same category:

> nine applicants
> 11 tons of iron ore
>
> For the three shop positions, there were 7 women applicants and 13 men applicants.

General guidelines. 1. Use figures to express specific dates, measures, hours, addresses, page numbers, and coordinates:

> 10 percent (*or* 10%)
> January 22, 2001
> 808 (*or* 80 degrees) north latitude
> 4:00 P.M.
> 30 Rockefeller Plaza
> p. 12
> vol. 3 (*or* volume 3)
> 76 tons
> 0.5 microns
> 2.5 ml

2. Always spell out a number that is the first word or words in a sentence:

> Fifteen thousand feet of wire was lost.
>
> *But:* We lost 15,000 feet of wire.

3. If a calendar year falls at the beginning of a sentence, use figures, but add an introductory word or phrase before it so that the sentence doesn't begin with a figure:

> Next year, 1996, promises to have sales that are double this year's earnings.
>
> Fiscal year 1996 may have sales that are double this year's earnings.

4. Spell out approximations or numbers used casually:

> We hiked a couple miles yesterday.
>
> Thanks a million.

5. Spell out ordinals in text, but in correspondence address blocks, either spell out the ordinals or write them in figures according to the given street name or other information (see Chapter 9, "Correspondence," Inside address, for examples of writing numbers in street addresses):

> the twenty-first century
> the tenth meeting

> Fifth Avenue
> 31 East 14 Street

6. Sometimes numbers form part of a corporate name or a set phrase. Style corporate names and phrases associated with them exactly as shown on the organization's letterhead or in reference works such as *Thomas Register:*

> Ten Speed Press
> 20th Century-Fox Studios
> 42nd Street Photo
> Pier 1 Imports
> Saks Fifth Avenue
> Fortune 500

7. When possible, round off very large numbers and use the word *million* or *billion* in place of listing numerous zeros:

> $116.7 million in sales
> a $200 billion federal deficit

8. If digits must be used in one instance in a sentence, use them for the other large numbers too:

> $116,700,000 in sales and $2,000,000 in returns
> a $3,000,000 business with an inventory of $1,691,421

Write decimals, ratios, and percentages as figures in most cases:

> 2.6 and 0.9 percent
> 5:1 ratio
> 100 to 1 odds

Place a zero in front of a decimal fraction *only* if the quantity could or might exceed 1.00. Omit the zero if it will never exceed one:

> 0.6 factor
> R = .12

Spell out common fractions and references to fractional amounts in general text, unless the reference would be too long or awkward if spelled out:

> a two-thirds margin
> $8\frac{1}{2}$ by 11 inches

Abbreviate inclusive numbers in footnotes, invoices, and other material if desired:

> pp. 100-109, 109-10, 1186-87, 1301-1400
> A.D. 36-42, 430-22; B.C. 1890-1900, 1990-96

Symbols

1. Spell out most signs and symbols, such as *percent,* in general business writing. Use the symbolic representation (%) in most technical and scientific writing:

> *General:* 4 (*or* four) feet and 6 (*or* six) inches
> *Technical:* 4′ 6″
>
> *General:* section 32
> *Technical:* §32

2. When a measurement is stated using an abbreviation or symbol, use a figure with it:

> 60 mm (*not* sixty mm)
> $5 (*not* five $)

The forthcoming sections have tables illustrating common technical signs, symbols, and abbreviations.

Mathematical Material

Scientific notation. Because scientists often deal with very large or small numbers, they have developed a special *scientific notation* that enables them to name such numbers without using an excessive number of zeros. This notation is based on powers of 10 (10^n, where the exponent n is an integer, or natural number). For example, the number 1,000 (the number 1 followed by three zeros) can be written more compactly as 10^3 ("10 to the third power"), because $10 \times 10 \times 10 = 1,000$.

You can see the usefulness of this notation when you consider a larger number such as *one billion* (1,000,000,000, or the number *1* followed by 9 zeros). In scientific notation, this is written as 10^9. Using this notation, you can quickly write numbers as large as you please without bothering to count zeros, even numbers that are so large that they have no name, such as 10^{28} ("10 to the 28th power"), or the number *1* followed by 28 zeros.

You can also use this notation to write numbers less than *1*. The general form is 10^{-n} (read as "10 to the negative *n*"), where the minus sign means 1 divided by 10^n, or $1/10^n$. For example, *one billionth* is written 10^{-9} ($1/10^9$).

You can combine this notation with decimal numbers to express numbers that lie between powers of ten. This is done by multiplying the base number by another number or, in general, $m \times 10^n$, where *1* is less than or equal to *m*, which is less than *10*. For example, 240,000 may be written 2.4×10^5. This system of notation is very useful when you use the metric system of measurement, which is based on units of 10.

Mathematical expressions. In preparing mathematical material, you not only will be dealing with signs and symbols that may be unfamiliar, but you also may be working with handwritten drafts that are barely legible. The most effective way to cope with this situation is to familiarize yourself with the subject matter. If your office prepares a large amount of mathematical material, you will no doubt have a technical style guide, such as the American Mathematical Society's *Mathematics into Type,* explaining the presentation of such material. For limited work in this area, a general guide, such as *The Chicago Manual of Style,* which has a section on mathematical expressions, may be helpful.

If you can't identify a symbol in a handwritten draft, you can leave a space with a question mark, or ask the author. In the latter case, it's preferable, if there are several questionable symbols, to mark them for clarification in a single conference with the author.

If you're preparing a manuscript to be set by desktop publishing or by another means of composition and if numerous symbols and expressions are used, make a list of them and submit it with the manuscript. Also, identify each one the first time it's used in the manuscript (do this whether or not you provide a separate list). A compositor will find this information very helpful, and many journals and book publishers require it. Since publisher styles vary, follow the specifications of the individual organization in preparing a manuscript. As is the case with any document, neatness, legibility, and accuracy are paramount.

Mathematical expressions consist of various signs and symbols, including those in the following sections.

Letter symbols. The letters in a mathematical expression may stand for *variables* (whose values range over a set of numbers), *constants* (whose numerical values are fixed and must be specified in a particular context), abbreviations of English words, or other kinds of symbols, such as index numbers. Letters of the Greek alphabet also are used in mathematical expressions. (Greek letters are used for certain kinds of quantities for historical reasons.) See the list in Table 7.2.

Fences. Fences, sometimes called *symbols of inclusion,* are the punctuation marks of mathematics. Their role is to prevent ambiguity by setting off from one another the different terms in a mathematical expression. Fences include symbols such as the left and right parentheses ( ), brackets [ ], braces { }, and other specialized symbols. The accepted convention for the order in which fences are used is $\{[( )]\}$. If more fences are needed, this order may be repeated with larger fences: $\{[(n + 2)(n + 1)^2 - 2n + (a - 1)^3]u\} - n^2$.

Signs of operation. Signs of operation, sometimes called *operators* or *operational signs,* indicate specific mathematical operations, such as addition

Table 7.2 Greek Alphabet

UPPERCASE	LOWERCASE	NAME
A	α	alpha
B	β	beta
Γ	γ	gamma
Δ	δ	delta
E	ε	epsilon
Z	ζ	zeta
H	η	eta
Θ	θ	theta
I	ι	iota
K	κ	kappa
Λ	λ	lambda
M	μ	mu
N	ν	nu
Ξ	ξ	xi
O	o	omicron
Π	π	pi
P	ρ	rho
Σ	σ ς	sigma
T	τ	tau
Υ	υ	upsilon
Φ	φ	phi
X	χ	chi
Ψ	ψ	psi
Ω	ω	omega

($+$), subtraction ($-$), multiplication ($\times$), or division ($\div$). The signs $\times$ and $\div$ are usually implicit. Instead of writing $a \times b \times c$, you could write abc. Another way of indicating multiplication is by writing a^3 instead of aaa ("a cubed," or "a to the third power"). Similarly, in division, instead of writing $x \div y$, you could use the fractional form x/y ("x divided by y," or "x over y").

Operations are also indicated by the superscript (exponent) of a quantity. For example, a^n ("a raised to the nth power," or "a to the nth") means n of the quantities a multiplied together. The symbol for root of a quantity ($\sqrt{}$) is called the *radical* symbol, as in $\sqrt{X}$, read as "the square root of x."

Other signs stand for more complicated processes such as *differentiation* and *integration*. These are operations that change the *form* of a function. If an equation in functional form is $y = f(x)$, differentiation could be expressed as $dy/dx = f'(x)$. Because *integration* is the reverse of differentiation, it is sometimes known as *antidifferentiation*. Integration may be thought of as a procedure that sums up an infinite number of elements whose size becomes gradually smaller; it is indicated by the symbol $\int$.

Other signs of operation are the *product sign* Π (capital Greek *pi*) and the *summation symbol* Σ (capital Greek *sigma*). They're used when a series of mathematical terms is multiplied or added, respectively. *Trigonometric functions* specify operations performed on letter symbols that represent angles, for example: $\times = \sin \theta$, $y = \cos \theta$, and $z = \tan \theta$, where $\sin =$ "sine," $\cos =$ "cosine," $\tan =$ "tangent": and θ is an angle.

Another sign is the *factorial* symbol !, as in $n!$ (read as "n factorial"). The *!* indicates the product of all integers from n to 1. For examples of mathematical operators, see Table 7.3.

Signs of relation. In contrast to signs of operation, signs of relation indicate the relationships among the various terms in a mathematical expression. In addition to the equality sign, other often-used signs of relation play similar roles. For example, $<$ and $>$ mean "less than" and "greater than," respectively. The expression $a < b$ is read as "a is less than b," and $a > b$ is read as "a is greater than b." For examples, see Table 7.4.

Spacing of symbols. Proper spacing of mathematical symbols is important both to avoid ambiguity and to give a clean, uniform appearance to a manuscript. Unless you know that an author is meticulous about writing mathematics, you can't rely on what you see, either in a handwritten draft or in one that has been computer generated by the author. You may be more familiar with the rules than the author is and thus can provide a valuable service.

In general, use *no space* in the following cases:

- Between quantities multiplied together when no multiplication sign is used: *xy; 2ab*

Table 7.3 Common Mathematical Operators

$+$	plus
$-$	minus
$\pm$	plus or minus
$\mp$	minus or plus
$\times$	multiplication sign
Σ	summation
Π	product symbol
∂	backcurling delta (partial differential sign)
∇	del (vector operator)
$\boldsymbol{\nabla}$	bold del
$\forall$	inverted sans serif aye (for all)
$\exists$	inverted sans serif ee (there exists)
$\wedge$	wedge, roof (outer product sign; conjunction sign)
$\vee$	inverted wedge or roof (disjunction sign)
$\cap$	intersection sign
$\cup$	union sign
$\sqrt{}$	radical
$\int$	integral
$\oint$	contour integral

- Between a symbol and its subscript and superscript: x^n, x^{2y+c}; Q_{max}
- Before and after fences: $(2x + b)(6y + c)$; $[(x^2 - 2y^2)(x + 2)]u_i$
- In names of functions or between names of multiplied functions: $f(x)$; $f(x)f(y)$
- Between a sign and its quantity in signed quantities: ± 6, -7, $\mid 10$
- When a sign of relation is used with a single quantity: "a value >6," "a length of ~ 3 meters"

Table 7.4 Common Mathematical Signs of Relation

=	equals; double bond
≠	not equal to
≙	corresponds to
≡	identically equal to; equivalent to; triple bond
≢	not identically equal to; not equivalent to; not always equal to
~	asymptotically equal to; of the order of magnitude of
≈	approximately equal to
≃	approximately equal to
≅	congruent to; approximately equal to
∝	proportional to; variation
<	less than
>	greater than
≮	not less than
≯	not greater than
≪	much less than
≫	much greater than
≤	less than or equal to
≥	greater than or equal to
≲	less than or approximately equal to
≳	greater than or approximately equal to
⊂	included in, a subset of
⊃	contains as a subset
⊄	not included in, not a subset of
⊆	contained within
⊇	contains
∈	an element of

Table 7.4 (continued)

∋	contains as an element
∉	not an element of
→	approaches, tends to; yields; is replaced by
↔	mutually implies
⊥	perpendicular (to)
∥	parallel (to)

Use *one space* in the following cases:

- Before and after a binary sign of operation (an operation involving two quantities): $a + b$; $a - b$ (note that this is different from a signed quantity). An exception is when a binary operator or sign of addition appears in a superscript, subscript, or limit, in which case no spaces are used: u^{n-1}, $\sum_{i=1}^{\infty}$.

- Before and after a sign of relation: $a = 2b$, $x < y$, $g \subset r$.

- Before and after abbreviations that are set in roman type: $2 \sin \theta$, $\log b$, $2x \exp 4y$. An exception to this is when the abbreviation is preceded or followed by an expression in fences or a superscript or subscript. In such case, use no space: $(6n - m)\log a$, $\exp[(2x - y)/4]$, $\sin^2 \theta$.

- Before and after a unary sign of operation (an operation on one expression):

$$\omega \int_0^{\infty} (6x^2 - 4y)dx, \ iq\frac{\partial \psi}{\partial t}, \ \sum_{n=1}^{\infty} x_n; \ \frac{dy}{dx}f(x).$$

- If an expression includes limits, count one space before and after the beginning and end of the limit:

$$\lim_{y \to \infty} f(x).$$

- If limits are written as superscripts or subscripts, count one space after the last character to the right:

$$g(t) = \frac{1}{2\pi i}\int_{a - i\infty}^{a + i\infty} e^{xt}f(x)dx.$$

- After commas in sets of symbols: (r, θ, ϕ); $f(x, y)$.

Use *three spaces* between elements in the following cases:

- Between two or more equations that are in sequence on the line:
$$z = a^2 + b^2 + c^2, \qquad x = 2a + 3b + c$$
- Between an equation and a condition on that equation:
$$d = u_a k \qquad (a = 1, 2, 3, \cdots, n)$$
- Between an equation and any parenthetical unit of measure:
$$a = v/t \qquad (m \cdot s^{-2})$$
- Between an equation and a following phrase in a displayed expression:
$$f(x) \to 0 \qquad \text{as } x \to \infty$$

Breaking equations. To avoid awkwardness as well as to conserve space, equations or expressions set in text are often formatted differently from equations set on a separate line (displayed). For example, in text, an equation containing a fraction should be written with a slash instead of a horizontal fraction bar: $h^2/4^2 ke^2 m = a_0/Z$.

Displayed equations are often numbered. Usually, if a displayed equation is subsequently cited, it should be numbered. All numbered equations should be displayed, but not all displayed equations need be numbered. If they will not fit on a single line, lengthy displayed equations may be broken (carried over to the next line). If possible, an equation should be broken only preceding a sign of relation (equal, less than, and so on) or preceding a sign of operation (plus, minus, integral symbol, and so on). The second line may be a standard indent and the equation number flush right:

$$
\begin{aligned}
u'(t) = {} & b^0 a_0^{-1} \sum_{r=1}^{\infty} \exp(s_r t) p_r t \\
& - b_1 a_0^{-1} \sum_{r=1}^{\infty} \exp[s_r(t - \omega)] p_r(t - \omega). \qquad (2)
\end{aligned}
$$

Fractions, expressions within fences, and expressions within a radical sign ($\sqrt{\ }$) should not be broken unless necessary. Don't break an expression containing an integral sign until d (variable) occurs:

$$
\begin{aligned}
\overline{K}(s, t) = {} & - K(s, t) + \int_a^b K(s, r) K(r, t) dr \\
& - \int_a^b \int_a^b K(s, r) K(r, w) K(w, t) dr \, dw.
\end{aligned}
$$

Where lists. Displayed equations are often followed by lists that define the symbols they contain, called "where lists" since they are preceded by the word *where*. When a list is lengthy, such as four or more lines, or itself contains built-up expressions, it should be displayed separately and the definitions aligned with the equal sign. The symbol definitions should be listed in the same order in which they appear in the equation. For example, an author might state the following:

We may write:

$$F^{3/4} = \left(\frac{bW_v - c}{2yL} \right)^m,$$

where b = proportionality constant,
         W_v = vapor mass rate,
         c = intercept as W_v = 0,
         $2yL$ = cross-sectional area normal to flow,
         L = tube length per crosspass,
         m = positive exponent.

Chemical Material

Chemical notation. Chemists generally divide all chemical compounds into two major kinds, inorganic and organic compounds. *Inorganic compounds* are those that are composed of elements other than the element carbon (atomic number 12). *Organic compounds* are those that contain carbon atoms. The reason for this division is twofold. Historically, the first carbon compounds studied were products of the human body; hence, they were called "organic" compounds. Second, because of its chemical properties, the element carbon forms a countless variety of different compounds, and the molecules of carbon compounds can be very large. Such compounds have given rise to a separate field of study.

The language of chemistry includes certain essential terms and principles:

- The basic unit of matter is the *atom.*
- There are many different kinds of atoms, and each kind is called an *element.*
- The chemical properties of an element are governed by its atomic structure. For example, every atom has a central part, the *nucleus,* in which most of its mass (or weight) is concentrated.
- The nucleus consists of two kinds of particles: the *proton,* which has one positive unit of electrical charge, and the *neutron,* which is electrically neutral.

- The number of protons in the nucleus is called its *atomic number*.
- The total number of neutrons and protons in a nucleus is called its *atomic mass number*.
- In nature, the nuclei of atoms of the same element can contain different numbers of neutrons (such atoms are called *isotopes*). The *average* mass of an element as it is found in nature is called the *atomic weight*.
- The nucleus is surrounded by a swarm of much lighter, fast-moving particles called *electrons*, each of which carries one negative unit of electrical charge. The electrons are bound to the nucleus by the attractive force between their negative charges and the positive charge on the nucleus.
- As we increase the number of protons and electrons in an atom, the number of electrons in the valence shell repeats in a regular pattern. (*Valence* is the combining power of an atom or ion expressed as a positive number.) Atoms having the same number of valence electrons tend to have similar chemical properties. This periodic pattern enables us to group elements with similar chemical properties. See the Periodic Table of the Elements.

The Periodic Table of Elements lists the names of the elements, their chemical symbols, and their atomic numbers. Since a chemical symbol isn't an abbreviation, it's *not* followed by a period. (Note that elements above 103 are synthetic rather than natural.)

Inorganic chemistry. The *name* of a chemical element appearing in text should be spelled out the first time it is used. The name of an element is not capitalized (unless it is the first word in a sentence):

Oxygen and hydrogen react to form water.

However, the first letter of each chemical *symbol* is always capitalized. The second letter, if there is one, is never capitalized:

The material was found to consist of C, H, Cl, and Br.

Indicating the atomic number, atomic mass number, ionic charge, and number of atoms of an element in a compound is done by the use of appropriate index numbers (superscripts and subscripts) attached to the chemical symbol. As in mathematical notation, there is no space between a chemical symbol and its index number:

- The atomic number is indicated by a lower-left index number: $_1$H, $_8$O, $_{12}$Mg, $_{50}$Sn. (The atomic number is usually omitted in a chemical formula, as it is unique to an element.)
- The atomic mass number is indicated by an upper-left index number ^{1}H, ^{16}O, ^{24}Mg, ^{118}Sn. Another way of indicating the atomic mass number of an element, usually when it stands alone or is mentioned in text, is to place it after the name or chemical symbol of the element: uranium 238, curium 247, carbon 14.
- To determine the number of neutrons in a nucleus, subtract the atomic number from the atomic mass number. Hence the isotope ^{235}U has 143 neutrons (235 minus 92), and ^{238}U has 146 neutrons (238 minus 92).
- Ionic charge is indicated by an upper-right index number: H^+, F^-, O^{2-}, Fe^{3+}, Co^{3+}, U^{5+}, Mn^{4+}. If an ion has only one plus or minus charge, the numeral *1* is omitted.
- When an atom gives up valence electrons, it is said to be *oxidized,* or in an *oxidation state.* Some atoms can give up different numbers of valence electrons. The *oxidation number,* which specifies how many electrons have been given up, is indicated by a roman numeral in parentheses following the chemical symbol: Fe(II), Fe(III), Co(III), U(V), Mn(IV). There is no space between the chemical symbol and the parenthetical numeral.
- The number of atoms of an element in a molecule is indicated by a lower-right index number: H_2, O_2, C_{16}, H_{34}, K_2CO_3.
- The same notation, with some additional features, is used for chemical compounds or molecules. Such an expression is known as a *chemical formula.* For example, the formula for the water molecule, which consists of two atoms of hydrogen and one atom of oxygen, is expressed in chemical notation as H_2O.

Organic chemistry. Because a carbon atom can form covalent bonds with as many as four other atoms, it is known as a *tetravalent* element. The spatial orientation of other atoms when they bond to carbon, and the number of bonds they form with carbon, strongly affect the properties of the resulting molecule.

For example, two molecules containing carbon may have the same chemical formula (with regard to the total number of atoms in the molecule) but quite different physical or chemical properties because of the way the other atoms are attached to the carbon atoms. For this reason, formulas describing carbon compounds are often given in structural form.

PERIODIC TABLE OF THE ELEMENTS

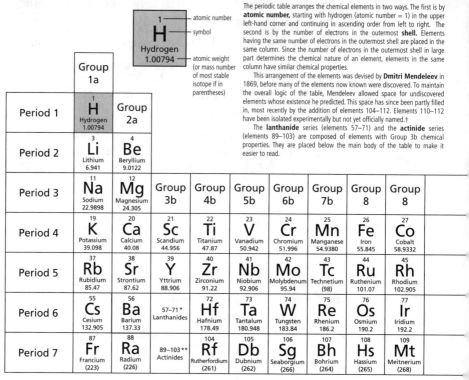

The periodic table arranges the chemical elements in two ways. The first is by **atomic number,** starting with hydrogen (atomic number = 1) in the upper left-hand corner and continuing in ascending order from left to right. The second is by the number of electrons in the outermost **shell.** Elements having the same number of electrons in the outermost shell are placed in the same column. Since the number of electrons in the outermost shell in large part determines the chemical nature of an element, elements in the same column have similar chemical properties.

This arrangement of the elements was devised by **Dmitri Mendeleev** in 1869, before many of the elements now known were discovered. To maintain the overall logic of the table, Mendeleev allowed space for undiscovered elements whose existence he predicted. This space has since been partly filled in, most recently by the addition of elements 104–112. Elements 110–112 have been isolated experimentally but not yet officially named.†

The **lanthanide** series (elements 57–71) and the **actinide** series (elements 89–103) are composed of elements with Group 3b chemical properties. They are placed below the main body of the table to make it easier to read.

atomic number — 1
symbol — H
Hydrogen
atomic weight — 1.00794
(or mass number of most stable isotope if in parentheses)

Period	Group 1a	Group 2a	Group 3b	Group 4b	Group 5b	Group 6b	Group 7b	Group 8	Group 8
Period 1	1 **H** Hydrogen 1.00794								
Period 2	3 **Li** Lithium 6.941	4 **Be** Beryllium 9.0122							
Period 3	11 **Na** Sodium 22.9898	12 **Mg** Magnesium 24.305							
Period 4	19 **K** Potassium 39.098	20 **Ca** Calcium 40.08	21 **Sc** Scandium 44.956	22 **Ti** Titanium 47.87	23 **V** Vanadium 50.942	24 **Cr** Chromium 51.996	25 **Mn** Manganese 54.9380	26 **Fe** Iron 55.845	27 **Co** Cobalt 58.9332
Period 5	37 **Rb** Rubidium 85.47	38 **Sr** Strontium 87.62	39 **Y** Yttrium 88.906	40 **Zr** Zirconium 91.22	41 **Nb** Niobium 92.906	42 **Mo** Molybdenum 95.94	43 **Tc** Technetium (98)	44 **Ru** Ruthenium 101.07	45 **Rh** Rhodium 102.905
Period 6	55 **Cs** Cesium 132.905	56 **Ba** Barium 137.33	57–71* Lanthanides	72 **Hf** Hafnium 178.49	73 **Ta** Tantalum 180.948	74 **W** Tungsten 183.84	75 **Re** Rhenium 186.2	76 **Os** Osmium 190.2	77 **Ir** Iridium 192.2
Period 7	87 **Fr** Francium (223)	88 **Ra** Radium (226)	89–103** Actinides	104 **Rf** Rutherfordium (261)	105 **Db** Dubnium (262)	106 **Sg** Seaborgium (266)	107 **Bh** Bohrium (264)	108 **Hs** Hassium (265)	109 **Mt** Meitnerium (268)

*LANTHANIDES	57 **La** Lanthanum 138.91	58 **Ce** Cerium 140.12	59 **Pr** Praseodymium 140.908	60 **Nd** Neodymium 144.24	61 **Pm** Promethium (145)	62 **Sm** Samarium 150.36	63 **Eu** Europium 151.96
**ACTINIDES	89 **Ac** Actinium (227)	90 **Th** Thorium 232.038	91 **Pa** Protactinium 231.036	92 **U** Uranium 238.03	93 **Np** Neptunium (237)	94 **Pu** Plutonium (244)	95 **Am** Americium (243)

ALPHABETICAL TABLE OF THE ELEMENTS

Element	Symbol	Atomic Number	Element	Symbol	Atomic Number	Element	Symbol	Atomic Number	Element	Symbol	Atomic Number
Actinium	Ac	89	Cadmium	Cd	48	Element 110	–	110	Helium	He	2
Aluminum	Al	13	Calcium	Ca	20	Element 111	–	111	Holmium	Ho	67
Americium	Am	95	Californium	Cf	98	Element 112	–	112	Hydrogen	H	1
Antimony	Sb	51	Carbon	C	6	Erbium	Er	68	Indium	In	49
Argon	Ar	18	Cerium	Ce	58	Europium	Eu	63	Iodine	I	53
Arsenic	As	33	Cesium	Cs	55	Fermium	Fm	100	Iridium	Ir	77
Astatine	At	85	Chlorine	Cl	17	Fluorine	F	9	Iron	Fe	26
Barium	Ba	56	Chromium	Cr	24	Francium	Fr	87	Krypton	Kr	36
Berkelium	Bk	97	Cobalt	Co	27	Gadolinium	Gd	64	Lanthanum	La	57
Beryllium	Be	4	Copper	Cu	29	Gallium	Ga	31	Lawrencium	Lr	103
Bismuth	Bi	83	Curium	Cm	96	Germanium	Ge	32	Lead	Pb	82
Bohrium	Bh	107	Dubnium	Db	105	Gold	Au	79	Lithium	Li	3
Boron	B	5	Dysprosium	Dy	66	Hafnium	Hf	72	Lutetium	Lu	71
Bromine	Br	35	Einsteinium	Es	99	Hassium	Hs	108	Magnesium	Mg	12

Metals	Nonmetals	Noble gases

							Group 0
		Group 3a	Group 4a	Group 5a	Group 6a	Group 7a	2 **He** Helium 4.0026
		5 **B** Boron 10.811	6 **C** Carbon 12.011	7 **N** Nitrogen 14.0067	8 **O** Oxygen 15.9994	9 **F** Fluorine 18.9984	10 **Ne** Neon 20.183
Group 8	Group 1b	Group 2b	13 **Al** Aluminum 26.9815	14 **Si** Silicon 28.086	15 **P** Phosphorus 30.9738	16 **S** Sulfur 32.066	17 **Cl** Chlorine 35.453	18 **Ar** Argon 39.948
28 **Ni** Nickel 58.69	29 **Cu** Copper 63.546	30 **Zn** Zinc 65.39	31 **Ga** Gallium 69.72	32 **Ge** Germanium 72.61	33 **As** Arsenic 74.9216	34 **Se** Selenium 78.96	35 **Br** Bromine 79.904	36 **Kr** Krypton 83.80
46 **Pd** Palladium 106.4	47 **Ag** Silver 107.868	48 **Cd** Cadmium 112.41	49 **In** Indium 114.82	50 **Sn** Tin 118.71	51 **Sb** Antimony 121.76	52 **Te** Tellurium 127.60	53 **I** Iodine 126.9045	54 **Xe** Xenon 131.29
78 **Pt** Platinum 195.08	79 **Au** Gold 196.967	80 **Hg** Mercury 200.59	81 **Tl** Thallium 204.38	82 **Pb** Lead 207.2	83 **Bi** Bismuth 208.98	84 **Po** Polonium (210)	85 **At** Astatine (210)	86 **Rn** Radon (222)
110† (269)	111† (272)	112† (277)

† Until official names are given to new elements, names based on a Latin translation of the atomic number are used; e.g. *ununbium* (Latin *unus* '1' + *unus* '1' + *bi-* '2') for element 112.

64 **Gd** Gadolinium 157.25	65 **Tb** Terbium 158.925	66 **Dy** Dysprosium 162.50	67 **Ho** Holmium 164.930	68 **Er** Erbium 167.26	69 **Tm** Thulium 168.934	70 **Yb** Ytterbium 173.04	71 **Lu** Lutetium 174.97
96 **Cm** Curium (247)	97 **Bk** Berkelium (247)	98 **Cf** Californium (251)	99 **Es** Einsteinium (252)	100 **Fm** Fermium (257)	101 **Md** Mendelevium (258)	102 **No** Nobelium (259)	103 **Lr** Lawrencium (262)

Element	Symbol	Atomic Number	Element	Symbol	Atomic Number	Element	Symbol	Atomic Number	Element	Symbol	Atomic Number
Manganese	Mn	25	Palladium	Pd	46	Ruthenium	Ru	44	Terbium	Tb	65
Meitnerium	Mt	109	Phosphorus	P	15	Rutherfordium	Rf	104	Thallium	Tl	81
Mendelevium	Md	101	Platinum	Pt	78	Samarium	Sm	62	Thorium	Th	90
Mercury	Hg	80	Plutonium	Pu	94	Scandium	Sc	21	Thulium	Tm	69
Molybdenum	Mo	42	Polonium	Po	84	Seaborgium	Sg	106	Tin	Sn	50
Neodymium	Nd	60	Potassium	K	19	Selenium	Se	34	Titanium	Ti	22
Neon	Ne	10	Praseodymium	Pr	59	Silicon	Si	14	Tungsten	W	74
Neptunium	Np	93	Promethium	Pm	61	Silver	Ag	47	Uranium	U	92
Nickel	Ni	28	Protactinium	Pa	91	Sodium	Na	11	Vanadium	V	23
Niobium	Nb	41	Radium	Ra	88	Strontium	Sr	38	Xenon	Xe	54
Nitrogen	N	7	Radon	Rn	86	Sulfur	S	16	Ytterbium	Yb	70
Nobelium	No	102	Rhenium	Re	75	Tantalum	Ta	73	Yttrium	Y	39
Osmium	Os	76	Rhodium	Rh	45	Technetium	Tc	43	Zinc	Zn	30
Oxygen	O	8	Rubidium	Rb	37	Tellurium	Te	52	Zirconium	Zr	40

A *structural formula* displays the spatial relationships among the atoms in a unique and unambiguous way.

In general, a carbon atom can bond to its neighbors in four ways. Each kind of bond is represented by a special notation.

Single bond. A single bond, in which two electrons are shared, is represented by a single line drawn from the carbon atom to another atom:

$$
\begin{array}{c}
\text{H} \\
| \\
\text{H} - \text{C} - \text{H} \\
| \\
\text{H}
\end{array}
$$

Double bond. A double bond, in which four electrons are shared, is represented as follows:

$$
\begin{array}{ccc}
\text{H} & & \text{H} \\
\diagdown & & \diagup \\
& \text{C} = \text{C} & \\
\diagup & & \diagdown \\
\text{H} & & \text{H}
\end{array}
$$

Triple bond. A triple bond, in which six electrons are shared, is represented as follows:

$$\text{H} - \text{C} \equiv \text{C} - \text{H}$$

Hydrogen bond. A hydrogen bond is represented by a dotted line in which a hydrogen atom bonded to atom *A* in one molecule makes an additional bond to atom *B* in either the same or another molecule:

$$
\begin{array}{ccc}
& \text{O} & \\
\diagup & & \diagdown \\
\text{H} & & \text{H} \\
\vdots & & \\
\text{O} & & \\
\diagup & & \diagdown \\
\text{H} & & \text{H}
\end{array}
$$

The Metric System

The metric system, also called the *International System of Units (SI)*, is a standardized system of expressing units of measurement. SI units have been officially adopted in nearly every country in the world because of

Table 7.5 SI Base and Supplemental Units

QUANTITY	UNIT	SYMBOL
length	meter	m
mass	kilogram	kg
time	second	s
electric current	ampere	A
thermodynamic temperature	kelvin	K
amount of substance	mole	mol
luminous intensity	candela	cd
plane angle	radian	rad
solid angle	steradian	sr

their simplicity and ease of manipulation. Although the use of metric weights and measures was legalized in the United States as long ago as 1866, Americans have in general preferred the traditional English system of measurement (such as *foot, pound,* and *degree Fahrenheit*), and conversion to SI has been slow.

Base units. Table 7.5 gives the SI base and supplemental units and their abbreviations. You may find that the SI units for mass (the kilogram), length (the meter), and time (the second) are the most familiar. However, the other base units (and their derived units) are used extensively in scientific literature. Each SI base unit has been defined with great precision in terms of measurable physical quantities. As measuring techniques become more precise, the base units occasionally have been redefined by decision of international scientific meetings. To deal with very large and very small measurements, SI provides prefixes for the base units. Table 7.6 gives the SI prefixes, their equivalents in scientific notation, and their official symbols.

Conversion from U.S customary units to SI. Tables 7.7 and 7.8 list common SI units and U.S. customary equivalents. To convert from U.S. customary to SI, you would multiply the number of U.S. customary units by the equivalent in SI units. For example, to convert 6 miles to kilometers, multiply 6 by 1.61 to obtain 9.66 kilometers.

Table 7.6 SI Prefixes

SYMBOL	PREFIX	MULTIPLICATION FACTOR
E	exa	10^{18}
P	peta	10^{15}
T	tera	10^{12}
G	giga	10^{9}
M	mega	10^{6}
k	kilo	10^{3}
h	hecto	10^{2}
da	deca	10^{1}
d	deci	10^{-1}
c	centi	10^{-2}
m	milli	10^{-3}
μ	micro	10^{-6}
n	nano	10^{-9}
p	pico	10^{-12}
f	femto	10^{-15}
a	atto	10^{-18}

SI style. Because a small change in the way SI units are written or printed can change their meaning completely, it's important to style them correctly. Following a few simple rules will help to avoid confusion:

- Write the full names of SI units in lowercase letters (unless they're the first word in a sentence). An exception is the (non-SI but commonly used) unit for temperature, the *degree Celsius,* which is always capitalized. Also, some SI units (*Newton, Kelvin, Watt, Pascal*) are named after famous scientists and therefore are capitalized. In such cases, begin the *symbol* with an uppercase letter too.

- Don't italicize or put a period after SI units (they're not mathematical symbols).

Table 7.7 Measurement

US CUSTOMARY SYSTEM (COMPARISON OF UNITS)

Unit	US	Metric	Unit	US	Metric
LENGTH			**VOLUME OR CAPACITY (LIQUID MEASURE)**		
inch	1/12 foot	2.54 centimeters	ounce	1/16 pint	29.574 milliliters
foot	12 inches or 1/3 yard	0.3048 meter	gill	4 ounces	0.1183 liter
yard	36 inches or 3 feet	0.9144 meter	pint	16 ounces	0.4732 liter
rod	16 1/2 feet or 5 1/2 yards	5.0292 meters	quart	2 pints or 1/4 gallon	0.9463 liter
furlong	220 yards or 1/8 mile	0.2012 kilometer	gallon	128 ounces or 8 pints	3.7854 liters
mile (statute)	5,280 feet (1,760 yards)	1.6093 kilometers	oil barrel	42 gallons	158.99 liters
mile (nautical)	6,076 feet (2,025 yards)	1.852 kilometers			
WEIGHT			**VOLUME OR CAPACITY (DRY MEASURE)**		
grain	1/7000 pound	64.799 milligrams	pint	1/2 quart	0.5506 liter
dram	1/16 ounce	1.7718 grams	quart	2 pints	1.1012 liters
ounce	16 drams	28.350 grams	peck	8 quarts or 1/4 bushel	8.8098 liters
pound	16 ounces	453.6 grams	bucket	2 pecks	17.620 liters
ton (short)	2,000 pounds	907.18 kilograms	bushel	2 buckets or 4 pecks	35.239 liters
ton (long)	2,240 pounds	1,016.0 kilograms			

UNITS OF THE INTERNATIONAL SYSTEM

The **International System** (abbreviated **SI**, for Système International, the French name for the system) was adopted in 1960 by the 11th General Conference on Weights and Measures. An expanded and modified version of the metric system, the International System addresses the needs of modern science for additional and more accurate units of measurement. The key features of the International System are decimalization, a system of prefixes, and a standard defined in terms of an invariable physical measure.

BASE UNITS

Unit	Quantity	Symbol
meter	length	m
kilogram	mass	kg
second	time	s
ampere	electric current	A
kelvin	temperature	K
mole	amount of matter	mol
candela	luminous intensity	cd

SUPPLEMENTARY UNITS

Two units are based on abstract geometry, not physical standards.

Unit	Quantity	Symbol
radian	plane angles	rad
steradian	solid angles	sr

PREFIXES

A multiple of a unit in the International System is formed by adding a prefix to the name of that unit. (**MF** = Multiplying Factor)

Prefix	Symbol	MF	Prefix	Symbol	MF
yotta-	Y	10^{24}	deci-	d	10^{-1}
zetta-	Z	10^{21}	centi-	c	10^{-2}
exa-	E	10^{18}	milli-	m	10^{-3}
peta-	P	10^{15}	micro-	μ	10^{-6}
tera-	T	10^{12}	nano-	n	10^{-9}
giga-	G	10^{9}	pico-	p	10^{-12}
mega-	M	10^{6}	femto-	f	10^{-15}
kilo-	k	10^{3}	atto-	a	10^{-18}
hecto-	h	10^{2}	zepto-	z	10^{-21}
deca-	da	10	yocto-	y	10^{-24}

BRITISH IMPERIAL SYSTEM (COMPARISON OF UNITS)

VOLUME OR CAPACITY (LIQUID MEASURE)				VOLUME OR CAPACITY (DRY MEASURE)			
Unit	Other British	US	Metric	Unit	Other British	US	Metric
pint	1/2 quart	1.201 pints	0.5683 liter	peck	1/4 bushel	1.0314 pecks	9.087 liters
quart	2 pints (1/4 gallon)	1.201 quarts	1.137 liters	bushel	4 pecks	1.0320 bushels	36.369 liters
gallon	8 pints (4 quarts)	1.201 gallons	4.546 liters				

- Don't mix unit names and their symbols. For example, don't write "km/second." Write either "km/s" or "kilometers per second."

- Don't make symbols plural (800 km, *not* 800 kms). Make full unit names plural in the usual way, by adding an *s*: meters, kilograms.

- Always space between a symbol and its numerical value: 500 s, *not* 500s, which would appear to be the plural of 500. An exception is the degree Celsius (°C) for which the degree sign and the Celsius symbol are written flush with the numerical value (40°C).

Table 7.8 Metric Conversion Chart

CONVERSION BETWEEN METRIC AND US CUSTOMARY UNITS					
When you know	**multiply by**	**to find**	**When you know**	**multiply by**	**to find**
inches	25.4	millimeters	millimeters	0.04	inches
	2.54	centimeters	centimeters	0.39	inches
feet	30.48	centimeters	meters	3.28	feet
yards	0.91	meters		1.09	yards
miles	1.61	kilometers	kilometers	0.62	miles
teaspoons	4.93	milliliters	milliliters	0.20	teaspoons
tablespoons	14.79	milliliters		0.07	tablespoons
fluid ounces	29.57	milliliters		0.03	fluid ounces
cups	0.24	liters	liters	1.06	quarts
pints	0.47	liters		0.26	gallons
quarts	0.95	liters		4.23	cups
gallons	3.79	liters		2.12	pints
cubic feet	0.028	cubic meters	cubic meters	35.31	cubic feet
cubic yards	0.76	cubic meters		1.35	cubic yards
ounces	28.35	grams	grams	0.035	ounces
pounds	0.45	kilograms	kilograms	2.20	pounds
short tons (2,000 lbs)	0.91	metric tons	metric tons (1,000 kg)	1.10	short tons
square inches	6.45	square centimeters	square centimeters	0.155	square inches
square feet	0.09	square meters	square meters	1.20	square yards
square yards	0.84	square meters	square kilometers	0.39	square miles
square miles	2.59	square kilometers	hectares	2.47	acres
TEMPERATURE CONVERSION BETWEEN CELSIUS AND FAHRENHEIT					
$°C = (°F - 32) \div 1.8$			$°F = (°C \times 1.8) + 32$		

- When a prefix symbol (M, G, and so on) is combined with a unit symbol, don't leave a space between them: GHz, *not* G Hz.

- Separate derived units involving multiplication, such as the Newton meter, from one another with a raised dot (N·m) or, if your software element lacks this symbol, with a period (N.m).

- Write derived units involving division either with a slash (/) or the negative exponent combined with the dot multiplier. For example, kilograms per cubic meter may be written as kg/m^3 or $kg \cdot m^{-3}$. When preparing a manuscript for a publisher, consult the organization's style specifications on this point. Whatever style is used, it's important to use it consistently.

- When numerical values are written in SI, use a space rather than a comma to separate groups of three digits to the left and to the right of the decimal point. Thus *ten thousand* is written as 10 000, *not* 10,000, and *one millionth* is written as 0.000 000 1, *not* 0.000,000,1.

- Numbers with only four digits to the right or left of the decimal point are written without either a space or a comma: 9856 and 0.0011. (This SI style should not be confused with the traditional business style for writing numbers with commas: 1,342,784.69.) In decimal numbers less than 1, the decimal point is *always* preceded by a zero: 0.068, *not* .068.

Business English

Office professionals spend most of each day using some form of communication. Whether the communication is oral or written, it must contain correct grammar and appropriate word choice. Office professionals must therefore have an above-average command of the English language so that their oral and written messages are accurate and effective. Errors in grammar and word usage will not only decrease the effectiveness of a message but will cast the user, their supervisors, and their companies in an unfavorable light.

RULES OF ENGLISH

Grammatical Terms

Grammatical terms are used to describe the function of parts of speech and other words in a sentence. This chapter describes the eight parts of speech and the phrases, clauses, sentences, and paragraphs in which they're used. For definitions of the following terms, refer to the appropriate section:

Term	Section
Abstract noun	Noun
Active voice	Verb
Adjective	Adjective
Adverb	Adverb
Affirmative adverb	Adverb
Auxiliary verb	Verb
Case	Pronoun
Clause	Phrases, Clauses, Sentences, and Paragraphs
Collective noun	Noun
Common noun	Noun
Comparative degree	Adjective; Adverb

Term	Section
Complex sentence	Phrases, Clauses, Sentences, and Paragraphs
Compound sentence	Phrases, Clauses, Sentences, and Paragraphs
Compound and complex sentence	Phrases, Clauses, Sentences, and Paragraphs
Concrete noun	Noun
Conjunction	Conjunction
Conjunctive adverb	Adverb
Coordinate conjunction	Conjunction
Correlative conjunction	Conjunction
Declarative sentence	Phrases, Clauses, Sentences, and Paragraphs
Definite pronoun	Pronoun
Demonstrative pronoun	Pronoun
Dependent (subordinate) clause	Phrases, Clauses, Sentences, and Paragraphs
Exclamatory sentence	Phrases, Clauses, Sentences, and Paragraphs
Gerund	Verb
Imperative mood	Verb
Imperative sentence	Phrases, Clauses, Sentences, and Paragraphs
Inactive voice	Verb
Indefinite pronoun	Pronoun
Independent clause	Phrases, Clauses, Sentences, and Paragraphs
Indicative mood	Verb
Infinitive	Verb
Interjection	Interjection
Interrogative adverb	Adverb
Interrogative pronoun	Pronoun
Interrogative sentence	Phrases, Clauses, Sentences, and Paragraphs
Intransitive verb	Verb
Irregular verb	Verb
Modifier	Adjective; Adverb
Mood	Verb
Negative adverb	Adverb
Nominative case	Pronoun
Nonrestrictive clause	Phrases, Clauses, Sentences, and Paragraphs
Noun	Noun
Objective case	Pronoun

Term	Section
Participle	Verb
Passive voice	Verb
Person	Verb
Personal pronoun	Pronoun
Phrase	Phrases, Clauses, Sentences, and Paragraphs
Positive degree	Adjective; Adverb
Possessive case	Pronoun
Predicate adjective	Adjective
Preposition	Preposition
Prepositional phrase	Preposition
Principal verb	Verb
Pronoun	Pronoun
Proper adjective	Adjective
Proper noun	Noun
Reciprocal pronoun	Pronoun
Reflexive pronoun	Pronoun
Regular verb	Verb
Relative adjective	Adjective
Relative pronoun	Pronoun
Restrictive clause	Phrases, Clauses, Sentences, and Paragraphs
Sentence	Phrases, Clauses, Sentences, and Paragraphs
Sentence adverb	Adverb
Simple sentence	Phrases, Clauses, Sentences, and Paragraphs
Subjunctive mood	Verb
Subordinate conjunction	Conjunction
Superlative degree	Adjective; Adverb
Tense	Verb
Transitive verb	Verb
Verb	Verb
Verbal	Verb
Voice	Verb

The following 15 terms will also help you better understand the basics of grammar:

Antecedent: The word, phrase, or clause to which a pronoun refers: *Mr. Parsons* [antecedent-noun] entered *his* [pronoun] office.

Appositive: A noun or noun phrase that explains another word(s): Phyllis Rogers, *president,* will retire this month.

Article: An adjective such as the indefinite articles *a* and *an* or the definite article *the:* She received *a* promotion.

Complement: A word(s) used after a verb to complete its meaning: The overactive economy caused the *inflation.*

Compound predicate: Two or more connected verbs or verb phrases: He *studied* and *analyzed* the problem.

Compound subject: Two or more words in the subject that are connected by conjunctions such as *and, or,* and *nor:* The *assistant* and the *executive* have adjoining offices.

Dangling modifier: A word or words that do not modify or logically refer to any other word: *Having completed the letter* [dangling], the fax was transmitted. *Better: Having completed the letter, she* transmitted the fax.

Direct object: A word or phrase referring to the person or thing receiving the action of a verb. Frequently, it answers the question "what" or "whom": She opened [what?] the *letter.*

Expletive: A word such as *there* that is placed where the subject normally would be positioned: *It* was caused by a computer malfunction. *Better: A computer malfunction* caused it.

Idiom: An expression that is peculiar to a particular language and also is peculiar to itself grammatically or cannot be understood from the individual meanings of the elements: The company was prepared to *see it through.* Idioms are often confusing to people in other countries and should be avoided in international correspondence.

Indirect object: An object *indirectly* affected by the action of a verb: Mr. Schwartz gave [verb] his *assistant* [indirect object] a new computer [direct object].

Misplaced modifier: A word positioned so that it modifies the wrong word or changes the meaning of the sentence. The proper position depends on the intended meaning: He *only* writes [doesn't do anything else] technical reports. He writes *only* technical [but not nontechnical] reports.

Predicate: The part of a sentence, including the verb, objects, or phrases governed by the verb, that modifies the subject: He *joined the committee.*

Split infinitive: An infinitive verb form that has an element, such as an adverb, interposed between *to* and the verb form: *to firmly unite.* Although this position is avoided by some writers, it's more desirable than creating an awkward construction by trying to avoid it: They want *to unite firmly* [awkward] the two factions.

Subject: The part of a sentence, including the noun, noun phrase, or pronoun, that denotes the doer of the action, the receiver of the action, or what is described by the predicate: *He* joined the committee.

Parts of Speech

The eight parts of speech that are described here are the noun, pronoun, verb, adjective, adverb, preposition, conjunction, and interjection. Knowing how these parts should be used in a sentence will help you avoid mistakes that detract from both your message and your image as an office professional.

Noun. A *noun* is a word that names a person (*Joe*), place (*New York*), thing (*book*), or abstraction (*theory*). *Proper nouns* name specific persons, places, or things (*Silicon Valley*; the *Internet*). *Common nouns* are sometimes classified as *concrete nouns* that name tangible things (*computer*) and *abstract nouns* that name ideas, beliefs, or qualities (*capitalism*).

The forms of a noun can show possession (the *treasurer's report*) and number, singular or plural (*company, companies*), as explained next.

Number. A noun may be either singular (*telephone*) or plural (*telephones*). Some may look or sound plural but may be either singular or plural, depending on the intended meaning (*politics*). (See Chapter 7, "Business Style Guide," Spelling, for more about spelling plurals and the use of variant forms.) Some irregular nouns indicate the plural by a change in the base form (*child, children*) or vowel (*mouse, mice*). Some have more than one acceptable plural form (*phenomena, phenomenons*), and others undergo no change (*sheep, sheep*).

Collective nouns. A *collective noun* denotes a collection of persons or things regarded as a unit. It takes a singular verb when it refers to the collection as a whole and a plural verb when it refers to the members of the collection as separate persons or things: The *committee was* in executive session. The *committee have* all left for the day. (In British usage, collective nouns are most often construed as plural: The *government are* committed to a liberal policy.) A collective noun should not be treated as both singular and plural in the *same* construction: The *company is* determined to press *its* [not *their*] claim. Examples of collective nouns are *clergy, company, family, group, public,* and *team.*

Use of nouns. A noun may be any of the following: the *subject of a sentence* (The *company* is in trouble), the *direct object of a verb* (Spiraling interest rates and inflation have affected the *company*), the *object of a preposition* (This is one of the most controversial issues in the *company*), or the *indirect object of a verb* (Give the *company* a chance, and it may recover).

Pronoun. A *pronoun* is a word substituted for a noun. It refers to a person or thing that has been named or understood in a particular context. Pronouns have grammatical case (nominative, possessive, or objective), number (singular or plural), person (first, second, or third), and gender (masculine, feminine, or neuter).

Case. The case of a pronoun is determined by its function in the sentence. The following pronouns are used in each case:

Nominative: I, we, you, he, she, it, they, who

Possessive: my, mine, our, ours, your, yours, his, her, hers, its, their, theirs, whose

Objective: me, us, you, him, her, it, them, whom

The *nominative case* is used in these instances:

- When the pronoun is used as the subject: *We* are ready.
- After a form of the verb *be* (in formal writing): It is *I*.
- After the conjunctions *as* and *than* (in formal writing): She is a better computer operator than *I* [am].
- When the pronoun is used in apposition to the subject noun or a predicate noun: The two employees [subject noun] — Brad and *he* — were transferred.

The *possessive case* is used in these instances:

- To show relationships such as possession, source, or authorship: *Their* work is outstanding.
- Before a gerund (in formal writing): The article was complimentary to Mr. Lewis concerning *his* working hard on the project.

The *objective case* is used in these instances:

- When the pronoun is the object of a verb: The high absenteeism disturbed *him*.
- When the pronoun *whom* is the object of a verb (in formal writing): Mrs. Priestly is the speaker *whom* we most admired.
- When the pronoun is the object of a verbal, such as a participle or gerund: Meeting *her* was interesting.

- When the pronoun is the object of a preposition: Between you and *me,* the office is in chaos.
- After the conjunctions *as* and *than* when the pronoun is the object of a verb omitted from the sentence: Her supervisor praised her as much as [he praised] *him.*
- When the pronoun is used in apposition to a noun that is an object: The company promoted two sales representatives — Jennifer Black and *me*—last week.

Number. Pronouns may be singular or plural and should agree with their verbs accordingly: *He has* a good job. *They have* good jobs.

Person. Pronouns may be classified by person (first, second, third) and must agree with their verbs accordingly:

First person: I am, *we* are

Second person: You are

Third person: He/she is, *they* are, *it* is

Gender. Pronouns may be classified by gender, with *he* being masculine; *she,* feminine; and *it,* neuter. Contemporary writing favors a nonsexist application of these personal pronouns, using *he and she* or *they* when appropriate, rather than *he* alone. In any case, the property of gender must be consistent between a pronoun and its antecedent: The company [antecedent] has benefited from *its* [possessive pronoun] new location.

Classes of pronouns. The following are the seven main classes of pronouns:

Personal pronoun: A pronoun that stands for the names of persons, places, or things (*I, you, he, she, it, we,* and *they*): *We* will produce the program, and *they* will distribute it. See also *Reflexive pronoun.*

Relative pronoun: A pronoun such as *who, what, that,* and *which* that refers to an antecedent and introduces a dependent clause. *Who* is used with persons; *that* with persons, animals, or inanimate objects; *what* with things; and *which* with animals or inanimate objects: She [antecedent] is a leader *who is destined for greatness* [dependent clause].

Interrogative pronoun: A pronoun such as *who, which,* and *what* that is used in a direct question: *What* do you want us to do?

Demonstrative (definite) pronoun: A pronoun such as *this, that, these,* and *those* that points definitely to persons or things to which the pronoun refers: *That* is the latest policy directive.

Indefinite pronoun: A pronoun that, like a demonstrative pronoun, also points out persons and things but does so less definitely. Examples are *all, any, anybody, anyone, anything, each, either, everybody, everything, few, neither, nobody, none, one, several,* and *some: Some* will no doubt drop out at the last minute.

Reflexive pronoun: A pronoun used as the direct or indirect object of a verb or as the object of a preposition: He bought *himself* a new computer. Reflexive pronouns may also be used for emphasis (I *myself* prefer a traditional office), although this construction should be avoided in business writing and particularly in international correspondence.

Reciprocal pronoun: A pronoun such as *each other* that expresses mutual action or relationship: They helped *one another* during the power failure.

Verb. A *verb* expresses action (*open*) or state of being (*is*). It may make a statement, ask a question, or give a command:

> The office *is* open from 9 A.M. to 5 P.M.
>
> *Do* you *have* the new catalog?
>
> *Take* the requisition to the purchasing department.

Classification of verbs. Verbs may be classified as transitive or intransitive, as principal or auxiliary, and as regular or irregular:

Transitive: A verb is *transitive* when it has an object: She *worked* the keyboard [object] with nimble fingers.

Intransitive: A verb is *intransitive* when it has no object: She *worked* hard.

Principal: A *principal verb* is complete in itself: The executive *uses* a formal writing style.

Auxiliary: An *auxiliary verb* accompanies the main verb and helps express its meaning: The executive *will* [auxiliary verb] *write* [main verb] the report in a formal style. Examples of auxiliary verbs are *be, can, do, have, may, must, ought, should, shall, will, would.*

Regular: A *regular verb* usually forms the past tense and the past participle by adding *-d* or *-ed* to the present tense: He *called* this morning. Verb tenses are discussed later in this section.

Irregular: An *irregular verb* forms the past tense and the past participle in different ways: *begin, began, begun; draw, drew, drawn; meet, met, met; spread, spread, spread:* He *did* [past tense] the work. He *has done* [past participle] the work.

Voice. When the *active voice* is used, the verb is performing the action: He *signed* the contract. Writers use the active voice to give strength and directness to their messages.

When the *passive,* or *inactive, voice* is used, the subject is acted on: The contract [subject] *was signed* by him. Since the passive voice is weaker than the active voice, writers generally avoid it unless they *don't* want to be direct: An error *was made* on page 5 (not, *You* made an error on page 5).

Mood. Verbs are used in one of three moods, the indicative, subjunctive, or imperative mood:

Indicative: States a fact or asks a question: You *know* the procedure.

Subjunctive: Expresses wishes, commands, or conditions contrary to fact. Often, the verb is preceded by a conjunction such as *if, though, lest, that, till,* or *unless:* If I *were* you [but I'm not], I would recommend a change in that policy.

Imperative: Expresses a request or command, often with the subject omitted: [You] *Hand* me the new manual, please.

Tense. The tense of a verb specifies the time or nature of the action that occurs. When present, past, or future action is described as completed, or *perfected,* it's in the *present perfect, past perfect,* or *future perfect* tense:

Present (action occurring now): I *am* in the conference room.

Past (action that occurred in the past): I *was* in the conference room.

Future (action that is expected to take place in the future): I *will be* in the conference room.

Present perfect: I *have been* on my vacation.

Past perfect: I *had been* on my vacation when you called last week.

Future perfect: I already *will have been* on my vacation by the time we next meet.

The following table shows the various forms of the verb *write* in the past, present, and future tenses. It includes the *present* and *past progressive* tenses in which the action is expressed as being in progress:

Tense	I	He/She/It	We/You/They
present	write	writes	write
present progressive	am writing	is writing	are writing
past	wrote	wrote	wrote
past progressive	was writing	was writing	were writing
present perfect	have written	has written	have written
past perfect	had written	had written	had written
future	will write, am going to write	will write, is going to write	will write, are going to write
future perfect	will have written	will have written	will have written

Person and number. A verb must agree with its subject in person (first, second, third) and number (singular, plural):

Person	Singular	Plural
First person	I send	We send
Second person	You send	You send
Third person	He/she/it sends	They send

The verb *be* has various forms such as *am, are,* and *is:* She *is* the best programmer in the department.

Certain words and expressions sometimes pose problems in connection with subject-verb agreement. For example, a verb must agree with the subject even when a singular or plural prepositional phrase intervenes: He is *one* of those people who *has* always maintained a positive attitude. Therefore, if a sentence has a singular subject, a verb must agree with it and not with a plural phrase that follows the verb: The *theme* of my lectures *is* fiscal irresponsibility and managerial incompetence.

The word *there* sometimes precedes a linking verb such as *is, seem,* or *appear.* In such cases, the subject or predicate nominative follows the verb: There *is* a *storage facility.* There *are* many *options.*

Extraneous expressions that intervene between a verb and its subject should be ignored in deciding upon subject-verb agreement: The *executive,* with a receptionist and two assistants, *is* in charge of registrations.

A singular subject preceded by *each, every, many a, such a,* or *no* takes a singular verb even when two or more of such subjects are linked by *and:* *Each* manager and *each* division chief *has urged* the employees to invest in the thrift plan.

When *either-or* and *neither-nor* are used, the verb should agree with the subject closest to it: Neither the supervisor nor the union *members are* willing to negotiate.

Verbals. *Verbals* are forms derived from verbs that are used as nouns or adjectives. They are called "verbals" rather than "verbs" because they have the properties of both noun and verb and adjective and verb.

Both *infinitives* and *gerunds* are *verbal nouns.* The word *to,* originally a preposition but now treated as part of the infinitive, may be included or omitted: *To decide* is the first step. Please *[to] decide.* Infinitives may also be used as adjectives and adverbs.

Gerunds, formed by adding *-ing* to the root or stem of a verb, are used like nouns: He teaches *programming.*

Participles are verbal adjectives. Although, like a gerund, the present participle of a regular verb is also formed by adding *-ing* to the stem, it's used as an adjective modifying a noun rather than as a noun: *Racing* machines droned on endlessly.

Adjective. *Adjectives* modify words, phrases, and clauses that serve as nouns and pronouns. An adjective describes, qualifies, limits, or makes a word distinct and separate from something else: a *tall* building, a *reasonable* offer, a *two-story* house.

Kinds of adjectives. *Proper adjectives* are derived from proper nouns: *German* industry. A *relative adjective* is a relative pronoun used as an adjective: She is the one *whose* telephone is out of order. A *predicate adjective* usually follows a linking verb but always modifies a noun or pronoun: The director is [linking verb] *happy* [describes the noun *director*].

Comparison of adjectives. Adjectives may occur in the *positive, comparative,* or *superlative* degree. The regular forms of comparison are made by adding *-er* (comparative) or *-est* (superlative) to the positive form of the adjective:

> *Positive:* An *easy* method
> *Comparative:* The *easier* of the two methods
> *Superlative:* The *easiest* of all methods

If a word has more than one syllable, comparison is usually made by adding *more* or *most,* rather than *-er* or *-est:*

> *Positive:* A *reliable* source
> *Comparative:* The *more reliable* of the two sources
> *Superlative:* The *most reliable* of all sources

Irregular adjectives have different forms than regular adjectives have, and comparison must be made by using the correct form rather than by adding *-er* or *-est* or *more* or *most:*

> *Positive:* A *good* suggestion
> *Comparative:* A *better* suggestion
> *Superlative:* The *best* suggestion

Adverb. An *adverb* may modify a verb (read *fast*), an adjective (a *very* fast reader), or another adverb (read *very* fast). A *sentence adverb* modifies an entire clause or sentence: *Unfortunately,* the stock split didn't have the desired effect. An *interrogative adverb* is used in asking or stating a direct or indirect question: *How* are you feeling? *Yes* is an *affirmative adverb,* and *no* and *not* are *negative adverbs. Conjunctive adverbs* connect sentences: The conference is over; *therefore,* work can return to normal.

Some adverbs may be identified by determining if they express time (when), place (where), manner (how), degree (to what extent), cause or purpose (why), or number (first, firstly, and so on). The following are examples of adverbs that fit these categories:

Time: already, finally, lately, never, now, then

Place: above, far, here, there, upstairs, where

Manner: easily, otherwise, surely, well

Degree: equally, fully, less, much, too

Cause or purpose: consequently, since, therefore, why

Number: first/firstly, second/secondly, third/thirdly

Comparison of adverbs. Like adjectives, regular and irregular adverbs may be compared by using the comparative or superlative form of the positive adverb. Regular adverbs commonly add the words *more* and *most* or *less* and *least* to make the comparison, although a few may add the word endings *-er* (*sooner*) and *-est* (*soonest*):

Positive: He is *often* available on Fridays.
Comparative: He is *more often* available on Fridays.
Superlative: He is *most often* available on Fridays.

Also like adjectives, some adverbs use different forms to indicate comparison, rather than add a word ending such as *-er* or a word such as *more:*

Positive: He did *badly* on the test.
Comparative: He did *worse* on the test than she did.
Superlative: Of everyone in class, he did the *worst* on the test.

Adverbs ending in -ly. Some adverbs are formed by adding *-ly* to an adjective, and some adjectives are formed by adding *-ly* to a noun. Often you can decide if a word is an adverb or an adjective by determining whether the root word, without the *-ly* added, is a noun or an adjective. For example, the root word in these cases is an adjective. The result is therefore an adverb:

sang *beautifully*
sighed *calmly*
beamed *eagerly*
laughed *happily*
spoke *harshly*
walked *rapidly*

The word to which *-ly* has been added in the following cases is a noun. The result is therefore an adjective:

brotherly concern
earthly vision

friendly employee
lovely decor
neighborly attitude
saintly demeanor

A common mistake is the use of an adverb when an adjective is intended. See bad, badly in A Concise Guide to Usage.

Preposition. A preposition connects and shows the relationship between a noun or pronoun and other words or expressions in a sentence. The noun or pronoun is the *object* of the preposition. The preposition together with the noun or pronoun is a *prepositional phrase: in the office.* Prepositional phrases may indicate a variety of situations or conditions:

> *Accompaniment:* Joe attended the meeting *with several colleagues.*
> *Cause:* The trip was canceled *because of bad weather.*
> *Support:* Those who are not *for us* are *against us.*
> *Destination:* We drove *to the city.*
> *Exception:* I have everything *but a private office.*
> *Possession:* The arrogance *of that official* defies description.
> *Composition or makeup:* I want a desk *of polished mahogany.*
> *Means or instrument:* I worked out the problem *with a spreadsheet program.*
> *Manner:* Treat all visitors *with courtesy.*
> *Direction:* I ran *across the hall* to find you.
> *Location:* John is *in the office.*
> *Purpose or intention:* They'll do anything *for a quick profit.*
> *Origin:* The new manager is *from Chicago.*
> *Time:* Call me *at noon.*

In addition to having easily recognized prepositions such as *in, to,* and *with,* the English language includes a variety of other prepositions, some of which also function as other parts of speech. *Above,* for example, may be used as a noun, adjective, and adverb as well as a preposition. The following are examples of single-word prepositions:

across	concerning	out	toward
along	during	over	under
before	except	regarding	without
between	inside	since	
but	near	till	

The following phrasal, or compound, prepositions consist of more than one word but are treated as single prepositions:

according to	contrary to	in lieu of	on behalf of
along with	from between	in place of	out of
aside from	in addition to	in regard to	regardless of
as well as	in case of	in spite of	with reference to

When two or more phrases used together share the *same* preposition, without intervening words, it isn't necessary to repeat the preposition: The testimony is *equal [to]* and *tantamount to* perjury. If two different prepositions are required, however, retain both of them: Our *interest in* and *concern for* the welfare of our employees has led us to take steps to improve their working conditions.

Conjunction. A *conjunction* links words, phrases, clauses, or sentences and is used to show how one sentence is related to another. The three principal types of conjunctions are coordinate, subordinate, and correlative conjunctions. *Conjunctive adverbs,* such as *besides, however,* and *nevertheless,* described in Adverbs, also connect sentences and words.

Coordinate conjunction. *Coordinate conjunctions,* such as *and, or, but, yet, for, nor,* and *so,* connect elements of equal value:

> He's the president of the company, *and* he's also her supervisor.
>
> She's successful *but* modest.

Subordinate conjunction. *Subordinate conjunctions,* such as *as if, because, in case, inasmuch as, provided that, since, when,* and *where,* connect a subordinate element to another element in a sentence:

> *Because* the report is late [subordinate element], the meeting will have to be postponed.
>
> Andrew is a skilled writer, *although* he has difficulty researching com plex subjects [subordinate element].

Correlative conjunction. *Correlative conjunctions,* such as *neither-nor,* are used in pairs or a series. Correlatives are intended to connect elements of equal value and must be positioned correctly in the sentence to avoid confusion:

> *Either* the executive *or* the assistant is coming.
>
> Overpopulation has been a problem *both* in India *and* in China.

The following are common correlative conjunctions:

although ... yet	if ... then	so ... as
as ... as	neither ... nor	though ... yet
as ... so	not only ... but also	whereas ... therefore
both ... and	now ... now	whether ... or
either ... or	now ... then	

Other parts of speech used as conjunctions. Pronouns and adverbs are also used as conjunctions to show the relation of one clause to another in a sentence. Refer to the description of relative pronouns and conjunctive adverbs in Pronoun and Adverb.

Interjection. An *interjection* is a word or words commonly used to express emotion. It may be used alone (*Oh!*) or as part of a sentence: *Oh, come on!*

Phrases, Clauses, Sentences, and Paragraphs

Phrases. A *phrase* is a group of words that does not have both a subject and verb and cannot stand alone:

> *Having addressed the sales force,* we then took questions from the floor.
>
> *Approaching that issue* was tricky.
>
> We will be delighted *to attend the meeting.*

Clauses. A *clause* is a group of words that has both a subject and a predicate and may or may not be able to stand alone. A sentence, for example, is a clause that can stand alone, but not all clauses are sentences:

> *If you have performed unsatisfactorily,* it will be reflected in your performance review.

A *restrictive clause* is essential to the meaning of the sentence and should not be set off with commas:

> The employees *who have signed their performance reviews* will receive salary adjustments on schedule.

A *nonrestrictive clause* is not essential to the meaning of the sentence and should be set off with commas:

> Seven employees, *who have known each other for many years,* are participating in the review program.

A *dependent clause* occupies a subordinate position in a sentence and cannot stand alone:

> *When the meeting adjourns,* we will listen to the recording of the proceedings.

An *independent clause* is a complete sentence in itself and can stand alone. This example has two independent clauses joined by the conjunction *and:*

> The supply of stationery is running low, *and* it's time for me to place a new order.

Sentences. A *sentence* is a group of words that has a subject and a verb and can stand alone. It begins with a capital letter and ends with concluding punctuation, such as a period, question mark, or exclamation point: The Board of Directors has unanimously voted a dividend increase. When it does not have a complete subject or predicate but is punctuated as if it were complete, it's known as a *sentence fragment:* The Board of Directors having unanimously voted [predicate is missing].

A sentence may be declarative (make a statement), interrogative (ask a question), imperative (request or command), or exclamatory (express strong feeling):

> *Declarative:* The applicants signed the forms.
> *Interrogative:* Did you sign the form?
> *Imperative:* Sign the form here.
> *Exclamatory:* I wish they'd hurry up and sign the forms!

A sentence may also be classified as simple, compound (two or more connected sentences), complex (containing a clause), or a combination of compound and complex:

> *Simple:* Some people complain a lot.
> *Compound:* Some people complain, some brood, and others don't care at all.
> *Complex:* When people become dissatisfied with their jobs, they often complain.
> *Compound-complex:* When people become dissatisfied with their jobs, they often complain, and management then has a problem that it must address.

A CONCISE GUIDE TO USAGE

Word Choice

Office professionals and their employers both know that correct word choice is an important ingredient in business communication. Using the wrong word in conversation or written messages may cause someone to reach the wrong conclusion, or it may make the user appear unprofessional. To avoid this, be alert to the following commonly misused words. Although many words, such as *ability* and *capacity,* are loosely used interchangeably in casual domestic conversation or writing, it's important to consider even subtle differences when composing international messages or formal domestic correspondence. Foreign readers, for example, often know English only as a second language and take even slight differences in meaning into account in their translations.

a, an   *A* is used before a word beginning with a consonant (*a* building) or a consonant sound (*a* university); *an* is used before a word beginning with a vowel (*an* employee) or a vowel sound (*an* hour). *A* rather than *an* should be used before words like *historical* (*a* hysterical employee) unless the *h* is not pronounced (*an* herb).

about   The construction *not about to* is sometimes used informally to express determination: We are *not about to* negotiate with strikebreakers. However, this usage should be avoided in business writing and, particularly, in international communication.

above   The use of *above* as an adjective or noun in referring to preceding text is common in some business and legal writing. In general writing, its use as an adjective (the *above* figures) is acceptable, but its use as a noun (read the *above*) should be avoided.

acquiesce   When *acquiesce* takes a preposition, it's usually used with *in* (*acquiesced in* the ruling) but sometimes with *to* (*acquiesced to* management's wishes).

admission, admittance   *Admission,* "achieving entry to a group or institution," has a more general meaning than *admittance,* "obtaining physical access to a place"; to gain *admission* to the board is to become a member; to gain *admittance* to the board is to enter its chambers. One pays *admission* to a theater (a price paid to become a member of the audience) to be allowed *admittance* (physical entry to the theater itself).

advance, advancement   *Advance,* as a noun, is used for forward movement (the *advance* of our salespeople into the new market) or for progress or improvement in a figurative sense (a sales *advance* of 35 percent this year). *Advancement* is often used in the figurative sense: career *advancement.* In that sense, there's a distinction between the two terms deriving from the transitive and intransitive forms of the verb *advance.* The noun *advancement* (unlike *advance*) often implies the existence of an agent or outside force. Thus the *advance* of research and development means simply the progress of the company's R & D efforts, whereas the *advancement* of research and development implies progress resulting from the action of an agent or force: The addition of $1.5 million to last year's budget has resulted in the *advancement of* our research efforts.

adverse   See averse, adverse.

advise   *Advise* in the sense "to counsel or give advice" is always acceptable in business contexts: The president *advised* employees to observe the new regulations. However, avoid the pretentious use of *advise* for *say, tell,* or *let you know* in business correspondence.

affect, effect   *Affect* and *effect* have no sense in common. As a verb, *affect* is most commonly used in the sense "to influence": How will bad weather *affect* deliveries? *Effect* as a verb means "to bring about or execute": The lay-offs are designed to *effect* savings. As a noun, it means "a result": We don't know what the *effect* of the new policy will be.

affinity   *Affinity* may be followed by *of, between,* or *with: affinity* of persons; *affinity* between two persons; *affinity* with another person. In technical writing, *affinity,* meaning "a chemical or physical attraction," is followed by *for:* a dye with an *affinity* for synthetic fabrics. In general usage, *affinity* should not be used as a simple synonym for *liking: affinity* for living in California.

affirmative   The expressions *in the affirmative* and *in the negative* (The client answered in the *affirmative*) are generally regarded as pompous. *Better:* The client answered *yes.*

agenda   *Agenda,* meaning "list" or "program," is well established as a singular noun. Its plural form is *agendas.*

ago   *Ago* may be followed by *that* or *when:* It was a week *ago* that [*or* when] I saw the invoice. It should not be followed by *since:* It was a week ago that [not *since*] the order arrived. *Since* is properly used without *ago:* It has been a week *since* the order arrived.

all, all of, all that   Constructions such as *all us* should be avoided. Use *all of us: all of us* employees. The construction *all that* is used informally in questions and negative sentences to mean "to the degree expected": The annual meeting was not *all that* exciting this year. However, this usage is generally unacceptable in business writing and, particularly, in international correspondence.

alleged   An *alleged burglar* is someone who is said to be a burglar but against whom no charges have yet been proved. An *alleged incident* is an event that is said to have taken place but which has not yet been verified. In their zeal to protect the rights of the accused, newspapers and law enforcement officials sometimes misuse *alleged.* A man arrested for murder may be only an *alleged murderer,* for example, because the charge of murder has yet to be proved. However, he is a *real,* not an *alleged, suspect* in that his status as a suspect is not in doubt. Similarly, if a murder is known to have taken place, there is nothing *alleged* about the crime.

all of   See all, all of, all that.

all right, alright   It's incorrect to write *all right,* meaning "in proper working order," as one word, *alright,* despite the parallel to words like *already* and *altogether* and despite the fact that in casual speech the expression is often pronounced as if it were one word.

all that   See all, all of, all that.

all together   See altogether, all together.

allude/allusion, refer/reference   *Allude* and *allusion* are often used when the more general terms *refer* and *reference* would be preferable. *Allude* and *allusion* apply to indirect reference that does not identify specifically: He *alluded* to her drug habit when he described the problems of dangerous outside forces. *Refer* and *reference,* unless qualified, usually imply direct, specific mention: She made *reference* to the book *ABCs of Teleconferencing* in her speech.

alternative   *Alternative* is widely used to denote simply "one of a set of possible courses of action," but many traditionalists insist that its use be restricted to situations in which only two possible choices present themselves: The *alternatives* are to attend a traditional college or to enter a vocational school. Used in this narrow sense, *alternative* would be incompatible with all numerals above *two* (there are *three alternatives*), and the use of *two*, in particular, would be redundant (the *two alternatives* are life and death). Similarly, *other* is unnecessary with *alternative:* There is no [*other*] *alternative.*

altogether, all together   *Altogether* should be distinguished from *all together.* As two words, *all together* is used with a group to indicate that its members performed or underwent an action collectively: The new computers were stored *all together* in an empty office. *All together* should be used only if it's possible to rephrase the sentence so that *all* and *together* may be separated by other words: The new computers were *all* stored *together.* As one word, *altogether* is used to mean "entirely" or "completely": It's *altogether* possible that we will lose the contract.

alumni   *Alumni* is commonly used to refer to both the *alumni* (masculine plural) and *alumnae* (feminine plural) of a coeducational institution.

A.M.   See ante meridian.

among   See between, among.

and   Although *and* has been used throughout history to begin sentences, businesspeople should avoid this practice in all but very casual writing. See also but.

and/or   Although *and/or* is widely used to mean "one or the other or both," business writers should avoid this usage, particularly in international correspondence, where it may not be understood. Usually, it's sufficient to use either the word *and* or the word *or.*

ante meridian   In general, *12 A.M.* denotes midnight, and *12 P.M.* denotes noon. However, sufficient confusion exists to make it advisable to say *12 noon* and *12 midnight* when absolute clarity is required.

anticipate, expect   Some traditionalists hold that *anticipate* should not be used simply as a synonym for *expect*. They restrict its use to senses in which it suggests some advance action, either to fulfill (*anticipate* my desires) or to forestall (*anticipate* the competition's next move). Others accept the word's use in the senses "to feel or realize beforehand" and "to look forward to" (often with the implication of foretasting pleasure): They are *anticipating* [*expecting*] a sizable dividend increase.

any   The phrase *of any* is sometimes used in informal contexts to mean "of all": That scientist is the best *of any* living authority on the subject. However, many find this construction unacceptable. *Any* is used to mean "at all" before a comparative adjective: Are the field office reports *any* better [comparative degree]this month? The related use of *any* by itself to mean "at all" should be avoided: It didn't matter at all [not *any*] to the supervisor.

anyone, any one   The one-word form *anyone* is used to mean "whatsoever person or persons." The two-word form *any one* is used to mean "whatever one [person or thing] of a group." "*Anyone* may join" means that admission is open to everybody. "*Any one* may join" means that admission is open to any one person of all the people who are applying for admission. When followed by *of*, only *any one* (two words) should be used: *Any one* of the employees could do the job. *Anyone* is often used in place of *everyone*: Dale is the most thrifty person *of anyone* I know. But the words *of anyone* are unnecessary in this context: Dale is the most thrifty person I know.

apparent   Used before a noun, *apparent* means "seeming": For all its *apparent* wealth, the company was leveraged to the hilt. Used after a form of the verb *to be*, however, *apparent* may mean either "seeming" (The virtues of the deal were only *apparent*) or "obvious" (The effects of the drought are *apparent* to anyone seeing the parched fields). Writers should take care that the intended meaning is clear from the context.

as . . . as, so . . . as   In current usage, comparisons with *as . . . as* are proper in any context, positive or negative: Their marketing is *as* good *as* ours. The *so . . . as* construction, although not required, should be applied only to negative comparisons, especially when the word *not* is used: Their marketing is not *so* good *as* [or *as* good *as*] ours.

as, since   Both *as* and *since* are used informally to mean "because" or "inasmuch as." When used in this way, *since* is preferred, and *as* should be avoided: *Since* [because] you're not interested, I'll remove your name from the mailing list. *As* has numerous other uses as a conjunction, adverb, pronoun, and preposition.

assure, ensure, insure   *Assure, ensure,* and *insure* all mean "to make sure or certain." Only *assure* is used with references to a person in the sense "to set the mind at rest": They *assured* the leader of their loyalty. Although *ensure* and *insure* are generally interchangeable, only *insure* is used in the commercial sense "to guarantee persons or property against risk." In the sense "to make certain," the British preference is *ensure;* American usage includes both *ensure* and *insure;* To *ensure* [or *insure*] success, the company did a thorough market study.

as well as   *As well as* in the sense "in addition to" does not have the conjunctive force of *and.* Consequently, the singular subjects remain singular and govern singular verbs: The *parent company, as well as its affiliate,* was named in the indictment. *As well as* is redundant in combination with *both*: The idea is unsound, *both* [or *as well as*] in practice.

averse, adverse   *Averse* and *adverse* are often confused. *Averse* indicates opposition or strong disinclination on the subject's part: The graduate was *averse* to joining the company. *Adverse* refers to something that opposes or hinders progress: an *adverse* economy; *adverse* circumstances.

awhile, a while   *Awhile,* an adverb, is never preceded by a preposition such as *for,* but the two-word form *a while* may be preceded by a preposition. Each of the following is therefore acceptable: *stay awhile; stay a while; stay for a while.*

back   The expression *back of* is an informal variant of *in back of* and should be avoided: There was a small loading dock *in back of* [not *back of*] the factory.

backward   The adverb may be spelled *backward* or *backwards,* and the forms are interchangeable: stepping *backward;* a mirror facing *backwards.* Only *backward* is an adjective: a *backward* view.

bad, badly   The adverb *badly* should not be used as an adjective: I felt *bad* [not *badly*] about the ruined press run. Also, *bad* and *good* should not be used as adverbs. Formal usage requires an adverb in these sentences: My tooth hurts *badly* [not *bad*]. He drives *well* [not *good*]. But when a word modifies the subject, it should be an adjective: She feels *bad* [or *good*].

because, due to, owing to   *Because* is used with nonlinking verbs: He was exhausted *because* of lack of sleep. *Due to* means "caused by" and may follow a linking verb: His exhaustion was *due to* lack of sleep. *Owing to* is used as a compound preposition: His policies were successful *owing to* his firm commitment to progress.

behalf   *In behalf of* and *on behalf of* have distinct senses and should not be used interchangeably. *In behalf of* means "in the interest of" or "for the benefit of": We raised money *in behalf of* the United Way. *On behalf of* means "as the agent of" or "on the part of": The lawyer signed the papers *on behalf of* the client.

beside, besides   In modern usage, the senses "in addition to" and "except for" are conveyed more often by *besides* than *beside:* We had few options *besides* the course we ultimately took. *Beside,* as a preposition, means "next to": His computer is positioned *beside* the scanner.

better, best   *Better* is used in a comparison of two: Which of the two accounting firms does the *better* job? *Best* is used to compare three or more: Which of these four methods works *best? Best* is also used idiomatically with reference to two in certain expressions: May the *best* man or woman win!

between, among   *Between* must be used when only two entities are involved: the rivalry *between* Ford and General Motors. When more than two entities are involved, the choice of *between* or *among* depends on the intended meaning. *Among* is used to indicate that an entity has been chosen from the members of a group: *Among* the three executives, Pat seems most likely to become the next president. *Among* is also used to indicate a relation of inclusion in a group: He is *among* the best engineers of our time. *Between* is used to indicate the area bounded by several points: We have narrowed the search to the area *between* Philadelphia, New York, and Scranton. In other cases, either *between* or *among* may be used. For example, one may say either that a telephone pole is lost *among* the trees (in the area of the trees) or lost *between* the trees (the trees have hidden the pole from sight).

bias   *Bias* defined as "a preference or inclination" may operate either for or against someone or something. But *bias* is now often used to refer to an unfair preference: Congress included a provision in the Civil Rights Act of 1964 banning racial *bias* in employment.

bimonthly, semimonthly   *Bimonthly* and *biweekly* mean "once every two months" and "once every two weeks." For "twice a month" and "twice a week," the words *semimonthly* and *semiweekly* should be used. But there is a great deal of confusion over the distinction, and a writer is well advised to substitute expressions such as "every two months" or "twice a month" whenever possible. However, the word *bimonthly* is unavoidable when used as a noun to mean "a publication that appears every two months."

black   When used to refer to an African-American, the noun and the adjective *black* are often capitalized. Writing authorities recommend that you avoid color labels and instead refer to a person's heritage, such as *Asian-American.*

blatant, flagrant   *Blatant* and *flagrant* are often confused. In the sense that causes the confusion, *blatant* has the meaning "totally or offensively conspicuous or obtrusive." *Flagrant* emphasizes wrong or evil that is glaring or notorious. Therefore, one who blunders may be guilty of a *blatant* (but not a *flagrant*) error; one who intentionally and ostentatiously violates a pledge commits a *flagrant* act.

born, borne   In its literal sense, the past participle *born* is used only of mammals and only in constructions with *to be:* The baby was *born*. It may also be used figuratively: A great project was *born*. *Borne,* said of the act of birth, refers only to the mother's role, but it can be used actively or passively: She has *borne* three children. Three children were *borne by* her [but not *borne to* her]. In all other senses of *bear,* the past participle is *borne:* The soil has *borne* abundant crops. Such a burden cannot be *borne* by anyone.

borrow   In many American English dialects, the expression *borrow off* is used in place of *borrow from*. This usage should be avoided, however. One writes: Gale *borrowed* $500 *from* [not *off*] the bank.

both   *Both* underscores that the activity or state denoted by a verb applies equally to two entities. Saying that *both* employees have exasperated you emphasizes that neither escapes your impatience. As such, *both* is improperly used with a verb that can apply only to two or more entities. It is illogical to say they're *both* alike, since neither could be "alike" if the other were not. Similarly, *both* is unnecessary in a sentence saying that they *both* appeared together, since neither one can "appear together" by himself or herself. The expression *the both* (the office manager gave it to *the both* of them) should be avoided. In possessive constructions, *of both* is usually preferred: the shareholders *of both* companies (rather than *both* their shareholders).

bring, take   In most American English dialects, *bring* is used to denote movement *toward* the place of speaking or the point from which the action is regarded: *Bring* the letter to me now; The newspaper *brought* good news about the economy. *Take* denotes movement away from such a place. Thus one normally *takes* checks to the bank and *brings* home cash though (from the banker's point of view, one has *brought* checks to the bank in order to *take* away cash).

but   *But* is used to mean "except" in some sentences: No one *but* a company officer can read it. In the sentence "No one *but* me can read it," *but* is treated as a preposition, and the pronoun *me* is in the objective case. *But* is redundant when combined with *however*: *But* [or *however*] the division went on with its own plans. Using *but* with a negative is unnecessary: It will take only an hour [not *but an hour*]. *But what* should also be avoided: I don't know whether [not *but what*] we'll arrive first. Don't substitute *but* for *than* in this type of sentence: It no sooner started than [not *but*] it stopped. Beginning a sentence with *but* is now widely accepted. See also and.

can, may   Traditionally, *can* has been used to express the capacity to do something and *may* to indicate permission: The supervisor said that anyone who wants an extra day off *may* have one. *May* I have that pencil? In informal speech, however, *can* is often used to express permission, and this usage is even more frequent in British English. The negative contraction *can't* is frequently used in coaxing and wheedling questions: *Can't* we have the day off?

cannot   In the phrase *cannot but*, which is criticized as a double negative, *but* is used in the sense of "except": One *cannot but* admire the takeover strategy [one cannot do otherwise than admire the strategy]. Alternative phrasings are *can but* admire, *can only* admire, *cannot help* admiring.

capital, capitol   The term for a town or city that serves as a seat of government is spelled *capital*. The term for the building in which a legislative assembly meets is spelled *capitol*. It is capitalized (*Capitol*) in reference to the seat of the U.S. Congress.

celebrant, celebrator   *Celebrant* should be reserved for an official participant in a religious ceremony or rite (the *celebrant* of a Mass). It's also considered acceptable in the general sense of "participant in a celebration": New Year's Eve *celebrants*. *Celebrator* is an acceptable alternative.

center   As an intransitive verb, *center* may be used with *on, upon, in,* or *at.* Logically, it shouldn't be used with *around,* since the word *center* refers to a point of focus: The discussion *centered on* [not *around*] the meaning of the law (with a possible alternative being *revolved around*). Some business authorities object to both *centered on* and *revolved around* in this context and prefer *involved, concerned,* or *focused on:* The discussion *focused on* the meaning of the law.

ceremonial, ceremonious   *Ceremonial* (adjective) is applicable chiefly to things; *ceremonious* (also an adjective), to persons and things. *Ceremonial* means simply "having to do with ceremony": *ceremonial* occasions; *ceremonial* garb. *Ceremonious,* when applied to a person, means "devoted to forms and ritual" or "standing on ceremony": a *ceremonious* chief of protocol.

certain   Although *certain* appears to be an absolute term (Nothing is more *certain* than death and taxes), it's frequently qualified by adverbs: *fairly* certain.

cite See quote, cite.

common See mutual, common.

compare, contrast *Compare* means "to examine something for similarity or difference" and is followed by *with* or *to*. Use *with* when you examine two things for similarities or differences: We compared our program *with* theirs. Use *to* when you compare dissimilar things: They *compared* the old mimeograph *to* a turtle. The verb *contrast* means "to show only differences." It is often followed by *with:* His views *contrast* sharply *with* his predecessor's views. The noun form is often followed by *to:* The next generation fax machines, in *contrast* to those of the previous generation, will operate at exceptionally high speeds.

complement, compliment *Complement* and *compliment,* though distinct in meaning, are sometimes confused. *Complement* means "something that completes or brings to perfection": The thick carpet was a perfect *complement* to the executive suite. *Compliment* means "an expression of courtesy or praise": We paid them a supreme *compliment* at the testimonial banquet.

complete *Complete* is generally held to be an absolute term like *perfect* or *chief,* which is not subject to comparison. It is sometimes qualified by *more* or *less,* however: A more *complete* failure I could not imagine; That book is the most *complete* treatment of the subject available today.

comprise, compose The traditional rule states that the whole *comprises* the parts, and the parts *compose* the whole: The Union *comprises* 50 states. Fifty states *compose* [*constitute; make up*] the Union. Although *comprise* is used informally, especially in the passive, in place of *compose* (The Union is *comprised* of 50 states), businesspeople should retain the traditional distinction.

continuance, continuation, continuity *Continuance* is sometimes used interchangeably with *continuation. Continuance,* however, refers to the duration of a state or condition: the president's *continuance* in office. *Continuation* applies especially to prolongation or resumption of action (a *continuation* of the board meeting) or to physical extension (the *continuation* of the railroad spur beyond our plant). *Continuity* refers to consistency over time: the *continuity* of foreign policy. The *continuity* of a story is its internal coherence from one episode to the next. The *continuation* of a story is that part of the story that takes up after a break in its recitation.

contrast See compare, contrast.

convince, persuade Traditionally, one *persuades* someone to act but *convinces* someone of the truth of a statement or proposition: By *convincing* me that no good could come of continuing the project, the director *persuaded* me to shelve it altogether. If this distinction is accepted, *convince* should not be used with an infinitive: They *persuaded* [not *convinced*] me to go.

council, counsel, consul   *Council, counsel,* and *consul* are never interchangeable, although their meanings are related. *Council* and *councilor* refer principally to a deliberative assembly, such as a city *council* and one of its members. *Counsel* and *counselor* pertain chiefly to advice and guidance and to a person who provides it: *counsel* of an attorney. *Consul* denotes an officer in the foreign service of a country: the *consul* in Bogota.

couple   *Couple,* when used to refer to a man and a woman together, may take either a singular or a plural verb. Whatever the choice, usage should be consistent: The *couple are* now finishing their joint research [*or* The *couple is* now finishing its joint research].

criteria, criterion   *Criteria* is a plural form only (*criteria* for making a decision *are*) and should not be substituted for the singular *criterion*: His *criterion is* ambiguous.

critique   *Critique* is widely used as a verb (*critique* the survey) but, as such, is regarded as pretentious jargon. The use of it as a noun in phrases such as *give a critique* or *offer a critique* is acceptable.

data   *Data* is the plural of the Latin word *datum* and may be used with either a singular or plural verb: The *data are* [*is*] nonconclusive.

debut   *Debut* is widely used as a verb, both intransitively in the sense "to make a first appearance" (The play *debuts* at our new downtown theater tonight) and transitively in the sense "to present for the first time": We will *debut* a new product line next week. However, both of these uses are widely objected to because traditionalists do not like the shift of *debut* from a noun to a verb.

depend   *Depend,* indicating condition or contingency, is always followed by *on* or *upon*: It *depends on* who is in charge. In casual speech, the preposition is sometimes omitted: It *depends* [on] who is in charge.

dilemma   *Dilemma* applies to a choice between evenly balanced alternatives, often unattractive ones: He faced the *dilemma* of choosing between a higher salary in another state or a lower salary close to home. It is not properly used as a synonym for *problem* or *predicament*: Hijacking has become a big *problem* [not *dilemma*] for our trucking subsidiary.

disinterested, uninterested   Traditionally, a *disinterested* party is one who has no stake in a dispute and is therefore presumed to be impartial. One is *uninterested* in something when one is indifferent to it. These two terms should not be used interchangeably, particularly in international correspondence.

distinct, distinctive   A thing is *distinct* if it's sharply distinguished from other things: a *distinct* honor. A property or attribute is *distinctive* if it enables us to distinguish one thing from another: This carpeting has a *distinctive* feel to it, meaning that the feel of the carpet enables us to distinguish it from other carpets. By contrast, thick-pile carpeting is a *distinct* type of floor covering, meaning that the thick-pile carpeting falls into a clearly defined category of floor coverings.

done   *Done* means "completely accomplished" or "finished": The entire project will not be *done* until next year. In some contexts, however, this use of *done* may be unclear: The work will be *done* next week. Does that mean that the work will be *finished* next week or that someone will *do* it next week? Alternatives, dependent on the meaning, would be: The work *will get done* next week; The work *will be done* by next week.

doubt, doubtful   *Doubt* and *doubtful* are often followed by clauses introduced by *that, whether,* or *if.* Often *that* is used when the intention is to express more or less complete rejection of a statement: I *doubt that* they will even try. In the negative, it's used to express more or less complete acceptance: I don't *doubt that* you are right. When the intention is to express real uncertainty, the choice is usually *whether:* We *doubt whether* they can succeed. In fact, *whether* is the traditional choice in such examples, although some experts would accept *if* (which is more informal) or *that. Doubt* is frequently used in informal speech, both as a verb and as a noun, together with *but:* I *doubt but* [or *but what*] they will come. However, *doubt but* and *doubt but what* should be avoided in business writing.

due, due to   The phrase *due to* is always acceptable when *due* functions as a predicate adjective following a linking verb: Our hesitancy was *due to* fear. But when *due to* is used as a prepositional phrase (We hesitated *due to fear*), the construction is unacceptable. Generally accepted alternatives are *because of* or *on account of.* See also because, owing to.

each   When the subject of a sentence begins with *each,* it is grammatically singular, and the verb and pronouns that follow must be singular as well: *Each* of the designers *has his or her* distinctive style. When *each* follows a plural subject, however, the verb and pronouns generally remain plural: The assistants *each have their* jobs to do. The redundant expression *each and every* should be avoided.

each other, one another   Traditionally, *each other* refers to two, and *one another* refers to more than two: Bob and Jane wrote to *each other;* The workers help *one another.* When speaking of an ordered series of events or stages, only *one another* can be used: The Caesars exceeded *one another* in cruelty, meaning that each Caesar was crueler than the previous one. *Each other* should not be used as the subject of a clause: We know what *each other* are thinking. *Better: Each of us* knows what *the other* is thinking. The possessive forms of *each other* and *one another* are written *each other's* and *one another's:* The machainists wore *each other's* hardhats.

effect   See affect, effect.

either   *Either* is primarily used to mean "one of two," although it's sometimes used for three or more: *either* corner of the triangle. When referring to more than two, *any* or *any one* is preferred. *Either* takes a singular verb: *Either* plant *grows* in the shade; I doubt whether *either* of them *is* available.

else   *Else* is often used redundantly in combination with prepositions such as *but, except,* and *besides:* No one [not *no one* else] but that witness saw the accident. When a pronoun is followed by *else,* the possessive form is generally written *someone else's,* not *someone's else.* Both *who else's* and *whose else* are used, but not *whose else's: Who else's* appointment book could it have been? *Whose else* could it have been?

emigrate   See migrate, emigrate, immigrate.

ensure   See assure, ensure, insure.

errata   The plural *errata* is sometimes used in the collective sense of a list of errors. Nevertheless, *errata* always takes a plural verb: The *errata are* noted in an attached memo.

everyplace, every place   *Everyplace* and *every place,* used adverbially for *everywhere,* are found principally in informal writing or speech: *Everyplace* [or *every place*] I go, I hear raves about our product. *Better: Everywhere* I go. *Every place,* as a combination of adjective and noun, is standard English: I searched in *every place* possible.

except   *Except* in the sense "with the exclusion of" or "other than" is generally construed as a preposition, not a conjunction. A personal pronoun that follows *except* is therefore in the objective case: No one *except* them knew it; Every member of the committee was called *except* me.

excuse   The expression *excuse away* has no meaning beyond that of *excuse* (unlike *explain away,* which has a meaning different from *explain*). *Excuse away* is unacceptable: The general manager's behavior cannot be *excused* [not *excused away*].

expect   See anticipate, expect.

explicit, express   *Explicit* and *express* both apply to something that is clearly stated rather than implied. *Explicit* applies more particularly to that which is carefully spelled out: the *explicit* terms of ownership contained in the licensing agreement. *Express* applies particularly to a clear expression of intention or will: The corporation made an *express* prohibition against dealers' selling cars below list prices.

farther, further   Traditionally, *farther* has been used for physical distance: The train backed *farther* down the line. *Further* has been used for nonphysical distance, as when referring to degree or time: *further* in debt; *further* steps to advertise our product. In some cases, however, especially in contemporary writing, either word is acceptable. One may say *further* from the truth or *farther* from the truth.

fault   *Fault* used as a transitive verb meaning "to criticize or find fault with" is now widely acceptable: One cannot *fault* management's performance; To *fault* them is unfair.

fewer, less   *Fewer,* referring to a smaller number, is correctly used in writing only before a plural noun: *fewer* reasons; *fewer* gains on the stock market. *Less,* referring to not as great an amount or quantity, is used before a mass noun: *less* music; *less* sugar; *less* material gain. *Less than* is also used before a plural noun that denotes a measure of time, amount, or distance: *less than* three weeks; *less than* 60 years old; *less than* $400.

finalize   *Finalize* is business jargon that is avoided by many careful writers: We will complete [not *finalize*] plans to remodel twelve stores this year.

firstly   *Firstly, secondly, thirdly,* and so on are less desirable substitutes for *first, second, third,* and so on.

flagrant   See blatant, flagrant.

flammable, inflammable   *Flammable* and *inflammable* mean the same thing. *Flammable* has been adopted by safety authorities for the labeling of combustible materials because the *in-* of *inflammable* was incorrectly believed by some people to mean "not": The liquid is *flammable.*

flaunt, flout   *Flaunt* and *flout* are often confused. As a transitive verb, *flaunt* means "to exhibit ostentatiously": The manager *flaunted* a corporate credit card and expense account. To *flout* is "to defy openly": They *flouted* all social conventions.

flounder   See founder, flounder.

forbid   *Forbid* may be used with an infinitive: The company *forbids* employees to smoke in the elevators. It may also be used with a gerund: They *forbid* your smoking. Avoid using it with *from:* They *forbid* your [not *forbid* you from*] smoking.

forceful, forcible, forced   *Forceful, forcible,* and *forced* have distinct, if related, meanings. *Forceful* is used to describe something that suggests strength or force: a *forceful* marketing campaign. *Forceful* measures may or may not involve the use of actual physical force. *Forcible* is most often used concerning actions accomplished by the application of physical force: There had clearly been a *forcible* entry into the storeroom; The suspect had to be *forcibly* restrained. *Forced* is used to describe a condition brought about by control or by an outside influence: *forced* labor; a *forced* landing, a *forced* smile.

former   *The former* is used when referring to the first of two persons or things mentioned: Bill and Max agreed; the *former* hesitated, however. When three or more people or items are involved, refer to the first by name: Computers, scanners, and copiers are integrated in many offices, with *computers* representing the dominant technology.

fortuitous, fortunate   *Fortuitous* is often confused with *fortunate*. *Fortuitous* means "happening by chance." *Fortunate* means "having unexpected good fortune." A *fortuitous* meeting may have either *fortunate* or *unfortunate* consequences. In common usage, some of the meaning of *fortunate* has rubbed off on *fortuitous,* so even when it's properly used, *fortuitous* often carries an implication of lucky chance rather than unlucky chance. But the word is not synonymous with *fortunate* and is best used when it refers to something that came about by chance or accident: The meeting proved *fortuitous,* and I came away with a much better idea of my responsibilities.

forward, forwards   *Forwards* should not be used in place of *forward,* except in the adverbial sense of "toward the front": move *forward* [or *forwards*]. In specific phrases, the choice of one or the other is often idiomatic: Look *forward;* from that day *forward;* backward(s) and *forward(s).*

founder, flounder   The verbs *founder* and *flounder* are often confused. *Founder* comes from a Latin word meaning "bottom" (foundation) and originally referred to knocking enemies down. It's now used to mean "to sink below the water" and "to fail utterly; collapse." *Flounder* means "to move clumsily; thrash about," and hence "to proceed in confusion." If the railroad's business between Chicago and Peoria is *foundering,* expect the line to be shut down. If the run is *floundering,* improved operating procedures and pricing policies may still save the service.

further   See farther, further.

get   *Get* has many uses, some of which are acceptable at all levels and others of which are generally thought to be informal. Avoid the use of *get* in place of *be* or *become:* The supervisors become [not *get*] angry when their assistants are late. Avoid the use of *get* or *get to* in place of *start* or *begin:* Let's start [not *get to*] work now. Also, avoid the use of *have got* or *have got to* in place of *must:* I must [not *have got to*] go now.

gift   *Gift* as a verb has traditionally been used in the sense "to present as a gift; to endow": We *gifted* the charity with a $1,000 donation. In current use, *gift* in this sense is considered affected and should be avoided. However, *gift* as a noun meaning "a present" is standard: We received your *gift*.

good, well   *Good* is used as an adjective with a linking verb, such as *be, seem,* or *appear:* The future looks *good. Well* should be used as an adverb: The plant runs *well.*

government   In American usage, *government* always takes a singular verb: The *government is* too bureaucratic. In British usage, *government,* in the sense of a governing group of officials, is usually construed as a plural collective and therefore takes a plural verb: The *government are* determined to maintain strict reins on industry.

group   *Group* as a collective noun may be followed by a singular or plural verb. It takes a singular verb when the persons or things that make up the group are considered collectively: The planning *group is* ready to present its report. *Group* takes a plural verb when the persons or things that make it up are considered individually: The *group were* divided in their sympathies.

half   The phrases *a half, half of,* and *half a* are all correct, although they may differ slightly in meaning. For example, *a half day* is used when *day* has the special sense "a working day," and the phrase then means about "4 hours." *Half of a day* and *half a day* are not restricted in this way and may therefore mean either 4 or 12 hours. When the accompanying word is a pronoun, however, the phrase with *of* must be used: *half of* them. The phrase *a half a* is unacceptable.

hardly   *Hardly* has the force of a negative. Therefore, it shouldn't be used with another negative: I could *hardly* see [not *couldn't hardly* see]. A clause following *hardly* is introduced by *when* or, less often, by *before:* We had *hardly* merged with one restaurant chain *when* [or *before*] a second chain made us an attractive offer. Such a clause is not introduced by *than,* except informally: *Hardly* had I walked inside *when* [not *than*] the downpour started.

head, headed up   The phrase *headed up* is sometimes used informally in place of the verb *head:* The committee is *headed up* by the city's most esteemed business leader. Use *head,* however, in business writing: The city's most esteemed business leader will *head* the committee.

headquarter, headquarters   The verb *headquarter* is used informally in both transitive and intransitive senses: The management consulting firm *has headquartered* its people in the New York Hyatt; Our European sales team *will headquarter* in Paris. However, both examples should be avoided in business writing. As a noun, *headquarters* is properly used with either a singular or a plural verb, although the plural is more common: Corporate *headquarters are* in Boston. The singular is sometimes preferred when reference is to authority rather than to physical location: *Headquarters has* approved the purchase of additional desktop computers for our engineers.

help　　*Help* in the sense "avoid" or "refrain from" is frequently used in an expression such as *I cannot help but think.* In formal writing, use either *I cannot help thinking* or *I cannot but think.* Another idiomatic use of *help* is exemplified by this sentence: Don't change it anymore than you can *help* [anymore than you have to]. Some grammarians condemn this usage on the ground that *help* in this sense means "avoid" and logically requires a negative.

here　　In constructions introduced by *here is* and *here are,* the number of the verb is governed by the subject, which appears after the verb: *Here is* the annual report. *Here are* the quarterly reports.

historic, historical　　*Historic* and *historical* are differentiated in usage, although their senses overlap. *Historic* refers to what is important in history: the *historic* first voyage to outer space. It's also used in regard to what is famous or interesting because of its association with persons or events in history: Edison's *historic* lab. *Historical* refers to whatever existed in the past, whether or not regarded as important: a *historical* character. Therefore, events are *historical* simply if they happened but *historic* only if they're regarded as important. *Historical* also refers to anything concerned with history or the study of the past: a *historical* society; a *historical* novel.

hopefully　　The use of *hopefully* to mean "it is to be hoped" (*Hopefully* [I hope], we'll exceed last year's sales volume) is sometimes justified by analogy to the similar uses of *happily* and *mercifully.* However, it's best to avoid using *hopefully* this way in business writing because some people consider it improper.

how　　The use of *as how* for *that* in sentences should be avoided: They said that [not *as how*] they would go. Similarly, the expressions *seeing as how* and *being as how* should be avoided.

however　　*However* is redundant in combination with *but.* One or the other should be used: We had an invitation *but* didn't go. We had an invitation; *however,* we didn't go. The use of *however* as the first word of a sentence is widely accepted.

identical　　Some authorities specify *with* as the preferred preposition after *identical.* However, either *with* or *to* is acceptable in business: a model *identical with* [or *to*] last year's.

idle *Idle* may be used in the transitive sense "to make idle." The following example is acceptable: The dock strike *had idled* many crews and their ships.

if *If* may be substituted for *whether* to introduce a clause indicating uncertainty after a verb such as *ask, doubt, know, learn,* or *see:* We shall soon learn *if* [whether] it's true. *If* should be avoided when it may be ambiguous: Please let us know *if* you agree. (Does that mean let us know *whether or not* — either way — you agree, or let us know *only if* you agree but not if you disagree?) Often, *if not* is also ambiguous: The discovery offered persuasive, *if not* conclusive, evidence. This could mean persuasive and *perhaps conclusive* or persuasive *but not conclusive.* Traditionally, the subjunctive (*if I were*) is used for a situation contrary to fact: If I *were* the president, I would [*or* should] make June 1 a national holiday. The indicative is required when the situation described by the *if* clause is assumed to be true: *If I was* [not *were*] short with you a moment ago, it's only because I wasn't paying attention. When an *if* clause is preceded by *ask* or *wonder,* use the indicative: He asked *if Napoleon was* [not *were*] a great general. Using *would have* in place of the subjunctive in contrary-to-fact *if* clauses is incorrect: *if I had* been [not *if I would have* been] promoted.

immigrate See migrate, emigrate, immigrate.

impact *Impact* as a verb may be used transitively: These taxes *impact* small businesses. Some authorities consider the use of *impact on* unacceptable.

imply See infer, imply.

important The following sentence may be written with the adjective *important:* The shareholders' opinion is evident; more *important,* it will prevail. It also may be written with an adverb: The shareholders' opinion is evident; more *importantly,* it will prevail. Most grammarians prefer the adjective form, in which *important* stands for "what is important."

impractical, impracticable *Impractical* refers to that which is not sensible or prudent: Your suggestion that we use balloons to convey messages across town is amusing but *impractical. Impracticable* applies to that which is not capable of being carried out or put into practice: Building a traditional highway to the moon is obviously *impracticable.* Therefore, a plan might be *impractical* because it involves undue cost or effort, but even if it didn't, it might still be *impracticable.* The distinction between these words is so subtle that *impractical* is often used when *impracticable* would be more precise.

infer, imply *Infer* is sometimes confused with *imply,* but the distinction between the two words is useful. To *imply* is "to state indirectly." To *infer* is "to draw a conclusion." One should therefore write: The quarterly report *implies* that sales are down because of the recession. Because of that implication, investors have *inferred* that we have something to hide, and our stock has fallen three points.

inflammable   See flammable, inflammable.

input   *Input* is technical and business jargon referring to information fed into a computer. Careful writers avoid it in other contexts, particularly in formal writing and international correspondence: The nominee declared that he had no *information* [not *input*] about the adoption of the plank on abortion.

inside, inside of   *Inside* and *inside of* have the same meaning. *Inside* is generally preferred, especially in writing, when the reference is to position or location: *inside* the warehouse. *Inside of* is used more acceptably when the reference is to time: The 300-page report was photocopied *inside of* 10 minutes. *Better:* The 300-page report was photocopied *in less than* 10 minutes.

insure   See assure, ensure, insure.

intense, intensive   *Intensive* is often used interchangeably with *intense.* However, *intensive* refers especially to the strength or concentration of an activity when imposed from without. Thus one speaks of *intense* dislike but an *intensive* study.

intrigue   *Intrigue* is fully established as a noun and a verb in all meanings except "to arouse the interest or curiosity of." In that sense, it has been resisted by some authorities, who regard it as an unnecessary French substitute for an English word such as *interest* or *fascinate.* Nevertheless, it has gained increasing acceptance, probably because no single English word has precisely the same meaning. The following usage is therefore common: The announcement of a special press conference *intrigued* the financial writers in the manner of a good suspense novel.

its, it's   *Its,* the possessive form of the pronoun *it,* is never written with an apostrophe. The contraction *it's* (for *it is* or *it has*) is always written with an apostrophe.

joint   See reciprocal, joint.

kind   The use of the plurals *these* and *those* with *kind* (*these kind* of films) has been defended by some as a sensible idiom, but it should be avoided in business writing. Substitute *this* (or *that*) *kind of* or *these* (or *those*) *kinds of,* and be certain that the following nouns and verbs agree in number with *kind: This kind of* film *has had* a lot of success in foreign markets. *Those kinds of* books *capture* the public imagination. When *kind of* is used to mean "more or less," it's properly preceded by the indefinite article *a* in formal writing: *a kind of* genius [not *kind of a* genius]. The use of *kind of* to mean "somewhat" should be avoided: We were somewhat [not *kind of*] sleepy.

kudos   *Kudos* is one of those words, like *congeries,* that looks plural but is historically singular. Therefore, it's correctly used with a singular verb: *Kudos is* due the committee for organizing a successful company picnic.

lack   As an intransitive verb meaning "to be deficient," *lack* is used chiefly in the present participle with *in:* You'll be *lacking in* support from the finance committee. In the sense "to be in need of something," it requires no preposition but is sometimes used with *for:* You'll not *lack* [or *lack for*] support from the finance committee. In that example, *lack* is preferred over *lack for.* In some cases, however, the two phrasings may convey different meanings: The millionaire *lacks* nothing [has everything imaginable]. The millionaire *lacks for* nothing [has everything he needs or wants].

latter   *Latter,* as used in contrast to *former,* refers to the second of two: Jones and Smith have been mentioned for transfer to our London office, but the *latter* [Smith] may decline the post. *Latter* is not appropriate when more than two are named. Refer to the person by name: Jones, Smith, and Kowalski were nominated, and *Kowalski* was elected.

lay, lie   *Lay,* "to put, place, or prepare," and *lie,* "to recline or be situated," are frequently confused. *Lay* is a transitive verb and takes an object. *Lay* and its principal parts (*laid, laid, laying*) are correctly used in the following examples: Please *lay* the books on the table. He *laid* the books on the table. He *has laid* the books on the table. He *was laying* the books on the table. *Lie* is an intransitive verb and does not take an object. *Lie* and its principal parts (*lay, lain, lying*) are correctly used in the following examples: She often *lies* down after lunch. When she *lay* down, she fell asleep. She *had lain* down for only a few minutes before falling asleep. She *was lying* down when the phone rang.

leave alone, let alone   *Leave alone* may be substituted for *let alone* in the sense "to refrain from disturbing or interfering": *Leave* the employees *alone,* and they'll produce. *Left alone,* they've always been productive. Those who don't accept these examples generally believe that *leave alone* should be restricted to the sense "to depart and leave one in solitude": They were *left alone* in the wilderness. In formal writing, *leave* is not an acceptable substitute for *let* in the sense "to allow or permit." Only *let* is acceptable in these examples: *Let* me be. *Let* us not quarrel. *Let* matters stand.

lend   See loan, lend.

less   See fewer, less.

let's   In colloquial speech, *let's* is sometimes used as a mere indicator that a suggestion is being proffered, and its connection with the more formal *let us* has become correspondingly attenuated. One hears usages such as *Let's us go, Don't let's get all excited,* and *Let's get* yourself ready. Such casual usage should be strictly avoided in business writing.

lie   See lay, lie.

lighted, lit   *Lighted* and *lit* are both past tense and past participle forms of *light.* Both are also well established as adjectives also: a *lighted* [or *lit*] cigarette.

like   *Like* should be avoided as a conjunction: The machine responds as [not *like*] it should. Constructions such as *looks like, sounds like,* and *tastes like* are less offensive, but *as if* should be substituted in business writing: It looks *as if* no action will be taken on the bill before Congress recesses. There is less objection to the use of *like* as a conjunction when the verb following it is not expressed: The paper said that the new senator took to politics *like* a duck [takes] to water.

likewise   *Likewise* is not a conjunction and cannot take the place of a connective such as *and* or *together with:* The mayor risked his credibility and [not *likewise* or *and likewise*] his honor.

literally   *Literally* means "in a manner that accords precisely with the words": The tornado *literally* turned the house on its side. However, it's often used as if it meant "figuratively" or "in a manner of speaking," which is contrary to its true meaning: The supervisor was *literally* spitting fire. *Better:* The supervisor was *furious.*

loan, lend   *Loan* is used as a verb, especially in business, although some hold that *lend* is the preferred form in all writing. *Lend* is preferred over *loan* in the following examples: One who *lends* money to a friend may lose the friend. When I refused to *lend* my car, I was left out of the carpool. Many phrases and figurative uses require *lend: lend* an ear; distance *lends* enchantment.

lost   The phrase *lost to* can sometimes be ambiguous: As a result of poor preparation, the court battle was *lost to* the defense attorney. Was it lost by the defendant's attorney or lost by the plaintiff's attorney to the defendant's attorney? Unless the context makes the meaning clear, the sentence should be reworded: As a result of poor preparation, the court battle was *lost by* the defense attorney.

majority   When *majority* refers to a particular number of votes, it takes a singular verb: Her *majority was* five votes. When it refers to a group of persons or things that are in the majority, it may take either a plural or singular verb, depending on whether the group is considered as a whole or as a set of people considered individually. When, for example, we refer to an election accomplished by a group as a whole, we might say: The *majority elects* the candidate it wants. When we refer to a number of individuals, we might say: The *majority* of our employees *live* within five miles of the office. *Majority* is often preceded by *great* (but not by *greater*) in emphatically expressing the sense of "most of": The *great majority has* decided not to throw good money after bad. The phrase *greater majority* is appropriate only when considering two majorities: A *greater majority* of the workers accepted this year's contract than accepted last year's.

man   Unless they are referring to a male human being, business writers should substitute a nonsexist reference for *man,* such as *one, man or woman, human, person, police officer, firefighter, humankind,* and *member of Congress:* Every *citizen* [not *man*] should have a right to work.

materialize   *Materialize* as an intransitive verb (without an object) has the primary sense "to assume material form" or, more generally, "to take effective shape": If our plans *materialize,* we'll be ready to corner the market. Although *materialize* is widely used informally in the sense "appear" or "happen," such usage should be avoided: Three more witnesses testified, but no new evidence was presented [not *materialized*].

may   See can, may.

means   In the sense "financial resources," *means* takes a plural verb: Our *means are* adequate for this acquisition. In the sense "a way to an end," it may take a singular or plural verb. The choice of a modifier such as *any* or *all* generally determines the number of the verb: *Every means was* tried; There *are* s*everal means* at our disposal.

meantime, meanwhile   *Meantime* is more common than *meanwhile* as a noun: He completed filing the papers; in the *meantime,* we made plans for an unfavorable ruling. In expressing the same sense as "in the meantime" as a single adverb, *meanwhile* is more common than *meantime:* He completed filing the papers; *meanwhile,* we made plans for an unfavorable ruling — just in case.

might   In many Southern varieties of English, *might* is used in a "double" construction with *could:* We *might could* build over there. Less frequently, one hears *may can* and *might should.* These constructions are not familiar to the majority of Americans in other regions or to individuals in other countries and hence should be avoided in business writing.

migrate, emigrate, immigrate   *Migrate* is used with reference to both the place of departure and the destination and may be followed by *from* or *to.*

It is said of persons, animals, and birds and sometimes implies a lack of permanent settlement, especially as a result of seasonal or periodic movement. *Emigrate* pertains to a single move by a person and implies permanence. It refers specifically to the place of departure and emphasizes movement from that place. If the place is mentioned, the preposition is *from:* Since many people have *emigrated from* Russia, we see a new demand for Russian-language books. *Immigrate* also pertains to a single move by persons and likewise implies permanence. However, it refers to destination, emphasizes movement there, and is followed by *to:* Many illegal aliens have *immigrated to* the United States in recent months.

minimize According to traditional grammar, *minimize* can mean only "to make as small as possible" and is therefore an absolute term, which cannot be modified by *greatly* or *somewhat:* He tried to *minimize* [not minimize somewhat] the waiting period. The modifiers *greatly* and *somewhat* are appropriately used only with verbs such as *reduce* and *lessen.* The informal use of *minimize* to mean "to make smaller than before," which can be so modified, should be avoided in business writing.

mobile See movable, mobile.

most, mostly The adverb *most* is sometimes used informally in the sense of "almost": *Most* all the clients accepted the provisions in the contract. However, this usage should be avoided in business writing. In the sense "very," as an intensive where no explicit comparison is involved, *most* is acceptable: a *most* ingenious solution. The adverb *mostly* means "for the greatest part; mainly," or "generally; usually": The trees are *mostly* evergreens. In writing, one should say: *for the most part* [not *mostly*] in sentences such as this: *For the most part,* Universal Telecom is the supplier of our communications equipment.

movable, mobile Something is *movable* if it can be moved: *movable* office furniture; a *movable* partition. It's *mobile* if it's designed for easy transportation (a *mobile* electric generating unit) or if it moves frequently (a *mobile* drilling rig).

mutual, common *Mutual* is often used to describe a relation between two or more things, and in this use, it can be paraphrased with expressions involving *between* or *each other:* their *mutual* relations, meaning "their relations with each other" or "the relations between them." *Common* describes a relationship shared by the members of a group to something else (their *common* interest in accounting) or in the expression *common knowledge,* "the knowledge shared by all." The phrase *mutual friend,* however, refers to a friend of each of the several members of a group: The business partners were originally introduced by a *mutual friend.*

nauseous, nauseated   Traditionally, *nauseous* has meant "causing nausea." *Nauseated* has meant "suffering from nausea." The use of *nauseous* in the sense of *nauseated* should be avoided: She was *nauseated* after eating in the cafeteria; His crude behavior is *nauseous*.

need   The regular form of *need* must agree with its subject and is followed by *to:* He *needs to* go. The irregular form primarily occurs in questions, negations, and *if* clauses. It doesn't agree with its subject and isn't followed by *to:* He *need* not go. *Need* it be done in a hurry? The irregular form means "to be obliged to": You *needn't* come [are under no obligation to come]. In this case, there's an externally imposed obligation on the subject *you*. If there were no externally imposed obligation, the regular form could be used: Since I was there when it happened, I don't *need* to hear the television news account.

neither   *Neither* is construed as singular when it occurs as the subject of a sentence: *Neither* of the reports *is* finished. Accordingly, a pronoun with *neither* as an antecedent also must be singular: *Neither* of the doctors in the lawsuit *is* likely to reveal his or her identity.

no   When *no* introduces a compound phrase, its elements should be connected with *or* rather than with *nor:* The candidate has *no* experience *or* interest in product development. *No* modification *or* change in operating procedures will be acceptable to them.

nominal   *Nominal* in one of its senses means "in name only." Hence a nominal payment is a token payment, bearing no relation to the real value of what is being paid for. The word is often extended in use, especially by sellers, to describe a low or bargain price: We acquired 600,000 barrels of new oil reserves at a *nominal* extra cost.

no sooner   *No sooner,* as a comparative adverb, should be followed by *than,* not *where: No sooner* had I arrived *than* I had to leave for an emergency meeting. I had *no sooner* made an offer *than* they said the property had been sold to another person.

not   Care is needed in placing *not* and other negatives in a sentence to avoid ambiguity. "All issues are *not* speculative" could be taken to mean that *no issues* are speculative or that *some* are not speculative but some are. Similarly, "we *didn't* sleep until noon" could mean that we didn't fall sleep *until noon* or that we got up sometime *before* noon. When there is any doubt, reposition the negative, or reword the sentence.

nothing   *Nothing* takes a singular verb, even when it's followed by a phrase containing a plural noun or pronoun: *Nothing* except your fears *stands* in your path.

number   As a collective noun, *number* may take either a singular or a plural verb. It takes a singular verb when it's preceded by the definite article *the: The number* of skilled workers *is* small. It takes a plural verb when it's preceded by the indefinite article *a: A number* of the workers *are* unskilled.

odd   *Odd,* when used to indicate a few more than a given number, should be preceded by a hyphen to avoid ambiguity: She had *30-odd* sales yesterday. *Odd* in that sense is used only with round numbers.

off   *Off* shouldn't be followed by *of* or *from:* The speaker stepped *off* [not *off of* or *off from*] the platform. Nor should *off* be used instead of *from* to indicate a source in a sentence: I got a loan *from* [not *off*] the credit union.

on, upon   To indicate motion toward a position, both *on* and *onto* may be used: The dog jumped *on* [or *onto*] the counter. *Onto* is more specific, however, in indicating that the motion was initiated from an outside point, such as from the floor. In constructions in which *on* is an adverb attached to a verb, it shouldn't be joined with *to* to form the single word *onto:* The meeting moved on to [not *onto*] the next subject. In their uses to indicate spatial relations, *on* and *upon* are often interchangeable: The container was setting *on* [or *upon*] the table. To indicate a relation between two things, however, instead of between an action and an end point, *upon* cannot always be used: Hand me the book *on* [not *upon*] the file cabinet. Similarly, *upon* cannot always be used in place of *on* when the relation is not spatial: We'll be in Des Moines *on* [not *upon*] Tuesday.

One another   See each other, one another.

onetime, one-time   *Onetime* (single word) means "former." *One-time* (hyphenated) means "only once." Thus a *onetime* employee is a former employee. A *one-time* mayor was mayor only once.

only   When used as an adverb, *only* must be positioned in a sentence with care to avoid ambiguity. Generally, this means placing *only* next to the word or words that it limits: Dictators respect *only* force [they don't, for example, respect words]. Dictators *only* respect force [they don't *worship* it]. She picked up the receiver *only* when he entered [never at any other time]. She *only* picked up the receiver when he entered [didn't dial a number or do anything else]. *Only* is often loosely used as a conjunction equivalent to *but* in the sense "were it not that": They would have come, *only* they were snowed in. However, this usage should be avoided in business writing.

oral   See verbal, oral.

ought   *Ought to* is sometimes used without a following verb if the meaning is clear: Should we begin soon? Yes, we *ought to.* The omission of *to* (No, we *ought* not), however, is not standard. Informal usages such as "one *hadn't ought to* come" and "one *shouldn't ought to* say that," which are common in certain varieties of American English, should be avoided in business writing.

owing to   See because, due to, owing to.

pair   *Pair* as a noun may be followed by a singular or plural verb. The singular is always used when *pair* denotes the set taken as a single entity: This *pair* [set] of shoes *is* a year old. A plural verb is used when the members are considered as individuals: The *pair* [both] *are* working more harmoniously now. After a numeral other than *one, pair* itself may be either singular or plural, but the plural is more common: Six *pairs* of stockings *are* defective.

party   A person may be called a *party* in the sense of "participant": a *party* to the industrial espionage ring. But except in legal usage, *party* should not be used as a general synonym for *person:* The *person* [not *party*] who ordered the copier is no longer with our company.

pass   The past tense and past participle of *pass* is *passed:* They *passed* [or *have passed*] by the front gate. *Past* is the corresponding adjective (in centuries *past*), adverb (drove *past*), and preposition (*past* midnight; *past* the crisis).

peer   *Peer* is sometimes misused in the sense of "a superior": That manager is the equal, if not the *peer*, of any executive on the committee. Since *peer* refers to an equal, not a superior, it's redundant to use both *equal* and *peer* in the preceding sentence. *Peer* is properly used in the expressions *peer group* and a *jury of one's peers*.

people, persons   Traditionally, *people* and *persons* have been distinguished in usage. *People* is the proper term when referring to a large group of individuals, collectively and indefinitely: *People* use a wide variety of our products at work and at home. *Persons* is applicable to a specific and relatively small number: Two *persons* were hired. In modern usage, however, *people* is also acceptable with any plural number: I counted two *people*. The possessive form is *people's* (the *people's* rights), except when *people* is used in the plural to refer to two or more groups considered to be political or cultural entities: the Slavic *peoples'* history.

per   *Per* is used with reference to statistics and units of measurement: *per* mile; *per* day; *per* person. In nontechnical writing, it's preferable to substitute *a* or *each* for *per:* a dozen persons *a* [or *each*] day. More informal, general use, such as *per the terms of this contract,* should be avoided in business writing.

percent, percentage   *Percent* is written as one word in business material and should be spelled out in nontechnical work: 20 *percent*. The number of a noun that follows it or is understood to follow it governs the number of the verb: *A conglomerate owns 20* percent *of the stock. Consumer appliances account for 47* percent *of our sales.* Percentage, *when preceded by* the, takes a singular verb: *The percentage of unskilled workers* is *small.* When it's preceded by *a,* it takes either a singular or plural verb, depending on the number of the noun in the prepositional phrase that follows: *A small percentage of the workers* are *unskilled. A large percentage of the defective press run* was *never shipped.* When the word *of* follows, *percentage,* rather than *percent,* should be used: *percentage of sales.*

perfect, perfectly *Perfect* has been traditionally considered an absolute term, like *unique, chief,* and *prime,* and therefore has not been subject to comparison with *more, less, almost,* and other modifiers of degree. The comparative form nonetheless is used in the United States Constitution in the phrase *a more perfect union.* Although logically, something that's already *perfect* cannot be more so, it's generally regarded as correct to make comparisons when *perfect* is used to mean "ideal for the purposes": *A more perfect* spot for our broadcasting station could not be found. *Perfectly* is used informally as a mere intensive denoting "quite," "altogether," or "just": *perfectly* good; *perfectly* dreadful. However, this casual use should be avoided in business writing.

permit *Permit of* is sometimes used to mean "to allow for": *permits of* two interpretations. However, this usage should be avoided in business writing.

person *Person* is increasingly used to create compounds that may refer to either a man or a woman: *chairperson; salesperson; serviceperson.* These forms may be used when one is referring to the position itself, regardless of who might hold it: *The company should appoint a new* spokesperson. They're also appropriate when speaking of the specific individual holding the position: *She was the best* anchorperson *the local station had ever had.* In such cases, referring to *he* or *she,* the alternatives *anchorwoman* and *anchorman* would also be acceptable and might be preferred by the holder of the position.

persons See people, persons.

personality *Personality,* meaning "a celebrity" or "a notable," is widely used in speech and journalism. However, it should be avoided in this sense in business writing.

persuade See convince, persuade.

plead In strict legal usage, one is said to *plead* guilty or not guilty but not to *plead* innocent. In nonlegal contexts, however, *plead innocent* is sometimes used.

plus When *plus* is used after a singular or plural subject, the verb traditionally remains singular: Two *plus* two equals four. Our production efficiency *plus* their excellent distribution system *gives* us a competitive advantage. *Plus* is sometimes used loosely as a conjunction to connect two independent clauses: We had terrible weather this year, *plus* the recession affected us adversely. However, this use should be avoided in business writing.

P.M. See ante meridian.

poor In correct usage, *poor* should be used as an adjective, not an adverb: a *poor* person. It should not be used to qualify a verb: *did poor; never worked poorer. Poorly* and *more poorly* are required in such cases.

practical, practicable *Practical* describes that which is sensible and useful: a *practical* [sensible] approach. *Practicable* means "usable" and "workable": Your idea is *practicable* [will work]. The distinction, however, is often subtle, and many writers use *practical* in both cases. This example illustrates the traditional distinction: It might be *practicable* [could be done] to build a bullet train between New York and Omaha, but it would not be *practical* [sensible].

practically, virtually The primary sense of *practically* is "in a way that is practical": handle the project *practically*. It has also become almost interchangeable with *virtually,* meaning "in fact or to all purposes": The city was *practically* [or *virtually*] paralyzed by the strike. Thus a man whose liabilities exceed his assets may be said to be *practically* bankrupt, even though he has not legally been declared insolvent. By a slight extension of this meaning, *practically* is often used to mean "nearly" or "all but": They had *practically* closed the deal by the time I arrived. However, such use should be avoided in business writing.

precipitate, precipitant, precipitous *Precipitate* (and *precipitately*) often refers to rash, overhasty human actions: a *precipitate* decision. *Precipitant* (and *precipitantly*) is also used in the foregoing sense, with stress on rushing forward or falling headlong (literally or figuratively): *precipitant* action. *Precipitous* (and *precipitously*) is used primarily in reference to physical steepness (a *precipitous* slope) or in the figurative extensions of such literal uses (a *precipitous* drop in interest rates).

premiere *Premiere* is primarily used as a noun meaning "the first public performance": the *premiere* of the new movie. It's generally unacceptable as a verb, despite its wide use in the world of entertainment.

presently *Presently* is used primarily in the sense "soon": She'll arrive *presently*. It's also used in the sense "at the present time": He's *presently* [now] living in Chicago. Writers who use the word should be certain that the meaning is clear from the context.

principle, principal   *Principal* and *principle* are often confused but have no meanings in common. *Principle* is only a noun, and all its senses are abstract: *principles* of nuclear physics. *Principal* is both a noun and an adjective. As a noun (aside from its specialized meaning in law and finance), it generally denotes a person who holds a high position or plays an important role: a meeting between all *principals* in the transaction. As an adjective, it has the related sense "chief" or "leading": *principal* candidates.

protagonist   *Protagonist* denotes the leading figure in a theatrical drama or, by extension, in any work or undertaking. Sometimes in modern usage, the sense of singularity is lost: There are three *protagonists* in the takeover fight. This watered-down meaning should be avoided. *Protagonist* is sometimes also used to indicate a champion or advocate, another usage that should be avoided.

prove, proved, proven   The regular form *proved* is the preferred past participle: You have *proved* your point. The theory *has been proved* by our physicists. In such examples, the alternative, *proven*, is unacceptable to many experts. *Proven* is a Scots variant made familiar through its legal use: The charges *were* not *proven*. But *proven* is more widely used as an adjective directly before a noun: a *proven* talent; a *proven* point.

quick, quickly   Both *quick* and *quickly* are used as adverbs. *Quick* is more frequent in conversation: Come *quick!* In writing, *quickly* is preferred: When the signal was relayed to our parts center, we responded *quickly.* In the latter example, *quick* would be unacceptable to most grammarians.

quote, cite   *Quote* is appropriate when words are being given exactly as they were originally written or spoken: He *quoted* the first paragraph of the report. When the reference is less exact, *cite* is preferable: He *cited* an advertising study. *Quote* as a substitute for *quotation* should be avoided: the *quotation* [not *quote*] from Milton.

raise, rise   *Raise* is properly used as a transitive verb (with an object): *Raise* the loading bay doors. For intransitive (no object) uses, *rise* is standard: The platform *rises*. However, *raise* is sometimes used as an intransitive verb: The window *raises* easily. *Raise*, rather than *rise*, is now standard in the United States for an increase in salary, although one still speaks of a *rise* in prices.

rare, scarce   *Rare* and *scarce* are sometimes interchangeable, but *scarce* carries an additional implication that the quantities involved are insufficient or inadequate. Thus we speak of *rare* books or of the *rare* qualities of someone we admire, but we refer to increasingly *scarce* oil reserves.

rarely, seldom   The use of *ever* after *rarely* or *seldom* is considered redundant: He *rarely* [not *rarely ever*] makes a mistake. The following constructions, using either *rarely* or *seldom,* are standard, however: *rarely if ever; rarely or never* [not *rarely or ever*].

rather   *Rather* is usually preceded by *should* or *would* in expressing preference: They *would rather* not diversify the company. But *had* is equally acceptable: I *had rather* be dead than be unemployed. In a contraction such as *he'd,* either *would* or *had* can be understood: *He'd rather* [He would *or* had rather] be dead than be unemployed. As a modifier, *rather* is frequently unnecessary and overused: *rather* nice; *rather* cold; *rather* important.

reciprocal, joint   *Reciprocal,* like *mutual,* described earlier, may apply to relations between the members of a group, often with reference to an exchange of goods or favors: *reciprocal* trade. *Joint* is often used to describe an undertaking in which several partners are involved: The *joint* efforts of federal and local officials will be required to eradicate acid rain.

refer, reference   See allude/allusion, refer/reference.

regard, respects   *Regard* is traditionally singular in the phrase *in* (or *with*) *regard to* (but not *in regards to*). *Regarding* and *as regards* are used in the same sense as "with reference to" but are not as widely acceptable. In the same sense, *with respect to* is acceptable, but *respecting* is not. *Respects* is sometimes preferable to *regards* in the sense of "particulars": *In some respects* [not *regards*], we're similar to our competition.

relatively   *Relatively* is appropriate when a comparison is stated or implied: The first question was *relatively* easy (that is, in comparison to the others). *Relatively* should not be used to mean simply "fairly": I'm fairly [not *relatively*] sure of it.

repel, repulse   The verbs *repel* and *repulse* both have the physical sense of "to drive back or off." They also may apply to rebuffing or rejecting discourteously, but only *repel* is used in the sense of "to cause distaste or aversion": Your arrogance *repelled* us. He *repulsed* with rudeness all our attempts to help him.

replete   *Replete* means "abundantly supplied": a takeover battle *replete* with scandal, mudslinging, and threats. It shouldn't be used to mean simply "complete" or "equipped": a club complete [not *replete*] with pool, tennis courts, and golf courses.

responsible   Some usage experts believe that *responsible* should be used only with reference to persons, since only persons can be held accountable. The word is widely used, however, with reference to things: Defective welding was *responsible* for the buckled axle.

restive, restless   *Restive* and *restless* are used as equivalent terms. *Restive,* however, implies more than simply "nervous" or "fidgety." It implies resistance to some sort of restraint. Thus a patient who is sleeping poorly may be *restless,* but the same patient is *restive* only if the person is kept in bed against his or her will.

rise   See raise, rise.

sacrilegious   The adjective *sacrilegious* is often misspelled through confusion with *religious.* It refers to gross irreverence toward something sacred: His profanity in church was *sacrilegious.*

said   As an adjective, *said* is seldom appropriate to any but legal writing, where it is equivalent to *aforesaid:* the *said* [aforesaid] tenant (named in a lease); *said* [aforesaid] property. In similar contexts in general usage, *said* should be omitted: the tenant; the property.

same   Only in legal writing is *the same* or just *same* used as a substitute for *it* or *them.* In general writing, one should be specific: The charge is $5. Please send your payment [not *the same*] today.

scarce   See rare, scarce.

scarcely   *Scarcely* has the force of a negative. Therefore, it's not properly used with another negative: I could scarcely [not *couldn't scarcely*] believe it. A clause following *scarcely* is introduced by *when* or, less often, by *before* but not by *than:* The meeting had *scarcely* begun *when* [or *before*] it was interrupted.

seasonal, seasonable   *Seasonal* and *seasonable,* though closely related, are differentiated in usage. *Seasonal* applies to what depends on or is controlled by the season of the year: a *seasonal* rise in unemployment. *Seasonable* applies to what is appropriate to the season (*seasonable* clothing) or timely (a *seasonable* intervention in the dispute). Rains are *seasonal* if they occur at a certain time of the year. They're *seasonable* at any time if they save the crops.

see that   The phrase *see where* sometimes occurs in conversation as an informal equivalent of *see that:* I *see that* [*see where*] everything is running smoothly at the office. The same applies to *read where.* However, these informal usages should be avoided in business writing.

seldom   See rarely, seldom.

semimonthly   See bimonthly, semimonthly.

set, sit   Originally, *set* meant "to cause (something) to sit," so it's now in most cases a transitive verb: The worker *set* his shovel down. She *set* the table. *Sit* is generally an intransitive verb: He *sits* at the microphone.

However, some exceptions exist: The sun *sets* [not *sits*]. A hen *sets* [or *sits*] on her eggs.

shall, will   In formal writing, *shall* is used in the first person to indicate futurity: I *shall* leave tomorrow. In the second and third persons, the same sense of futurity is expressed by *will:* He *will* come this afternoon. Use of the auxiliaries *shall* and *will* is reversed when the writer wants to indicate conditions, such as determination, promise, obligation, command, compulsion, permission, or inevitability: I *will* leave tomorrow. In informal, contemporary writing, *will* is used in all three persons to indicate futurity: We *will* be in New York next week. *Shall* is still used in first-person interrogatives (*Shall* we go? Where *shall* we have our sales conference this year?) and in a few set phrases (We *shall* overcome). A condition other than mere futurity is often expressed more clearly by an alternative to *shall* or *will*, such as *must* or *have to* (indicating determination, compulsion, or obligation) or by use of an intensifying word, such as *certainly* or *surely*, with *shall* or *will*. Informally, contractions such as *I'll, we'll*, and *you'll* are generally used without distinction between the functions of *shall* and *will* as formally defined.

should, would   Traditionally, the rules governing the use of *should* and *would* have been based on the rules governing the use of *shall* and *will*. These rules have been relaxed even more in the case of *should* and *would*. Either *should* or *would* is now used in the first person to express conditional futurity: If I had known that, I *would* [or *should*] have made a different reply. In the second and third persons, only *would* is acceptable: If he had known that, he *would* have made a different reply. *Would* cannot always be substituted for *should*, however. *Should* is used in all three persons in a conditional clause: if I [or you; he or she] *should* decide to go. *Should* is also used in all three persons to express duty or obligation (the equivalent of *ought to*): I [or you; he or she] *should* go. *Would* is used to express volition or promise: I agreed that I *would* do it. Either *would* or *should* is possible as an auxiliary verb with *like, be inclined, be glad, prefer*, and related verbs: I *would* [or *should*] *like* to call your attention to an oversight in the accountant's report. But *would* is more common than *should*. *Should have* is sometimes incorrectly written *should of* by writers who have mistaken the source of the spoken contraction *should've*.

since   See as, since.

sit   See set, sit.

slow, slowly   *Slow* is used as a colloquial or an informal variant of the adverb *slowly* when it comes after the verb: We drove the car *slow*. But *slowly* should be used in business writing. *Slow* is also often used informally when brevity and forcefulness are sought: Drive *slow! Slow* is the established idiomatic form with certain senses of common verbs: The watch runs *slow.* Take it *slow.* It, too, should be avoided in business writing.

so   The conjunction *so* is followed by *that* when it introduces a clause stating the purpose of or reason for an action: The supervisor stayed late *so that* [in order that] he could catch up on his paperwork. *So* can stand alone, however, when it is used to introduce a clause that states the result or consequence of something: The canning process kills much of the flavor of the food, *so* salt is added.

so . . . as   See as . . . as, so . . . as.

sometime   *Sometime* as an adjective is properly used to mean "former." It's also used colloquially with the meaning "occasional": the team's *sometime* pitcher. This latter use, however, should be avoided in business writing.

stratum   The standard singular form is *stratum.* The standard plural is *strata* and, less commonly, *stratums* (but not *stratas*).

take   See bring, take.

tend   *Tend* is an informal variant of *attend* in the phrase *tend to,* meaning "to apply one's attention to": A special session of the legislature has been called to *tend to* [attend to] the question of a windfall profits tax. This usage should be avoided in international correspondence.

than, as   In comparisons, a pronoun following *than* or *as* may be taken as either the subject or the object of a "missing" verb whose sense is understood: John is older *than* I [am]. The nominative *I* is required since the verb *am* is implied. *But:* It doesn't surprise me as much *as* [it surprises] him.

this, that   *This* and *that* are both used as demonstrative pronouns to refer to a thought expressed earlier: The door was unopened; *that* [or *this*] in itself casts doubt on the guard's theory. *That* is sometimes the better choice in referring to what has gone before (as in the preceding example). When the referent is yet to be mentioned, only *this* should be used: *This* is what bothers me — we have no time to consider late applications. *This* is often used in speech as an emphatic variant of the indefinite article *a: This* friend of mine inquired about working here. I have *this* terrible headache. However, such informal usage should be avoided in business writing.

tight   *Tight* as an adverb appears after the verb when it follows verbs such as *squeeze, shut, close, tie,* and *hold:* hold on *tight;* close it *tight.* In most cases, the adverb *tightly* also may be used in this position: close it *tightly.* In a few cases, *tight* is the only form that may be used: sit *tight;* sleep *tight.* Before a verb, only *tightly* should be used: The money supply will be *tightly* controlled.

together with   *Together with*, like *in addition to*, is often employed following the subject of a sentence or clause to introduce an addition. The addition, however, does not alter the number of the verb, which is governed by the subject: The senator [singular], *together with* two aides, *is* expected in an hour. The same is true of *along with, as well as, besides, in addition to*, and *like*: Common sense *as well as* training *is* a requisite for a good job.

too   *Too* preceded by *not* or another negative is frequently used informally as a form of understatement to convey humor or sarcasm: The workers were not *too* pleased with the amount of their raises. This applicant is not *too* computer literate. *Not too*, when used to mean "not very," is also considered informal: Passage of the bill is *not* now considered *too* likely. However, such informal usage should be avoided in business writing. *Too* can often be eliminated from such sentences without loss, but if deletion gives undue stress to the negative sense, you may find *not very* or *none too* preferable choices: The applicant is *not very* computer literate.

torn   *Torn*, never *tore*, is the standard past participle of the verb *tear*. I have *torn* the book.

tortuous, torturous   Although *tortuous* and *torturous* have a common Latin source, their primary meanings are distinct. *Tortuous* means "twisting" (a *tortuous* road) or by extension "extremely strained or devious" (*tortuous* reasoning). *Torturous* refers primarily to the pain of torture. However, *torturous* also can be used in the sense of "twisted" or "strained," and *tortured* is an even stronger synonym: *tortured* reasoning.

transpire   *Transpire* has long been used in the sense "to become known": It soon *transpired* that they intended to gain a controlling interest in the corporation. The meaning "to happen" or "to take place" has come into use more recently: The board wondered what would *transpire* next. This latter use, however, should be avoided in business writing, particularly in international correspondence.

try and, try to   *Try and* is common in informal conversation for *try to*, especially in established combinations such as *try and stop me* and *try and get some rest*. In most contexts, however, it's not interchangeable with *try to* unless the level is clearly informal. In business writing, *try to* is appropriate: It's a mistake to *try to* [not *try and*] force compliance with a regulation that's so unpopular.

type   *Type* is followed by *of* in constructions such as *that type of leather*. The variant form in which *of* is omitted, as in *that type leather*, is generally unacceptable. *Type* is most appropriate when reference is being made to a well-defined or sharply distinct category: that *type* of chassis; this *type* of pain reliever. When the categorization is vaguer or less well accepted, *kind* or *sort* is preferable. See also kind.

under way   See way, under way.

unexceptional, unexceptionable   *Unexceptional* is often confused with *unexceptionable.* When the desired meaning is "not open to objection" or "above reproach," the term is *unexceptionable: unexceptionable* arguments. *Unexceptional* should be used to mean "not exceptional": an *unexceptional* student.

uninterested   See disinterested, uninterested.

upon   See on, upon.

various   *Various,* sometimes appearing as a collective noun followed by *of,* is unacceptable usage: He spoke to *various* [not *various of*] the members. *Various* is correct in the sense "of diverse kinds": for *various* reasons.

verbal, oral   In the sense "by word of mouth," *verbal* is synonymous with *oral.* In other senses, *verbal* has to do with words, whether written or spoken: *verbal* communication (as opposed to communication by body language, for example). *Verbal,* when applied to terms such as *agreement, promise, commitment,* and *understanding,* is well established as a synonym of *oral.* However, to avoid ambiguity, use *oral:* an *oral* [verbal] agreement.

virtually   See practically, virtually.

wait on, wait for   *Wait on* is correctly used in the sense "to serve": *wait on* customers in the restaurant. *Wait for* is used to mean "awaiting": We'll *wait for* the purchaser's decision.

want   When *want* and an infinitive are separated in a sentence, *for* is used: What I *want* is *for* you to finish that letter first. I *want* very much *for* you to take the company's offer. In other cases, *for* should not be used: I *want* to go to the exhibit next month.

-ward, -wards   Since the suffix *-ward* indicates direction, there's no need to use *to* with it: The cargo ship is sailing *westward* [or *to the west*].

way, under way   *Way,* not *ways,* is the generally accepted form in writing when the term refers to distance: a long *way* to go. The phrase *underway,* meaning "in motion" or "in progress," may be written as one word or two: The project is *under way* [or *underway*].

well   See good, well.

what   When *what* is the subject of a clause, it's singular if it's taken as equivalent to *that which* or *the thing which: What* seems to be a mechanical problem in the stamping equipment *is* creating defective panels. It is plural if it is equivalent to *those which* or *the things which: What were* at first minor incidents *have become* major problems in the chemical disposal system. In other cases, when a *what* clause is the subject of a sentence, it's usually plural if the clause indicates plurality. Since the conditions governing this choice are complicated, consult an authority, such as *The American Heritage Dictionary of the English Language,* for further information.

whatever   *Whatever* (pronoun) and *what ever* (two words) are used in questions and statements: *Whatever* [or *what ever*] made them say that? Both forms are used, although the one-word form is more common. (The same is true of *whoever, whenever, wherever,* and *however* when used in corresponding senses.) As an adjective, only the one-word form is used: Take *whatever* office supplies you need. When the phrase preceding a restrictive clause is introduced by *whatever, that* should not be used. *Whatever* book [not *whatever book that*] you want to look at will be sent to your office.

where   When *where* refers to "the place *from* which," it requires the preposition *from: Where* did you come *from?* When it refers to "the place *to* which," no preposition is needed: *Where* did they go [not go *to*]? Also, when *where* refers to "the place *at* which" no preposition is needed: *Where* are they [not where are they *at*]?

which   *Which* sometimes refers to an entire preceding statement rather than to a single word: The drilling failed to turn up any new reserves, *which* disturbed the geologist. In this acceptable example, the reference is clear. However, when *which* follows a noun, the antecedent may be in doubt and ambiguity may result: The inspector filed the complaint, *which* was a surprise. If *which* is intended to refer to the entire first clause rather than to the complaint, the desired sense would be expressed more clearly by this construction: We learned that the inspector had filed the complaint, *and that discovery* came as a surprise to us.

whose   *Whose,* as the possessive form of a relative pronoun, can refer to both persons and things. Thus it functions as the possessive of both *who* and *which.* The following example, in which *whose* refers to an inanimate object, is acceptable: The car, *whose* design is ultramodern, is typical of the new styles. The alternative possessive form *of which* is also used in referring to things but is sometimes cumbersome in application.

why   *Why* is redundant in *the reason why:* The reason [not reason *why*] they opposed the new policy is not clear. The sentence could also be recast: Their reasons for opposing the new policy are not clear.

will   See shall, will.

win   *Win* used as a noun in the sense of "victory" or "success" is frequently seen in sports reporting and other informal contexts. However, it shouldn't be used in this sense in business writing: An impressive *victory* [not *win*] in the primary would strengthen his position greatly.

-wise   The suffix *-wise* has long been used to mean "in the manner or direction of": *clockwise, likewise, otherwise,* and *slantwise.* It's particularly overused as business jargon meaning "with relation to" and is excessively attached to a variety of nouns: *saleswise, inflationwise, interestwise.* Generally considered vague and pretentious, the *-wise* suffix should be avoided in all forms of domestic and international communication: The report is not encouraging in terms of potential sales [not *saleswise*]. For tax savings [not *Taxwise*] however, it's an attractive arrangement.

with   *With* does not have the conjunctive force of *and.* Consequently, in the following example, the verb is governed by the singular subject and remains singular: The governor, *with* his aides, is expected at the trade show on Monday.

would   See should, would.

wreak   *Wreak* is sometimes confused with *wreck,* perhaps because the *wreaking* of damage may leave a *wreck:* The storm *wreaked* havoc along the coast. The past tense and past participle forms of *wreak* are *wreaked,* not *wrought,* which is an alternative past tense and past participle of *work:* The Bible says God *wreaked* punishment on sinners, and Samuel F. B. Morse properly asked, "What hath God *wrought?*"

Cliches

Although many cliches began as proverbs representing the wisdom of various cultures, their overuse has rendered them stale and ineffective. Because of this, they're viewed as trite expressions that weaken messages and make the writer appear unimaginative and unprofessional. They're especially troublesome in international correspondence since foreign readers tend to translate everything literally. Office professionals can be of immense help to their employers by remaining alert to cliches that may inadvertently be used in conventional and electronic messages. The following list contains examples of the kinds of expressions that should never be used in business:

a little (of that) goes a long way	all in the same boat
add insult to injury	all/other things being equal
agonizing reappraisal	all things considered
agree to disagree	all things to all men/people
albatross around one's neck	all work and no play
all in a day's work	armed to the teeth
all in all	as luck would have it

as the crow flies
at/never at a loss for words
at this point in time
ax to grind
bag and baggage
battle royal
beat a dead horse
beat a hasty retreat
beat around the bush
beg to disagree
bend/lean over backwards
best foot forward
best-laid plans
best of all possible worlds
best of both worlds
better late than never
bite off more than one can chew
bite the bullet
black-and-white issue
boggle the mind
bolt from the blue
bone of contention
bright future
budding genius
by leaps and bounds
by the same token
case in point
clear as a bell
clear as mud
dead giveaway
dead in the water
die is cast
draw the line
easier said than done
far be it from me
few and far between
few well-chosen words
fill the bill
first and foremost
food for thought
foot in the door
foot the bill
foregone conclusion
frame of reference

get a jump on the competition
get down to brass tacks
get one's feet wet
get/start the ball rolling
graphic account
grind to a halt
handwriting on the wall
hard row to hoe
have a foot in the door
high and dry
hit the nail on the head
in no uncertain terms
in one fell swoop
in on the ground floor
in the final/last analysis
in the long run
it goes without saying
it is interesting to note
it stands to reason
keep a low profile
last but not least
leave no stone unturned
let well enough alone
light at the end of the tunnel
make a long story short
meaningful dialogue
method in one's madness
mince words
miss the boat
moment of truth
moot question/point
more easily said than done
more than meets the eye
necessary evil
needs no introduction
neither here nor there
no sooner said than done
not worth its salt
nothing new under the sun
of a high order
on the ball/stick
on the other hand
open and shut case
opportunity knocks

other side of the coin
over a barrel
part and parcel
pillar to post
plain and simple
play hardball
play it by ear
pull no punches
put best foot forward
red-letter day
render a decision
rest assured
save for a rainy day
second to none
shot in the arm
show one's hand
small world
strictly speaking
sweet smell of success
take a dim view of
take a raincheck

take it easy
take the bull by the horns
take with a grain of salt
that is to say
throw caution to the wind
tip the scales
too little, too late
tried and true
uncharted waters
up to one's ears
usually reliable source(s)
viable option
view with alarm
wash one's hands of
well worth one's while/trouble
when all is said and done
when you come right down to it
without a doubt
without further ado
worst-case scenario

Redundant Expressions

Redundancy—needless repetition of words and ideas—is one of the principal obstacles to preparing clear, precise prose. The following list gives some common redundant expressions. The elements that are italicized in the phrases should be deleted:

advance planning
anthracite *coal*
ascend *upward*
assemble *together*
basic fundamental
big *in size*
bisect *in two*
blend *together*
capitol *building*
chief/leading/main protagonist
close *proximity*
coalesce *together*
collaborate *together/jointly*
completely unanimous
congregate *together*
connect *together*

consensus *of opinion*
continue to persist
courthouse *building*
current/present incumbent
descend *downward*
doctorate *degree*
endorse a check *on the back*
erupt *violently*
explode *violently*
fellow colleague
few *in number*
first beginning
founder *and sink*
free gift
from whence
fuse *together*

gather *together*
habitual custom
hoist *up*
individual person
join *together*
knots *per hour*
large *in size*
merge *together*
necessary *need*
new innovation
new recruit
old antique
opening gambit
original prototype
passing fad
past history

pointed barb
protrude *out*
real fact
recall *back*
recoil *back*
recur *again/repeatedly*
revert *back*
short *in length/height*
shuttle *back and forth*
skirt *around*
small *in size*
tall *in height*
temporary reprieve
two twins
universal panacea
visible *to the eye*

Correspondence

Office professionals spend substantial time every day preparing electronic and traditional correspondence. They may compose and send their own messages or create messages for someone else. They also may edit long report-style messages drafted by their supervisors. In each case, both the physical appearance of the message (format, neatness, and overall visual impact) and content (accuracy, tone, clarity, and general effectiveness) will determine how favorably or unfavorably the recipient will view the sender and his or her company. Correspondence, therefore, has a major impact on an organization's image and its dealings with customers, clients, and the public.

Although no one denies the crucial role that correspondence has in modern business, the pressure of an overfilled workday leads many busy businesspeople to conclude that they don't have time for the traditional niceties of correspondence. Yet a confusing, terse, or unattractive communication may cost the company more in lost business than the writer saves in time by rushing with his or her correspondence. In many companies, in fact, management spends considerable time trying to win back customers who went elsewhere because they were offended by an employee's abrupt, rude message or by the employee's failure to respond at all.

Communication experts agree that the business world is moving at an extraordinarily rapid pace and that employees have too much to do and too little time to do it. Nevertheless, they believe that poorly written messages are unnecessary, that it's a bogus excuse to say that one doesn't have time to be polite or careful. Rather, they argue that it takes no more time to say something politely and to construct a message the right way than it takes to say something impolitely and craft a message the wrong way. This chapter presents information that should make it easier for busy communicators to handle their correspondence "the right way."

STATIONERY

Traditional mail is sometimes used in place of electronic mail for messages that must be prepared in paper form and sent in a sealed envelope, such as an important letter of agreement (contract). The selection of stationery is therefore as important today as it was in the past, and quality stationery still reflects a company's concern about its public image. Since office professionals are usually responsible for ordering stationery and sometimes help to select the paper, it's helpful to learn something about weight, texture, and color. A printer who handles stationery (letterhead, business cards, and so on) can be very helpful, and you shouldn't hesitate to ask for detailed information before placing an order.

Letterhead

The paper you select for your traditional letter and memo stationery will probably be used in a laser or ink-jet printer. It may also be used in your office copier or your fax machine. (See the descriptions of equipment in Chapter 1, "The Online Office," Basic Technologies.) Most manufacturers recommend a 20- or 24-pound weight for these machines, and paper manufacturers designate the appropriate uses on the packages of paper. (Paper weight refers to the weight in pounds of one ream, or about 500 sheets, cut to standard size.) If the paper is too light, it may not be strong enough to feed properly. If it's too heavy, the thickness may cause paper jams.

Since stationery is often folded to fit into a standard No. 10 envelope (about 4 1/8 by 9 1/8 inches), it should form a clean, even crease. (See Envelope Formats.) Also, the ink from the printed letterhead must not bleed through to the reverse side. The color and texture must allow the printed characters and handwritten signatures to be clean and clear, without blotches.

Letterhead should be printed on the felt side of the paper — the side from which you can read the watermark (a marking or design in quality paper that is visible when held up to the light). All continuation sheets and envelopes should match the letterhead in color, texture, and weight.

Business Cards

Business cards may be prepared in any format desired, and they may be printed with any color combination and on any size card stock (heavy paper), although 3½ by 2 inches is a standard wallet size. Executives usually select a somewhat conservative style, often an off-white card, dark ink, and a traditional arrangement of data. For example, the person's name may be placed in the middle of the card, with the job title, department, and firm name in the lower left corner. The street address, e-mail address, telephone-fax numbers, and website may be in the lower right corner. Staff members may have their firm names, rather than their own names, in the center. Cards used internationally should have the data duplicated on the reverse side in the language of the country (avoid abbreviations on that side of the card). For further ideas, look at the many samples that printers display, and follow the preference of your employer.

Commercial Cards

Although a personally prepared message is good public relations and is always appropriate, commercial cards, with generic printed messages, may be used for certain informal occasions, such as for sending holiday greetings. Even then, however, it's important to add a few handwritten words beneath the printed message and to sign one's name beneath the printed company name.

Commercial cards for business use are available in office-supply stores, certain stationery stores, and other retail outlets. In addition, various websites have a wide selection of styles and e-messages. With the right software, you can also create and print your own cards in-house.

COMMON FORMATS

Letter Formats

For traditional, hard-copy letters, the three most common business formats are the full-block, modified-block, and simplified-block formats. A personal style, used on smaller-size, personal (noncompany) stationery, is appropriate for certain personal or social business letters, such as a thank you for a gift or a sympathy message to a coworker or customer. This type of letter may be prepared in either a full-block or modified-block style, according to preference. Some companies also use a variation of one of the three standard formats or a combination of two or more formats.

The models in this chapter (Full-Block Format, Modified-Block Format, and Simplified-Block Format) indicate their principal differences and format specifications, such as the proper line spacing to use between elements. Once you've selected a format (if your employer has no preferred format), store the specifications, described in the following sections, in your computer as a template for future use.

Major Parts of a Letter

The major parts of a traditional business letter—usually presented in the following order—are the date, confidential notation, inside address, attention line, salutation, subject, body, complimentary close, signature,

COMPANY LETTERHEAD

February 4, 2001

Mr. William C. Cross
ABC Chemicals Ltd.
321 Park Avenue East
City, ST 98765

Dear Mr. Cross:

FULL-BLOCK LETTER FORMAT

This is a full-block letter format, featuring all elements aligned with the left margin.

The date is placed two or more lines below the letterhead, and the inside address begins three or more lines below the date. The salutation appears two lines below the inside address and the subject two lines below the salutation. The body begins two lines below the subject. The complimentary close is placed two lines below the last line of the message body, and the printed signature is about four lines beneath it.

Concluding notations may be single- or double-spaced, depending on available space.

Sincerely,

John M. Swanson
Executive Vice President

rs

Encs.: 4

cross.ltr

Full-Block Format

COMPANY LETTERHEAD

1-PAGE FAX TO 800-555-6543

February 4, 2001

Dr. David J. Peters
State Insurance Corporation
4556 Hightower Boulevard
City, ST 98765

Dear Dr. Peters:

MODIFIED-BLOCK LETTER FORMAT

This is a modified-block letter format, which is a more traditional style than the full-block format. The date, complimentary close, and signature block are all aligned at or just past the center of the page.

A fax notation may be placed at the top of the letter or with the other end-of-letter notations. When it's placed at the top, the date begins two lines below the notation, and the inside address and salutation are positioned as they would be in a full-block format. The subject, however, is indented.

Except that the complimentary close and signature block are aligned under the date, at or just past the page center, the spacing is the same as that used in the full-block format. Concluding notations may be single- or double-spaced.

Cordially,

Donna W. Reardon
Human Resources Manager

Enc.: Brochure

cc: Jim Hartley

Modified-Block Format

COMPANY LETTERHEAD

February 4, 2001

Ms. Barbara C. Mackie
HCI Corporation
One State Street
City, ST 98765

SIMPLIFIED-BLOCK LETTER FORMAT

Ms. Mackie, this is a model of the simplified format. It's a clean, modern style designed for easy formatting and composition.

The date is flush with the left margin two or more lines beneath the letterhead. The inside address, also flush left, is two or more lines below the date. The salutation is omitted in this format, but the addressee's name is often mentioned in the first and last paragraphs to personalize the letter.

The subject is placed three lines below the inside address, and the message begins three lines after that. Since there's no complimentary close, Ms. Mackie, the signature is placed about five lines below the message. The traditional concluding notations are handled the same as in other formats.

Jane M. Wright
Senior Editor

By UPS Next-Day Air

P.S. You may enjoy reading the enclosed booklet about formatting letter reports. JMW

Simplified-Block Format

reference initials, filename notation, enclosure notation, delivery notation, copy notation, postscript, and continuation-page heading. These elements must be properly arranged on the page with ample margins (usually a minimum of 1 inch top and bottom and about 1 1/2 inches on both sides).

Date. The date includes the month, day, and year: *September 4, 2001.* In military style, the day is placed before the month and no comma is used: *4 September 2001.* All numerals (*9/4/01*) should be avoided since people may not read the numbers in the same way. In some countries, for example, *9/4/01* would be read as *April 9, 2001,* rather than *September 4, 2001.*

Place the date two or more lines below the last line of the letterhead, flush left in the full-block and simplified-block formats and at the page center or slightly right of it in the modified-block format.

Confidential notation. Use a confidential, or personal, notation on a letter and envelope when you don't want anyone other than the addressee to open the letter. Place the word *Confidential* or *Personal* in all capital letters or with an initial capital two to four lines below the date (also on the envelope [see Envelope Formats] below the return address):

> January 4, 2001
>
>
> CONFIDENTIAL

Inside address. Place the inside address flush left, regardless of the letter format, three or more lines below the date, depending on the length of the letter. Include all data necessary for correct identification and delivery of the letter. This may include the recipient's name; job title; company name; department; street address; suite or other number; and city, state, and ZIP code, as well as the country in the case of international mail. (See also Attention line.) If you write often to the same person, you can create a macro to reenter the data automatically with only a keystroke or two so that you won't have to rekey all the information each time you write.

If two names are given in the inside address, place the name of the person of higher rank first. If both are equal, list the names alphabetically. If the people are at different addresses, also arrange them by rank or alphabetically but as two separate inside address blocks, one stacked above the other, separated by a blank line (and mail an original printout of each letter to each person).

You may omit the job title if an address is particularly long, although often the title is helpful for delivery in a very large company. If you include it, place a short version on the same line as the name and a long version on the next line. When any information is too long to fit on one line of the inside address, indent the carryover line.

Use a personal or professional title before the addressee's name: *Mr., Ms., Dr., Professor,* or other title. (Since *Ms.* is not used in other countries, use the country's equivalent of *Miss* or *Mrs.*) If you don't know if a person is a man or a woman, omit the title: *A. J. Wilson.* Place scholastic abbreviations, such as *Ph.D.,* after the name. If a person has more than one degree, place the one pertaining to the person's profession first. (See Forms of Address for more about the use of personal and professional titles.) Spell out all numerical street names through *ten* (*14 Tenth Avenue*), but use figures for house and building numbers, except the number *one* (*One McKenzie Street*), and separate a house or building number from a street number with a hyphen (*2 - 17 Street*). Room and suite numbers should be on the same line as the street address:

Ms. Joan Goodwin,
Vice President, Sales
CCC Corporation
1234 Matthews Street, Suite 4
City, ST 98765

Dr. Beverly G. Ryan, President
CCC Corporation, Inc.
12 - 34 Street
City, ST 98765

Mr. J. H. Parsons, Manager
CCC Corporation Ltd.
Research and Development Division
One Boyleston Avenue, Room 10
Ottawa, ON K1A OB1
CANADA

Dr. Beverly G. Ryan, President
Mr. J. H. Parsons, Manager of
Research and Development
CCC Corporation, Inc.
34 West 15 Street, NW
City, ST 98765

Business Manager
CCC Corporation, Inc.
Sales and Marketing Department
2000 Second Avenue
City, ST 98765

Attention line. Address your letter to the company, and use an attention line on both the envelope and the letter when you want to be certain that someone else will open and read the letter if the person named in the attention line is absent. You may also address a letter to one person and name another in the attention line. Then if the addressee is absent, the person named in the attention line will open the letter.

Position the attention line flush left within the inside address — on the first line if the letter is addressed generally to a firm or after the addressee's name if the letter is addressed to a person. Spell out the word *Attention,* and use the person's full name without a title: *Attention Jim Hendricks.* See Salutation for the proper greeting when an attention line is used:

> Attention Ellen Parker
> ABC Incorporated
> 567 Tower Court
> City, ST 98765
>
> Mr. John Grayson
> Attention Julia Morris
> ABC Incorporated
> 567 Tower Court
> City, ST 98765

Salutation. Place the salutation, or greeting, two lines below the inside address, flush left in the full-block and modified-block formats. Omit the salutation in the simplified-block format. Capitalize the word *Dear* and the words of a formal title such as *Your Excellency,* and place a colon after the last word.

In letters addressed to a company or department, with or without an attention line, use a general greeting, such as *Ladies and Gentlemen* or *Dear Members of the Sales Department,* but not *Dear ABC Incorporated* or *Dear Sales Department.* Use first names only when you're certain a recipient wants to be addressed that way. Use first names in international correspondence only when the recipient has specifically asked to be addressed that way. Refer to Forms of Address for information on the use of personal and professional titles in salutations:

> Dear Ms. Smith:
> Dear Ms. Kline and Mr. Thomas:
> Dear Dr. Wilson and Ms. Adams:
> Dear Mss. Smith, Thomas, and Osmon:
> Dear Dr. Browne, Ms. Hendricks, and Mr. Rider:
> Dear Jan:
> Dear Jan and Phil:
> Dear A. B. Renfro: (*gender unknown*)

Dear Professor Lee:
Dear Major Benson:
Dear Señora Gonzalez: (*letter to other country*)
Ladies and Gentlemen: (*letter to company*)
Dear Sales Manager: (*name unknown*)
Dear Sir: (*very formal*)
Dear Madam: (*very formal*)
Most Reverend Sir: (*very formal*)
To Whom It May Concern: (*letter to unknown recipients*)
Dear Friends: (*letter to group of people*)

Subject. A subject summarizes the main topic of a message and makes it unnecessary for the writer to announce the subject in the first paragraph. Place the subject flush left, two lines below the salutation in the full-block format and three lines below the salutation in the simplified-block format. Place it two lines below the salutation and indent it the same as the paragraphs in the modified-block format.

Often the word *Subject* is omitted. If it's used, however, put a colon after it, and write it and the words that follow in all capital letters or capitalize each important word, as preferred. (Law offices commonly use the words *In re* or *Re*, with no colon after them, rather than the word *Subject*. In this case, the line should be placed *above*, rather than after, the salutation.) If possible, use a single subject and focus on that one main topic in the letter:

NOVEMBER SALES MEETING
SUBJECT: NOVEMBER SALES MEETING
SUBJECT: November Sales Meeting
Subject: November Sales Meeting

Body. Single-space the body, or the discussion part of the message, and leave one blank line between the paragraphs. Begin the body two lines below the subject or the salutation in the full-block and modified-block formats and three lines below the subject in the simplified-block format. Place paragraphs flush left in the full-block and simplified-block formats, and indent them about ½ inch in the modified-block format.

Business reports (see Chapter 6, "Document Creation," Report Preparation) prepared as letters may have subheads and other features, such as lists. If headings are used (see the examples in Chapter 6, "Document Creation," Formal Report, Body), place them flush left or centered, with one or more blank lines above and below each head, or position them run in with the first line of a paragraph. Write the headings in all capitals, with important words capitalized, or with an initial capital only, as preferred, and print them in a larger size or in an italic or bold face, if desired. Although they should be distinctive, it's usually best to avoid distracting design flairs and flourishes in business correspondence.

Lists in a letter should be set off from the rest of the body, usually with one blank line before and after the list and sometimes with a space between each list item. A list may also be indented from the left (or from both the left and right) as a block, using the same amount of indention as that used for any paragraph, often about ½ inch. Single-space the items in a list, the same as the rest of the message.

Quotations in a letter that exceed four or five lines should be set off from the rest of the body as a blocked quotation, or extract. (Chapter 7, "Business Style Guide," Quotation marks, explains the proper use of quotation marks.) An extract is usually indented the same as a paragraph, or about ½ inch. Leave one blank line before and after an extract.

If a letter runs over to a second page, follow the instructions in Continuation-page heading.

Complimentary close. A complimentary close is used in all formats except the simplified-block format. Place the close two lines below the message body, flush left in the full-block format and at the page center or slightly right of it in the modified-block format.

Capitalize the first word of the close, and place a comma after the last word. A close should be selected based on the relationship between the writer and the recipient. Although friendly, familiar closes are common in domestic letters, more formality is required in international letters.

Those who are on a first-name basis and have a close, personal relationship or a long working relationship commonly use informal closes, such as *Regards* and *Best regards*. When the persons have a friendly relationship but are not on a first-name basis, a close such as *Cordially* or *Cordially yours* is appropriate. The most neutral and most widely used closes are *Sincerely* and the somewhat more formal version *Sincerely yours*. When writing to a dignitary or high-ranking official and greater deference is needed, use a formal close such as *Respectfully* or *Respectfully yours*. (Whenever the word *yours* is added to a close, it tends to make it more formal.)

Signature. The signature block consists of the sender's printed name and, possibly, job title, as well as the handwritten signature. The information is positioned flush left in the full-block and simplified-block formats and at the page center or slightly right of it (aligned with the date at the top of the page) in the modified-block format.

When the signature block consists of the sender's name and, possibly, job title, place it about four lines below the complimentary close or five lines after the message body in the simplified-block format. If the sender's name is included with the letterhead data, however, it's not necessary to repeat it at the bottom of the page in the signature block.

When a company name is included (not common in the simplified format), place it two lines below the complimentary close, and place the person's name and job title about four lines below the company name. This form is used by accountants and others who want to make clear that the letter represents the company's, not the person's, opinion or report:

> Sincerely yours,
>
> WADE & SONS ACCOUNTING, INC.
>
> *Henry McCauley*
>
> Henry McCauley, CPA
> General Manager

Write the handwritten signature the same as the printed signature. Thus if the printed signature is *Barry M. McCoy,* the letter shouldn't be signed *B. M. McCoy.*

Place a personal title, such as *Ms.,* in parentheses before the printed name only if the recipient otherwise would not know that the sender wants to be addressed that way (such as in international correspondence) or if gender isn't clear from the name alone. If you don't include a title, and if a recipient has no way of knowing if you hold a title such as *Dr.,* the recipient (in the United States) will assume that a man should be addressed as *Mr.* and a woman as *Ms.* However, recipients in other countries will address a woman as *Miss* or *Mrs.* if she doesn't put *Ms.* in front of her name in the signature block:

> *P. R. Thompson*
>
> (Mr.) P. R. Thompson [*gender unclear*]
>
> *Rhoda Crossman*
>
> (Ms.) Rhoda Crossman [*letter to another country*]

If desired, include academic initials (*Ph.D.*), initials designating a religious order (*SJ*), or evidence of certification (*CPA*) after the printed signature, even if a job title is also included. Place *Esq.* (*Esquire*), which is seldom used in the United States, after the name of a prominent professional man or woman if you know that the person prefers it:

> *Roger K. Sanders*
>
> Roger K. Sanders, Sc.D.
> Professor of Molecular Physics

Nadine M. Michaels

Nadine M. Michaels, Esq.
Attorney at Law

The following examples are acceptable business forms of the printed signature following a complimentary close. In the last example, the title *Ms.* is included because the gender is unclear from the name alone:

Adam S. Goldberg

Adam S. Goldberg
Vice President, New Product Development

Benjamin D. Ralston

Benjamin D. Ralston
Customer Representative

Courtney J. Stiller

Courtney J. Stiller
Administrative Assistant

C. J. Stiller

(Ms.) C. J. Stiller
Administrative Assistant

In the first of the next three examples, the assistant signs her own name to her own letter. In the second example, she signs her own name to a letter she composed at someone else's request. In the third example, the person who dictated or composed the letter isn't there to sign it. Since the assistant has been asked to sign the writer's name, she places her initials below the person's last name or in parentheses after the name to signal that she is signing the writer's name in his or her absence:

Amanda Wilson

Amanda Wilson
Assistant to Mr. Steinberg

Amanda Wilson

Amanda Wilson
For Arnold K. Steinberg

Arnold K. Steinberg (aw)

Arnold K. Steinberg
Director of Human Resources

Even though the complimentary close is omitted in the simplified format, the signature lines — name and title — are included. Style them the same as for the full-block and modified-block formats, as indicated in the preceding examples.

Reference initials. The reference initials indicate who signs, dictates, and prepares the printout of a letter. Although this information is useful only to the sender, companies often put it on all copies, including the recipient's copy, to avoid having to add it later only on the file copies.

Place the initials two lines below the signature block. The computer operator's initials are written in lowercase letters. The composer/dictator and signer's initials are written in all capital letters. The reference initials and any notations that follow may all be single- or double-spaced, depending on the length of the letter and personal preference. In either case, position the information flush left in all formats.

If the person who composes and signs a letter is the same, his or her initials are usually omitted. If the signer doesn't want to have them listed, you would note only the initials of the computer operator who prepares the printed letter. If different people compose, sign, and prepare the printout, all initials are usually given. Place the signer's initials first, then those of the person who composed or dictated the letter, and last those of the computer operator:

> mj (*composer/dictater and signer are the same, and this person doesn't want his or her initials listed*)
>
> AV:mj (*composer/dictator and signer are the same, and this person does want his or her initial listed*)
>
> AV:MT:mj (*composer/dictator and signer are different, and each person's initials are therefore listed*))

Filename notation. Offices and file departments may find it helpful to have the filename added to a letter at the time of preparation to facilitate later storage and retrieval. If you include the name under which the letter will be filed, place the notation below the reference initials. If during an exchange of correspondence with an addressee you also include that person's filename, place it below yours. Add *Our file/ref.* and *Your file/ref.* for clarity:

> mjacobs.ltr
>
> Our file: mjacobs.ltr
> Your file: bsimpson.doc

Enclosure notation. When you're enclosing other material, add a notation to that effect at the bottom of the letter, flush left, one or two lines below the filename or reference initials. (Space all notations consistently, either single- or double-spaced.)

Especially important enclosures should be identified. Spell out or abbreviate the words *Enclosure* (*Enc.*) and *Enclosures* (*Encs.*), as preferred. (Spell them out in international correspondence in case the recipient is unfamiliar with domestic U.S. abbreviations.)

Enc.

2 Encs.: P & L Statement
         Policy ABC- 123

Delivery notation. If you send a traditional letter by some means other than regular postal mail, add a notation below the enclosure notation specifying the form of delivery. If a letter is to be faxed and no cover sheet will be used (though a cover sheet is advisable), you may add a special fax notation centered two lines below the letterhead data or two lines above and aligned with the date. When the notation is in that position, write it in all capital letters or with an initial capital only, as preferred. Otherwise, write the notation with an initial capital only (except for proper nouns), and place it in the standard delivery-notation position below the enclosure notation:

By certified mail
By UPS Next-Day Air
By fax to 800-555-4170

Copy notation. The copy notation is used to show who, other than the addressee, will receive a copy of the letter. Place the notation below the delivery notation, single- or double-spaced, the same as the other notations.

Common designations are *Copy* or *c* for any type of copy, *cc* for computer copy (formerly carbon copy), *pc* for photocopy, and *fc* for fax copy. When you send a copy to someone and don't want the addressee to know about it, use a blind-copy notation (*bc*). Omit the *bc* designation on the addressee's copy, and include it only on your file copy and the blind-copy recipient's copy.

Copy: Marilyn Hartford

cc: Harold T. Martin

c: Lucille M. Baxter
   Benjamin R. Taylor
   Avery B. Wexler, Jr.

bc: Jean McGhee

Postscript. A postscript, introduced by the initials *P.S.* (or *PS*), is a brief, additional comment unrelated to the principal message. It shouldn't be something you forgot to include in the main message. Place the postscript two lines below the last notation, flush left in the full-block and simplified-block formats and with a paragraph indent in the modified-block format. Add the sender's initials at the end:

> P.S. Have you heard when the next meeting of the Science Club is scheduled? DVC

Although more than one postscript should be avoided, if it's necessary to include two, use the abbreviation *P.P.S.* (or *PPS*) for the second one.

Continuation-page heading. If your message exceeds one page, use paper for the additional pages that matches the letterhead stationery. If your company doesn't have printed continuation pages, use matching blank sheets. Always carry at least two lines of the letter body over to the continued page. Reformat the first page if necessary to allow for this. Place a continuation-page heading a half inch to an inch from the top edge of the paper. Begin the continued text of the letter body two to four lines below the continuation-page heading.

Format the heading in any basic style that you prefer, such as stacked or in a single line. Use the addressee's full name, without a personal title. Use figures or words for the page numbers, as preferred:

> Mary Dennison, January 4, 2001, page 2
>
> Mary Dennison
> January 4, 2001
> Page two

Memo and E-mail Formats

A memo or e-mail format differs from a letter format in that it lacks an inside address, salutation, and complimentary close. Instead, guidewords, or headings, such as *Date, To, From,* and *Subject* are written at the top of the page, and the sender fills in the appropriate information after each word. Sometimes other headings, such as *Order Number* or *Attention,* are added to the basic guidewords.

Although traditional memos are often prepared on regular business stationery (8 1/2 by 11 inches), commercial forms of various sizes are available in office-supply stores or can be ordered from printers. Commercial designs sometimes have ruled lines for the sender to hand-write a message rather than prepare it by computer. Certain styles have a carbonless attachment that the recipient can use for sending a reply on the same page as the sender's message. The model Traditional Memo Format would be appropriate for preparation on regular business letterhead. Although the E-mail Format is similar, the e-mail software provides a standard template with certain guidewords after which information is filled in by the sender. The computer automatically fills in the date and time and the sender's name and e-mail address.

COMPANY LETTERHEAD

DATE: February 4, 2001   FROM: Arthur J. Lee

TO: Janice B. Wilcox   SUBJECT: Memo Format

This is an example of a company memo with a displayed list. The other features and specifications are similar to those used for a traditional letter. The body also should be prepared the same as a traditional letter body.

Begin the message at least three lines below the last guideword (heading), and treat displayed lists something like this:

- Leave one blank line between the text and the first item in the list.

- Indent the list, or place it flush left, as desired.

- Leave one blank line between each item, if desired, but single-space within an item.

- Leave one blank line between the last line of the list and the first line of regular text.

You may—but need not—key in or hand-write your initials at the end of the message about two lines below the last line of text. Treat any concluding notations the same as those in a traditional letter.

AJL

jbwilcox.memo

cc: Mary Allen
    Sandra Kendall

Traditional Memo Format

Fax cover sheets are sometimes styled like memos. Although companies usually design their own cover sheets, standard commercial forms are also available. Like memos, most include headings (*Name, Date, Address, Fax Number,* and so on) followed by a designated area where the sender can write a brief message.

From: Arthur J. Lee <ajlassociates.com>
To: Janice B. Wilcox <jbwilcox.com>
Date: Thursday, February 4, 2001 2:25 PM
Subject: E-mail Format

Janice, this e-mail will serve as an example of a common e-mail format. It closely resembles a traditional memo format and also begins with guidewords, which are followed by the e-mail message.

As you can see, this message doesn't have any special text formatting. Although lists, headings, and other features are widely used in traditional memos, it's uncertain whether any formatting you do in an e-mail will be translated the same way—or at all—by the recipient's software.

E-mails may have attachments (called "enclosures" in traditional mail) and may have some of the other parts used in a traditional memo, such as a copy distribution. Since there's no letterhead, you may want to add a signature block with address data at the end of your e-mail.

Let me know if you have any questions, Janice, and good luck with your report about e-mail communication.

****

Arthur J. Lee
Director of Communications
Arthur J. Lee Associates
114 Adams Drive, Room 4000
City, ST 98765
Phone: 420.555.4200
Fax: 420.555.4201
Website: www.ajlassociates.com

2/4/01

E-mail Format

Major Parts of a Memo or E-mail

The following are the main parts of a memo or e-mail: the confidential notation (traditional memo only); guidewords (*Date*, *To*, and so on); message body; the same notations used in a letter (reference initials, filename notation, enclosure notation, delivery notation, and copy notation); postscript; and continuation-page heading.

Like traditional business letters, traditional memos should be properly positioned on the page, using margins similar to those of a letter on all sides. The computer automatically provides standard (default) settings in an e-mail message. Your ability to change the default settings depends on the options of your e-mail program. Although memos may vary in size and arrangement of certain elements, particularly the headings, a standard memo begins with the headings and ends with any notation or postscript.

Confidential notation. A confidential or personal notation may be used on a traditional memo if it contains sensitive material. Depending on the design of the memo, you might place the notation close to the top of the page, preferably above the guidewords. See the description of this notation in Parts of a Letter.

Guidewords. The most common memo headings are *Date, To, From,* and *Subject.* But others may be added, as desired. In some e-mail programs, the template lists headings such as *To, Cc, Bcc,* and *Subject,* after which you fill in the desired information. Other information, such as *From* and *Date* (including *time*), are automatically provided by the computer. Again, other headings may be added, as desired. You may, for example, need one for an Attention line.

If traditional memo letterhead doesn't provide a fax number, an office telephone extension, an e-mail address, or a website, this information may be added beneath the last line of the letterhead data. One purpose of a traditional memo or e-mail is to provide essential information quickly and easily, so there is no restriction, other than appearance or practicality, on the number and variety of guidewords you include.

Guidewords may be printed on special memo stationery or keyed in on your regular letter stationery. If you key in the headings, begin two to four lines below the letterhead data. Headings may be capitalized (*SUBJECT*), abbreviated (*SUBJ*), punctuated (*SUBJ.:*), or styled in some other way, according to preference. Each guideword, however, should be styled the same as the other guidewords.

To align the material that is filled in after each head on a traditional memo, begin writing one or two character spaces to the right of the longest head. In an e-mail message, the computer will align the information or set each item run on, depending on your program:

```
FROM:     Ann C. Messenger<acmessenger@universal.com>
TO:       Martin T. Phillips<mtphillips@northernlights.com>
DATE:     January 4, 2001 3:45 PM
SUBJECT:  Executive Bulletin–March
```

If you're printing out and sending an original copy of a traditional memo to numerous people, type the word *Distribution** with an asterisk after the guideword *To,* or write "See Distribution" after *To.* Then, two lines after the last notation or postscript of the memo, repeat the word *Distribution,* and list each intended recipient by rank or in alphabetical order:

TO: Distribution*
TO: See Distribution

Distribution:
Martin Phillips, President
Jennifer Abbott, Director of Research
Steven Bartlett, Executive Assistant
Kenneth Hall, Research Assistant
Paula Kincaid, Research Liaison
Dennis Wolf, Administrator, Science Lab

Style the *From* name(s) on a traditional memo the same as you style the *To* name(s). Thus if you use initials only (*M. R. Danson*) with the *To* name(s), also use initials only with the *From* name(s). Although a memo has no signature, the sender may add his or her initials two lines below the body, flush left or slightly to the right, as preferred. Style (capitalize and punctuate) the other guideword information (*Subject, Attention,* and so on) as described previously for these elements in Parts of a Letter.

Body. The body of a traditional memo or e-mail should be handled the same as the body of a letter, as described in Parts of a Letter. However, a traditional memo and, especially, an e-mail are often more succinct than a letter, focusing on a single topic, for example (particularly in an e-mail message, which should be as brief as possible for easy reading on a computer screen).

Nevertheless, as in a letter, paragraphs in a traditional memo may be flush left or indented, and you may use subheads, lists, abstracts, and other display features. In fact, such features are often more common in a memo, which is intended to distill and provide factual information in a clear, easy-to-read format. For this reason, the memo format is used for short reports more often than the letter format. However, keep in mind that such formatting may be lost in an e-mail message if the recipient's software doesn't print it out as you've set it up.

Notations. In both a traditional memo and an e-mail, the reference initials (traditional memo), filename notation, enclosure notation, delivery notation (traditional memo), and copy notation should be styled as described in Parts of a Letter. An enclosure notation, however, is usually described as an *Attachment* in an e-mail. Whether you can attach text only or both text and graphics depends on your software. Follow the instructions of your program for selecting the material (file) that you want to attach to your e-mail.

Postscript. Place the postscript flush left or with a paragraph indent, the same as the style used in the body of a letter (in most traditional memos and e-mails, everything is set flush left). Begin two lines below the last notation, and follow the instructions given previously for styling a postscript in Parts of a Letter.

Continuation-page heading. For a traditional memo, use printed or blank stationery, and always carry at least two lines of the memo body over to the continued page. Follow the instructions given previously for styling a continuation-page heading in Parts of a Letter. In an e-mail, the computer automatically adjusts the copy and identifies continued pages as, for example, *Page 1 of 3, Page 2 of 3,* and *Page 3 of 3.*

Envelope Formats

A wide variety of commercial envelope sizes and styles are available. Office-supply stores and printers can provide most of the standard regular and window envelopes. Regular business letterhead ($8\frac{1}{2}$ by 11 inches) can be folded in thirds to fit a No. 9 or a slightly larger No. 10 commercial envelope. (See Stationery.) Smaller sizes, such as $3\frac{5}{8}$ by $6\frac{1}{2}$ inches, can be used for notes, invoices, and other material that will easily fold to a smaller size. The U.S. Postal Service requires that envelopes measure no less than $3\frac{1}{2}$ by 5 inches.

Traditional letters and memos should be sent in envelopes that match the letterhead in color, texture, and weight. In-house paper memos, however, may be routed in larger, unsealed, string-tied interoffice mailers. These envelopes have lines on which you write the recipient's name and office. After the recipient removes his or her enclosure, the person's name is crossed off and the envelope reused.

Major Parts of Envelopes

The principal parts of a standard envelope consist of the sender's return address; postage and mail instructions, such as *Special Delivery;* special notations or other instructions, such as *Return Service Requested;* and the address block. The model Envelope Format illustrates the placement of data on an envelope addressed for sorting by the U.S. Postal Service's optical character reader equipment. See Address block for further information.

Return Address	Postage
RETURN SERVICE REQUESTED	SPECIAL DELIVERY

*(top line of
address block
no more than
2¾" from
bottom of
envelope)*

ABC 123-S
ATTN MS MC ADAMSON
HEATHERVILLE INDUSTRIES
1891 WEST AVENUE
CITY, ST 98765

*(1/2" minimum
left margin)*   *(1/2" minimum
                                                        right margin)*
                (5/8" minimum bottom margin)

Envelope Format

Return address. The sender's return address is usually printed in the upper left corner of the envelope. Businesspeople who use company envelopes may add their department or room number above or below the return address if the printed data omits this.

Postage and mail instructions. Mail instructions are placed about two lines below the postage that is applied in the upper right corner. Write the instructions in all capital letters: *SPECIAL DELIVERY.*

Notations. Letter writers may add special notations or instructions about two lines below the sender's return address. Write the information in all capital letters:

[**Return Address**]
CONFIDENTIAL

[**Return Address**]
RETURN SERVICE REQUESTED

Address block. The traditional style is to write the person's name, job title, company and department, street, and city, state, and ZIP code centered on the envelope, capitalizing all important words:

Mr. J. G. Dougherty, Treasurer
RRR Corporation, Inc.
Business Department
13 Franklin Street
City, ST 98765

The U.S. Postal Service, however, prefers that addresses be positioned within a designated rectangular address area. See the margin requirements stated on the model Envelope Format. Envelopes so addressed can be more easily and quickly processed by equipment designed for automated handling.

The address block must be written at least $\frac{1}{2}$ inch from the left and right edges and at least $\frac{5}{8}$ inch from the bottom edge of the envelope. Your software may automatically place the address in the proper position.

Write the address in all capital letters without punctuation, or capitalize each important word. Place unit numbers, such as a room number, after the street on the same line, and put a box number before a station name. Place a post office box on the line below the street address (mail is delivered to whichever is listed last, the street or the post office box address). Place optional nonaddress data, such as a date or reference number, on the first line of the address. Place an attention line immediately above a company name but on the line below a person's name.

For further information, refer to a current edition of the U.S. Postal Service's *Domestic Mail Manual* and *International Mail Manual.* These publications are available by subscription from the Superintendent of Documents in Washington, D.C., in print copies and as CD-ROMs. See Chapter 5, "Mail Processing," Postal Mail and Types of Postal Mail, for additional information about the U.S. Postal Service and classes of mail, and visit the Postal Service website.

Table 9.1 lists the authorized two-letter abbreviations for U.S. states and dependencies. Table 9.2 lists acceptable postal abbreviations for streets and words often appearing in place names. Table 9.3 provides the accepted two-letter abbreviations for Canadian provinces.

ZIP Codes

The first three digits of a ZIP code identify the delivery area of the sectional center facility (SCF) or major city post office (unique three-digit ZIP code office) serving the area where the address is located. The next two (the fourth and fifth) digits identify the delivery area of an associate post office or a branch or station of a major city post office. All post offices are assigned one or more unique five-digit ZIP codes. Post offices usually have a copy of the *National ZIP Code and Post Office Directory* available for customer use. Copies are also for sale at the National Information Data Center (NIDC) in Washington, D.C. (see also the NIDC's website). In addition, various (sometimes smaller) commercial directories may be purchased online or in bookstores.

The most complete ZIP code is a nine-digit number consisting of five numbers, a hyphen, and four numbers, which the United States Postal Service describes by its trademark ZIP + 4. Together, the final four digits

Table 9.1 Two-Letter Abbreviations of U.S. States and Dependencies

STATE	ABBREV.	STATE	ABBREV.
Alabama	AL	Montana	MT
Alaska	AK	Nebraska	NE
Arizona	AZ	Nevada	NV
Arkansas	AR	New Hampshire	NH
California	CA	New Jersey	NJ
Canal Zone	CZ	New Mexico	NM
Colorado	CO	New York	NY
Connecticut	CT	North Carolina	NC
Delaware	DE	North Dakota	ND
District of Columbia	DC	Ohio	OH
Florida	FL	Oklahoma	OK
Georgia	GA	Oregon	OR
Guam	GU	Pennsylvania	PA
Hawaii	HI	Puerto Rico	PR
Idaho	ID	Rhode Island	RI
Illinois	IL	South Carolina	SC
Indiana	IN	South Dakota	SD
Iowa	IA	Tennessee	TN
Kansas	KS	Texas	TX
Kentucky	KY	Utah	UT
Louisiana	LA	Vermont	VT
Maine	ME	Virginia	VA
Maryland	MD	Virgin Islands	VI
Massachusetts	MA	Washington	WA
Michigan	MI	West Virginia	WV
Minnesota	MN	Wisconsin	WI
Mississippi	MS	Wyoming	WY
Missouri	MO		

Table 9.2 Street and Place-Name Abbreviations

NAME	ABBREV.	NAME	ABBREV.
Academy	ACAD	Central	CTL
Agency	AGNCY	Church	CHR
Air Force Base	AFB	Churches	CHRS
Airport	ARPRT	Circle	CIR
Alley	ALY	City	CY
Annex	ANX	Clear	CLR
Arcade	ARC	Cliffs	CLFS
Arsenal	ARSL	Club	CLB
Avenue	AVE	College	CLG
Bayou	BYU	Common	CMM
Beach	BCH	Corner	COR
Bend	BND	Corners	CORS
Big	BG	Course	CRSE
Black	BLK	Court	CT
Bluff	BLF	Courts	CTS
Bottom	BTM	Cove	CV
Boulevard	BLVD	Creek	CRK
Branch	BR	Crescent	CRES
Bridge	BRG	Crossing	XING
Brook	BRK	Dale	DL
Burg	BG	Dam	DM
Bypass	BYP	Depot	DPO
Camp	CP	Divide	DV
Canyon	CYN	Drive	DR
Cape	CPE	East	E
Causeway	CSWY	Estates	EST
Center	CTR	Expressway	EXPY

NAME	ABBREV.	NAME	ABBREV.
Extended	EXT	Highlands	HGLDS
Extension	EXT	Highway	HWY
Fall	FL	Hill	HL
Falls	FLS	Hills	HLS
Farms	FRMS	Hollow	HOLW
Ferry	FRY	Hospital	HOSP
Field	FLD	Hot	H
Fields	FLDS	House	HSE
Flats	FLT	Inlet	INLT
Ford	FRD	Institute	INST
Forest	FRST	Island	IS
Forge	FRG	Islands	IS
Fork	FRK	Isle	IS
Fountain	FTN	Junction	JCT
Freeway	FWY	Key	KY
Furnace	FURN	Knolls	KNLS
Gardens	GDNS	Lake	LK
Gateway	GTWY	Lakes	LKS
Glen	GLN	Landing	LNDG
Grand	GRND	Lane	LN
Great	GR	Light	LGT
Green	GRN	Little	LTL
Ground	GRD	Loaf	LF
Grove	GRV	Locks	LCKS
Harbor	HBR	Lodge	LDG
Haven	HVN	Loop	LOOP
Heights	HTS	Lower	LWR
High	HI	Mall	MALL

Table 9.2 (continued)

NAME	ABBREV.	NAME	ABBREV.
Manor	MNR	Place	PL
Meadows	MDWS	Plain	PLN
Memorial	MEM	Plains	PLNS
Middle	MDL	Plaza	PLZ
Mile	MLE	Point	PT
Mill	ML	Port	PRT
Mills	MLS	Prairie	PR
Mines	MNS	Radical	RADL
Mission	MSN	Ranch	RNCH
Mound	MND	Ranches	RNCHS
Mount	MT	Rapids	RPDS
Mountain	MTN	Resort	RESRT
National	NAT	Rest	RST
Naval Air Station	NAS	Ridge	RDG
		River	RIV
Neck	NCK	Road	RD
New	NW	Rock	RK
North	N	Row	ROW
Orchard	ORCH	Run	RUN
Oval	OVAL	Rural	R
Palms	PLMS	Saint	ST
Park	PARK	Sainte	ST
Parkway	PKY	San	SN
Pass	PASS	Santa	SN
Path	PATH	Santo	SN
Pike	PIKE	School	SCH
Pillar	PLR	Seminary	SMNRY
Pines	PNES	Shoal	SHL

NAME	ABBREV.	NAME	ABBREV.
Shoals	SHLS	Tower	TWR
Shore	SHR	Town	TWN
Shores	SHRS	Trace	TRCE
Siding	SDG	Track	TRAK
South	S	Trail	TRL
Space Flight Center	SFC	Trailer	TRLR
		Tunnel	TUNL
Speedway	SPDWY	Turnpike	TPKE
Spring	SPG	Union	UN
Springs	SPGS	University	UNIV
Spur	SPUR	Valley	VLY
Square	SQ	Viaduct	VI
State	ST	View	VW
Station	STA	Village	VLG
Stream	STRM	Ville	VL
Street	ST	Vista	VIS
Sulfur	SLFR	Walk	WALK
Summit	SMT	Water	WTR
Switch	SWCH	Way	WAY
Tannery	TNRY	Wells	WLS
Tavern	TVRN	West	W
Terminal	TERM	White	WHT
Terrace	TER	Works	WKS
Ton	TN	Yards	YDS

identify geographic units, such as a side of a street between intersections, both sides of a street between intersections, a building, a floor or group of floors in a building, a firm within a building, a span of boxes on a rural route, or a group of post office boxes to which a single U.S. Postal Service employee makes delivery.

Table 9.3 Abbreviations of Canadian Provinces

PROVINCE	ABBREV.	PROVINCE	ABBREV.
Alberta	AB	Nova Scotia	NS
British Columbia	BC	Ontario	ON
		Prince Edward Island	PE
Manitoba	MB		
New Brunswick	NB	Quebec	PQ
Newfoundland	NF	Saskatchewan	SK
Northwest Territories	NT	Yukon Territory	YT

International and Overseas Military Mail

U.S. Postal Service publications provide full instructions for addressing mail and preparing material for recipients in other countries, including U.S. military personnel who are stationed outside the United States. Consult a current copy of the *Direct Mail Manual,* mentioned earlier, which has extensive addressing information. The *International Mail Manual* has detailed information about mailing to other countries. In the case of mail to civilian personnel, the following general guidelines apply:

- At least the entire right half of the address side of the envelope, package, or card should be reserved for the destination address, postage, labels, and postal notations.
- Addresses in Russian, Greek, Arabic, Hebrew, Cyrillic, Japanese, or Chinese characters must bear an interline translation of the names of the post office and country of destination in English. If the English translation is not known, the foreign language words must be spelled in Roman characters (print or script).
- Mail may not be addressed to a person in one country "in care of" a person in another country.
- The name of the sender or addressee may not be in initials except where they are an adopted trade name.
- Mail may not be addressed generally to the titles *Boxholder* or *Householder,* without a name.
- The house number and street address or box number must be included when mail is addressed to towns or cities.

- The bottom line of the address must show only the country name, written in full (no abbreviations) and in capital letters.

The following examples use the optional full capitalization style, without punctuation. However, this style should be used only with envelope addresses. The corresponding inside address of a traditional letter should be capitalized and punctuated normally. (*Note:* Full capitalization is no longer required for Postal Service optical character reader [OCR] scanning equipment, which can read even handwritten uppercase-lowercase addresses.)

MR THOMAS CLARK
117 RUSSELL DRIVE
LONDON WIP 6HQ
ENGLAND

For mail to Canada, either of the following address formats may be used when the postal delivery zone number is included in the address:

MS HELEN SAUNDERS
CANADIAN ENTERPRISES
1010 CLEAR STREET
OTTAWA ON K1A 0B1
CANADA

MS HELEN SAUNDERS
CANADIAN ENTERPRISES
1010 CLEAR STREET
OTTAWA ON CANADA
K1A 0B1

In general, overseas military addresses must conform to domestic addressing standards. Mail addressed to military personnel within the United States must include the name of the military installation, state, and either the correct ZIP code or ZIP + 4 code. When applicable, the address must also include the name of a ship (if any) and any pertinent numbers, such as the unit number, the Consolidated Mail Room (CMR) number, the Postal Service Center (PSC) number, or any assigned box number.

The last line of an overseas military address must contain the person's APO (army/air force post office) or FPO (navy post office) and the customary two-letter state abbreviation (see Table 9.1) and ZIP code. The abbreviations *AA* (area Americas), *AE* (area Europe), and *AP* (area Pacific) should be written in front of ZIP codes that have these prefixes: 340 (*AA*), 090-098 (*AE*), and 962-966 (*AP*). Refer to the *Direct Mail Manual* for instructions.

FORMS OF ADDRESS

The correct forms of address must be used in the inside address, salutation, and envelope address. The following sections describe the proper forms of personal, scholastic, official, and honorary titles.

Women

In domestic business correspondence, the most common title for single, married, widowed, and divorced women is *Ms.* (plural, *Mss.*) However, you may use the title *Mrs.* if you know that the woman prefers it. Don't address women in other countries by the title *Ms.* Instead, use the country's equivalent of *Miss* or *Mrs.* Most foreign titles, such as *Señora* or *Frau,* are spelled in full. The French *Madame,* however, should always be abbreviated before a personal name:

> Ms. Angela McCarthy and Ms. Laura Phelps
> Mss. Angela McCarthy, Laura Phelps, Dana Caruthers, and Nadene Pritkin
> Mme. Andrea Paix

The title *Madam* (plural *Mesdames*) is used primarily in formal correspondence to government officials and diplomats:

> Madam Ambassador
> Madam Prime Minister

If a woman holds another title, such as a religious, military, or scholastic title, use it in business correspondence rather than *Ms.,* unless you know that the woman prefers the personal title:

> The Reverend Angela McCarthy
> Captain Angela McCarthy
> Dr. Angela McCarthy

If you can't determine whether an addressee is a man or woman, omit the title:

> A. R. McCarthy
> [Address]
> Dear A. R. McCarthy:

Men

The title *Mr.* (plural *Messrs.*) should be used unless a man has earned another title:

Mr. Leonard Eastman and Mr. Walter Grey
Senator Leonard Eastman and Mr. Walter Grey
Messrs. Leonard Eastman, Walter Grey, John Hudson, and Wesley Stowe

Spouses

When addressing a business letter to spouses, use the same title for each spouse that you would use if you were writing a business letter to each person alone:

Mr. Leonard Eastman
Ms. Angela McCarthy-Eastman
Trinity Publishing
[Address]

Dear Mr. Eastman and Ms. McCarthy-Eastman:

Dr. Leonard Eastman
Dr. Angela McCarthy-Eastman
Trinity Publishing
[Address]

Dear Dr. Eastman and Dr. McCarthy-Eastman:

Dr. Angela McCarthy-Eastman
Mr. Leonard Eastman
Trinity Publishing
[Address]

Dear Dr. McCarthy-Eastman and Mr. Eastman:

Officials and Dignitaries

Esquire (*Esq.*) is not common in the United States; however, it is occasionally used among attorneys and people in the consular corps. Omit the personal or other title when *Esq.* follows the name:

Angela McCarthy, Esq.
[Address]

Dear Ms. McCarthy:

The Honorable is used before the names of certain prominent officials. Refer to Table 9.4 for further examples:

The Honorable Leonard Eastman
[Address]

Dear Governor Eastman:

Use of the title *Reverend* versus *The Reverend* depends on the person's religious affiliation. Some religious persons do not place *The* before *Reverend,*

Table 9.4 Forms of Address

The following list gives the appropriate name and title to use in an inside address and the appropriate salutation for business correspondence. In a few cases, a more formal salutation is also given when it, too, is appropriate or may be preferred for very high ranking dignitaries. Use an official's business address for business and business-related social correspondence and the official's home address (when known) for social or personal letters and invitations. When a person holds a scholastic degree or honorary title, such as *Dr.,* substitute it for *Mr.* or *Ms.*

GOVERNMENT OFFICIALS

President	The President The White House Dear Mr. President:
President-elect	The Honorable Marcus Shipley The President-elect Dear Mr. Shipley:
Former president	The Honorable Marcus Shipley Dear Mr. Shipley:
Vice president	The Vice President Old Executive Office Building Dear Mr. Vice President:
Speaker of the House	The Honorable Jean Shipley Speaker of the House of Representatives Dear Ms. Shipley: Dear Madam Speaker: (*formal*)
Former speaker	The Honorable Marcus Shipley Dear Mr. Shipley:
Cabinet officer	The Honorable Jean Shipley Secretary of _____ Dear Madam Secretary:
Former cabinet officer	The Honorable Marcus Shipley Dear Mr. Shipley:
Undersecretary, department	The Honorable Jean Shipley Undersecretary of _____ Dear Ms. Shipley: Dear Madam Undersecretary: (*formal*)
Attorney general	The Honorable Marcus Shipley Attorney General of the United States Dear Mr. Attorney General:

GOVERNMENT OFFICIALS

U.S. senator	The Honorable Jean Shipley United States Senate Dear Senator Shipley:
Senator-elect	The Honorable Jean Shipley Senator-elect Dear Ms. Shipley:
Former U.S. senator	The Honorable Jean Shipley Dear Ms. Shipley:
U.S. Senate, committee, subcommittee chair	The Honorable Marcus Shipley Chairman _____ Committee United States Senate Dear Mr. Chairman:
U.S. representative	The Honorable Jean Shipley United States House of Representatives Dear Ms. Shipley:
Former U.S. representative	The Honorable Marcus Shipley Dear Mr. Shipley:
Territorial delegate	The Honorable Marcus Shipley Delegate of _____ House of Representatives Dear Mr. Shipley:
Heads of independent U.S. organizations	The Honorable Jean Shipley Postmaster General Dear Madam Postmaster General:
State governor	The Honorable Marcus Shipley Governor of _____ Dear Governor Shipley:
State lieutenant governor	The Honorable Jean Shipley Lieutenant Governor of _____ Dear Ms. Shipley:
State secretary of state	The Honorable Marcus Shipley Secretary of the State of _____ Dear Mr. Shipley:
State attorney general	The Honorable Jean Shipley Attorney General State of _____ Dear Ms. Shipley:

Table 9.4 (continued)

GOVERNMENT OFFICIALS (continued)

State senate president	The Honorable Marcus Shipley President of the Senate of the State of _____ Dear Mr. Shipley:
State speaker of assembly, house	The Honorable Jean Shipley Speaker of the Assembly/House of Representatives of the State of _____ Dear Ms. Shipley:
State treasurer, auditor, comptroller	The Honorable Marcus Shipley Treasurer of _____ Dear Mr. Shipley:
State senator	The Honorable Jean Shipley The Senate of _____ Dear Senator Shipley:
State representative assemblyman/woman, delegate	The Honorable Marcus Shipley House of Delegates State of _____ Dear Mr. Shipley:
State district attorney	The Honorable Jean Shipley District Attorney State of _____ Dear Ms. Shipley:
City mayor	The Honorable Marcus Shipley Mayor of _____ Dear Mayor Shipley: Dear Mr. Mayor: (*formal*)
City board of commissioners	The Honorable Jean Shipley President Board of Commissioners of the City of _____ Dear Ms. Shipley:
City attorney, counsel, corporation counsel	The Honorable Marcus Shipley City Attorney Dear Mr. Shipley:

GOVERNMENT OFFICIALS

Alderman/woman	Alderwoman Jean Shipley City Hall Dear Ms. Shipley:

COURT OFFICIALS

Chief justice of U.S. Supreme Court	The Chief Justice of the United States The Supreme Court Dear Mr. Chief Justice:
Associate justice of U.S. Supreme Court	Justice Shipley The Supreme Court Dear Justice Shipley: Dear Madam Justice: (*formal*)
Retired associate justice of U.S. Supreme Court	The Honorable Marcus Shipley Dear Justice Shipley:
Chief justice, judge, of state supreme court	The Honorable Jean Shipley Chief Justice Supreme Court of _____ Dear Madam Chief Justice:
Associate justice of state's highest court	The Honorable Marcus Shipley Associate Justice Supreme Court of _____ Dear Justice Shipley:
State presiding justice	The Honorable Jean Shipley Presiding Justice, Appellate Division Supreme Court of _____ Dear Justice Shipley:
Judge of court	The Honorable Marcus Shipley Judge of the United States District Court for the District of _____ Dear Judge Shipley:
Clerk of court	The Honorable Jean Shipley Clerk of the Superior Court of _____ Dear Ms. Shipley:

Table 9.4 (continued)

DIPLOMATIC AND FOREIGN OFFICIALS

When officials are not at their posts, add the name of the country where they are based (*American Ambassador to Great Britain*). For officials who hold military rank, use their military title instead of *The Honorable*. (Americans are never addressed as *His* or *Her Excellency*). The words *United States* should be used instead of the word *American* when a U.S. official is assigned to a country in South or Central America (*The Ambassador of the United States*). In other countries, the phrase *American Ambassador* may be used. When foreign officials have personal or other professional titles such as *Dom* or *Dr.,* that title may be combined with the diplomatic title (*His Excellency Dr. Marcus Shipley*).

U.S. ambassador	The Honorable Jean Shipley The Ambassador of the United States American Embassy Dear Madam Ambassador:
U.S. chargé d'affaires, consul general, consul, vice consul	Mr. Marcus Shipley Chargé d'Affaires of the United States Dear Mr. Shipley:
Foreign ambassador	Her Excellency Jean Shipley The Ambassador of _____ Dear Madam Ambassador: Excellency: (*formal*)
Foreign minister in the United States	The Honorable Dr. Marcus Shipley Minister of _____ Dear Mr. Minister:
Prime minister	Her Excellency Jean Shipley Prime Minister of _____ Dear Madam Prime Minister: Excellency: (*formal*)
Canadian or British prime minister	The Right Honorable Jean Shipley, C.M.G. Prime Minister of _____ Dear Madam Prime Minister:
President, premier, of a nation	His Excellency Marcus Shipley President of _____ Dear Mr. President: Excellency: (*formal*)
Foreign chargé d'affaires ad interim in the United States	Ms. Jean Shipley Chargé d'Affaires ad Interim of _____ Dear Ms. Shipley:

UNITED NATIONS OFFICIALS

In the United Nations, as elsewhere, American citizens are addressed as *The Honorable,* rather than as *His* or *Her Excellency.*

Secretary general	His Excellency Marcus Shipley Secretary General of the United Nations Dear Mr. Secretary General: Excellency: (*formal*)
Under Secretary	The Honorable Jean Shipley Under Secretary of the United Nations Dear Ms. Under Secretary:
U.S. representative to the United Nations, ambassadorial rank	The Honorable Marcus Shipley United States Representative to the United Nations Dear Mr. Ambassador:
Foreign representative to the United Nations, ambassadorial rank	Her Excellency Jean Shipley Representative of _____ to the United Nations Dear Madam Ambassador: Excellency: (*formal*)

MILITARY SERVICES: ARMY, AIR FORCE, MARINE CORPS

The same titles are used in the army, air force, and Marine Corps, although the designation for each branch of service differs: *USA* (U.S. Army), *USAF* (U.S. Air Force), *USMC* (U.S. Marine Corps). The reserve is indicated by adding *R* to the service designation: *USAFR* (U.S. Air Force Reserve).

General, lieutenant general, major general, brigadier general	General Marcus Shipley, USA Dear General Shipley:
Colonel, lieutenant colonel, major, captain	Colonel Jean Shipley, USMC Dear Colonel Shipley:
First lieutenant, second lieutenant	First Lieutenant Marcus Shipley, USAF Dear Lieutenant Shipley:
Warrant officer	Chief Warrant Officer Jean Shipley, USA Dear Ms. Shipley:
Retired officer	Colonel Marcus Shipley, USMC, Retired Dear Colonel Shipley:
Enlished personnel	Private First Class Jean Shipley, USA Dear Private Shipley:

Table 9.4 (continued)

MILITARY SERVICES: NAVY, COAST GUARD

The same titles are used in the navy and Coast Guard, although the designation for each branch of service differs: *USN* (U.S. Navy); *USCG* (U.S. Coast Guard). The reserve is indicated by adding *R* to the service designation: *USNR* (U.S. Navy Reserve).

Admiral, vice admiral rear admiral	Admiral Marcus Shipley, USN Dear Admiral Shipley:
Captain, commander	Captain Jean Shipley, USCG Dear Captain Shipley:
Lieutenant commander, lieutenant, lieutenant (jg), ensign	Lieutenant Commander Marcus Shipley Dear Commander Shipley:
Warrant officer	Chief Warrant Officer Jean Shipley, USCG Dear Ms. Shipley:
Retired officer	Commander Marcus Shipley, USN, Retired Dear Commander Shipley:
Enlisted personnel	Petty Officer First Class Marcus Shipley, USCG Dear Petty Officer Shipley:

RELIGIOUS OFFICIALS

Churches follow different practices in the use of *The* preceding *Reverend.* Some organizations have dropped *The,* although most have retained it. Follow the organization's preference. Many men and women religious now prefer to be addressed by their last names (*Dear Sister Shipley*), rather than their first names (*Dear Sister Jean*). Some heads of congregations have adopted a title such as *President* or *Director,* rather than the traditional *Father* or *Mother Superior.* Follow the person's preference in individual cases.

The pope	His Holiness, The Pope *or* His Holiness, Pope [Name] Vatican City, Italy Your Holiness: *or* Most Holy Father:

RELIGIOUS OFFICIALS

Apostolic pro-nuncio	His Excellency The Most Reverend Marcus Shipley Titular Archbishop of _____ The Apostolic Pro-Nuncio Dear Archbishop Shipley: Your Excellency: (*formal*)
Roman Catholic cardinal in the United States	His eminence Marcus Cardinal Shipley Archbishop of _____ Dear Cardinal Shipley: Your Eminence: (*formal*)
Roman Catholic archbishop in the United States	The Most Reverend Marcus Shipley, D.D. Archbishop of _____ Dear Archbishop Shipley: Most Reverend Sir: *or* Your Excellency: (*formal*)
Anglican archbishop	The Most Reverend Marcus Shipley Archbishop of _____ Dear Archbishop Shipley: Your Grace: (*formal*)
Roman Catholic bishop in the United States	The Most Reverend Marcus Shipley Bishop of _____ Dear Bishop Shipley: Most Reverend Sir: (*formal*)
Protestant Episcopal bishop	The Right Reverend Marcus Shipley, D. D., LL.D. Bishop of _____ Dear Bishop Shipley: Right Reverend Sir: (*formal*)

Protestant Episcopal
presiding bishop
	The Most Reverend Marcus Shipley,
	  D.D., LL.D.
	Presiding Bishop of the Protestant
	  Episcopal Church in Amercia
	Dear Bishop Shipley:
	Most Reverend Sir: (*formal*)

Anglican bishop	The Right Reverend Marcus Shipley The Lord Bishop of _____ Dear Bishop Shipley: Right Reverend Sir: (*formal*)

Table 9.4 (continued)

RELIGIOUS OFFICIALS (continued)

Methodist bishop	The Reverend Marcus Shipley, D.D. Methodist Bishop Dear Bishop Shipley: *or* Dear Dr. Shipley:
Protestant Episcopal dean	The Very Reverend Marcus Shipley, D.D. Dean of _____ Dear Dean Shipley:
Roman Catholic monsignor (higher rank)	The Right Reverend Marcus Shipley Dear Monsignor Shipley: Right Reverend Monsignor: (*formal*)
Roman Catholic priest	The Reverend Marcus Shipley, S.C. Dear Dr. Shipley:
Episcopal priest, high church	The Reverend Marcus Shipley, D.D., Litt.D. Dear Dr. Shipley:
Protestant minister	The Reverend Jean Shipley, D.D., Litt.D. Dear Dr. Shipley:
Jewish rabbi	Rabbi Marcus Shipley, D.D. Dear Rabbi Shipley:
Roman Catholic brother	Brother Marcus Shipley Dear Brother Marcus: *or* Dear Brother Shipley:
Roman Catholic sister	Sister Jean Shipley Dear Sister Jean: *or* Dear Sister Shipley:

COLLEGE AND UNIVERSITY OFFICIALS

President, chancellor	Dr. Jean Shipley, President Dear Dr. Shipley:
Dean, assistant dean	Dr. Marcus Shipley, Dean School of _____ Dear Dr. Shipley:
Professor, assistant professor, associate professor	Dr. Jean Shipley Professor of _____ Dear Dr. Shipley: Dear Professor Shipley: (*if no doctorate*)
Instructor	Mr. Marcus Shipley Dear Mr. Shipley:

---

although most retain *The*. The examples in Table 9.4 use the traditional *The Reverend:*

> The Reverend Leonard Eastman
> First Unity Church
> [Address]
>
> Dear Dr. Eastman:

> Reverend Leonard Eastman
> First Unity Church
> [Address]
>
> Dear Dr. Eastman:

Use *Reverend* alone with a surname (no first name) only if a personal or scholastic title intervenes:

> The Reverend Dr. Eastman
>
> The Reverend Ms. McCarthy

MODEL LETTERS

Effective Messages

An effective message, whether prepared for traditional delivery or electronic transmission, should follow the correct style and format described in this chapter and in Chapter 7, "Business Style Guide," Guide to Capitalization and Punctuation and Guide to Composition. Each message should be consistent with the rules of grammar and composition described in Chapter 8, "Business English," Rules of English. The message should also have an appropriate tone for the intended reader and comment on an intellectual level that is suitable for the reader. Although messages may differ in some respects, such as in the degree of formality used, depending on how well you know the recipient and what your objective is, the following strategies will in general make them more effective:

- Get right to the point. Businesspeople are very busy, and the recipient may have many more messages to read.
- Avoid overly long, complex sentences and paragraphs, particularly in international correspondence.
- Use the active voice ("We are excited about your proposal") instead of the passive voice ("Your proposal has been met with excitement on our part"), unless you have a special reason to be indirect.
- Precede bad news with good news, or at least begin a bad-news letter with a pleasant comment (a *buffer*). This will make the recipient feel better: "Thanks, Bob, for your suggestion about a product marketing

survey. It would be wonderful if we could use the FRT sampling techniques you suggested. Unfortunately, we don't have enough money in this year's budget to adopt that plan."

- Avoid bureaucratic jargon ("Operational life-cycle statistics re the configuration of this system belie the system's estimated utility vis-a-vis strategic plans"). However, don't be too casual ("You bet! We'd love to talk to you guys about your marketing techniques"). A straightforward, businesslike approach is always preferred.

- Arrange your thoughts and the paragraphs containing them in a logical, coherent manner. See Chapter 7, "Business Style Guide," Paragraph style.

- Use a very short, to-the-point concluding paragraph to state any action you want the reader to take, to thank the reader, or to summarize the main point of your letter.

- Avoid conversational abbreviations, such as *BTW* for "by the way," and symbols for emotion (*emoticons,* also called *smileys*), such as *: (* for "frowning." This type of informal shorthand is appropriate only in personal messages.

The following models are examples of messages about common business topics. Many of them are repetitive-type messages in which only names, dates, monetary amounts, and other such facts change each time. The basic message could thus be stored in your computer, ready to be copied and edited each time you need to send a similar message, rather than rekey the entire new message:

Adjustment

Thank you for returning the fax machine (Model C1000) that you ordered on September 3. You're right — the rollers are not working properly. I've asked our shipping department to send you a replacement model immediately at no additional cost.

We realize the inconvenience you've experienced and are therefore sending the replacement by overnight express. We're also enclosing in the shipment a small gift to thank you for your patience.

Please let me know, Ms. Schorsch, if you have any problems with the replacement machine. We value your business and look forward to working with you again.

Application

It was a pleasure meeting with you and Leslie Maguire during lunch Tuesday. It's always nice to find other Brooklyn Medical School graduates in our city.

I was particularly impressed with what you had to say about the Society of Medical Practitioners, and I'm accepting your offer to become a member. My application is enclosed, along with a copy of my resume and several letters of recommendation.

Thanks so much for offering to sponsor me, Dave. I appreciate your interest and am eagerly looking forward to becoming a member of your organization.

Appointment

Bill Walsh would like to know if you could meet him in his office (Room 1421) on Friday, August 7, at 4 o'clock.

He's reviewed your proposal to enlarge our company library and wants to discuss possible cost and staff requirements for such an expansion. I know that he's eager to learn more about your idea.

Please let me know (extension 7600) whether this time is convenient. Thanks very much.

Appreciation

Thank you for your recent order, Dr. Nelson, which we've shipped by Walton Transport Services, as you requested. It's always a pleasure to welcome a new customer to Legg & Greene.

We know the extent to which joint business practices such as yours are expanding, and we're ready to fill whatever equipment needs you may have in the months and years ahead. I'm enclosing a copy of our spring-summer catalog.

Please let us know if you have any questions about your order. We look forward to hearing from you again.

Collection

We're sorry that, effective today, we must close your credit line to further purchases. We've written to you several times and have also telephoned to remind you of the importance of keeping your account current. Unfortunately, the amount of $639.98 is now four months past due.

We urge you to protect your credit rating and avoid the additional costs you'll incur if legal action is required. Please call or write today, Mr. Lewitt, to discuss your past-due account and how you can meet your obligations.

Complaint

I'm returning for a refund one self-inking stamp and stamp pad. They were ordered from your catalog on April 24 and paid for by my check No. 6161 for $16.98. Although the product was advertised on your website and in your catalog as self-reinking, the ink is too faint to produce an effective imprint.

Please send a refund check of $16.98 to Ms. Cynthia Edison at the letterhead address. Thank you.

Congratulations

All of us at Stevens & Stevens are happy to send you and your associates our sincerest congratulations on the tenth anniversary of Ergonomic Designers!

Your collection of ergonomic products has been a much-needed solution to cumulative trauma disorders in the workplace. Our own employees once suffered from this serious problem before discovering your back supports and other ergonomic aids.

We've enjoyed preparing your annual Ergonomic Series catalogs and new product advertisements, and we want to wish you and everyone else at Ergonomic Designers many more years of progress and prosperity.

Follow-up

Arlene, have you had a chance to think about addressing my data processing class at our June seminar? Since we expect to send the program to our desktop publishing group on May 1, I'd appreciate receiving your decision on this by Tuesday, April 22 (hope it'll be yes).

Thanks much.

Inquiry

Do you have any booklets or other literature about health-care financing? If so, please send an order form, as well as any free material that you have on this subject. If you have nothing available, could you direct me to another source?

Thank you.

Introduction

I'm happy to introduce James Newton, who has worked for this firm during the past two years. Jim is interested in joining the Council of City Trial Attorneys, and I wholeheartedly endorse his application.

He's a capable, hard-working attorney who has taken on several difficult cases for us and has performed superbly. His credentials and law school record are impeccable, and he is well versed in your state law, having served as a judicial assistant to criminal court Judge Elizabeth M. Mahoney before being employed in our firm.

If you need any further information, please call me at 123-555-5000. I'll appreciate any consideration you can give to Jim's application.

Invitation

Roy, I'd like you to be my guest for lunch along with Cindy Medline on Thursday, August 7. I've made reservations at the Bar and Grill, and we could meet in the lobby about noon on Thursday.

Could let me know by Tuesday if you'll be available? Both Cindy and I hope you can join us. We're eager to hear about your tour of Europe last month and want to catch up on other news too.

Order

Please send the following item to my attention at Shipley Associates, 12 State Street, City, ST 98765:

> One (1) #133-6466-01 balance-beam $250 scale (to 400 pounds)

Since we need this item on or before March 6, 2001, please ship it by UPS Next-Day Air.

Thank you.

Sales

Thank you for participating in our cartridge-recycling program. We're happy to enclose your refund check for $5. To receive this refund in the future, follow these two simple steps:

> 1. Go to any authorized Powermate store where your refund check may be applied toward the purchase of your next Powermate dry-ink cartridge.
>
> 2. Present the refund check when you purchase your next cartridge, and $5 will be deducted from the purchase price.

Thanks to environmentally conscious customers like you, our cartridge-recycling program is a huge success — and as long as you keep recycling cartridges, we'll keep sending you refund checks!

If you have any questions about our program, call us anytime between 9 and 5 Eastern time at 800-555-1201. We're always happy to hear from you.

Transmittal

Thank you, Ms. Dennison, for asking about our easel pads. Here's the brochure you requested.

Presentations for Business offers a complete line of easel products, including the unique static image pad described in the enclosed brochure. This pad can be used with dry-erase or permanent markers, so it's perfect for meetings, presentations, brainstorming sessions, signs, and messages.

If we can answer any questions, Mrs. Dennison, or help you select the right products for your meetings, please call a customer representative at 800-555-7707. We appreciate your interest in Presentations for Business products.

Information Management

Office professionals are often responsible for directing and controlling the flow of information in and out of and within an office. Other chapters have focused on specific types of movement, such as the delivery of voice messages (Chapter 4, "Telecommunications") and the transmission of e-mails and faxes and the delivery of traditional letters and memos (Chapter 5, "Mail Processing"). Incoming information and copies of outgoing information must also be stored in an office in a logical manner and in a secure place that provides not only for temporary or permanent storage but also for rapid retrieval.

Records management is an area of information management involving the systematic analysis and control of all types of records, including paper records, magnetic media, optical media, and microforms. The management of paper records is the most challenging task in many offices, and the problem of finding adequate storage space has led organizations to develop further procedures for handling nonpaper records.

In some organizations, large quantities of machine-readable magnetic or optical disks and tapes are maintained by centralized computing facilities, and such records account for a rapidly growing percentage of the information resources in those organizations. However, like their paper counterparts, photographic and machine-readable records require appropriate storage facilities, must be carefully prepared for effective retrieval, and must be protected from inadvertent damage or destruction.

RECORDS MANAGEMENT

The size of an organization often determines what type of records-management program exists. Some mid- to large-size corporations, government agencies, and other organizations have formal, centralized programs staffed by one or more full-time professionals. In such organizations, departmental assistants typically serve as liaisons who provide the records-management staff with essential information about departmental files and record-keeping requirements. They help prepare inventories of records, implement records-retention schedules (usually prepared or approved by an attorney), prepare records for delivery to off-site archival storage, identify potential storage applications, help select manual and automated filing equipment, and help develop appropriate filing systems. In most departments, office professionals are familiar with record-keeping practices, and their liaison role is critical to the success of a records-management program.

Many smaller organizations and some larger ones may have no formal information-management or records-management program. Consequently, office professionals must assume responsibility for such activities in their offices or departments. Although some aspects of records management require technical expertise, many concepts are based on common sense and an orderly approach to problem solving that is characteristic of much of an office professional's work.

Active Records

Organizing files for easy retrieval of material later is a primary concern in records management. Often, though, the need to improve a filing system isn't apparent until it becomes increasingly difficult to find material. In addition, computer software already has a built-in document-management feature, and the filing of paper copies, often considered low-priority work, is given little attention. When inattention and disinterest exist, they pose a serious obstacle to the design, functioning, and maintenance of an effective and efficient system.

Official files. Records managers often insist that an *official file* be established. The official-file concept emphasizes that an official file will be the sole, complete, and authoritative accumulation of an organization's records.

Official files are common in insurance claims processing, accounts receivable, purchasing, and other transaction-oriented activities, where work is performed in readily identifiable stages by office employees, each of whom contributes information to the file. Official files are found less frequently in scientific research, engineering, architecture, law, and other project-oriented activities, where the work is performed in a discretionary manner by office professionals.

Personal files. In project-oriented settings, individual employees often need to maintain *personal files*. These files, stored in individual offices or in adjacent work areas, offer the convenience of close proximity, but they may vary greatly in scope and content. Often, they're incomplete, and they may be set up so that only the creator or principal user can comprehend them. As a result, they're largely inaccessible to other workers who may need to retrieve information when the creator or principal user is out of the office. If the creator or main user leaves the organization before completing a project or other activity, it can be very difficult for others to reconstruct what was done.

Dual files. One way to solve the problem of only the creator or principal user knowing how to use his or her personal file is to establish this clear guideline: All participants in project-related activities must route all documents associated with the project to a single official file, even if copies are temporarily retained in the participant's personal file. Having one official file will eliminate time-consuming searches in multiple personal files, and having one complete file will increase the likelihood of retrieving accurate information. However, this practice also will result in the storage of numerous duplicate copies, creating a greater need for additional storage space, particularly if the duplicates are in paper form.

Centralization. An official file may be centralized or decentralized. Centralization typically occurs at the department or division level, less often at the organization level. A common pattern is a centralized repository for the official files of all projects undertaken by a given department or division.

Centralization encourages the development of filing systems and the standardization of filing practices. Staff training is simplified, and work performance is enhanced. Compared to having a number of scattered files (decentralization), centralization usually requires fewer file-maintenance personnel. In addition, file control and security are usually improved.

FILING SYSTEMS

Filing Procedures

The steps taken in filing paper material differ from those taken in filing documents electronically, as the following sections indicate.

Manual filing. In most cases, follow these steps in filing paper material: After the material has been released for filing, separate it into obvious categories, such as correspondence and reports. Alphabetize the individual items in each category, or code them numerically, depending on your filing system. If you need to set up a new file folder, make the filename consistent with the corresponding electronic filename, if any, or first select an electronic version. Follow office policy in regard to writing on or highlighting words on the material. If this isn't permitted, attach removable, self-adhesive notes on which you can write the appropriate filename or code, if having this information would be helpful.

Remove staples and paper clips, and prepare file folder, guide, container, and other labels, as needed. Also, fill out any necessary cross-reference sheets. Finally, insert the documents into the appropriate file folders. Usually, in the case of correspondence and similar material, put the items with the most recent date on top.

Electronic filing. Although your software will direct the computer to organize your files and store them electronically, users still must take certain steps to ensure that a document is named properly and stored where desired (hard disk, floppy disk, tape, and so on) and can easily be found and retrieved. Follow the requirements of your software in naming your files, and set up general electronic "directories" or "folders" to which you can send the particular documents. For example, if you exchange numerous messages with a client named Jane Arnold, you may want a separate "folder" called *jane arnold* or *jarnold* to which you'll direct the computer to send all messages and documents involving Ms. Arnold.

Similarly, direct the computer to file e-mail attachments that you send or receive to the appropriate electronic folders, and enter the filenames and other required data on any computer indexes that you maintain. Also, just as you might prepare cross-reference sheets for a paper file, add any necessary cross-references to your electronic filename index. For example, if you use social security or other numbers for filenames, you'll also need an alphabetical index to tell you which number belongs with a particular person's name (or file). To keep coworkers who also access the same electronic files informed about the location of such electronically filed material (folder name, filename of individual items, and so on), regularly print out and distribute revised indexes to them, and they should do the same for you.

To reduce the accumulation of material on your hard disk, periodically transfer inactive files to removable floppy disks or other forms of storage (follow company policy). Prepare labels as needed for floppy disks, tapes, and their containers (with filenames that match those on your hard disk). When possible, save your files in a format or medium that won't readily be obsolete. In any case, include with your floppy disks copies of the software that was used to create the material.

Filing Systems

A variety of manual, electronic, and other filing systems are available, and different offices may use one or more systems. For example, an office may have an alphabetical personal file and also use the numerical official file of a particular department or division in which the office is located. Most offices or departments devise a system that is best suited for their specific type of activity. It may be a combination of standard alphabetical or numerical systems or some other adaptation of a standard system.

Regardless of the general location of containers, and regardless of whether the files are paper, magnetic, microform, or optical, a manageable system must be developed not only to accommodate current records but also to allow for future expansion. The principal authority consulted by many systems designers is the Association of Records Managers and Administrators (ARMA International) in Prairie Village, Kansas. The ARMA publishes numerous books, reports, guidelines, standards, audiovisual aids, and home-study material. Office professionals who are helping to devise or redesign a manual or electronic filing system should request a free Technical Publications Catalog from the association and visit its website.

Since a computer program has an already-established file-management system, it's usually more practical to design the paper system (filenames, indexing, alphabetizing method, and so on) so that it's consistent with the electronic system. If the electronic and paper systems are as consistent as possible, users won't have to learn different filenames and two unrelated systems. This in turn should make it easier to locate the same information in either system.

In naming your electronic files, follow the requirements of your software in regard to the number of characters allowed, characters that may *not* be used, required spacing, and punctuation, capitalization, and so on. Although most programs don't require the addition of a three-letter extension, you may find it useful to include such an extension to designate the type of file, such as a letter or financial statement. Thus you might name the file for a letter to Jeffrey Smith as *jsmith.ltr* and file the hard copy of the letter in a corresponding paper file folder labeled *Smith Jeffrey.*

Alphabetical Files

Some form of alphabetical filing may be applied to names, places, and other subjects. Although the same words may be used in both paper and computer filing, they may be abbreviated on a disk file. *Property Management,* for example, may be written in full on the label of a paper file folder or a paper file-division guide but may be abbreviated as *Ptymgmt* or something else in a computer filename.

Alphabetical filing methods. Alphabetical methods of filing may be either *letter by letter,* which is the method commonly used in a dictionary or encyclopedia, or *word by word,* which is the method most often used in a manual office filing system. Notice the difference in the order of filenames, depending on whether they're arranged letter by letter or word by word:

Letter by letter: travelerschecks	*Word by word:* travel schedule
travelschedule	travelers check

Alphabetizing rules. Although general A-to-Z alphabetizing rules are familiar, special rules apply in certain situations.

- Transpose personal names for filing, with the last name first (unit number 1), followed by the first name (unit number 2), and ending with the middle name or initial (unit number 3): (1) Jones (2) John (3) W. Some foreign names are already written with the family name first. *Ho Kai Lin,* for example would be arranged as *Ho Lin Kai* for filing. *Ho* is the last name, and *Lin* is the first name in this case. If *Kai* might be the first name, include a cross-reference under *Ho Kai Lin* directing the user to *Ho Lin Kai.*

- Leave company names that are formed with a personal name as is, without reversing the order as you would do with a personal name alone. *John Hill & Sons* would therefore be treated as *John Hill[&] Sons,* not as *Hill John[&] Sons.* Notice that the ampersand (*&*) is disregarded.

- Disregard an article, preposition, or conjunction in arranging words for filing unless it's part of a foreign name (*LeCar*) and unless it's joined to a main word or letter by a hyphen. Thus *J and K Computers* would be treated as *J[and] K Computers,* ignoring the *and.* However, *J-and-K Computers* would be alphabetized as *J and K Computers,* keeping the *and* and treating it as the second alphabetizing unit.

- Ignore the hyphens, and alphabetize each part of a hyphenated company name as a separate word. *You-Know-It Preschool* would therefore be treated as *You Know It Preschool.* However, treat a hyphenated personal name as one word, not as separate words. *Madeline Hill-Saunders* would thus be alphabetized as *HillSaunders Madeline.*

- Arrange names with numbers in numerical order, and place them as a group in front of any names with words only: *3 Flower Decorating, 4 Cheese Pizza,* and so on.

- Treat words representing numbers that are joined by a hyphen (*Seventy-two Place*) as one word in filing: *Seventytwo Place.*

- Treat names beginning with prefixes such as *De, Des, La, Las, Van,* and *Von* as one-word filing units. *DesMoines* (but *New York* — two words).

- Place names beginning with *Mc* or *Mac* in front of other words beginning with *M* or in alphabetical order within the *M* listings, as preferred: *McDermitt Henry, Madison Edward, Morgan Charles,* or *Madison Edward, McDermitt Henry, Morgan Charles.*

- File all initials or abbreviations, such as *SAM* (sequential access method), in alphabetical order as a group in front of other full-word names in that alphabetical section. Or file them within the appropriate alphabetical section, treating each one as a regular word, if preferred.

- Spell out abbreviations, such as *Chas.* (*Charles*), when space allows, and file them as a full word.

- Omit accents (diacritical marks) and apostrophes in foreign words (*Chargé d'Affaires*) when writing filenames: *Charge dAffaires.*

- Ignore titles of persons, unless you need them to distinguish people with the same name. In that case, add the titles as written — spelled out or abbreviated — without punctuation, and place them in parentheses as the last filing unit: *Foster James (Colonel), Foster James (Dr).*

- When someone is always known by a title (*Sister Annette*), retain it and treat it as the first filing unit. Similarly, if someone doesn't use a last name for business purposes (*Madame Mysteria*), also treat the title as the first filing unit. If the person uses a nickname for a first name (*Babe Rutherford*), treat the nickname as the person's given first name: *Madame Mysteria, Rutherford Babe, Sister Annette.*

- Use cross-reference cards or sheets in the paper files in the alphabetical location of an alternative name or an abbreviation to direct users to the name under which material is filed. You can use the same type of cross-references in an alphabetical computer index.

Applying the preceding rules to the words and names that were given as examples (listed in column 1), you would arrange them in word-by-word units and alphabetize them as indicated in column 2:

Words and Names	Alphabetize As
Edward Madison	3 Flower Decorating
Seventy-two Place	4 Cheese Pizza
Dr. James Foster	Charge dAffaires
Ho Kai Lin	DesMoines

John Hill & Sons	Foster James (Colonel)
Des Moines	Foster James (Dr)
Chargé d'Affaires	HillSaunders Madeline
J and K Computers	Ho Lin Kai
Sister Annette	J and K Computers
John W. Jones	J[and] K Computers
Madame Mysteria	John Hill[&] Sons
You-Know-It Preschool	Jones John W
Babe Rutherford	Madame Mysteria
New York	Madison Edward
Madeline Hill-Saunders	McDermitt Henry
4 Cheese Pizza	Morgan Charles
J-and-K Computers	New York
3 Flower Decorating	Rutherford Babe
Henry McDermitt	Seventytwo Place
Charles Morgan	Sister Annette
Colonel James Foster	You Know It Preschool

Folders, tabs, and guides. In paper files, alphabetical filing is compatible with both drawer- and shelf-type filing equipment, using folders and guides with tabs. File folders may have top or side tabs, and the top style may be a third cut, half cut, fifth cut, two-fifths cut, or full (straight) cut. Labels containing the individual filenames are affixed to these tabs, and labels designating major sections are affixed to the guide tabs. (Guides in an alphabetical file are often printed with each letter of the alphabet.)

Alphabetical filing systems may also use color coding (different colors for the labels, folders, or guides) as a means of making it easier to identify at a glance specific files or sections of files. For example, labels in an *A* section may have a red border, those in the *B* section a blue border, and so on. Sometimes color is used to distinguish between different people who have the same name. The potential uses of color are almost limitless, and in general, different colors help filers avoid misfiles and more easily locate specific information.

Cross-references. When you might logically find something filed under any one of two or more names, it's necessary to insert cross-reference sheets or cards in the paper files for the alternative names. These cross-reference sheets or cards will direct the user to the actual name under which the material is filed:

Harris B M	Steubing-Harris Marjorie (Mrs.)
SEE Harris Benjamin M	SEE Harris Benjamin M

Cross-reference sheets may also include other information, if desired, such as the date and subject of the filed material. Indexes prepared for documents filed electronically may have similar cross-references and information.

Subject Files

A-to-Z filing. A simple A-to-Z filing system is often the easiest type of system to use for organizing material by subject. Little training is needed for setup or maintenance. This type of system becomes more complex, though, as alphabetic or numeric codes are added. For example, two- to six-letter alphabetic codes may be added to the subjects, as in *SCH SCHEDULE.* Or a combination letter-number code may be used, as in *SCH-01 DIRECTORS MEETING SCHEDULE, SCH-02 STOCKHOLDERS MEETING SCHEDULE.* In a decimal-numeric coding system, only numbers are used, as in *100 SCHEDULE, 100.1 DIRECTORS MEETING SCHEDULE, 100.2 STOCKHOLDERS MEETING SCHEDULE.*

When this system causes both general and specific headings to be mixed, however, a more complex variation may be needed. For example, consider a hypothetical subject filing system used by the marketing department of an electronics company. This subject file contains product literature and published articles pertaining to various microcomputer products and components. Therefore, a section of such a file might include these headings:

Anadex Printers	Input Peripherals
Application Software	Laser Printers
Auxiliary Storage Devices	Microprocessors
BASIC Interpreters	Microsoft BASIC Interpreter
Central Processing Units	Minifloppy Disk Drives
Compilers and Interpreters	Operating Systems
Dienet Printers	Output Peripherals
Display Terminals	Printers
Hard-Disk Drives	Read-Only Memories
Hertz Display Terminals	System Software
Ink-Jet Printers	Winchester Disk Drives

As you can see, this list contains an odd mixture of general and specific headings. Material on related subjects — the various types of printers, for example — is scattered throughout the list. None of the general headings is subdivided to reflect specialized facets of a given topic, and there's no broad framework for establishing new headings. In practice, some subjects will likely contain many documents while others may contain only a few pages.

Hierarchical filing. A more complex subject system, sometimes called an *hierarchical subject system* or a *classification system,* is designed to address these problems. Rather than having topical headings arranged in conventional alphabetical sequence, the documents are arranged in a network of logically interrelated subdivisions representing general and specific facets of a given subject or activity. The first step in designing this type of customized subject file is to subdivide all records into very broad groups called *series.* In the microcomputer information file example, the subject file might include the following series:

> Central Processing Units
> Input Peripherals
> Output Peripherals
> Auxiliary Storage Devices
> System Software
> Application Software

Each of these series might be subdivided into two or more primary categories as in this example:

> Output Peripherals
> > Printers
> > Display Terminals

A primary category could be further subdivided into secondary categories as follows:

> Printers
> > Ink-Jet Printers
> > Laser Printers

You can keep subdividing categories in this way to the extent that it's necessary or desirable.

Advantages of hierarchical filing. The subject system just described is truly systematic, because it reflects the structure of the activity through which the documents themselves were created. These systems are well suited to browsing since related documents are grouped together in the file. For the same reason, they allow you to retrieve documents at varying levels. In the previous example, all information about microcomputer output devices can be obtained in one location.

Disadvantages of hierarchical filing. A major problem in hierarchical filing is that this type of system is time-consuming to construct and typically requires a thorough understanding of the activity by which the documents were created. Thus to design a subject file for a marketing department that maintains information about microcomputers, you need to know a substantial amount about the microcomputer industry. An office professional may lack the time and background required to design such a system, although it might be initially designed by a records manager or other trained specialist with the office professional's assistance. Once such a system has been designed, you should be able to maintain and, if necessary, modify it.

Another drawback is that this type of system provides only one place to file a given document, even though the document's contents may reflect several different subjects or several facets of the same subject. This limitation can be overcome, though, by duplicating documents for filing in multiple locations or by creating a cross-index. Neither method is entirely satisfactory, however. The obvious shortcoming of filing duplicate copies is that they substantially increase the filing time and the size of the files. Although an index provides a means of accessing documents by subjects other than the one under which the document is filed, it also can prove time-consuming to maintain.

Geographic Files

A geographic arrangement is a variant form of alphabetical filing and is sometimes used in sales offices, distribution outlets, and similar organizations. The typical geographic file is initially subdivided by state or other territorial grouping, and the state or other names are arranged alphabetically. Each state name, for example, might be subdivided into cities or regions, again arranged alphabetically. Within each of these subdivisions, names of correspondents or customers might be arranged alphabetically. The purpose of geographic files is to cluster together the records pertaining to particular sales or distribution territories.

Numeric Files

As the name suggests, numeric systems are widely used for case files, transaction files, financial records, and similar applications in which documents are numbered and requested by an identifying number. In some cases, name files or other alphabetical files are converted to numeric codes to ensure privacy or to decrease filing labor. Compared with alphabetical systems, numeric systems require fewer rules to cover special situations, although a name-to-file number index must be maintained. For example, if you wanted to review the file for John Jones, you would first have to look up *Jones John* in an alphabetical index to find out the number under which the material is filed.

Sequential numeric files. Sequential, or consecutive, numeric filing is the simplest and most widely encountered type of numeric system. It features a basic consecutive arrangement (1, 2, 3, and so on), with the highest numbers being added to the end of the file. Like alphabetical systems, sequential numeric systems are compatible with drawer- and shelf-type filing equipment. Printed or customized number guides can be used to subdivide the file into readily identifiable segments, and color-coded guides are available as well to simplify misfile detection.

Sequential numeric filing systems are easily learned and implemented, but several significant disadvantages limit their utility in certain situations. For example, all recently added numbers fall at the end of the file. In large, centralized filing situations, therefore, personnel often must wait to file or retrieve documents.

Terminal-digit files. Terminal-digit systems are well suited to large, centralized records-management applications where reference activity must be distributed throughout a file and responsibility for particular file segments will be assigned to specific people. Terminal-digit techniques are especially useful in accounts payable, accounts receivable, insurance claims adjustment, and similar transaction-processing applications. They're also widely used in medical records management.

The terminal-digit system requires an identifier of six or more digits. When shorter record numbers are involved, the number sequences can be padded with zeros to increase the length. For filing purposes a number is rewritten as three pairs of two digits each, with the resulting pairs being separated by hyphens:

- The number *365461* is subdivided as *36-54-61*, where *61* is described as the primary pair of digits, *54* as the secondary pair, and *36* as the tertiary pair.

- The file drawer or shelf is labeled *61* and the file guide *54-61*. The folders that are filed in or on drawer or shelf *61* are numbered *00-54-61, 01-54-61, 02-54-61*, and so on to *99-54-61*.

The scattering of sequentially numbered files allows for a more equitable distribution of filing, reference, purging, and other file-maintenance activity. Furthermore, the need to backshift folders following purging is eliminated. As with sequential numeric systems, terminal-digit systems commonly have printed or customized numeric guides in the paper files to divide a file into easily recognizable segments. Color-coded folders may also be used.

Middle-digit files. Middle-digit systems, a variant form of nonsequential numeric filing, also require a six-digit record identifier divided into three pairs of two digits each.

- The number *365461* is again subdivided as *36-54-61*, but in this case, *54* is the primary pair of digits, *36* is the secondary pair, and *61* is the tertiary pair.

- The file drawer or shelf is labeled *54* and the file guide *36-54*. The folders that are filed in or on drawer or shelf *54* are numbered *36-54-00, 36-54-01, 36-54-02*, and so on to *36-54-99*.

As with terminal-digit filing, printed or customized guides and color-coded folders can be used in the paper files. In large, centralized applications where even distribution of filing activity is desired, a middle-digit arrangement results in a scattering effect similar to, but somewhat less radical than, that of terminal-digit filing.

Chronological Files. Chronological filing, a variation of numeric filing, is widely used in small personal files. In chronological filing, records are arranged by date, with the most recent date at the beginning. This type of file is commonly used for correspondence and transaction files.

Decimal files. An older system based on the Dewey Decimal System, decimal filing classifies records under ten or fewer main categories that are numbered *000* to *900*. Each main division may be subdivided into nine or fewer subdivisions (*800, 810, 820,* and so on to *890*). The various subdivisions may each again be subdivided (*810, 811, 812, 813,* and then *813.1, 813.2,* and so on).

Duplex-numeric files. This system of filing uses numbers that are each divided into two groups of digits and separated by a space, hyphen, or other punctuation, as in *40-1,* where *40* is the main division, and *40-1* is a subdivision. Thus if *40* referred to *Computers, 40-1* might refer to *Computer Maintenance.*

Block numeric files. In a block system, a block of numbers is assigned to major functions or areas of activity. Thus the numbers *300-500* might be assigned to the subject *Computers.* Subdivisions would be treated the same as in a duplex-numeric system, so *300-17* might refer to *Computer Maintenance.* Block systems are complex and often difficult to set up.

Alphanumeric Files. Alphanumeric systems, in which the file identifier contains a mixture of alphabetical characters and numeric digits, combine alphabetical and sequential numeric filing techniques. Depending on the procedure used, numerals may be sorted before or after alphabetical characters.

The primary names or subjects are arranged alphabetically and each given a number. Thus if *100 Computers* is a primary subject, it would be filed alphabetically in the *C* section of the files. Its subdivision *Computer Maintenance,* however, would be assigned a number, such as *103,* and would be filed numerically after *100 Computers.* (Other ways of combining numbers and letters are also possible.) Like many numerical systems, an alphanumeric system allows for indefinite expansion but can be difficult to set up and learn.

Phonetic Filing

A less common system, phonetic filing, is designed for large name files in which last names may sound alike but have variant spellings or frequent misspellings (*Smith, Smythe*). In a primitive form of phonetic filing, one of the spellings of a given name is selected for use, and all variant spellings are filed under that form. Cross-references are placed in the file to direct the user to the right spelling. If every variant spelling of *Smith* is filed under the spelling *Smith,* for example, there should be a cross-reference in the *Smythe* location referring the user to *Smith.*

Electronic Files

Your electronic files include the technologies, devices, and media that make electronic storage and retrieval possible. The two main forms of storage are magnetic and optical storage. *Magnetic storage* refers to hard disks, floppy disks, and tapes. *Optical storage* refers to optical disk and tape formats, such as CD-ROM (compact disk — read-only memory), WORM (write once — read many times), CD-DA (compact disk — digital audio), and CD-R (compact disk — recordable). The process of transferring an image to a computer-readable format, such as an optical disk, is known as *electronic document imaging (EDI).*

Although the concept of electronic filing is attractive and is being applied more widely as space for paper files diminishes, the data stored on computer-processable magnetic and optical media are not stable enough for permanent archiving and must be recopied periodically to prevent loss from deterioration. Also, the data generated by one computer system may be incompatible with other systems or with newer versions of the same system, thereby complicating the electronic transfer of documents from one system to another.

Magnetic storage. The highest storage capacity is available on a *fixed,* or *permanent, hard drive.* This device consists of one or more magnetic platters and a read-write mechanism that allows you to read the contents on your computer screen and also insert new data on it. Other types of hard drives are also available, such as a *hard disk cartridge drive,* with removable recording media. Smaller, removable, relatively low storage capacity disks are called *floppy disks, flexible disks,* or *diskettes.* The name reflects a time when all such disks were flexible or bendable, but the 3.5-inch versions used nowadays are, in fact, durable and rigid. Floppy disks are commonly used for backup and short-term or sometimes long-term storage apart from the computer.

Magnetic tape is available in a variety of formats, such as large reels, small cartridges and cassettes and digital audiotape. Continuous-loop formats are commonly used in multiuser dictation systems and voice recordings. Removable tapes, like removable disks, are used for backup as well as short-term and long-term storage.

Optical storage. The most familiar form of optical disk storage is the small, read-only *CD-ROM* (compact disk — read-only memory). CD-ROMs are used to store large data collections, such as encyclopedias, as well as systems and applications software programs. A *read-only format* means that you can read the contents on your computer screen, but you can't insert (file) new data on the disk. Some optical disks are available in a *read-write format* that allows you to insert new data on it as well as read the contents on your computer screen. The *WORM* (write once — read many times) is an example. The *write-once* designation means that you can't repeatedly insert new data over the old, as you could do with a magnetic disk, but you can keep adding data at the end as long as space is available. Larger, higher storage capacity optical disks are also used for long-term storage. The smaller blank disks are more often used for backup but may also be used for short-term or long-term storage.

Other forms of optical media are large-capacity optical tapes and smaller cartridges, cassettes, digital-linear tapes, and optical memory cards. *Optical memory cards,* unlike the more common platter-shaped disks or the ribbonlike strips of tape, are small, rectangular storage media about the size of a credit card.

Like magnetic media, the various optical media must be operated by a read-write drive mechanism, which is typically added to the computer as a peripheral device. Unlike magnetic media, the optical media usually have higher recording densities and therefore can store more information.

Document Management System

Files and documents stored electronically need a document profile, or index, to provide a means to locate and retrieve the documents later.

A *document management system (DMS)* provides such a profile, or index. New and improved software is continually being developed for managing the various document formats, such as a report or a spreadsheet format. For purposes of retrieval, each profile attached to a document provides a coded form of index terms that enable you to find the document by entering a keyword.

In large, centralized filing facilities, retrieval is handled by authorized file personnel who follow established company procedures for retrieval and release to interested personnel. Passwords, antiviral programs, and other safeguards are part of any centralized electronic filing system. Individual offices in smaller organizations will be more directly involved in any document management system and may need additional training to use and maintain it.

Keyword retrieval. For keyword retrieval, an index consisting of key terms must be available. The index, consisting of *field data,* is developed so that you can find documents containing information related to a search parameter. *Field* refers to the specific location in a record where certain data are stored. Usually, keyword retrieval allows you to specify not only words that actually appear in a document but also similar words or words with related meanings.

A form of retrieval that uses field data, such as keyword retrieval, is faster than one using full-text, or full-document, retrieval (see the next section). Many systems, however, allow you to search for a subject by either a full-text or keyword method.

Full-text retrieval. This form of document retrieval uses an inverted index to find every document containing a specific word or words that you specify in the search parameter. The computer therefore creates an alphabetical index of all words in a document and their location (some systems ignore articles, such as *the,* and conjunctions, such as *and*).

Unlike keyword retrieval, described in the previous section, full-text retrieval is slower and isn't as precise. The system only looks for words that actually appeared in a document. Whereas systems providing keyword searching usually allow you to specify similar words or those with related meanings, full-text requires that you enter the *exact words* used in the document you want to find. However, as mentioned earlier, many systems have both full-word and keyword capability.

Reports Management System

A reports management system is a form of document management pertaining to paper and electronic reports of all sizes. Because organizations are producing massive numbers of reports—often daily—they must take special steps to control the production and disposition of them. Reports management is usually part of an organization's overall information-management program. However, the following steps apply especially to the management of reports:

- Periodically assess the need to continue issuing the type of reports that are currently being prepared, disseminated, and stored.
- Stop issuing reports that duplicate data already available elsewhere or easily obtained in a database.
- Stop issuing any report that is no longer mandatory or essential.
- Schedule periodic reports, such as quarterly reports, less often, such as annually or semiannually.
- Combine similar reports into a single report.
- Edit and condense lengthy reports to the smallest possible size.
- Distribute copies only to those who must have them.
- Never store extra printed copies for possible distribution later (print out another copy only as requested).
- Issue and file smaller reports only in electronic form, without printing paper duplicates for the paper files.

REMINDER AND FOLLOW-UP SYSTEMS

All businesses need some type of records for handling reminders and follow-ups. Usually, this involves paper and electronic calendars and various forms of follow-up files.

Executive-Assistant Communication

Communication between an executive and his or her assistant concerning calendar scheduling is imperative. Imagine the embarrassment that might be caused if the executive would schedule an appointment with one guest or client while you were scheduling another appointment for the same time. One way to avoid double bookings is to have an understanding with the executive whereby you schedule only *tentative* appointments unless there is an understanding to the contrary. For example, you would notify a visitor that a proposed conference or appointment is tentative and that confirmation will follow. After checking the date and time with the executive, you could then confirm the appointment and note it on both calendars. In addition, you should routinely check the executive's calendar early each morning and throughout the day, as warranted, to be certain that the items on your calendar correspond to those on the executive's calendar.

Calendar Management

Effective calendar management means having the right calendars and keeping notations consistent on both your calendar and the executive's calendar. It also means making the best possible use of the calendar as a reminder system, scheduling both short-term and long-term events.

Calendar entries. Many activities should be entered more than once. If a client's anniversary is August 9, you must make a notation on the page for August 9 and also note on August 1 or 2 that the executive should be reminded to prepare a letter. Then you should make a notation on your calendar to be certain that the letter is sent by August 4 or 5, depending on the client's location.

Using previous calendars, you can compile a list of annual events — holidays, tax dates, family birthdays, insurance-premium due dates, and so on. Add those that pertain only to your duties on your calendar, but put those that concern only the executive on both calendars. Don't worry if the dates change later. You can always change them on the calendar at that time. Until then, having them on the calendar will at least remind you and the executive that an activity is approaching.

Types of calendars. A wide variety of software is available for reminders and follow-ups. With multifunction programs, you can create calendars, schedule and set up daily reminder "alarms," and do a variety of other tasks. In general, you key in dates and other information, and the computer organizes it and prints or displays a copy when you need it. *Personal information managers (PIMs)* enable you to record names and addresses, schedule work and appointments, record and retrieve notes, and do an assortment of other tasks. Such organizers are usually small, hand-held devices, although you can also find Web-based (usually free) calendars and organizers. Some of the Web versions have other features, such as e-mail and encryption (coded or scrambled messages for security). However, electronic calendar and similar reminder systems can seldom replace their paper counterparts, the desk or pocket calendar. Often it's faster and easier to jot down something on paper than it is to go to the computer, call up the electronic calendar, key in a new entry, and print out a revised copy.

Office professionals still rely heavily on the traditional desk calendar, preferably one that opens flat on the desk to the current day. For scheduling numerous appointments or activities, a calendar with 15-minute time slots is helpful. Executives also use a desk calendar and, in addition, may carry a small pocket calendar while traveling or attending meetings. If your supervisor has two calendars, desk and pocket, both should be consistent with your calendar. Depending on the type of work in your office, you may also be required to maintain an oversize wall or desk calendar showing special dates, such as meeting dates, for a week, a month, or even a year.

Follow-up Files

Types of follow-up files. The two standard types of conventional follow-up files are letter-size and card-size files. The card-size files are often kept on top of a desk, and the letter-size files may be kept in a desk file drawer or other nearby file. Both are set up in a similar manner. A letter-size follow-up file needs 12 monthly folders and 31 daily folders, placed behind the folder for the current month, as well as 1 folder for future years. Copies of correspondence or memo reminders that need follow-up on a certain day are dropped into the folder for that day. The folder for future years is usually placed behind all other folders.

As each day arrives, you should check the folder for that day and send out follow-up notices as needed. Place the new follow-up copy and the previous copy in the folder for another day to be followed up again if no reply is received. As soon as a reply is received, remove all initial and follow-up copies, and place them in the regular files. If only duplicates were used in the follow-up file, with the originals or primary copies in the regular files, destroy the duplicates when they're no longer needed.

Card tickler files. A card tickler file is arranged the same way as a letter file, except that copies of full-size letters cannot be dropped in folders. Instead, brief notations are written on the cards, and the cards are then filed behind numbered daily guides (1 through 31), a future monthly guide, or the single guide for future years.

INACTIVE RECORDS

Some inactive records must be kept to meet legal requirements, because of their historical significance, or simply in case they need to be consulted in the future. Often such records accumulate in office work areas and occupy valuable space needed for the active files. This creates overcrowding, an increase in the potential for misfiles, and wasted time in handling filing duties.

Organizations with numerous records to store usually have records-management software. When bar codes are affixed to containers, the computer can track material to and from storage areas or to and from borrowers who have removed material. Depending on the software, you may be able to use your computer to classify, code, and track items; develop a retention schedule; and manage other aspects of records storage.

Records Inventory

Taking inventory of existing records is a necessary first step before plans to store or dispose of the records can be put into effect. In organizations with formal, centralized records-management programs, a departmental assistant may be asked to complete inventory worksheets specifically designed to gather essential data about the department's records. In some cases, a records-management staff will interview office personnel. In the absence of a centralized records-management program, office professionals usually prepare their own survey instruments and conduct their own inventories. In either case, records are commonly inventoried at the series level.

A *record series* is a group of related documents supporting a common activity and usually having a common name, such as general correspondence, budget reports, purchase orders, and human resources files. For each series, the following information is commonly collected:

- The name by which the series is known to department members and other users
- The form name and number if the series consists of standardized forms
- A brief description and statement of purpose, indicating the functions that the series supports
- Physical location — the address of the office or other facility where the records are stored
- Inclusive dates
- Physical format: paper, microfilm, videotape, floppy disks, and so forth
- The arrangement of documents or other records within the series, such as alphabetical by patient name for a medical record series or numerically by claim number for a series of insurance files
- Series volume, expressed in terms of the number, type, and condition of the file cabinets or storage containers occupied by the records

- Annual growth rate, typically estimated by comparing file segments for different years or, if necessary, by counting documents from a representative sample of the series
- Physical attributes, such as the size of documents or other media condition, color, and texture
- Frequency of reference and names of user departments

In most cases, this information can be determined by carefully examining the records or by interviewing appropriate personnel. If desired, inventory results may be summarized on a tabular worksheet by listing the individual series in rows and the categories of information in columns.

Records Scheduling

For legal and other reasons, records may not be destroyed without company authorization, and a properly developed schedule will help to prevent such mistakes.

Retention schedule. A schedule should list all record series and state the retention period for each type of record and where it is to be stored. If something is to be destroyed, the schedule should also state the authorized date and method of destruction. Confidential records, for example, might have to be shredded, whereas surplus conference programs, which provide public information, might be delivered intact to a recycling site.

Most schedules indicate whether a record series or type of document should be held for a short, medium, or long term. It should also identify *vital records,* such as a copyright, which must be kept permanently.

- *Short-term retention:* Many records are needed for a brief period but have little continuing utility and will be destroyed within a short time, perhaps several months to two years after their creation or receipt. Such records are typically retained in office locations until discarded.
- *Medium-term retention:* Other records must be retained for a specified period, perhaps for one to ten years, but eventually will be destroyed. Such records are often retained in office locations during a relatively brief initial period of active reference and, when reference activity subsides, are transferred to lower-cost, off-site storage facilities.
- *Long-term retention:* A final, often large, group of records must be retained indefinitely. In many cases, such records are put on magnetic or optical disks or tapes or on microfilm to save space, and the

original paper documents are destroyed. Some may be stored in office locations or off-site, depending on the possibility that they may be consulted from time to time.

Legal requirements for retaining records may relate to tax records, pension funds, waste disposal, and other activities subject to government regulation. Often, government contracts have clauses that specify what has to be retained and for how long. State statutes, which vary from state to state, also specify minimum or maximum retention periods for certain records.

Because of the legal requirements for some records, retention and disposal schedules are usually developed by or at least reviewed by an attorney. However, because office professionals work with files and other records almost daily, the information they can provide is very valuable in any records-management program. In addition, records-management handbooks and other publications provided by the ARMA and other professional groups are available to help those who need guidance in developing a retention and disposal schedule.

Periodic review. Developing a retention and disposal schedule is only the first step, albeit an important one. Once a schedule has been prepared, it should be open to periodic review and modification as needed. This type of schedule must be revised periodically as new records series are created and as experience reveals the need for modification of previously established retention periods. An annual review of retention schedules is strongly recommended.

The actual implementation of retention schedules is typically the responsibility of office professionals. Some prefer to allot a specific period during the summer or other slack periods for this purpose. In some organizations, a records-management unit performs compliance audits to determine that retention schedules are being appropriately implemented.

Records Centers

A records center is an off-site warehouse designed specifically to store inactive records until they are destroyed. This type of storage facility may differ from one providing permanent storage. For example, some records centers won't accept records that don't have a destruction date. Others, however, will additionally house permanent records if they have been placed on disks, tapes, or microform media.

Inactive records storage. Whether the records are in the form of hard copy, magnetic or optical media, or film, they must be placed in suitable boxes or other containers. Each container must then be labeled, and the records must be described on a special inventory form. This form should indicate not only the contents but the location of the storage container in the warehouse. Those who are involved in transferring inactive records should follow the organization's instructions for packing, labeling, and inventorying.

Strict measures are necessary to protect the documents from theft or from damage or destruction caused by fire, humidity, water, or other peril. Protection, therefore, is a principal consideration in selecting a storage site. Certain crucial, irreplaceable items may be copied and stored in two locations in case something causes destruction in one of them.

Inactive records retrieval. Some inactive items will occasionally be needed by the transmitting department. Specific reference arrangements vary considerably. In the absence of a formal records-management program, for example, a records center may be shared by several departments, each of which services its own records. When a formal records-management program exists, the records center is usually operated by a small staff. In such organizations, the records center functions as a custodial agency rather than a generally accessible reference library.

Records center storage is commonly considered an extension of the transmitting department's own filing space, and the department controls access to the transmitted records just as if they had never left its own offices. Reference requests generally require departmental approval. Before contacting the records center, the department will consult its copies of the records inventory sheets to determine the shipment number and container location of the desired records. The records center typically responds to reference requests by returning the requested containers or file folders to the transmitting office. If only a few items are involved, some records centers will provide photocopies.

Microstorage

If an organization is storing massive amounts of paper documents, the space requirements and the cost will eventually become overwhelming. Many organizations, therefore, must copy paper records onto a reduced-size media (*document imaging*). The most popular media for reduced-size storage are magnetic and optical media, described earlier; videodisks; and microforms. Some of these media are more suitable for long-term storage than others. Some disks and tapes, for example, hold relatively little information, and usually, they must be recopied periodically because of deterioration. Microforms, on the other hand, are relatively more permanent, although a secure and protected environment is needed for all types of permanent records.

Storage formats. Records stored on computer disks and tapes can be easily copied from hard-disk files or scanned from hard-copy sources. The more durable, noncombustible microforms can be created from paper documents or from computer-processed data. The common film formats are *microfilm* (rolls of film) and *microfiche* (sheets of film). *Superfiche* and *ultrafiche* are forms of microfiche that have smaller images and can hold more information per sheet. A disadvantage of film compared with magnetic and optical media is that information must be recorded on additional rolls or sheets, increasing the time for search and retrieval. With magnetic and optical media, new information can be inserted at any desired location within a document.

Microfilm cameras and other equipment are needed for source-document microfilming. The processed film is then duplicated to provide an extra security (or working) copy. The process of *computer-output microfilming (COM)* transfers computer-processed, machine-readable data directly onto microfilm or microfiche. Organizations may have their own COM recorders or retain a service bureau specializing in COM production.

Display and printing. Although microforms are intended for permanent storage, certain records must be recalled from time to time, and the process of locating records is much slower than it is with magnetic and optical media. However, with computer-aided search and retrieval, the process of locating documents stored on microfilm can be somewhat reduced. Once a document is located, special display and printing equipment is then needed to enlarge and read the microimages. Microform readers are a type of projection device used for this purpose. Since most equipment both reads and prints, you can either view a document on a screen, similar to a computer display, or print out a hard copy of it.

Unlike microforms, magnetic tapes and disks don't require additional equipment. They can be viewed on the computer monitor and printed out on the computer printer the same as any freshly created computer document. Equipment needs and costs are, therefore, an important consideration in developing an appropriate records-management program.

Meetings and Conferences

Few businesses can exist without meetings to exchange information and decide on necessary actions. However, the participants don't have to be assembled in the same room or location for a meeting to take place. Other alternatives to a face-to-face, in-person discussion include audioconferences, computer conferences, and videoconferences. (See Teleconferences.) Often such alternatives are more time- and cost-efficient ways to discuss issues and make decisions.

When someone proposes a meeting — whether it's a small, local meeting of a few people or a gathering of numerous participants for a large conference — many factors should be considered to determine whether the meeting is truly necessary. You may not be in a position to evaluate those factors to make the determination, but you'll probably have information about schedules and other matters, such as available meeting rooms, that are very helpful to executives.

Generally, the person in charge will have to decide if the proposed meeting has a legitimate objective and what will be accomplished as a result of the meeting. If no concrete actions will be taken or if the participants won't leave the meeting better informed, the meeting may be unnecessary. However, if it's decided that a meeting will be useful, the strategies described in the next sections will help you make it more efficient, controlled, and effective.

TYPES OF MEETINGS

On-Site Meetings

The most common meetings are the frequent on-site staff and executive meetings held in most businesses. As suggested in Meeting Preparation, you may be expected to prepare and distribute notices and agendas for these meetings, collect files and other information, take notes, and prepare the formal minutes. On-site meetings might include some or all of the following:

- *Departmental meetings held at company headquarters:* These meetings may involve hotel, restaurant, travel, and entertainment arrangements, as indicated in Meeting Arrangements.
- *Shareholders' and directors' meetings:* These meetings, whether on-site or in other locations, are more formal than routine departmental and staff meetings.
- *Regularly scheduled management and executive committee meetings:* Most organizations always hold certain meetings periodically (weekly, monthly, quarterly, annually, or at other set times).
- *Special staff, management, and executive meetings:* When something important arises, it may be necessary to call a special meeting apart from the regularly scheduled meetings.
- *Employee meetings:* Some meetings are called by management or by an employee leader to make important announcements to all personnel.

Refer to Meeting Arrangements for a description of large conferences and other meetings held in facilities away from the company offices.

Informal Meetings

Traditional meetings. Most staff, departmental, and executive meetings are informal. In such cases, the meeting notice and agenda, or list of topics, don't follow a prescribed pattern. The minutes may consist only of informal notes and a follow-up e-mail to participants from the person in charge (see Facilitator), confirming any decisions that were made. Even in such an informal atmosphere, though, the person guiding a meeting needs to have a list of matters to discuss and needs to lead the discussion and maintain order among the participants. The office professional's role in this type of meeting is often defined more by office practices than by formal meeting procedure.

Facilitator. Many meetings, such as staff meetings, don't have an elected or assigned chairperson. The one who requests the meeting or a senior employee may simply take charge and thereby become the meeting's *facilitator.* This person will call the meeting to order, open discussions, encourage broad participation, try to settle conflicts that arise, and generally guide the group toward consensus (general agreement) on the issues being discussed. After the meeting, the facilitator will see that decisions are recorded in writing and that summaries are sent to attendees.

Consensus. The aim of a facilitator, or the one presenting topics for discussion, is to bring about a general agreement in principle. Reaching consensus doesn't mean that all attendees will enthusiastically support a decision but rather that they'll agree to abide by it. This is important for the sake of harmony and cooperation. In formal meetings, a majority (or other number) must vote on a decision for the decision to be adopted.

Conflict resolution. Facilitators generally deal with disagreements by encouraging people to express their opposing views and respectfully listen to the views of others. They encourage those in disagreement to explore different solutions and to look for common ground or a basis on which they can find a mutually satisfactory resolution to the conflict.

Roundtable meetings. Although most informal meetings are small office meetings, some organizations occasionally hold companywide roundtable meetings — with no agenda and no assigned speakers. In these open-space, interactive meetings, the participants are typically seated in a large circle, signifying an equal status for all, and the participants, not a meeting chair or company management, decide what they want to talk about. Later, participants may be able to sign up for smaller, individual discussion groups.

Typically, a facilitator (see Facilitator) leads with a comment or question. This person may have been asked to guide the discussion or perhaps was merely the first person to speak and thereby became the unofficial group leader. Although the company may set certain ground rules, such as how long someone may speak, the success of the meeting largely depends on the mature, orderly behavior of the participants. It's therefore characterized more by the lack of a rigid structure than by any adherence to traditional meeting rules or conventions.

Such an unstructured meeting is not suitable when a particular outcome is desired or when on-the-spot decisions must be made. Nevertheless, since it encourages the free exchange of ideas, it's useful for collecting a wide range of information and discovering more about the participants' interests and needs.

Formal Meetings

A formal meeting follows prescribed rules, beginning with the purpose for holding the meeting. Each step thereafter must also meet the requirements of the organization. Often an organization's bylaws state who shall call a meeting, when and where it may be held, who is entitled to attend, what form of notice must be given, how many votes are required to pass an issue, how the minutes shall be maintained, and so on. Some formal meetings, such as an annual conference or convention (see Meeting Arrangements), are large. Others, such as a directors' meeting (which may not be strictly formal), are small.

Shareholders' meetings. Invitations to shareholders' meetings are very formal and are usually printed. They're issued on behalf of the company officers about four weeks before the event or at a set time stipulated in the company's bylaws. A proxy form usually accompanies the invitations for use by the shareholders who cannot attend in person. A *proxy* designates someone (such as an officer) who may cast the absent member's vote. The corporate secretary or general counsel typically handles invitations to a formal meeting. Office professionals, however, help make arrangements for things such as printing and mailing.

Directors' meetings. Directors' meetings are usually either formal or semiformal, depending on the size of the organization. Unlike a shareholders' meeting, a directors' meeting may not require a printed notice or proxy. Like a shareholders' meeting, a directors' meeting often must be held as directed by the organization's bylaws. For more about duties and procedures, refer to Meeting Preparation.

Teleconferences

People who need to discuss something or make decisions about something can do so in many ways, such as by face-to-face meetings, telephone calls, e-mail exchanges, or video transmissions. The teleconference, which may take many forms, is a sophisticated version of electronic communication and telecommunication designed primarily to link participants in groups of all sizes for discussion and decision making.

Audioconference. Teleconferences may consist of some form of audioconference, computer conference, or videoconference. The simplest form of conference—a small *audioconference* (conference call)—might involve three people in different cities who use the conference-call feature of their telephone company to establish a three-way connection similar to the traditional two-way connection. For more about telephone communication and telephone company services, refer to Chapter 4, "Telecommunications," Telephone Techniques and Telephone Company Services.

Computer conference. In a *computer document conference,* meeting participants use their computers, with conferencing software, and modems to call each other over their network lines. Once a connection has been established among all participants, the same document, such as a spreadsheet or report, can be called up on everyone's computer screen. Using a keyboard or mouse, a participant can then change the document while the others watch the changes being made on their own screens. In some cases, users select or are assigned different color type that differentiates their annotations from those of the other participants. When a small microphone is attached to the computer, users can discuss the document as well as work on it on screen. When a camera is added, they can also see each other.

Like any type of conference, a computer document conference requires preparation and planning. Participants must be notified of the time and place of the intended computer link and should be advised about the material or documents to be displayed or discussed. Office professionals are usually actively involved in preparing schedules and sending notices, as well as in processing the printouts resulting from the document conference.

Videoconference. The term *videoconference* covers a wide range of long-distance visual conferencing. When a computer conference, described in the previous section, includes cameras and microphones, it becomes a mini-videoconference. Also, some on-site and remote (telecommuter; field) office PCs are routinely equipped with cameras and microphones, enabling users to "stop by each other's office" without ever leaving their own offices. With inexpensive digital video cameras and video chat services offered by Internet service providers, almost anyone with a PC can participate in a form of videoconferencing.

When larger groups are involved, a meeting room specially equipped with television cameras, microphones, speakers, electronic visual aids, and other equipment is usually required. Some hotel chains and other service organizations offer such facilities. A firm with adequate space can also rent or build its own large-scale videoconferencing system, using transmission facilities provided by communications companies.

For convenience, you might classify videoconferences as three main types, depending on the specific features and the number of participants:

- A *desktop conference* consists of telephone calls combined with video, or picture, capability. Participants must have the right software and hardware for their PCs, including cameras, to both see and hear each other.

- A *group videoconference* consists of small groups of people gathered in rooms in different locations that have the necessary desktop or other audio and video equipment in each room to enable them to talk to and see each other.

- A *large videoconference* consists of large groups of people gathered in conference-size rooms in different locations that have sophisticated audio and video equipment set up in videoconferencing facilities and providing high-quality broadcast transmission from each location.

Arrangements. If you're helping with the arrangements for a teleconference, get cost estimates and a list of available services and equipment from several teleconference service companies. (Check the yellow pages and the Internet for sources.) You'll also need to do the following: find out when participants are available, schedule the conference, prepare programs and agendas, send meeting notices, inspect the conference room, arrange for delivery of required equipment and supplies, arrange for a recording or minutes of the conference, and handle postconference duties, such as returning supplies and sending a transcript to each participant.

Teleconferencing service companies will set up the type of conferencing arrangement that you need and provide the equipment and transmission link between locations that you designate. Some will videotape or make another type of record of the proceedings or will provide someone qualified to make such a recording.

Videoconference etiquette. Although microphones other than the one being used by the speaker are usually muted, attendees should be considerate of others and avoid talking, whispering, tapping fingers, rustling papers, and making other noise. Participants must remember that there is a slight delay in relaying video through a network and therefore must give speakers enough time to finish their sentences before replying. Also, before transmitting graphics, senders should alert other participants so that everyone doesn't transmit at once and tie up a network.

PARLIAMENTARY PROCEDURE

Parliamentary procedure refers to the steps that meeting participants must take to adhere to the rules, precedents, and customary practices that apply to meeting conduct. Together, these "rules, precedents, and customary practices" are known as *parliamentary law.* Office professionals who conduct meetings with assistants and other coworkers or who attend and take minutes at other meetings must be familiar with proper parliamentary procedure. Although very small, informal meetings usually dispense with formal motions and standard parliamentary practice, more formal meetings, such as a directors' meeting, must follow parliamentary guidelines.

The most familiar, detailed guide is *Robert's Rules of Order,* available in various paperback editions. Smaller, quick-reference guides are also available. Such books describe the proper conduct of meetings according to parliamentary rules similar to those used by the U.S. House of Representatives.

Duties of Officers

President. The president, or chair (*also:* chairman, chairperson), opens a formal or semiformal meeting and calls it to order, announcing business in the order listed on the agenda. The presiding officer also puts motions to a vote and announces the results. If points of order arise, the presiding officer decides those questions (subject to possible appeal by any two members). A chair may vote when voting is by ballot or, otherwise, only when his or her vote is needed to change the outcome. In addition to conducting the meetings, a president may have many other duties, such as signing legal documents and representing the organization at ceremonial functions.

Vice president. The vice president, or vice chairman, assists the president and may assume the chair when the president is absent. Vice presidents often head various committees and handle special assignments for the organization.

Secretary. The meeting secretary (*also:* clerk, recording secretary) maintains the organization's official records and often must sign all important papers. When both the president and vice president are absent, the meeting secretary calls the meeting to order and asks the group to elect a chair pro tem. When the positions of secretary and treasurer are combined, the meeting secretary also has the financial responsibilities described for the treasurer. The most important duty of the meeting secretary, however, is recording the proceedings of the meeting and preparing and maintaining the minutes. (See The Minutes.) Thus if it's your job to take or prepare the minutes, this task usually must be done according to the instruction of the elected corporate secretary.

Treasurer. The treasurer maintains the organization's financial records, including the checkbook and checking or savings accounts. The treasurer also must pay all bills and arrange for the filing of tax returns and the handling of bookkeeping and auditing activities. Usually, the treasurer must prepare monthly or quarterly financial reports and present them at the appropriate meetings. (Some organizations hire outside management, and the treasurer then would supervise the financial services that this management provides.) If you work for the treasurer of an organization, part of your duties will include helping to maintain the necessary records and preparing and distributing the treasurer's periodic financial reports.

Committees. Although they're not officers of the organization, committee chairs often perform the same duties as those of a regular chair while the committee is in session. Committee chairs may be appointed by the president, or the first person named to serve on a committee may become its chair. In other cases, the committee members may elect their own chair. Frequently, the person elected or chosen names another committee member as secretary to record the proceedings of committee meetings and prepare minutes, which should be kept separate from the minutes of the parent organization.

Introducing Business

In an informal meeting, matters are often decided by consensus. (See Consensus.) In a formal meeting, business is introduced and transactions decided by way of motions. A member, after being recognized by the chair, "moves" that some resolution be approved or that some action be taken:

> I move that we adopt the following resolution: RESOLVED That . . .

The chair then asks for a second to the motion ("I second the motion") and asks for discussion:

> It has been moved [by . . .] and seconded [by . . .] that we adopt the following resolution: . . . Is there any discussion?

After discussion appears to be over, the chair puts the question to a vote by voice, show of hands, secret ballot, or other approved method:

> Is there any further discussion? [*none requested*] All those in favor of the motion to . . . say aye; those opposed, no. [*pause for vote*] The noes have it. The motion has failed.

Motions. In very formal meetings, motions must be stated formally, and the rules developed in *Robert's Rules of Order* or another approved parliamentary guide must be followed. Numerous restrictions and qualifications apply to the important motions that are used, and a meeting secretary should have a rules-of-order book available for reference during the meeting.

Classes of motions. Both the meeting chair and the meeting secretary must be familiar with the main types of motions, and other participants will also benefit from knowing which motions may or may not be used at different times. Generally, there are four classes of motions:

- A *privileged motion* is the highest-ranking motion and takes precedence over any other motion currently being discussed. You might, for example, ask the chair to return to the specified order of business or set the time for adjournment.

- A *subsidiary,* or *secondary, motion* is one that's applied to another motion currently being considered as a means of disposing of the other motion. Hence you might move to table (lay aside) the other motion.

- An *incidental motion* is one that arises from or is prompted by another motion and has to be decided before a vote can be taken on the other motion. You might, for example, move to withdraw the other motion.

- A *main,* or *principal, motion* is any motion used to introduce business. You might, for example, move that a person be appointed to study recycling in the office. The description of this type of motion (*principal motion*) is misleading because main, or principal, motions yield to all other motions and therefore are really of lower rank than the other three types of motions.

MEETING PREPARATION

Your role in planning and participating in any meeting that involves your supervisor is instrumental in ensuring a successful meeting. Once your supervisor has instructed you to set up a meeting, you should determine the date, time, and place that the meeting is to be held. Often these criteria will depend on the availability of a meeting room. You may be required to shop around for a room, present alternatives to the executive, and proceed with plans according to his or her decision.

Next, you need to know who should attend the meeting and if any of the participants are required to bring specific documents or present a report. You'll also need to know what your recourse should be if one or more of the people on the attendance list are unable to attend. Can the meeting take place without those people? Should the meeting be postponed to a time more convenient to them? Can a substitute sit in for those unable to attend? You also need to know what, if any, equipment will be needed during the meeting.

Although guests may be invited, or the meeting may be declared open to the public or to all employees, usually only those who are essential to the objective of a meeting should attend. In most cases, no more than 10 to 12 people should attend a discussion-style meeting. However, if the intent is to give or hear a speech, with or without a question-and-answer period, the number of participants is usually restricted only by seating and space availability. See also Roundtable meeting.

The Agenda

Preliminary agenda. After determining the number of participants, prepare an *agenda*—a list of topics in the order to be presented at the meeting. For some meetings, a preliminary (or working) agenda is circulated in advance to the prospective participants. In some cases, the host may want to solicit further agenda topics from the ones who receive the preliminary draft. Use of a preliminary agenda enables the host to cut out as much extraneous subject matter as possible. The final agenda is developed from the preliminary model, and it, too, is often distributed to the participants in advance so that they'll be prepared to discuss and act on the various topics.

How to set up an agenda. Prepare the agenda double- or triple-spaced in numbered or unnumbered outline style. Include as much or as little detail as the executive requires. For example, you may be required to list specific items under each agenda category, such as under "unfinished business." In that case, you could read the previous minutes to see which items were unresolved at the last meeting and therefore should be listed on the current agenda under "unfinished business." In a large organization, it's also helpful to include the names of people presenting reports or any other detail that may be useful to the participants.

The illustration Agenda is an example of an agenda for a small, informal staff meeting, but the same type of outline style would be appropriate for a formal meeting. Excessive detail is omitted in the agenda for a small, informal meeting because the participants are used to working together, know each other, and are generally familiar with the meeting activity and topics.

Meeting Notice

Types of notification. Once you've done the preliminary work for the meeting, you're ready to inform the participants. Seven to ten business days' (sometimes less) notice is considered appropriate for an in-house staff or executive meeting. When attendees must travel from other locations, including out of state, they'll need two to four weeks' notice to make travel reservations and prepare to be away from their offices.

Depending on the level of formality in your company or the formality and nature of the meeting, you might telephone the participants' offices and then confirm the verbal notification in writing, such as by e-mail or

---

AGENDA

Editorial Meeting
April 14, 2001

1. Call to order

2. Roll call

3. Minutes of previous meeting (corrections, omissions)

4. Directors' report

5. Publisher's report

6. Production manager's report

7. Unfinished business

    a. Works in progress

    b. Proposals before the board

    c. Staff

8. New business

    a. Budget

    b. New proposals

9. Announcements (including date of next meeting)

10. Adjournment

Agenda

fax. State the date, time, location, and nature of the meeting along with the agenda and any special requests of the individual. For example, alert the participants or presenters about any special materials they should bring with them. Also, ask the participants to let you know if they'll attend, and notify the chair of any prospective absences as soon as you receive the replies.

Sometimes only the members of high-level corporate committees receive copies of an agenda and the minutes of previous meetings. In such cases, you would send only a brief memo to the presenters and other participants, informing them of the date, time, and location of the meeting and the time at which presenters are expected to make their presentation(s):

TO:	Jim Hartley
FROM:	Deanne Reese
SUBJECT:	Budget Committee Meeting
PURPOSE:	Approve Revised Budget
DATE:	May 23, 2001
TIME:	9:30 a.m.
PLACE:	Board Room, 3rd Floor

Rod Smith wanted me to let you know that your presentation is scheduled between 9:35 and 9:50 a.m. Let us know (extension 721) if you have any questions. Also, if you can't attend, please let Rod or me know by Friday, May 12. Thanks very much.

If you work in the office of the company president, you may be called on to issue formal notices of forthcoming meetings to the board of directors. These gatherings usually occur at a set time during the fiscal year, and the procedures in preparing for them are predetermined. Examine previous notices in the files for examples of content and format.

Directors' address list. Keep a current list of the directors' full names, corporate and home addresses, corporate titles, telephone and fax numbers, and e-mail addresses. Notify them of the meeting, preferably in writing (e-mail, fax, or traditional mail) at least two or three weeks in advance or according to the provisions of the company's bylaws. Keep a separate list of the directors in order of seniority on the board, with notations about the date on which they were notified of the meeting and a check mark indicating whether or not each person will or will not be able to attend. Total the number of attendees to determine whether a quorum will be present. Usually, the bylaws will tell you what number constitutes a quorum.

Other arrangements. You also may need to make arrangements in outside sites for shareholders' or other large meetings. With directors' meetings, you may be asked to make hotel reservations for those directors living out of town, and you may be expected to arrange dinners and lunches for them. This is very likely if your position is in the office of the president or the chair and chief executive officer.

Meeting-Room Preparation

Before the meeting begins, check the meeting room for lighting, temperature, and proper ventilation. Also check on the setup of fax machines, computers, visual aids, and any special equipment that you ordered. Test the audiovisual equipment to be certain that everyone can clearly see and hear the presentations, and test the electronic devices to be certain that ports, cords, and outlets are compatible and in proper working order. In addition, there should be a supply of pens and paper, water and glasses, wastebaskets, brochures or other handouts, and coat and hat racks. If you're having refreshments, check that tables or serving carts are available for snacks and beverages.

If you've prepared a meeting file (reports, pertinent correspondence, and so on) for your supervisor or anyone else, present it before the meeting or bring it to the meeting room, whichever the recipient prefers. If you must present a variety of material in different folders, use color-coded folders so that participants can quickly locate different items during the meeting. Some participants use three-ring binders, with different colored index tabs, that open easily to any page and will remain flat on the table at that page.

If place cards on the meeting table indicate where each person will sit, quickly draft a seating chart for your use later in identifying who is speaking as you take notes. If place cards aren't used, wait until everyone is seated to prepare a chart.

The Minutes

Preparation. If you're required to take the minutes of the meeting, bring along both pens and writing paper and, for backup, a tape or video recorder and blank cassettes. Arrive at the meeting site before everyone else does to ensure that everything is ready. To take the minutes, you should have plenty of materials (paper, cassettes, and so on) to get through a lengthy session. Be certain that you have a copy of the agenda, as well as any reports, financial statements, or other documents that may be referred to during the meeting.

What to record. The most difficult part of taking minutes is deciding what information has to be written down verbatim, what can be paraphrased, and what is nonessential for the official record. Minutes are meant to be concise, factual, and objective records of what has happened during a meeting. Therefore, you can't allow personal preferences to influence your note taking, and you can't give more weight to what certain people say than to what others say. You also must be able to interpret statements for what is truly being said, not what you think someone means because of the deliverer's voice inflections, intonations, or mannerisms.

It can be very difficult to discriminate from among all the opinions and facts just what should be recorded in the minutes. Yet, to record the proceedings fairly, it's necessary to take a disinterested position. As a recorder, you must listen carefully and take down information even when more than one person is talking at the same time, making sure that you attribute all statements to their correct sources. However, if you're uncertain about something, quietly ask someone about it at an opportune moment.

Motions and resolutions. In corporate or organizational meetings, it's necessary to record motions and resolutions verbatim as well as the names of those who made them. You may want to have blank copies of forms to use for this purpose on which you fill in names and motions:

Motion #1: _____

_____

_____

Made by: _____
Seconded by: _____

Recording guidelines. To begin your note-taking session, follow these guidelines:

- Write down the date, location, and time that the meeting begins.
- Record the names of those present and absent (if fewer than 20). A quorum check is necessary for larger meetings.
- Identify the type of meeting (such as regular, weekly, annual, special, or executive).
- Identify the presiding officer.
- Record the action. When the meeting begins, key your notes to match numbered items (if any) on the agenda. If the discussion is "works in progress" and this subject is item *a* under *7. Unfinished Business,* key your notes simply as *7a* and record the discussion. This relieves you of writing out the full title of number *7a.* When you're ready to put your notes on the computer, simply refer to the agenda to get the full wording for number *7a.*
- Record the time of adjournment.

Since the minutes serve as an official record of a meeting, it's imperative that they be objectively recorded and conscientiously transcribed into a final, formal document.

Drafts. You may prepare one or more drafts of the minutes before the meeting secretary approves a final version.

Preparation. Before you sit down at your computer, assemble the following materials:

- The agenda
- Your notes and recorded cassettes
- *Robert's Rules of Order* or other reference book on parliamentary procedure
- Any reports or other documents discussed or distributed at the meeting
- Verbatim copies of motions and resolutions
- The constitution or bylaws of the group (if applicable)

Format guidelines. Prepare the draft according to the following general guidelines. To determine the specific format used in your organization, examine previous copies of the minutes in the files:

- Double-space the draft, even if the final version will be single-spaced, so that you or the meeting secretary can make handwritten corrections between the lines.
- Number the pages consecutively at the top or bottom of the pages.
- Identify the meeting and date at the top of the page.
- Identify the participants (if no more than 20) and the presiding officer in the first paragraph, and state when the meeting was called to order.
- Use subheads for different topics if warranted by the length and complexity of the document.
- Conclude with the time of adjournment.
- Assemble all attachments for inclusion with the final copy.

Refer to Chapter 6, "Document Creation," for more about document preparation.

Copy distribution. It's good practice (and usually required) to present the presiding officer and the meeting secretary with a printout of the draft. If this isn't feasible, present the draft to your supervisor before preparing the final copy. Either person will be able to help you find misinterpretations or extremely sensitive material that should not be published.

Final copy. Check copies of previous minutes for your organization's preferred style, with single- or double-spacing. The paper used also depends on precedent. Some groups have specially printed stationery for their official minutes, whereas others use ordinary white bond paper.

Most minutes today, particularly those of an informal meeting, are written in a narrative style, and it's especially important that your summaries of the discussions succinctly express the scope of the conversations. See the illustration Minutes for an example of the minutes of a relatively informal meeting.

Editorial Scheduling Meeting
ABC PUBLISHERS
October 16, 2001

Call to Order: The weekly editorial scheduling meeting of Friday, October 16, convened at 10 a.m. in the conference room. The presiding officer was Amanda Billings. Staff members present included Robert Desmond, Carl Edwards, Denise Jameson, Martha Nichols, and Philip Thompson. Roger Lochman was unable to attend.

Minutes: The minutes of the previous meeting, October 9, were reviewed and approved.

Finances: Amanda Billings reported that the corporation is considering an office products line to balance the shortfall expected in the Secondary Education Division. Robert Desmond said that he is reviewing titles in progress and asked each editor to submit a cost summary of freelance services.

Production: Carl Edwards emphasized the need for improving the flow of manuscript to composition and offered to meet with those who wanted to discuss this.

Scheduling: Amanda Billings reminded the attendees that she will need their sections of the office products publishing plan by October 23.

Submissions: The staff voted to reject the manuscript *Dictionaries: Friends or Foe?*

Personnel: Denise Jameson raised the question again about when a new editor will be hired to replace Tom Westman, who left the company on March 6. She recommended that someone be found as soon as possible because of the upcoming ambitious production schedules.

Next Meeting: The next meeting of the editorial staff is set for Friday, October 23.

Adjournment: The meeting was adjourned at 11:30 a.m.

_____
Secretary

_____
Presiding Officer

Minutes

MEETING ARRANGEMENTS

The arrangements for an in-house staff or executive meeting are usually relatively simple. They may involve informally notifying participants, preparing a brief agenda, reserving the company conference room or asking to use someone's office, and ordering beverages and snacks (if any). By contrast, the arrangements for a large conference or convention or other such off-site meeting are very complex, usually involving a team of planners and arrangers, each with a specific duty such as program development or speaker invitations. Assistants to members of this team must help to prepare and maintain records of schedules, deadlines, hotel and other arrangements, registrations, and anything else pertinent to the particular meeting. With the appropriate calendar, scheduling, and desktop publishing software, most of the planning and publishing activities can be handled within the company.

Hotel Services

Setting up a formal meeting may be simple or complicated, depending on the nature of the event and the kind of planning that you do. The easiest and most direct way to plan off-site meetings is to get in touch with the hotel, convention center, or other facility where the event will be held.

Before a facility has been selected, you'll probably get bids from at least three possible facilities based on the data in your list of Advance Information as well as any other information supplied by the meeting planners. The authorized committee can then decide which hotel is the most competitive.

Meeting arrangement and coordination. Major domestic and foreign hotels and conference centers have individuals responsible for setting up and coordinating meeting arrangements. They're trained to suggest innovative arrangements and handle a myriad of details that would overwhelm most sponsoring organizations. Nevertheless, some meetings may require that all arrangements be made by the sponsoring organization. Regardless of whether this is the case or whether a hotel or conference-site representative does the coordinating, it's very important that all possible requirements be known well in advance of the event.

Advance Information

Information the hotel coordinator will need. Even when you use hotel services, some activities must be planned early so that you can tell the hotel coordinator the following essential things:

- The date(s) of the meeting
- The estimated number of participants and overnight room requirements
- The size of the meeting rooms and dining rooms needed
- The desired seating plans
- The meals (number, locations, times, and menus) required and whether an outside caterer is desired for refreshments (if allowed by the hotel)
- The special equipment required, in which rooms, and whether the organization will rent or bring its own equipment (if allowed by the hotel)
- The nonbusiness events (tours, dances, and so on) that are planned
- The registration and information booth requirements
- The airport courtesy car requirements
- The security requirements
- The organization's preferences for billing procedure, amount of deposit with the hotel, and other financial matters
- Any other special needs

Deadlines. You must know well in advance the inclusive dates of the event, since sites are sometimes reserved years ahead. The number of participants also must be confirmed in advance, for this figure affects all other planning — the budget for the entire event, the number of hotel reservations required, the selection of conference and dining rooms, the type of seating, the group rates for meals, and so on.

Determine with the hotel the final cut-off date for receipt of acceptances and changes in the list of participants and stick to it. Otherwise, chaos will ensue — rooms will not be available, the hotel staff will be upset, and participants arriving without reserved rooms will be angry.

Give the hotel representatives detailed information on a day-by-day chart showing exactly what is expected of them. Base your chart on the agenda that the executive has written for the meeting. See the illustration Meeting Activity Sheet for an example of one day's activities for a television affiliates meeting.

Conference Package
Mailing arrangements. A detailed conference package, with program and registration forms, must be mailed to all prospective participants in sufficient

---

COMPANY LETTERHEAD

TO:	International Hotel	**DATE:**	February 1, 2001

FROM: Janice Sale
Executive Assistant to
  Martin Miller
UBC TV Network

SUBJECT: Affiliates Meeting

**INCLUSIVE
DATES:**   May 1-4, 2001

DAY-BY-DAY ACTIVITY CHART

Date	Time	Room	Activity	Setup	Attendees	Equipment	Meals
5/4	9:00 a-noon	Blue	Ratings review	Seats for 200	200	1 dais mike, 25 aisle mikes, 4 video mach.	
	10:30 a-10:45 a	Red	Break	4 buffet tables	200		Fruit bowl, pastries, coffee, tea, milk, juice
	1:00 p-2:00 p	Lilac	Lunch	20 rnd. tables, 10 seats each	200		Vichyss., veal roast, green salad, rolls, apple pie, coffee, tea, milk
	2:15 p-5:00 p	Sand	New progs.	Same as 9-12	200		
	3:45 p-4:00 p	Red	Break	Same as 10:30-10:45	200		Cheese, crackers, coffee, tea, milk, juice
	6:00 p-7:30 p	White	Cock-tails	4 buffet tables, 4 bars	200		See attached lists

Meeting Activity Sheet

time for them to respond. For many meetings, it's necessary to make the first mailing several months before the meeting date. Some meeting planners select a particular airline as the "official airline" for the conference, and in return, the airline may fund or handle the mailing of the conference package.

What to include. A conference package may include some or all of this information:

- Program
- Registration materials, including a return confirmation form, nametag, and meal tickets
- A map indicating the location of the meeting site
- Ground transportation data
- Information about hotel check-in and check-out times, room reservations and costs, meal plans, and payment procedures
- A summary of electronic hookups available in sleeping rooms
- Description of planned entertainment and a summary of available activities and points of interest
- Activities available for spouses or other guests of meeting participants
- Description of available exercise and sports facilities
- List of doctors in the area
- Any other information a participant will need to know

Meeting Room

Seating plans. Various seating plans should be studied in relation to the nature of the meeting and the number of participants. Is it a panel discussion? A formal sales presentation? An informal brainstorming session? A meeting at which a prominent person will give a speech? The illustration Seating Plans for Meetings suggests possible seating plans.

Consider round tables for meals. Such tables allow for more relaxed conversation. The long rectangular tables of the T and U formations are more appropriate for formal gatherings, especially those during which video or slide shows are presented.

Supplies and equipment. Ensure that all tables are covered, if appropriate, and set with water pitchers, glasses, pens, and writing pads. If place cards are used, check them against your seating charts just before the meeting begins.

If electronic equipment, screens, flip charts and markers, slide projectors, lecterns, microphones, recorders, or video equipment is needed, give the hotel a list of these items and then ensure later that they are available in the right rooms at the right times. If the hotel cannot supply all the equipment you need, ask whether you may bring in other equipment, and check the yellow pages for nearby rental sites. *Reconfirm* delivery of all rental

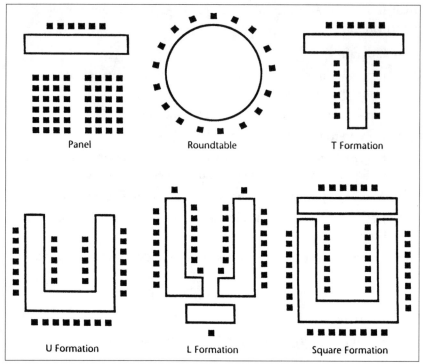

Seating Plans for Meetings

equipment. After the equipment arrives, test everything immediately so that if anything doesn't work, replacements can be ordered in time.

Refreshments. Companies usually plan morning and afternoon breaks during meetings, and tables should be set up in appropriate places for them. For the morning break, usually lasting 15 minutes, you may offer coffee and tea (including decaffeinated), juice, milk, bottled water, and soft drinks (regular and diet), as well as snacks. Avoid serving only sweet rolls at the morning break. A large crystal bowl of melon balls mixed with various other fresh fruits is a welcome alternative or at least an interesting supplement to the rolls. Hot turnovers are also appealing. For further ideas, consult with the hotel or an outside caterer (if the hotel allows outside services).

Your Role at a Large Conference

Preconference checks. If you attend a large meeting, you'll fulfill many responsibilities that are usual for an expediter or a troubleshooter. Devise checklists on which you have noted the particulars of the meeting plans for each day. Go to the meeting rooms and check the seating, the ventilation, the place cards, the positioning of the equipment, and the arrangements for morning and afternoon break refreshments. If other members of the conference team have this assignment, you may simply accompany them and offer assistance as needed.

Stay in contact with the hotel staff members assigned to your company's event, and work closely with them to resolve any last-minute problems. If registration is to take place the night before and early on the first official day of the meeting, be at the desk along with the other participants so that you can assist in getting the participants settled.

Speaker presentations. You may be asked to assist a speaker with certain equipment during a presentation. Take time in advance to familiarize yourself with the equipment so that the presentation will run smoothly and professionally. If possible, rehearse the presentation at least once before it's given. Be sure that all electrical cords are out of the way. Speakers have been known to become entangled in such wiring and fall while walking back and forth during presentations.

Hospitality suites. If the company has booked a hospitality suite for informal gatherings between events, request that the housekeeping staff clean and air the room at least one time, and preferably two times, during the day. Stale air and odors combine to create an unpleasant atmosphere for people who want to use the suite for telephone calls, small informal meetings, or simply relaxation.

Special services. You may have to arrange for special office assistance or translation services. Discuss these problems with the hotel. If no help is forthcoming, check the yellow pages for temporary agencies and for foreign-language translators or schools. Universities are also good sources for translators, as is the U.S. State Department, which maintains a list of qualified people to accompany foreign visitors on government-sponsored itineraries.

Special security requests. The meeting may feature someone from the private, political, governmental, or entertainment sector as a keynote speaker or performer. If so, talk to that person's staff and the hotel staff about any special security arrangements required.

Travel arrangements. For information on making travel arrangements to attend meetings both within the country and in other countries, see Chapter 12, "International and Domestic Travel," Travel Preparations and International Travel.

International and Domestic Travel

In many companies, a significant percentage of executive time is spent in travel, sometimes both domestic and international travel. Assistants to executives who travel have additional responsibilities involving both the arrangements for a trip and the follow-up activities after the trip.

TRAVEL PREPARATIONS

Sources of Information

The information you need to make arrangements for a trip is available through a wide variety of sources from travel agents to transportation companies to electronic and print guides. Although many large and medium-size companies have their own travel offices or use a travel agent, others use the Internet for both information (schedules, rates, and so on) and reservations.

Travel agent. One of the best sources of immediate, up-to-date information is the travel agent. If you're planning to use such services, find an agent who will spend enough time with you both to help you understand your business and to help you make the best possible arrangements. Don't hesitate to shop around and examine the agent's reputation by checking with other clients of the agent or even the Better Business Bureau. See Using a travel agent for further suggestions.

Transportation companies. Although businesses make most or all travel arrangements over the Internet and through commercial travel agencies or in-house travel departments, you may still want to call airlines, Amtrak, or other transportation companies (use the toll-free 800 numbers) to discuss a particular schedule or other matter with a representative. You'll find the numbers of major airlines and other transportation companies (rail, ship, bus, car rental, and so on) in the yellow pages. (Add any numbers that you call frequently to your electronic and print desk telephone list.)

Electronic systems. A number of electronic sources of information are available to users who have the right equipment. Your company may, for example, buy travel-planning software or lease a computerized travel system that will display flight numbers and other travel information meeting the guidelines you specify. Perhaps your supervisor travels only the first week of every month and prefers all flights to be between 6 P.M. and 1 A.M. You may also subscribe to an online database or an electronic travel service, in the same way that you would subscribe to a shopping or financial service. Or you may use the free information and reservations features of travel websites.

Print and electronic guides. The *Official Airline Guide,* which provides information about domestic and international flights, is available in print, online, and CD-ROM versions. The *Official Railway Guide* offers similar information about Amtrak and about other passenger trains in Canada and Mexico. Although print versions don't provide up-to-the minute information, you may want to build a print library of area or country travel guides for general reference. For instance, you should have a travel guide for each city and country that your supervisor regularly visits. Additionally, you may need road maps, hotel guides, and other local information, available in print or online guides or through the chamber of commerce in each city. The Internet also provides a variety of information about cities, areas, and countries.

Publications such as *The Hotel/Motel Red Book,* the *Hotel and Travel Index,* and the *Official Hotel and Resort Guide* have various information about hotels, airlines, car rental agencies, and railroads, sometimes with miscellaneous other data such as city and county maps and currency-conversion rates. Ask your travel agent, local reference librarian, or local bookstore if it has copies available that you can examine before buying one for the office.

For a variety of information on other countries, consider both the books that are written about a particular country and the guides that cover all countries, such as the *World Factbook* and *World Travel Guide.* You can also subscribe to regularly updated reports, such as the David M. Kennedy Center for International Studies' (Brigham Young University's) *Culturgrams,* which are newsletter-style reports on each major country of the world.

Reservations

Whether you make reservations directly over the Internet or through a commercial travel agent or in-house travel officer, you must always collect certain information in advance:

General Information

- What is the point of origin and the destination?
- How many stopovers will there be, where, and for how long?
- What are the preferred dates and times for departure and return?
- What means of transportation does the executive prefer (air, rail, car)?
- What time of day or night does the executive prefer to travel?
- What type of commuter connections does the executive prefer (bus shuttle, air shuttle)?
- What travel documents are needed (international trip)? See Travel Documents.
- What payment or billing method will the executive use?
- What is the currency exchange rate (international trip)? See Currency.
- Will translation or other services be needed (international trip)? See Language.
- What portable equipment and supplies will the executive take along?

Air Travel

- Is there an airline or other transportation company that the executive prefers?
- What class of service (first, business, coach) does the executive prefer?
- What is the point of origin and the destination?
- Which dates and times does the executive prefer for departures and returns?
- Does the executive prefer a certain airline or flight number?
- Does the executive have special needs (airport lounges with electronic-equipment hookups, disability requirements, dietary requirements)? See Special Conveniences and Services.
- What are the limitations on luggage (size, pounds, number of carry-on pieces)? See Packing and Luggage.

Railway Travel

- What is the point of origin and destination?
- Which dates and times does the executive prefer for departures and returns?
- What type of railway accommodations (sleeping and dining) does the executive need?
- Does the executive have special needs (disability requirements, dietary requirements)?
- What business amenities, such as computer hookups, does the executive need?

Auto Travel

- What car-rental or courtesy-car service will the executive need?
- What pick-up and drop-off sites does the executive want?
- Does the executive prefer a certain make and size of car?
- On what days and at what times does the executive need the car?
- Will the executive need an international driver's license? See International driving permit.

Hotels

- What type of hotel/motel accommodations does the executive prefer? See Accommodations.
- What business amenities, such as computer hookups, does the executive need?
- What are the estimated arrival and departure dates and times?
- Are corporate rates or other discount features available?

Make a checklist, and collect as much information as possible before you contact a transportation company, hotel, or a travel agent. An agent may point out other information that you'll need to make the most appropriate overall arrangements, including air and rail connections, ground transportation, and suitable hotel accommodations. If you make any portion of the arrangements yourself, such as car rental or hotel accommodations, coordinate the times, dates, and locations with the main portion of the trip being arranged by a travel agent.

Using a travel agent. Most agents, depending on agency size and proximity to your office, will do the following: set up an account for billing purposes, look for discount fares and other cost savings, make all travel and travel-related arrangements, find out if e-tickets (paperless, online record) or print tickets are provided, deliver print tickets to your office or arrange for airport pickup, and assist you with international documentation, such as visas and tourist cards. They'll also provide itinerary sheets with day-by-day reservations and accommodations information.

However, before you contact a travel agent to make reservations, compile a list of the special services that the traveler will need, including unusual requests, and determine whether the agency can handle everything you require. Ask what kind of ongoing service will be provided, such as mileage-accumulation reporting and application for frequent-flier benefits. (Check your company's policy on frequent-flier miles — whether they belong to the company or the traveler. If they belong to the traveler, they may be a taxable benefit.) Even after you select an agent, continue to compare prices and services with other agents from time to time to be certain that you're getting the best possible rates and service.

Ask if the agent is a member of the American Society of Travel Agents (ASTA) and if he or she has a Certified Travel Counselor rating. Also find out if the agency specializes in business travel or deals only in leisure travel. Determine whether it will open a company account and provide the type of account summaries your office requires, and ask about charges for its services as well as any cost-cutting features that it may offer. Also inquire whether it has 24-hour emergency phone and fax numbers and an e-mail address for those who may need assistance after hours.

Special Conveniences and Services

Many executives have memberships in airline clubs, which provide specially equipped lounges at major airports. There, passengers can have beverages and snacks, watch television, use the telephone, plug in a notebook computer or portable fax, work while waiting for the flight to be announced, and often take care of other needs, such as cashing a check.

Many executives also expect to have special electronic and telecommunications facilities and other business amenities at their hotels. Large hotels generally have all necessary computer and fax hookups and offer many other services to executives, such as late checkouts, car-rental discounts, room upgrades, tour arrangements, and reservations for theater performances. The concierge, usually found near the front desk, can provide information about the specific services the hotel offers.

When documents need to be shipped while an executive is traveling, he or she can use a private delivery company or overnight courier services. (See the descriptions of mail and transportation services in Chapter 5.)

International passenger airlines frequently have a small-package service whereby a package can be shipped on the next flight for a nominal fee. Special customs clearances are included, but the package must be picked up promptly at the destination. Inquire at the airline for further information.

See Business Assistance for information about securing translators and interpreters and making other foreign contacts.

Packing and Luggage

Packing. Your travel agent, an airline reservations office, or a website may have up-to-date weather information and suggestions about the type of clothing that will be needed at the destination. Electronic and print guides also offer other information, such as general climatic summaries. Some countries, such as those in the Middle East and parts of Africa, have strict clothing requirements, especially for women. Study a guide to the area where the executive will be traveling for information about social and religious customs that affect attire. Your travel agent also may be able to advise you about the pertinent customs.

Some executives maintain a prepacked flight bag and overnight kit or, if this is not feasible, a series of packing lists — one for overnighters, another for two- or three-day trips, and still another for trips of four days or more. If you haven't prepared such lists before, ask the executive to tell you about or give you a list of the desired items, and be prepared to add your own suggestions. Prepacking or at least maintaining packing lists is a method that has been used for years by military personnel. It saves much time and last-minute rushing.

Supplies and equipment. A prepacked travel briefcase is another way of expediting take-off. Include in it items such as this: a copy of the itinerary; an appointment book; an address book; writing and mailing materials; notebook computer and supplies; other portable equipment, such as a cell phone, small fax, personal digital assistant (PDA), and calculator; and miscellaneous supplies such as prepaid phone cards, stamps, paper clips, and cellophane tape.

Electrical adaptors. Travelers in other countries should remember that throughout Europe, the Mediterranean, and the Far East, the standard electric current is generally 220 volts/50 hertz, and the plugs to appliances as well as the electrical outlets differ markedly from those in the United States. Therefore, if an electric appliance such as a shaver or hair dryer is carried along, the executive should take a lightweight, all-purpose transformer and plug adapter, available at most department or hardware stores.

Luggage. Executives usually prefer luggage of a size and weight that can be carried on board the flight. Ask the travel agent or check with the airline for regulations concerning size, weight, and number of carry-on pieces. With carry-on luggage, there's no need to wait at the baggage claim area upon arrival. If luggage is to be checked, the executive needs to allow additional time for airport check-in. Ask the travel agent or airline office about minimum check-in times. The travel agent or airline office also can tell you the maximum weight allowable and pieces that may be checked. This point applies especially to long trips or to trips in which the executive may have to transport special product samples in oversize bags. For additional suggestions, see Identification tags and cards.

Appointment Schedules and Itineraries

Appointment schedule. A traveling executive needs a schedule of all appointments that have been arranged. Prepare a tentative schedule, and continue to edit in changes until the last possible moment. Although you should use any format for the schedule that your supervisor prefers, appointment schedules are often prepared in table or list format. You might, for example, set up four columns headed as follows, and record the appropriate information under each heading:

> *Column 1:* Contact [*contact's name, company, and address*]
> *Column 2:* Numbers [*contact's telephone, fax, and other numbers and e-mail address*]
> *Column 3:* Date and time [*of appointment*]
> *Column 4:* Comments and Reminders [*miscellaneous information and remarks*]

If extensive comments or reminders are required concerning the appointments, you may want to have a separate sheet for each appointment or include only a couple appointments per page. In this case, you could list the following headings for each contact in a single left-hand column, and key in the appropriate data after each line (include the same information indicated in the preceding list of column heads):

> *Appointment Schedule: October 9, 2001*
> 1. Contact: ...
> 2. Numbers: ...
> 3. Date and Time: ...
> 4. Comments and Reminders: ...

It's always helpful to note time differences, if any, on the appointment schedule so that the executive will know what time it is at the home office. If something should arise during a business meeting that warrants a telephone call, the executive can more easily decide when to place the call.

If pertinent, use the Comments and Reminders space to include the name, address, and telephone number of the limousine service (if any) and the name of the driver (if known). When the place, phone number, and so on where the appointment will take place differs from the contact's company address and numbers, you can include the information for the appointment site here or beneath the company address information, as preferred.

Host data. You can also use the Comments and Reminders space to summarize notes about the person or company that the executive will visit. Sometimes information can be obtained from websites or business directories in your local library's reference room. Some information may be available from the person who originally set up or suggested the meeting. Depending on the prominence of the person, another source of information might be the international edition of *Who's Who.* If the host is a government official, the local consulate or embassy can usually provide appropriate personal background information. Having some knowledge of a foreign colleague's interests, social and religious customs, and family can be of great assistance in getting a meeting off to a pleasant, diplomatic start.

File material. Some of the information the executive needs, such as a report or brochure, may be too extensive to summarize on the appointment schedule or on a travel itinerary. In that case, you may want to collect the necessary information and organize it by topic in individual file folders. When practical, make photocopies of file material and leave the original in the files. If more than two folders are used, color-code the labels to help the executive locate information quickly and easily.

Itinerary. An itinerary is an essential document for the executive who travels. Frequently, the travel agent prepares the itinerary, which you can annotate if you have additional information that you would like to include. If you prepare the itinerary, set it up in your computer so that changes can be made at the last minute. Use column headings such as the following, and fill in the appropriate information below the headings. Include a footnote that explains whether all times that are listed are standard, daylight, or something else:

> Date
> Place of departure (city and terminal)
> Departure time
> Destination (city and terminal)
> Arrival time
> Type of transportation (plane, train, etc.)

Accommodation (flight, car, room number, and so on)
Meals or snack service
Car rental (type, agency, location, telephone)
Other ground transportation (shuttle bus, limousine, location, etc.)
Hotel (name, address, telephone, fax, e-mail address)

Ask your supervisor if he or she would like any other information on the itinerary. For example, you might include the emergency phone and fax numbers and e-mail address of the travel agent. If this type of additional information is desired, include it within the preceding categories, when appropriate, add more categories, or insert it at the beginning or end of the other data.

INTERNATIONAL TRAVEL

The executive who travels in other countries must consider everything just mentioned in this chapter as well as a host of other matters, such as a passport, foreign currency, a language translator, and customs. The role of those who assist a traveler becomes particularly important when helping the person prepare for an international trip. Because of the complexity of international travel, business travelers rarely attempt to make such arrangements without the assistance of a travel agent.

Travel Documents

Passport. A valid U.S. passport is needed when the executive is traveling in other countries. Although a few countries, such as Canada and Mexico, don't require a passport, almost all other countries do. You can get application forms from places that accept applications, or you may download them from the Internet.

Passport applications should be presented in person to the clerk of a federal, state, or probate court; in many post offices; certain libraries; and certain county and municipal offices. If the executive already has a passport, it may be renewed by mail in some cases. When applying for a passport, the traveler must submit proof of citizenship, proof of identity, two passport photographs, a social security number, and the required fee. The Superintendent of Documents in Washington, D.C., offers a free booklet titled *Your Trip Abroad,* which explains what travel documents are needed. If you have additional questions, ask your travel agent for assistance, or inquire at the nearest passport office.

Visas and tourist cards. Many countries require a visa or tourist card for entry. The visas are issued by the embassies and consulates of the various countries for a small fee or free of charge. Be certain to check with the appropriate consulate or embassy or with your travel agent to learn which visas or tourist cards are required for a particular trip. Regulations may change without notice. If a country requires a visa but the executive didn't obtain one, he or she may usually purchase a tourist card instead upon entering the country. It will be necessary to fill out an application, pay a fee, and present proper identification.

When applying for a visa before departure, it's important to allow sufficient time for securing application forms, completing them, and applying by mail, especially if several visas are required. Keep in mind that consulates aren't located in all U.S. cities. It's helpful to keep a current District of Columbia telephone book if the executive frequently travels in other countries. You'll find the addresses and telephone numbers of all embassies in Washington in that directory. For addresses of overseas consular offices, check the listings over the Internet, or ask your local reference librarian for directories that have this information, such as the *Congressional Directory.* Through the Superintendent of Documents, you can also subscribe to a small directory called *Key Officers of Foreign Service Posts.*

Health documents and medications. If the executive is taking special medication, he or she should carry enough of the medication for the duration of the trip, as well as a doctor's certificate verifying the need for the medication. The family physician can provide information relating to prescription refills in case of an emergency. It's a good idea to take along extra medication just in case a business trip lasts longer than expected or inclement weather or other circumstances delay the return schedule. Items such as passports, visas, and medication should never be packed in luggage that will be checked through, in case the luggage doesn't arrive on the same flight or is lost. For other tips, send for a copy of *Health Information for International Travel* from the Superintendent of Documents in Washington, D.C.

Under the World Health Organization regulations, many countries require that visitors be vaccinated against smallpox, cholera, and yellow fever. Although some vaccinations are not required by the World Health Organization, they may be recommended for the traveler's protection. Consult your local Public Health Service; the Centers for Disease Control and Prevention (CDCP) in Atlanta, Georgia; or your travel agent. (The CDCP website posts travel advisories about epidemics and recommendations for inoculations against malaria, hepatitis, and so on.) All vaccinations must be contained in a World Health Organization certificate, obtainable from the Public Health Service in your city.

Should the executive be concerned with the possibility of becoming ill during a foreign trip, you or the executive should contact Intermedic or the International Association for Medical Assistance to Travelers (IAMAT) before departure. Both organizations, located in New York City, publish international directories of English-speaking physicians. The executive should also ask his or her insurer whether an additional, temporary health policy will be needed for the trip.

International driving permit. Executives who plan to rent a car while traveling in other countries must have a current international driving permit. Applications, available from an American Automobile Association (AAA) office, should be submitted along with a valid U.S. driver's license, two passport photos, and the required fee. Ask your travel agent for assistance if you have further questions.

Business Assistance

Foreign contacts. Throughout the world, a traveler will rarely be too far from communication with an embassy or consulate where he or she can get expert assistance in arranging local business contacts. Many international cities also have U.S. Chamber of Commerce offices that can be helpful. Major sources of information in the United States include the U.S. Department of Commerce, U.S. Department of State, and U.S. Small Business Administration. Check the websites, or ask your local reference librarian to suggest a directory with current telephone numbers and addresses. If you need to contact a foreign embassy in the United States, refer to the embassy addresses and websites in the Country Profiles at the end of this chapter.

You can get information and guidance on the use of translators and interpreters from the economic or commercial attaché of any U.S. embassy or consulate, special overseas trade office, or Chamber of Commerce office abroad. Most hotels will also help you make arrangements for special assistance, such as translation services. See Language for further suggestions.

Letters of introduction. The executive may want to have individuals, banks, and other sources write letters of introduction, letters granting credit, or other letters that will be helpful while conducting business in the various countries. The Department of Commerce has commercial and market information that may be helpful in deciding what type of introductory letters will be needed. Foreign commercial officers in U.S. embassies and consulates can also provide help with business introductions.

Currency

Foreign currency. Before leaving home, the executive will need some currency of the host country. To determine current exchange rates, call the international department of the firm's bank, or consult websites or financial sections in newspapers. Most large banks maintain international departments and will exchange dollars for foreign currency. (Banks offer better exchange rates than airports, domestic or foreign hotels, and other services.)

If the executive already has some foreign currency in hand, it won't be necessary to wait at the airport or elsewhere to obtain it. Taxis, buses, and trains may be ready to depart for town and the hotel or for connections to other cities away from the airport, and it could be a problem to have to wait. Also, with local currency available on arrival, the executive will have money for tipping porters and bellhops, taking local transportation, using pay phones, and so on.

A bank, when exchanging dollars into foreign currency, may provide a guide on the foreign currency purchased, such as denominations and conversion rates. Conversion rates are based on the current buying rate and therefore fluctuate. One day's rates may be slightly more or less on another day.

Additional funds and credit. An executive should also have one or more company or personal credit cards and an appropriate supply of traveler's checks. These checks, available in various denominations, can be purchased from banks or from issuers such as American Express Company. In some cases, ATM cards may be used in other countries to get local currency. For additional funds, a letter of credit may be purchased from a bank, usually in an amount of $1,000 or more, on which the traveler can draw at foreign banks.

Language

Translators and interpreters. Although English is widely used around the world for business dealings, the executive who knows the language of other countries has an advantage. Even the use of a few common words and phrases will please the hosts. However, if the executive isn't fluent in the other language, a translator or interpreter will be needed, and when possible, these arrangements should be made before the executive leaves the United States.

Many companies prefer that the traveler take along an employee who is qualified to serve as a translator-interpreter, rather than trust an unknown person in the other country. If that's not possible and it's necessary to find someone in the other country, a U.S. embassy or consulate in the host country is often a more reliable source of assistance than a hotel or other foreign source. In addition, the executive should have an electronic or print version of a foreign language dictionary and phrase book for each country.

Language courses. If the company plans major commitments to a given country or area of the world, the executive may be required to take one or more language courses. Universities, colleges, and high schools frequently offer adult education language classes in the evenings and on weekends. Private and semiprivate classes are available through most language schools, which are advertised in the yellow pages or over the Internet. Self-teaching video- and audiocassettes are also available, as is private instruction from tutors. The amount of international corporate involvement will determine the amount of fluency required. However, learning a foreign language is never a wasted talent, and most executives believe it will serve them well.

Assisting the executive. You can help in many ways by finding sources of information on language (books, tapes, schools, and so on), by locating advertisements of electronic and print phrase dictionaries, and also by learning something of the language along with the executive. In addition, you'll probably be required to order a supply of business cards for the executive for the trip. The information on each card should also be printed in the language of the host country on the reverse side of the card (avoid abbreviations on that side), preferably by a printer that regularly handles foreign-language material.

Security

Security is a concern for any traveler both in the United States and in other countries. Most potential problems, however, can be avoided if practical steps are taken to avoid them.

Commonsense precautions. Established patterns or routines are a threat to personal security and safety. Hence a regular, predictable route and time of travel each day is a mistake. Frequent changes of direction, travel time, and mode of transportation, coordinated within an overall protection plan, will make it more difficult for a potential abductor or attacker to plan an ambush or interception.

Other commonsense precautions include keeping hotel keys with one at all times, securely holding personal handbags, wallets, and other cases close to one's body (tie a rubber band around wallets so that a pickpocket can't easily slide them out of a pocket). Also avoid wearing expensive jewelry or carrying designer luggage and other items that would tempt a thief. Prepay as much as possible so that it isn't necessary to carry a lot of cash. When using a pay phone or cell phone, never mention names, places, money, credit card numbers, or other revealing information that someone might overhear, and shield telephones and other equipment when you punch in numbers.

Release of travel information. One of the most important things to remember is not to announce travel plans. Travel information concerning the executive or the executive's family should *not* be released to the media until after the trip. Press releases with photographs and travel details could create unnecessary exposure and should be evaluated very carefully. Telephone calls, mail, or personal inquiries from unknown sources or persons seeking travel information or personal data about the executive and the family should be refused.

Use of names in making reservations. Whenever possible, especially in the case of high-level executives of multinational organizations, don't make bookings for hotels, rental cars, limousines, or chauffeur services in the executive's name. Make them in the name of the manager of the local office in the host country, in the company name only, or in a name other than the executive's (perhaps in the name of an associate traveling with the executive). (See also Accommodations.) This procedure will preclude unnecessary interest on the part of unknown people in the travel plans and whereabouts of the executive.

Executive-staff cooperation. An important safeguard is encouraged by clear and open communication between the executive and his or her assistant, as well as other staff members. Arrangements and agreements between the executive, an assistant, and other staff should be made with a view toward ensuring that everyone is continually aware of all itineraries, changes in itineraries (regardless of when any changes are made), and arrival times, destinations, departure times, excursions, and so on. The more you know about where an executive should be at any time, the easier it will be for you to recognize that something is wrong if the executive is long overdue.

Transportation. On arrival at a destination terminal, travelers sometimes fail to check whether taxis have identification numbers and shuttle drivers have valid identification. A traveler should not hesitate to ask for identification if any doubts exist. When possible, passengers also should verify the fare before leaving. Mass transit in some countries is faster than taxis and shuttles, but it can be dangerous at night. When using mass transit, travelers should avoid shoulder bags that can easily be pulled off. Instead, they should carry tokens or fare cards in a secure pocket. Especially, executives should avoid displaying identification or making comments in public that would reveal where they are staying.

Identification tags and cards. Airline regulations require that personal identification be carried on the outside of all checked luggage in the event that the luggage is misdirected at some point during the journey. Top executives should avoid using expensive designer luggage but should use combination locks and tags that conceal the person's name and company address. Some commercial identification tags bear only a name and an identification number. If the luggage is misdirected en route and is subsequently found, the airline locating the luggage will contact the other airline office named on the tags to determine how to reroute or return the luggage.

Accommodations. Travelers should take certain precautions in their hotels and the surrounding area. Before taking a drive or walk, for example, it's a good idea to ask the concierge if and where it's safe to be out alone. Even in recommended areas, a traveler needs to be alert to someone who might be following and to pickpockets and thieves that run or drive past, snatching purses and packages before the victim realizes what has happened. Important documents should be kept in the hotel safe and only photocopies carried in pockets or purses. Items that are taken along in a car and can't be carried with one should be locked in the trunk and the car parked in a well-lit area.

Travel guides recommend that guests register using only initials and ask for two keys, which suggests that the guest isn't alone. (See also Use of names in making reservations.) Speak in terms of *we:* "*We* prefer a third-floor room." Refuse rooms by an exit or elevator, but also avoid rooms in a sparsely populated wing. Test all locks, and be certain that the emergency exit is unlocked. Take the room key with you when you go out. Above all, don't hesitate to express concerns or ask hotel personnel for assistance.

Foreign political atmosphere. Evaluate the political atmosphere of a foreign government and the mood of its populace as they relate to Americans or American enterprise. If political or economic unrest is evident, check with the government's foreign affairs office or with the U.S. State Department before departure. The State Department also posts travel advisories on its website.

Suggest that the executive check in with foreign governmental representatives on arrival. When possible, give the U.S. embassy or consulate in the host country a copy of the executive's itinerary, at least on a per-city basis. Take the advice of the embassy or consulate personnel about any special security procedures.

For each country on the executive's itinerary, prepare a list of phrases in the local language, such as "I need the police [*or* doctor, telephone, ambulance, hospital, U.S. embassy, and so on]." Include numerals in the host country's language on the same list. For instance, 1, 2, 3, 4, and so forth are fine in most countries, but China, Japan, and most Middle Eastern countries have different numeral systems.

Prepare instructions on the use of local pay phones. Telephone services in many countries are not the same as services in the United States. The local consulate of the country being visited or the U.S. embassy or consulate in that country can offer valuable assistance in this regard. Also, remind the executive to keep a supply of local coins for use with pay phones and other vending machines. In addition, the executive should memorize or carry along the access code of his or her long-distance carrier and the country code of his or her home base (which may be another country — other than the United States — in which the executive has an office).

Customs

Executives who travel to other countries should be aware of the customs regulations covering purchases brought back to the United States. Some items that the executive takes along also may have to be declared before entering the destination country. Ask your travel agent for detailed information, and contact the nearest U.S. Customs office or visit its web site for current information. Request copies of *Know Before You Go, Customs Hints for Returning U.S. Residents, Customs Hints for Non-Residents,* and *GSP and the Traveler.* Travel guides also may have customs information for the countries covered in the guides.

TRIP FOLLOW-UP

Meet with the executive and go over the itinerary sheet as soon as possible after the trip. Having kept a copy of the itinerary and having made pertinent notes as the executive has called in during the trip, your own follow-up tasks now should be easier.

Expense Reports

No doubt the executive will have made notes on the itinerary regarding expenses. If additional currency exchanges took place while the executive was traveling, the rates will usually differ, either from day to day or from city to city. This factor will affect the bottom line of the expense reports. In converting foreign currency to dollars, use the currency conversion rate that was charged.

Remember to take into consideration tips for porters at airports and hotels and door attendants at hotels and clubs. Any cash paid out as tips should be noted. If you remind the executive about the tips, other cash expenses that are not supported by receipts may come to mind at the same time.

If payment for hotels, meals, or limousines was made with a major credit card, it's advisable to complete as much of the expense report as possible and hold it, pending receipt of the credit card charges. (The credit card accounting office converts the foreign currency to dollars for billing.) If your company prefers that all expenses be submitted immediately on return, always mention in the expense report that a supplemental expense record will follow as soon as all credit card billings have been received.

Follow-up Correspondence

While going over the itinerary with the executive after the trip, request all business cards that the executive has received during the trip. Add those names, addresses, corporate titles, telephone and fax numbers, and e-mail addresses to the executive's electronic and print address lists. During the review, make a note of any letters of appreciation that should be written to foreign hosts and other contacts. Were any special arrangements made by a host, such as limousine transportation, flowers or fruit baskets in the hotel room, dinners at the host's home or at a club or restaurant, or special tours? A short letter of thanks, such as the following, will suffice. (Avoid contractions, abbreviations, idioms, cliches, and so on in international correspondence.)

> I want to send you my sincere thanks for your kindness during my recent visit to Paris. The wonderful welcome that I received from you and your staff made me feel at home. It was especially thoughtful of you to provide the excellent bottle of wine, which made the long journey much less tiring.
>
> I greatly appreciated the help of your fine staff, and I am looking forward to returning to Paris soon.

If the executive called in during the trip, review any notes made during the conversations. Will some time elapse before plans or agreements made abroad can be put into final form? If so, send a message to this effect to reassure the foreign business colleague that although some work still may be pending, the arrangements discussed are nevertheless proceeding.

(For more about preparing correspondence, refer to Chapter 9, "Correspondence.") Again, avoid contractions, abbreviations, idioms, cliches, and so on in international correspondence:

> Thank you again for spending time with me on Thursday, January 19, to discuss our proposal. I have given the information and changes to our legal staff for incorporation into the final agreement. As soon as our board of directors has approved these changes, I will write to you again.
>
> I greatly appreciated your kindness and help during our discussions. Thank you very much.

Written Reports

While reviewing the itinerary, take the opportunity to transfer all notes or comments made by the executive to the computer. Prepare these notes immediately for the executive's review, together with a list of all business cards received. The executive will then have raw travel data in a readable, well-organized format for reference in writing any post-trip reports.

As soon as the executive has given you the full information for the post-trip report, prepare a draft for editing, additions, and other changes. Chapter 6, "Document Creation" (Style and Format), provides formatting and preparation guidelines for business reports. Chapter 7, "Business Style Guide" (Guide to Capitalization and Punctuation and Guide to Composition), provides information about proper business style.

COUNTRY PROFILES

In a global economy, office professionals need to become more familiar with the different countries and regions of the world that their employers visit. The following profiles therefore list basic information on most major countries worldwide:

Short name and official (long) name

Geographical location

Capital city

Nationality

Language

Religion

Currency

National holiday

Embassy address (in the United States)

Website (if available)

For some countries, certain information was not available at the time of preparing the following list and therefore is not included. For example, not all countries had websites. Also, some countries, such as Tajikistan, were relatively new republics, and others, such as Yugoslavia, were in political and economic turmoil. Any information given in such cases should be considered tentative, sometimes incomplete, and subject to change. Even in many stable, established countries, one should expect occasional social, political, and economic change.

Some of the information given in the profiles varies from year to year. Certain religions or languages, for example, may disappear over time, or others may emerge. Embassy addresses or websites may change. Thus the data in these profiles should be used as a general guide to help you become better acquainted with other countries around the world. Any specific facts or further information should be confirmed through an appropriate source, such as a U.S. embassy in the specific country, before making firm travel plans:

Afghanistan (Islamic State of Afghanistan)

Location: Southern Asia, north and west of Pakistan and east of Iran

Capital: Kabul

Nationality: Afghan(s)

Language: Pashtu, Afghan Persian (Dari), Turkic, other

Religion: Sunni Muslim (majority), Shi'a Muslim, other

Currency: afghani (AF) = 100 puls

National holiday: April 28, Victory of the Muslim Nation; May 4, Remembrance Day for Martyrs and Disabled; August 19, Independence Day

Embassy: 2341 Wyoming Avenue, NW, Washington, DC 20008

Website: http://www.afghan-web.com

Albania (Republic of Albania)

Location: Southeastern Europe, along Adriatic Sea between Greece and Serbia and Montenegro

Capital: Tirana

Nationality: Albanian(s)

Language: Albanian (official: Tosk dialect), Greek

Religion: Muslim (majority), Albanian Orthodox, Roman Catholic

Currency: lek (L) = 100 quintars

National holiday: November 28, Independence Day

Embassy: 2100 S Street, NW, Washington, DC 20008
Website: http://www.undp.tirana.al; http://www.albanian.com

Algeria (Democratic and Popular Republic of Algeria)
Location: Northern Africa, along Mediterranean Sea between Morocco and Tunisia
Capital: Algiers
Nationality: Algerian(s)
Language: Arabic (official), French, Berber dialects
Religion: Sunni Muslim (state religion, majority), Christian, Jewish
Currency: Algerian dinar (DA) = 100 centimes
National holiday: November 1, Anniversary of the Revolution
Embassy: 2118 Kalorama Road, NW, Washington, DC 20008

Andorra (Principality of Andorra)
Location: Southwestern Europe, between France and Spain
Capital: Andorra la Vella
Nationality: Andorran(s)
Language: Catalan (official), French, Castilian
Religion: Roman Catholic
Currency: French franc (F) = 100 centimes; peseta (Pta) = 100 centimos
National holiday: September 8, Mare de Deu de Meritxell
Embassy: 2 United Nations Plaza, New York, NY 10017
Website: http://www.andorra.ad/cniauk.html

Angola (Republic of Angola)
Location: Southern Africa, along South Atlantic Ocean
Capital: Luanda
Nationality: Angolan(s)
Language: Portuguese (official), Bantu and other African languages
Religion: Indigenous beliefs, Roman Catholic, Protestant
Currency: kwanza (NKz) = 100 lwei
National holiday: November 11, Independence Day
Embassy: 1050 Connecticut Avenue, NW, Washington, DC 20036
Website: http://www.angola.org

Antigua and Barbuda
Location: Between Caribbean Sea and North Atlantic Ocean, east-southeast of Puerto Rico
Capital: Saint John's
Nationality: Antiguan(s), Barbudan(s)

Language: English (official), local dialects
Religion: Anglican (majority), other Protestant sects, Roman Catholic
Currency: East Caribbean dollar (EC$) = 100 cents
National holiday: November 1, Independence Day
Embassy: 3216 New Mexico Avenue, NW, Washington, DC 20016
Website: http://www.antigua-barbuda.com

Argentina (Argentine Republic)

Location: Southern South America, along South Atlantic Ocean between
    Chile and Uruguay
Capital: Buenos Aires
Nationality: Argentine(s)
Language: Spanish (official), English, Italian, German, French
Religion: Roman Catholic (majority), Protestant, Jewish, other
Currency: nuevo peso argentino = 100 centavos
National holiday: May 25, Revolution Day
Embassy: 1600 New Hampshire Avenue, NW, Washington, DC 20009

Armenia (Republic of Armenia)

Location: Southwestern Asia, east of Turkey
Capital: Yerevan
Nationality: Armenian(s)
Language: Armenian (majority), Russian, other
Religion: Armenian Orthodox
Currency: dram = 100 luma
National holiday: September 21, Referendum Day
Embassy: 2225 R Street, NW, Washington, DC 20008

Australia (Commonwealth of Australia)

Location: Between Indian and South Pacific oceans
Capital: Canberra
Nationality: Australian(s)
Language: English, native languages
Religion: Anglican, Roman Catholic, other Christian, non-Christian
Currency: Australian dollar ($A) = 100 cents
National holiday: January 26, Australia Day
Embassy: 1601 Massachusetts Avenue, NW, Washington, DC 20036
Website: http://www.austemb.org; http://www.abs.gov.au

Austria (Republic of Austria)

Location: Central Europe, north of Italy and Slovenia
Capital: Vienna

Nationality: Austrian(s)
Language: German
Religion: Roman Catholic (majority), Protestant, other
Currency: euro (EUR); subdivision: Austrian schilling (AS) = 100 groschen
National holiday: October 26, National Day
Embassy: 3524 International Court, NW, Washington, DC 20008
Website: http://www.austria.org

Azerbaijan (Azerbaijan Republic)
Location: Southwestern Asia, along Caspian Sea between Iran and Russia
Capital: Baku (Baki)
Nationality: Azerbaijani(s)
Language: Azeri (majority), Russian, Armenian, other
Religion: Muslim (majority), Russian Orthodox, Armenian Orthodox, other
Currency: manat = 100 gopik
National holiday: May 28, Independence Day
Embassy: 927 15th Street, NW, Washington, DC 20005
Website: http://www.president.az/azerbaijan/azerbaijan.htm

Bahamas, The (Commonwealth of The Bahamas)
Location: Caribbean, North Atlantic Ocean islands southeast of Florida
Capital: Nassau
Nationality: Bahamian(s)
Language: English, Creole
Religion: Baptist, Anglican, Roman Catholic, Methodist, other Protestant, other
Currency: Bahamian dollar (B$) = 100 cents
National holiday: July 10, National Day
Embassy: 2220 Massachusetts Avenue, NW, Washington, DC 20008
Website: http://www.bahamas.net.bs/government; http://www.bahamas.net

Bahrain (State of Bahrain)
Location: Middle East, archipelago in Persian Gulf east of Saudi Arabia
Capital: Manama
Nationality: Bahraini(s)
Language: Arabic, English, Farsi, Urdu
Religion: Shi'a Muslim (majority), Sunni Muslim
Currency: Bahraini dinar (BD) = 1,000 fils

National holiday: December 16, Independence Day
Embassy: 3502 International Drive, NW, Washington, DC 20008

Bangladesh (People's Republic of Bangladesh)

Location: Southern Asia, along Bay of Bengal between Burma and India
Capital: Dhaka
Nationality: Bangladeshi(s)
Language: Bangla (official), English
Religion: Muslim (majority), Hindu, other
Currency: taka (Tk) = 100 poisha
National holiday: March 26, Independence Day
Embassy: 2201 Wisconsin Avenue, NW, Washington, DC 20007
Website: http://www.virtualbangladesh.com

Barbados

Location: Between Caribbean Sea and North Atlantic Ocean north of
   Venezuela
Capital: Bridgetown
Nationality: Barbadian(s)
Language: English
Religion: Protestant (majority), Roman Catholic, other
Currency: Barbadian dollar (Bds$) = 100 cents
National holiday: November 30, Independence Day
Embassy: 2144 Wyoming Avenue, NW, Washington, DC 20008

Belarus (Republic of Belarus)

Location: Eastern Europe, east of Poland
Capital: Minsk
Nationality: Belarusian(s)
Language: Byelorussian, Russian, other
Religion: Eastern Orthodox (majority), other
Currency: Belarusian rubel (BR)
National holiday: July 3, Independence Day
Embassy: 1619 New Hampshire Avenue, NW, Washington, DC 20009

Belgium (Kingdom of Belgium)

Location: Western Europe, along North Sea between France and the
   Netherlands
Capital: Brussels
Nationality: Belgian(s)
Language: Flemish (majority), French, German

Religion: Roman Catholic (majority), Protestant, other
Currency: euro (EUR); Belgian franc (BF) = 100 centimes
National holiday: July 21, National Day
Embassy: 3330 Garfield Street, NW, Washington, DC 20008
Website: http://www.belgium.fgov.be

Belize

Location: Middle America, along Caribbean Sea between Guatemala and
   Mexico
Capital: Belmopan
Nationality: Belizean(s)
Language: English (official), Spanish, Mayan, Garifuna (Carib)
Religion: Roman Catholic (majority), Protestant, other
Currency: Belizean dollar (Bz$) = 100 cents
National holiday: September 21, Independence Day
Embassy: 2535 Massachusetts Avenue, NW, Washington, DC 20008
Website: http://www.belizenet.csm

Benin (Republic of Benin)

Location: Western Africa, along North Atlantic Ocean between Nigeria
   and Togo
Capital: Porto-Novo (seat of government: Cotonou)
Nationality: Beninese (sing. and pl.)
Language: French (official), Fon, Yoruba
Religion: Indigenous beliefs (majority), Muslim, Christian
Currency: Communaute Financiere Africaine franc (CFAF) = 100
   centimes
National holiday: August 1, National Day
Embassy: 2737 Cathedral Avenue, NW, Washington, DC 20008

Bhutan (Kingdom of Bhutan)

Location: Southern Asia, between China and India
Capital: Thimphu
Nationality: Bhutanese (sing. and pl.)
Language: Dzongkha (official), Tibetan dialects, Nepalese
   dialects
Religion: Lamaistic Buddhist (majority), Hindu
Currency: ngultrum (Nu) = 100 chetrum (Indian currency is also legal
   tender)
National holiday: December 17, National Day
Website: http://www.bhutan.org

Bolivia (Republic of Bolivia)
Location: Central South America, southwest of Brazil
Capital: Sucre (seat of government: LaPaz)
Nationality: Bolivian(s)
Language: Spanish, Quechua, and Aymara (all official)
Religion: Roman Catholic (majority), Protestant
Currency: boliviano ($B) = 100 centavos
National holiday: August 6, Independence Day
Embassy: 3014 Massachusetts Avenue, NW, Washington, DC 20008
Website: http://www.ine.gov.bo

Bosnia and Herzegovina
Location: Southeastern Europe, along Adriatic Sea and Croatia
Capital: Sarajevo
Nationality: Bosnian(s) and Herzegovinian(s)
Language: Croatian, Serbian, Bosnian
Religion: Muslim, Orthodox, Catholic, Protestant, other
Currency: 1 convertible marka = 100 convertible pfenniga
National holiday: January 9, Republic Day; March 1, Independence Day;
    November 25, Bosnia Republic Day
Embassy: 1707 L Street, NW, Washington, DC 20036
Website: http://www.bosnianembassy.org

Botswana (Republic of Botswana)
Location: Southern Africa, north of South Africa
Capital: Gaborone
Nationality: Motswana (sing.), Batswana (pl.)
Language: English (official), Setswana
Religion: Christian, indigenous beliefs
Currency: pula (P) = 100 thebe
National holiday: September 30, Independence Day
Embassy: 3400 International Drive, NW, Washington, DC 20008

Brazil (Federative Republic of Brazil)
Location: Eastern South America, along Atlantic Ocean
Capital: Brasilia
Nationality: Brazilian(s)
Language: Portuguese (official), Spanish, English, French
Religion: Roman Catholic
Currency: real (R$) = 100 centavos
National holiday: September 7, Independence Day

Embassy: 3006 Massachusetts Avenue, NW, Washington, DC 20008
Website: http://www.ibge.gov.br; http://www.brasil.emb.nw.dc.us/

Brunei (Negara Brunei Darussalam)
Location: Southeastern Asia, along South China Sea and Malaysia
Capital: Bandar Seri Begawan
Nationality: Bruneian(s)
Language: Malay (official), English, Chinese
Religion: Muslim (official), Buddhist, Christian, indigenous beliefs
Currency: Bruneian dollar (B$) = 100 cents
National holiday: February 23, National Day
Embassy: 2600 Virginia Avenue, NW, Washington, DC 20037
Website: http://www.brunet.bn

Bulgaria (Republic of Bulgaria)
Location: Southeastern Europe, along Black Sea between Romania and
　Turkey
Capital: Sofia
Nationality: Bulgarian(s)
Language: Bulgarian, secondary languages
Religion: Bulgarian Orthodox (majority), Muslim, Jewish, Roman
　Catholic, Uniate Catholic, Protestant, Gregorian-Armenian
Currency: lev (Lv) = 100 stotinki
National holiday: March 3, Independence Day
Embassy: 1621 22nd Street, NW, Washington, DC 20008

Burkina Faso
Location: Western Africa, north of Ghana
Capital: Ouagadougou
Nationality: Burkinabe (sing. and pl.)
Language: French (official), ethnic languages (majority)
Religion: Indigenous beliefs, Muslim, Roman Catholic and other Christian
Currency: Communaute Financiere Africaine franc (CFAF) = 100 centimes
National holiday: August 4, Anniversary of the Revolution
Embassy: 2340 Massachusetts Avenue, NW, Washington, DC 20008

Burma. See Myanmar.

Burundi (Republic of Burundi)
Location: Central Africa, east of Democratic Republic of the Congo
Capital: Bujumbura

Nationality: Burundian(s)
Language: French and Kirundi (both official), Swahili
Religion: Christian (majority), indigenous beliefs, Muslim
Currency: Burundi franc (FBu) = 100 centimes
National holiday: July 1, Independence Day
Embassy: 2233 Wisconsin Avenue, NW, Washington, DC 20007

Cambodia (Kingdom of Cambodia)

Location: Southeastern Asia, along Gulf of Thailand between Thailand, Vietnam, and Laos
Capital: Phnom Penh
Nationality: Cambodian(s)
Language: Khmer (official), French
Religion: Theravada Buddhist (majority), other
Currency: new riel (CR) = 100 sen
National holiday: November 9, Independence Day
Embassy: 4500 16th Street, NW, Washington, DC 20011
Website: http://www.cambodia.org

Cameroon (Republic of Cameroon)

Location: Western Africa, along Bight of Biafra between Nigeria and Equatorial Guinea
Capital: Yaounde
Nationality: Cameroonian(s)
Language: French and English (both official), 24 major African language groups
Religion: Indigenous beliefs (majority), Christian, Muslim
Currency: Communaute Financiere Africaine franc (CFAF) = 100 centimes
National holiday: May 20, National Day
Embassy: 2349 Massachusetts Avenue, NW, Washington, DC 20008
Website: http://www.camnet.cm

Canada

Location: Northern North America, along North Atlantic and North Pacific oceans north of the United States
Capital: Ottawa
Nationality: Canadian(s)
Language: English and French (both official)
Religion: Roman Catholic, United Church, Anglican, other
Currency: Canadian dollar (Can$) = 100 cents

National holiday: July 1, Canada Day
Embassy: 501 Pennsylvania Avenue, NW, Washington, DC 20001
Website: http://www.statcan.ca; http://www.canada.gc.ca/main_e.html

Cape Verde (Republic of Cape Verde)

Location: Western Africa, islands in North Atlantic Ocean west of
   Senegal
Capital: Praia
Nationality: Cape Verdean(s)
Language: Portuguese, Criuolo
Religion: Roman Catholic, Protestant
Currency: Cape Verdean escudo (CVEsc) = 100 centavos
National holiday: July 5, Independence Day
Embassy: 3415 Massachusetts Avenue, NW, Washington, DC 20007

Central African Republic

Location: Central Africa, north of Democratic Republic of the Congo
Capital: Bangui
Nationality: Central African(s)
Language: French (official), Sangho, Arabic, Hunsa, Swahili
Religion: Indigenous beliefs, Protestant, Roman Catholic, Muslim, other
Currency: Communaute Financiere Africaine franc (CFAF) =
   100 centimes
National holiday: December 1, National Day
Embassy: 1618 22nd Street, NW, Washington, DC 20008

Chad (Republic of Chad)

Location: Central Africa, south of Libya
Capital: N'Djamena
Nationality: Chadian(s)
Language: French and Arabic (both official), Sara, Sango, numerous other
   languages
Religion: Muslim, Christian, indigenous beliefs
Currency: Communaute Financiere Africaine franc (CFAF) =
   100 centimes
National holiday: August 11, Independence Day
Embassy: 2002 R Street, NW, Washington, DC 20009

Chile (Republic of Chile)

Location: Southern South America, along South Atlantic and South Pacific
   oceans between Argentina and Peru

Capital: Santiago
Nationality: Chilean(s)
Language: Spanish
Religion: Roman Catholic (majority), Protestant, Jewish
Currency: Chilean peso (Ch$) = 100 centavos
National holiday: September 18, Independence Day
Embassy: 1732 Massachusetts Avenue, NW, Washington, DC 20036
Website: http://www.segegob.cl/seg-ingl/index2i.html

China (People's Republic of China)
Location: Eastern Asia, along East and South China seas between North
   Korea and Vietnam
Capital: Beijing
Nationality: Chinese (sing. and pl.)
Language: Standard Chinese or Mandarin, Yue, Wu, Minbei, Minnan,
   Xiang, Gan, Hakka dialects, minority languages
Religion: (Officially atheist), Taoist (Daoist), Buddhist, Muslim,
   Christian
Currency: yuan (¥) = 10 jiao
National holiday: October 1, National Day
Embassy: 2300 Connecticut Avenue, NW, Washington, DC 20008
Website: http://www.china-embassy.org

Colombia (Republic of Colombia)
Location: Northern South America, along North Pacific Ocean and
   Caribbean Sea between Panama and Venezuela
Capital: Bogota
Nationality: Colombian(s)
Language: Spanish
Religion: Roman Catholic
Currency: Colombian peso (Col$) = 100 centavos
National holiday: July 20, Independence Day
Embassy: 2118 Leroy Place, NW, Washington, DC 20008

Comoros (Federal Islamic Republic of the Comoros)
Location: Southern Africa, island group in Mozambique Channel between
   Madagascar and Mozambique
Capital: Moroni
Nationality: Comoran(s)
Language: French and Arabic (both official), Comoran (blend of Arabic
   and Swahili)

Religion: Sunni Muslim (majority), Roman Catholic
Currency: Comoran franc (CF) = 100 centimes
National holiday: July 6, Independence Day
Embassy: 336 East 45th Street, New York, NY 10017
Website: http://www.ksu.edu/sasw/comoros/comoros.html

Congo (Democratic Republic of the Congo), formerly Zaire
Location: Central Africa, northeast of Angola
Capital: Kinshasa
Nationality: Congolese (sing. and pl.)
Language: French (official), Lingala, Kingwana, Kikongo, Tshiluba
Religion: Roman Catholic, Protestant, Kimbanguist, Muslim
Currency: Congolese franc (CF) = 100 centimes
National holiday: June 30, Anniversary of Independence from Belgium
Embassy: 1800 New Hampshire Avenue, NW, Washington, DC 20009

Congo (Republic of the Congo)
Location: Western Africa, along South Atlantic Ocean between Angola and Gabon
Capital: Brazzaville
Nationality: Congolese (sing. and pl.)
Language: French (official), Lingala and Monokutuba, other
Religion: Christian, animist, Muslim
Currency: Communaute Financiere Africaine franc (CFAF) = 100 centimes
National holiday: August 15, Congolese National Day
Embassy: 4891 Colorado Avenue, NW, Washington, DC 20011
Website: http://www.gksoft.com/govt/en/cg.html

Costa Rica (Republic of Costa Rica)
Location: Middle America, along Caribbean Sea and North Pacific Ocean between Nicaragua and Panama
Capital: San Jose
Nationality: Costa Rican(s)
Language: Spanish (official), English
Religion: Roman Catholic, Protestant
Currency: Costa Rican colon (C) = 100 centimos
National holiday: September 15, Independence Day
Embassy: 2114 S Street, NW, Washington, DC 20008

Cote d'Ivoire. See **Ivory Coast.**

Croatia (Republic of Croatia)
Location: Southeastern Europe, along Adriatic Sea between Bosnia and Herzegovina and Slovenia
Capital: Zagreb
Nationality: Croat(s)
Language: Croation (majority), other
Religion: Roman Catholic (majority), Orthodox, Slavic Muslim, Protestant, other
Currency: Croatian kuna (HRK) = 100 lipas
National holiday: May 30, Statehood Day
Embassy: 2343 Massachusetts Avenue, NW, Washington, DC 20008

Cuba (Republic of Cuba)
Location: Island between Caribbean Sea and North Atlantic Ocean south of Florida
Capital: Havana
Nationality: Cuban(s)
Language: Spanish
Religion: Roman Catholic (majority), Protestant, Jehovah's Witness, Jewish, Santeria
Currency: Cuban peso (Cu$) = 100 centavos
National holiday: January 1, Liberation Day; July 26, Rebellion Day

Cyprus (Republic of Cyprus)
Location: Middle East, island in Mediterranean Sea south of Turkey
Capital: Nicosia
Nationality: Cypriot(s)
Language: Greek, Turkish, English
Religion: Greek Orthodox (majority), Muslim, Maronite, Armenian Apostolic, other
Currency: Cypriot pound (£C) = 100 cents; Turkish lira (TL) = 100 kurus
National holiday: October 1, Independence Day; Turkish Cypriot area celebrates on November 15
Embassy: 2211 R Street, NW, Washington, DC 20008

Czech Republic
Location: Central Europe, southeast of Germany
Capital: Prague

Nationality: Czech(s)
Language: Czech
Religion: Atheist, Roman Catholic, Protestant, Orthodox, other
Currency: koruna (Kc) = 100 haleru
National holiday: May 8, National Liberation Day; October 28, Founding of the Republic
Embassy: 3900 Spring of Freedom Street, NW, Washington, DC 20008

Denmark (Kingdom of Denmark)

Location: Northern Europe, along Baltic and North seas on peninsula north of Germany
Capital: Copenhagen
Nationality: Dane(s)
Language: Danish, Faroese, Greenlandic, German
Religion: Evangelical Lutheran (majority), other Protestant and Roman Catholic, other
Currency: Danish krone (DKr) = 100 oere
National holiday: April 16, Birthday of the Queen
Embassy: 3200 Whitehaven Street, NW, Washington, DC 20008
Website: http://www.denmark.org

Djibouti (Republic of Djibouti)

Location: Eastern Africa, along Gulf of Aden and Red Sea between Eritrea and Somalia
Capital: Djibouti
Nationality: Djiboutian(s)
Language: French and Arabic (both official), Somali, Afar
Religion: Muslim (majority), Christian
Currency: Djiboutian franc (DF) = 100 centimes
National holiday: June 27, Independence Day
Embassy: 1156 15th Street, NW, Washington, DC 20005

Dominica (Commonwealth of Dominica)

Location: Island between Caribbean Sea and North Atlantic Ocean between Puerto Rico and Trinidad and Tobago
Capital: Roseau
Nationality: Dominican(s)
Language: English (official), French patois
Religion: Roman Catholic (majority), Protestant, other
Currency: East Caribbean dollar (EC$) = 100 cents

National holiday: November 3, Independence Day
Embassy: 3216 New Mexico Avenue, NW, Washington, DC 20016

Dominican Republic
Location: Eastern two-thirds of island Hispaniola, between Caribbean Sea
   and North Atlantic Ocean east of Haiti
Capital: Santo Domingo
Nationality: Dominican(s)
Language: Spanish
Religion: Roman Catholic
Currency: Dominica peso (RD$) = 100 centavos
National holiday: February 27, Independence Day
Embassy: 1715 22nd Street, NW, Washington, DC 20008

Ecuador (Republic of Ecuador)
Location: Western South America, along Pacific Ocean at Equator between
   Colombia and Peru
Capital: Quito
Nationality: Ecuadorian(s)
Language: Spanish (official), Amerindian languages (especially Quechua)
Religion: Roman Catholic
Currency: sucre (S/) = 100 centavos
National holiday: August 10, Independence Day
Embassy: 2535 15th Street, NW, Washington, DC 20009

Egypt (Arab Republic of Egypt)
Location: Northern Africa, along Mediterranean Sea between Libya and
   Gaza Strip
Capital: Cairo
Nationality: Egyptian(s)
Language: Arabic (official), English, French
Religion: Muslim (majority; mostly Sunni), Coptic Christian, other
Currency: Egyptian pound (£E) = 100 piasters
National holiday: July 23, Anniversary of the Revolution
Embassy: 3521 International Court, NW, Washington, DC 20008
Website: http://www.idsc.gov.eg

El Salvador (Republic of El Salvador)
Location: Middle America, along North Pacific Ocean between Guatemala
   and Honduras
Capital: San Salvador

Nationality: Salvadoran(s)
Language: Spanish, Nahua
Religion: Roman Catholic (majority), Protestant
Currency: Salvadoran colon (C) = 100 centavos
National holiday: September 15, Independence Day
Embassy: 2308 California Street, NW, Washington, DC 20008

Equatorial Guinea (Republic of Equatorial Guinea)
Location: Western Africa, along Bight of Biafra between Cameroon and Gabon
Capital: Malabo
Nationality: Equatorial Guinean(s) *or* Equatoguinean(s)
Language: Spanish and French (both official), pidgin English, Fang, Bubi, Ibo
Religion: Roman Catholic (majority), other Christian, pagan practices
Currency: Communaute Financiere Africaine franc (CFAF) = 100 centimes
National holiday: October 12, Independence Day
Embassy: 1511 K Street, NW, Washington, DC 20005

Eritrea (State of Eritrea)
Location: Eastern Africa, along Red Sea between Djibouti and Sudan
Capital: Asmara
Nationality: Eritrean(s)
Language: Afar, Amharic, Arabic, Tigre and Kunama, Tigrinya, Cushitic
Religion: Muslim, Coptic Christian, Roman Catholic, Protestant
Currency: nafka = 100 cents
National holiday: May 24, National Day
Embassy: 1708 New Hampshire Avenue, NW, Washington, DC 20009
Website: http://www.NetAfrica.org/eritrea

Estonia (Republic of Estonia)
Location: Eastern Europe, along Baltic Sea and Gulf of Finland between Latvia and Russia
Capital: Tallinn
Nationality: Estonian(s)
Language: Estonian (official), Russian, Ukrainian, other
Religion: Evangelical Lutheran, Russian and Estonian Orthodox, other
Currency: Estonian kroon (EEK) = 100 cents
National holiday: February 24, Independence Day
Embassy: 2131 Massachusetts Avenue, NW, Washington, DC 20008

Website: http://www.ciesin.ee/undp/nhdr97/eng/index.html;
  http://www.vm.ee

Ethopia (Federal Democratic Republic of Ethiopia)
Location: Eastern Africa, west of Somalia
Capital: Addis Ababa
Nationality: Ethiopian(s)
Language: Amharic (official), Tigrinya, Orominga, Guaraginga, Somali,
  Arabic, English
Religion: Muslim, Ethiopian Orthodox, animist, other
Currency: Ethiopian birr (Br) = 100 cents
National holiday: May 28, National Day
Embassy: 2134 Kalorama Road, NW, Washington, DC 20008

Fiji (Republic of the Fiji Islands)
Location: Oceania, island group in South Pacific Ocean between Hawaii
  and New Zealand
Capital: Suva
Nationality: Fijian(s)
Language: English (official), Fijian, Hindustani
Religion: Christian (majority), Hindu, Muslim, other
Currency: Fiji dollar (F$) = 100 cents
National holiday: October 10, Independence Day
Embassy: 2233 Wisconsin Avenue, NW, Washington, DC 20007

Finland (Republic of Finland)
Location: Northern Europe, along Baltic Sea between Sweden and Russia
Capital: Helsinki
Nationality: Finn(s)
Language: Finnish (majority) and Swedish (both official), Lapp, Russian
Religion: Evangelical Lutheran (majority), Greek Orthodox, other
Currency: euro (EUR); subdivision: markka or finmark (FMk) = 100 pennia
National holiday: December 6, Independence Day
Embassy: 3301 Massachusetts Avenue, NW, Washington, DC 20008
Website: http://www.finland.org

France (French Republic)
Location: Western Europe, along Bay of Biscay, English Channel, and
  Mediterranean Sea between Spain and Germany
Capital: Paris
Nationality: Frenchman(men), Frenchwoman(women)

Language: French (official), declining regional dialects and languages
Religion: Roman Catholic (majority), Protestant, Jewish, Muslim, other
Currency: euro (EUR); subdivisioin: French franc (F) = 100 centimes
National holiday: July 14, National Day; Taking of the Bastille
Embassy: 4101 Reservoir Road, NW, Washington, DC 20007
Website: http://www.info-france-usa.org; http://www.france.org

Gabon (Gabonese Republic)

Location: Western Africa, along Atlantic Ocean at Equator between
    Republic of the Congo and Equatorial Guinea
Capital: Libreville
Nationality: Gabonese (sing. and pl.)
Language: French (official), Fang, Myene, Bateke, Bapounou/Eschira,
    Bandjabi
Religion: Christian (majority), Muslim, animist
Currency: Communaute Financiere Africaine franc (CFAF) = 100 centimes
National holiday: August 17, Independence Day
Embassy: 2034 20th Street, NW, Washington, DC 20009

The Gambia (Republic of The Gambia)

Location: Western Africa, along North Atlantic Ocean and Senegal
Capital: Banjul
Nationality: Gambian(s)
Language: English (official), Mandinka, Wolof, Fula, other
Religion: Muslim (majority), Christian, other indigenous beliefs
Currency: dalasi (D) = 100 butut
National holiday: February 18, Independence Day
Embassy: 1155 15th Street, NW, Washington, DC 20005
Website: http://www.Gambia.com

Georgia

Location: Southwestern Asia, along Black Sea between Turkey and Russia
Capital: T'bilisi
Nationality: Georgian(s)
Language: Georgian (official), Russian, Armenian, Azeri
Religion: Georgian Orthodox (majority), Muslim, Russian Orthodox,
    Armenian Apostolic, other
Currency: lari
National holiday: May 26, Independence Day
Embassy: (temporary) 1511 K Street, NW, Washington, DC 20005
Website: http://www.parliament.ge

Germany (Federal Republic of Germany)

Location: Central Europe, along Baltic and North seas between the
  Netherlands and Poland
Capital: Berlin
Nationality: German(s)
Language: German
Religion: Protestant, Roman Catholic, Muslim, other
Currency: euro (EUR); subdivision: deutsche mark (DM) = 100 pfennige
National holiday: October 3, German Unity Day
Embassy: 4645 Reservoir Road, NW, Washington, DC 20007
Website: http://www.undp.org/missions/germany;
  http://www.government.de/english/01/newsf.html

Ghana (Republic of Ghana)

Location: Western Africa, along Gulf of Guinea between Ivory Coast and
  Togo
Capital: Accra
Nationality: Ghanaian(s)
Language: English (official), African languages
Religion: Indigenous beliefs, Muslim, Christian, other
Currency: new cedi (C) = 100 pesewas
National holiday: March 6, Independence Day
Embassy: 3512 International Drive, NW, Washington, DC 20008

Greece (Hellenic Republic)

Location: Southern Europe, along Aegean, Ionian, and Mediterranean seas
  between Albania and Turkey
Capital: Athens
Nationality: Greek(s)
Language: Greek (official), English, French
Religion: Greek Orthodox (majority), Muslim, other
Currency: drachma (Dr) = 100 lepta
National holiday: March 25, Independence Day
Embassy: 2221 Massachusetts Avenue, NW, Washington, DC 20008
Website: http://www.hiway.gr/gi

Grenada

Location: Caribbean, island between Caribbean Sea and Atlantic Ocean
  north of Trinidad and Tobago
Capital: Saint George's
Nationality: Grenadian(s)

Language: English (official), French patois
Religion: Roman Catholic (majority), Anglican, other Protestant
Currency: EC dollar (EC$) = 100 cents
National holiday: February 7, Independence Day
Embassy: 1701 New Hampshire Avenue, NW, Washington,
   DC 20009
Website: http://www.grenada.org

Guatemala (Republic of Guatemala)
Location: Middle America, along Caribbean Sea and North Pacific Ocean
   between El Salvador and Mexico
Capital: Guatemala
Nationality: Guatemalan(s)
Language: Spanish (majority), Amerindian languages
Religion: Roman Catholic, Protestant, indigenous Mayan beliefs
Currency: quetzal (Q) = 100 centavos
National holiday: September 15, Independence Day
Embassy: 2220 R Street, NW, Washington, DC 20008

Guinea (Republic of Guinea)
Location: Western Africa, along North Atlantic Ocean between Guinea-
   Bissau and Sierra Leone
Capital: Conakry
Nationality: Guinean(s)
Language: French (official), individual ethnic languages
Religion: Muslim (majority), Christian, indigenous beliefs
Currency: Guinean franc (FG) = 100 centimes
National holiday: April 3, Anniversary of the Second Republic
Embassy: 2112 Leroy Place, NW, Washington, DC 20008

Guinea-Bissau (Republic of Guinea-Bissau)
Location: Western Africa, along North Atlantic Ocean between Senegal
   and Guinea
Capital: Bissau
Nationality: Guinean(s)
Language: Portuguese (official), Crioulo, African languages
Religion: Indigenous beliefs, Muslim, Christian
Currency: Communaute Financiere Africaine franc (CFAF) =
   100 centimes
National holiday: September 24, Independence Day
Embassy: 1511 K Street, NW, Washington, DC 20005

Guyana (Co-operative Republic of Guyana)

Location: Northern South America, along North Atlantic Ocean between
 Suriname and Venezuela
Capital: Georgetown
Nationality: Guyanese (sing. and pl.)
Language: English, Amerindian dialects, Creole, Hindi, Urdu
Religion: Christian (majority), Hindu, Muslim, other
Currency: Guyanese dollar (G$) = 100 cents
National holiday: February 23, Republic Day
Embassy: 2490 Tracy Place, NW, Washington, DC 20008

Haiti (Republic of Haiti)

Location: Caribbean, western third of island Hispaniola between
 Caribbean Sea and North Atlantic Ocean west of Dominican Republic
Capital: Port-au-Prince
Nationality: Haitian(s)
Language: French (official), Creole (official)
Religion: Roman Catholic (majority), Protestant, other
Currency: gourde (G) = 100 centimes
National holiday: January 1, Independence Day
Embassy: 2311 Massachusetts Avenue, NW, Washington, DC 20008
Website: http://www.haiti.org/embassy/

Honduras (Republic of Honduras)

Location: Middle America, along Caribbean Sea and North Pacific Ocean
 between El Salvador and Nicaragua
Capital: Tegucigalpa
Nationality: Honduran(s)
Language: Spanish, Amerindian dialects
Religion: Roman Catholic (majority), Protestant
Currency: lempira (L) = 100 centavos
National holiday: September 15, Independence Day
Embassy: 3007 Tilden Street, NW, Washington, DC 20008
Website: http://www.honduras.com

Hungary (Republic of Hungary)

Location: Central Europe, east of Austria and northwest of Romania
Capital: Budapest
Nationality: Hungarian(s)
Language: Hungarian (majority), other
Religion: Roman Catholic (majority), Calvinist, Lutheran, atheist, other

Currency: forint (Ft) = 100 filler
National holiday: August 20, St. Stephen's Day (National Day)
Embassy: 3910 Shoemaker Street, NW, Washington, DC 20008
Website: http://www.hungaryemb.org

Iceland (Republic of Iceland)

Location: Northern Europe, island between Greenland Sea and North
   Atlantic Ocean northwest of the United Kingdom
Capital: Reykjavik
Nationality: Icelander(s)
Language: Icelandic
Religion: Evangelical Lutheran (majority), other Protestant, Roman
   Catholic
Currency: Icelandic krona (IKr) = 100 aurar
National holiday: June 17, Anniversary of the Establishment of the
   Republic
Embassy: 1156 15th Street, NW, Washington, DC 20005
Website: http://www.iceland.org

India (Republic of India)

Location: Southern Asia, along Arabian Sea and Bay of Bengal between
   Myanmar (Burma) and Pakistan
Capital: New Delhi
Nationality: Indian(s)
Language: Hindi (national language); official languages: Assamese,
   Bengali, Gujarati, Kannada, Kashmiri, Malayalam, Marathi, Oriya,
   Punjabi, Sanskrit, Sindhi, Tamil, Telugu, Urdu; Hindustani; English
Religion: Hindu (majority), Muslim, Christian, Sikh, Buddhist, Jains,
   other
Currency: Indian rupee (Re) = 100 paise
National holiday: January 26, Anniversary of the Proclamation of the
   Republic
Embassy: 2107 Massachusetts Avenue, NW, Washington, DC 20008
Website: http://www.nic.in; http://www.indianembassy.org;
   http://www.tourindia.com/

Indonesia (Republic of Indonesia)

Location: Southeastern Asia, archipelago between Indian and Pacific
   oceans
Capital: Jakarta
Nationality: Indonesian(s)

Language: Bahasa Indonesia (official), English, Dutch, Javanese and other local dialects
Religion: Muslim (majority), Protestant, Roman Catholic, Hindu, Buddhist, other
Currency: Indonesian rupiah (Rp)
National holiday: August 17, Independence Day
Embassy: 2020 Massachusetts Avenue, NW, Washington, DC 20036

Iran (Islamic Republic of Iran)

Location: Middle East, along Gulf of Oman, Persian Gulf, and Caspian Sea between Iraq and Pakistan
Capital: Tehran
Nationality: Iranian(s)
Language: Persian and Persian dialects, Turkic and Turkic dialects, Kurdish, Luri, Balochi, Arabic, Turkish, other
Religion: Shi'a Muslim (majority), Sunni Muslim, Zoroastrian, Jewish, Christian, Baha'i
Currency: 10 Iranian rial (IR) = 1 toman
National holiday: April 1, Islamic Republic Day

Iraq (Republic of Iraq)

Location: Middle East, along Persian Gulf between Iran and Kuwait
Capital: Baghdad
Nationality: Iraqi(s)
Language: Arabic, Kurdish (official in Kurdish areas), Assyrian, Armenian
Religion: Shi'a Muslim (majority), Sunni Muslim, Christian, other
Currency: Iraqi dinar (ID) = 1,000 fils
National holiday: July 17, Anniversary of the Revolution
Website: http://www.Iraqi-mission.org

Ireland

Location: Western Europe, major part of island of Ireland in North Atlantic Ocean west of Great Britain
Capital: Dublin
Nationality: Irishman(men), Irishwoman(women)
Language: English, Irish (Gaelic)
Religion: Roman Catholic (majority), Church of Ireland, other
Currency: euro (EUR); subdivision: Irish pound (£Ir) = 100 pence
National holiday: March 17, Saint Patrick's Day
Embassy: 2234 Massachusetts Avenue, NW, Washington, DC 20008
Website: http://www.cso.ie/index.html; http://www.genuki.org.uk

Israel (State of Israel)

Location: Middle East, along Mediterranean Sea between Egypt and
   Lebanon
Capital: Jerusalem
Nationality: Israeli(s)
Language: Hebrew (official), Arabic (official for Arab minority), English
Religion: Jewish (majority), Muslim (mostly Sunni), Christian, Druze,
   other
Currency: new Israel shekel (NIS) = 100 new agorot
National holiday: May 14 (subject to Jewish calendar), Independence Day
Embassy: 3514 International Drive, NW, Washington, DC 20008
Website: http://www.israel.org

Italy (Italian Republic)

Location: Southern Europe, peninsula extending into central
   Mediterranean Sea south of France, Switzerland, and Austria
Capital: Rome
Nationality: Italian(s)
Language: Italian, German, French, Slovene
Religion: Roman Catholic (majority), Protestant, Jewish, Muslim
Currency: euro (EUR); subdivision: Italian lira (Lit) = 100 centesimi
National holiday: June 2, Anniversary of the Republic
Embassy: 1601 Fuller Street, NW, Washington, DC 20009
Website: http://www.istat.it

Ivory Coast (Republic of the Ivory Coast [Cote d'Ivoire])

Location: Western Africa, along North Atlantic Ocean between Ghana and
   Liberia
Capital: Yamoussoukro (administrative center: Abidjan)
Nationality: Ivorian(s)
Language: French (official), Dioula and numerous other native dialects
Religion: Muslim (majority), Christian, indigenous beliefs
Currency: Communaute Financiere Africaine franc (CFAF) = 100 centimes
National holiday: August 7, National Day
Embassy: 2424 Massachusetts Avenue, NW, Washington, DC 20008
Website: http://icweb2.loc.gov/frd/cs/citoc.html

Jamaica

Location: Caribbean, island in the Caribbean Sea south of Cuba
Capital: Kingston
Nationality: Jamaican(s)

Language: English, Creole
Religion: Protestant (majority), Roman Catholic, other
Currency: Jamaican dollar (J$) = 100 cents
National holiday: First Monday in August, Independence Day
Embassy: 1520 New Hampshire Avenue, NW, Washington, DC 20036
Website: http://www.jamaica.com

Japan
Location: Eastern Asia, islands between North Pacific Ocean and Sea of
   Japan east of Korea and Russia
Capital: Tokyo
Nationality: Japanese (sing. and pl.)
Language: Japanese
Religion: Shintoist and Buddhist (majority), other
Currency: yen (¥)
National holiday: December 23, Birthday of the Emperor
Embassy: 2520 Massachusetts Avenue, NW, Washington, DC 20008
Website: http://www.embjap.org; http://www.mofa.go.jp

Jordan (Hashemite Kingdom of Jordan)
Location: Middle East, northwest of Saudi Arabia
Capital: Amman
Nationality: Jordanian(s)
Language: Arabic (official), English
Religion: Sunni Muslim (majority), Christian
Currency: Jordanian dinar (JD) = 1,000 fils
National holiday: May 25, Independence Day
Embassy: 3504 International Drive, NW, Washington, DC 20008
Website: http://www.nic.gov.jo

Kazakhstan (Republic of Kazakhstan)
Location: Central Asia, northwest of China
Capital: Astana
Nationality: Kazakhstani(s)
Language: Kazakh (Qazaq) and Russian (both official)
Religion: Muslim, Russian Orthodox, Protestant, other
Currency: Kazakhstani tenge = 100 tiyn
National holiday: October 25, Independence Day
Embassy: (temporary) 3421 Massachusetts Avenue, NW, Washington,
   DC 20008
Website: http://www.undp.org/missions/kazakhstan

Kenya (Republic of Kenya)
Location: Eastern Africa, along Indian Ocean between Somalia and Tanzania
Capital: Nairobi
Nationality: Kenyan(s)
Language: Swahili and English (both official), numerous indigenous languages
Religion: Protestant, Roman Catholic, indigenous beliefs, Muslim, other
Currency: Kenyan shilling (KSh) = 100 cents
National holiday: December 12, Independence Day
Embassy: 2249 R Street, NW, Washington, DC 20008

Kiribati (Republic of Kiribati)
Location: Oceania, islands in Central Pacific Ocean along equator between Hawaii and Australia
Capital: Tarawa
Nationality: I-Kiribati (sing. and pl.)
Language: English (official), Gilbertese
Religion: Roman Catholic (majority), Protestant, Seventh Day Adventist, Baha'i, Church of God, Mormon
Currency: Australian dollar ($A) = 100 cents
National holiday: July 12, Independence Day

Korea, North (Democratic People's Republic of Korea)
Location: Eastern Asia, northern part of Korean peninsula along Korea Bay and Sea of Japan between China and South Korea
Capital: P'yongyang
Nationality: Korean(s)
Language: Korean
Religion: Buddhist, Confucianist, Christian, Chondogyo
Currency: North Korean won (Wn) = 100 chon
National holiday: September 9, Democratic People's Republic of Korea Foundation Day

Korea, South (Republic of Korea)
Location: Eastern Asia, southern part of Korean peninsula along Sea of Japan and Yellow Sea
Capital: Seoul
Nationality: Korean(s)
Language: Korean, English

Religion: Christian, Buddhist, Confucianist, folk religions (shamanism), Chondogyo, other
Currency: South Korean won (W) = 100 chun
National holiday: August 15, Liberation Day
Embassy: 2450 Massachusetts Avenue, NW, Washington, DC 20008

Kuwait (State of Kuwait)

Location: Middle East, along Persian Gulf between Iraq and Saudi Arabia
Capital: Kuwait
Nationality: Kuwaiti(s)
Language: Arabic (official), English
Religion: Sunni Muslim (majority), Shi'a Muslim, Christian, Hindu, Parsi, other
Currency: Kuwaiti dinar (KD) = 1,000 fils
National holiday: February 25, National Day
Embassy: 2940 Tilden Street, NW, Washington, DC 20008
Website: http://www.moc.kw/

Kyrgyzstan (Kyrgyz Republic)

Location: Central Asia, west of China
Capital: Bishkek
Nationality: Kyrgyzstani(s)
Language: Kirghiz (Kyrgyz) and Russian (both official)
Religion: Muslim (majority), Russian Orthodox, other
Currency: Kyrgyzstani som (KGS) = 100 tyiyn
National holiday: August 31, Independence Day; December 2, National Day
Embassy: 1732 Wisconsin Avenue, NW, Washington, DC 20007

Laos (Lao People's Democratic Republic)

Location: Southeastern Asia, northeast of Thailand and west of Vietnam
Capital: Vientiane
Nationality: Lao(s) *or* Laotian(s)
Language: Lao (official), French, English, ethnic languages
Religion: Buddhist (majority), animist, other
Currency: new kip (NK) = 100 at
National holiday: December 2, National Day
Embassy: 2222 S Street, NW, Washington, DC 20008
Website: http://www.laoembassy.com/discover/index.htm

Latvia (Republic of Latvia)
Location: Eastern Europe, along Baltic Sea between Estonia and Lithuania
Capital: Riga
Nationality: Latvian(s)
Language: Lettish (official), Lithuanian, Russian, other
Religion: Lutheran, Roman Catholic, Russian Orthodox
Currency: Latvian lat (LVL) = 100 santims
National holiday: November 18, Independence Day
Embassy: 4325 17th Street, NW, Washington, DC 20011
Website: http://www.latvia-usa.org; http://www.csb.lv

Lebanon (Lebanese Republic)
Location: Middle East, along Mediterranean Sea between Israel and
  Syria
Capital: Beirut
Nationality: Lebanese (sing. and pl.)
Language: Arabic (official), French, English, Armenian
Religion: Muslim (majority), Christian, Jewish
Currency: Lebanese pound (£L) = 100 piasters
National holiday: November 22, Independence Day
Embassy: 2560 28th Street, NW, Washington, DC 20008
Website: http://www.erols.com/lebanon/stat.htm

Lesotho (Kingdom of Lesotho)
Location: Southern Africa, enclave in South Africa
Capital: Maseru
Nationality: Mesotho (sing.), Basotho (pl.)
Language: English (official), Sesotho, Zulu, Xhosa
Religion: Christian (majority), indigenous beliefs
Currency: loti (L) = 100 lisente
National holiday: October 4, Independence Day
Embassy: 2511 Massachusetts Avenue, NW, Washington, DC 20008

Liberia (Republic of Liberia)
Location: Western Africa, along North Atlantic Ocean between Ivory Coast
  and Sierra Leone
Capital: Monrovia
Nationality: Liberian(s)
Language: English (official), ethnic languages
Religion: Indigenous beliefs, Christian, Muslim
Currency: Liberian dollar (L$) = 100 cents

National holiday: July 26, Independence Day
Embassy: 5201 16ᵗʰ Street, NW, Washington, DC 20011

Libya (Socialist People's Libyan Arab Jamahiriya)
Location: Northern Africa, along Mediterranean Sea between Egypt and
 Tunisia
Capital: Tripoli
Nationality: Libyan(s)
Language: Arabic, Italian, English
Religion: Sunni Muslim
Currency: Libyan dinar (LD) = 1,000 dirhams
National holiday: September 1, Revolution Day

Liechtenstein (Principality of Liechtenstein)
Location: Central Europe, between Austria and Switzerland
Capital: Vaduz
Nationality: Liechtensteiner(s)
Language: German (official), Alemannic dialect
Religion: Roman Catholic (majority), Protestant, other
Currency: Swiss franc, franken, or franco (SwF) = 100 centimes, rappen,
 or centesimi
National holiday: August 15, Assumption Day

Lithuania (Republic of Lithuania)
Location: Eastern Europe, along Baltic Sea between Latvia and Russia
Capital: Vilnius
Nationality: Lithuanian(s)
Language: Lithuanian (official), Polish, Russian
Religion: Roman Catholic (majority), Lutheran, Russian Orthodox,
 Protestant, evangelical Christian, Baptist, Muslim, Jewish
Currency: Lithuanian litas = 100 centas
National holiday: February 16, Statehood Day
Embassy: 2622 16ᵗʰ Street, NW, Washington, DC 20009
Website: http://www.std.lt

Luxembourg (Grand Duchy of Luxembourg)
Location: Western Europe, between France and Germany
Capital: Luxembourg
Nationality: Luxembourger(s)
Language: Luxembourgian German, French, English
Religion: Roman Catholic (majority), Protestant, Jewish

Currency: euro (EUR); subdivision: Luxembourg franc (LuxF) = 100 centimes
National holiday: June 23, National Day
Embassy: 2200 Massachusetts Avenue, NW, Washington, DC 20008

Macedonia (The Former Yugoslav Republic of Macedonia)
Location: Southeastern Europe, north of Greece
Capital: Skopje
Nationality: Macedonian(s)
Language: Macedonian (majority), Albanian, Turkish, Serbo-Croatian, other
Religion: Eastern Orthodox (majority), Muslim, other
Currency: Macedonian denar (MKD) = 100 deni
National holiday: September 8, Independence Day
Embassy: 3050 K Street, NW, Washington, DC 20007

Madagascar (Republic of Madagascar)
Location: Southern Africa, island in Indian Ocean east of Mozambique
Capital: Antananarivo
Nationality: Malagasy
Language: French and Malagasy (both official)
Religion: Indigenous beliefs (majority), Christian, Muslim
Currency: Malagasy franc (FMG) = 100 centimes
National holiday: June 26, Independence Day
Embassy: 2374 Massachusetts Avenue, NW, Washington, DC 20008
Website: http://www3.itu.ch/missions/Madagascar

Malawi (Republic of Malawi)
Location: Southern Africa, east of Zambia
Capital: Lilongwe
Nationality: Malawian(s)
Language: English and Chichewa (both official), other regional languages
Religion: Protestant (majority), Roman Catholic, Muslim, traditional indigenous beliefs
Currency: Malawian kwacha (MK) = 100 tambala
National holiday: July 6, Independence Day and Republic Day
Embassy: 2408 Massachusetts Avenue, NW, Washington, DC 20008

Malaysia
Location: Southeastern Asia, peninsula and northern part of island Borneo, along South China Sea, south of Vietnam and north of Indonesia

Capital: Kuala Lumpur
Nationality: Malaysian(s)
Language: Malay (official), English, Chinese dialects, Tamil, Mandarin, numerous ethnic languages
Religion: Muslim, Buddhist, Christian, Hindu, Confucianist, other
Currency: ringgit (M$) = 100 sen
National holiday: August 31, National Day
Embassy: 2401 Massachusetts Avenue, NW, Washington, DC 20008

Maldives (Republic of Maldives)
Location: Southern Asia, atolls in Arabian Sea and Indian Ocean south-southeast of India
Capital: Male (Maale)
Nationality: Maldivian(s)
Language: Maldivian Divehi, English
Religion: Sunni Muslim
Currency: rufiyaa (Rf) = 100 laari
National holiday: July 26, Independence Day
Website: http://www.maldives-info.com;
   http://www.undp.org/missions/maldives/

Mali (Republic of Mali)
Location: Western Africa, southwest of Algeria
Capital: Bamako
Nationality: Malian(s)
Language: French (official), Bambara, numerous other African languages
Religion: Muslim (majority), indigenous beliefs, Christian
Currency: Communaute Financiere Africaine franc (CFAF) = 100 centimes
National holiday: September 22, Anniversary of the Proclamation of the Republic
Embassy: 2130 R Street, NW, Washington, DC 20008

Malta (Republic of Malta)
Location: Southern Europe, islands in Mediterranean Sea south of Sicily
Capital: Valletta
Nationality: Maltese (sing. and pl.)
Language: Maltese and English (both official)
Religion: Roman Catholic
Currency: Maltese lira (LM) = 100 cents
National holiday: September 21, Independence Day

Embassy: 2017 Connecticut Avenue, NW, Washington, DC 20008
Website: http://www.magnet.mt/home/cos

Marshall Islands (Republic of the Marshall Islands)
Location: Oceania, atolls and reefs in North Pacific Ocean between Hawaii
  and Papua New Guinea
Capital: Majuro
Nationality: Marshallese (sing. and pl.)
Language: English (official), Marshallese dialects, Japanese
Religion: Protestant (majority), other Christian
Currency: U.S. dollar (US$) = 100 cents
National holiday: May 1, Proclamation of the Republic of the Marshall
  Islands
Embassy: 2433 Massachusetts Avenue, NW, Washington, DC 20008

Mauritania (Islamic Republic of Mauritania)
Location: Northern Africa, along North Atlantic Ocean between Senegal
  and Western Sahara
Capital: Nouakchott
Nationality: Mauritanian(s)
Language: Hasaniya Arabic and Wolof (both official), Pular, Soninke,
  French
Religion: Muslim
Currency: ouguiya (UM) = 5 khoums
National holiday: November 28, Independence Day
Embassy: 2129 Leroy Place, NW, Washington, DC 20008
Website: http://www.embassy.org/mauritania

Mauritius (Republic of Mauritius)
Location: Southern Africa, island in Indian Ocean east of Madagascar
Capital: Port Louis
Nationality: Mauritian(s)
Language: English (official), Creole, French, Hindi, Urdu, Hakka, Bojpoori
Religion: Hindu (majority), Christian, Muslim, other
Currency: Mauritian rupee (MauR) = 100 cents
National holiday: March 12, Independence Day
Embassy: 4301 Connecticut Avenue, NW, Washington, DC 20008

Mexico (United Mexican States)
Location: Middle America, along Caribbean Sea, Gulf of Mexico, and
  North Pacific Ocean between Guatemala and the United States

Capital: Mexico
Nationality: Mexican(s)
Language: Spanish, Mayan, Nahuatl, other regional indigenous languages
Religion: Roman Catholic (majority), Protestant, other
Currency: new Mexican peso (Mex$) = 100 centavos
National holiday: September 16, Independence Day
Embassy: 1911 Pennsylvania Avenue, NW, Washington, DC 20006
Website: http://www.inegi.gob.mx/homeing/homeinegi/homeing.html

Micronesia (Federated States of Micronesia)

Location: Oceania, island group in north Pacific Ocean between Hawaii and Indonesia
Capital: Palikir
Nationality: Micronesian(s)
Language: English (official), Trukese, Pohnpeian, Yapese, Kosrean
Religion: Roman Catholic, Protestant, other
Currency: U.S. dollar (US$) = 100 cents
National holiday: May 10, Proclamation of the Federated States of Micronesia
Embassy: 1725 N Street, NW, Washington, DC 20036

Moldova (Republic of Moldova)

Location: Eastern Europe, northeast of Romania
Capital: Chisinau
Nationality: Moldovan(s)
Language: Moldovan and Romanian (both official), Russian, Gagauz
Religion: Eastern Orthodox (majority), Jewish, Baptist
Currency: Moldovan leu (pl. lei) (MLD)
National holiday: August 27, Independence Day
Embassy: 2101 S Street, NW, Washington, DC 20008

Monaco (Principality of Monaco)

Location: Western Europe, along Mediterranean Sea on southern coast of France near Italy
Capital: Monaco
Nationality: Monacan(s) *or* Monegasque(s)
Language: French (official), English, Italian, Monegasque
Religion: Roman Catholic
Currency: French franc (F) = 100 centimes
National holiday: November 19, National Day

Mongolia
Location: Northern Asia, between China and Russia
Capital: Ulaanbaatar
Nationality: Mongolian(s)
Language: Khalkha Mongol, Turkic, Russian, Chinese
Religion: Tibetan Buddhist (majority), Muslim
Currency: tughrik (Tug) = 100 mongos
National holiday: July 11, National Day
Embassy: 2833 M Street, NW, Washington, DC 20007
Website: http://www.MongoliaOnline.mn/english

Morocco (Kingdom of Morocco)
Location: Northern Africa, along North Atlantic Ocean and
    Mediterranean Sea between Algeria and Sahara
Capital: Rabat
Nationality: Moroccan(s)
Language: Arabic (official), Berber dialects, French
Religion: Muslim (majority), Christian, Jewish
Currency: Moroccan dirham (DH) = 100 centimes
National holiday: March 3, National Day
Embassy: 1601 21st Street, NW, Washington, DC 20009

Mozambique (Republic of Mozambique)
Location: Southern Africa, along Mozambique Channel between South
    Africa and Tanzania
Capital: Maputo
Nationality: Mozambican(s)
Language: Portuguese (official), indigenous dialects
Religion: Indigenous beliefs, Christian, Muslim
Currency: metical (Mt) = 100 centavos
National holiday: June 25, Independence Day
Embassy: 1990 M Street, NW, Washington, DC 20036
Website: http://www.mbendi.co.za/cymzcy.htm

Myanmar (Union of Myanmar, formerly Burma)
Location: Southeastern Asia, along Andaman Sea and Bay of Bengal
    between Bangladesh and Thailand
Capital: Yangon (also known as Rangoon)
Nationality: Burmese (sing. and pl.)
Language: Burmese, minority languages and dialects
Religion: Buddhist (majority), Christian, Muslim, animist beliefs, other

Currency: kyak (K) = 100 pyas
National holiday: January 4, Independence Day
Embassy: 2300 S Street, NW, Washington, DC 20008
Website: http://www.myanmar.com/e-index.html

Namibia (Republic of Namibia)
Location: Southern Africa, along South Atlantic Ocean between Angola and South Africa
Capital: Windhoek
Nationality: Namibian(s)
Language: English (official), Afrikaans (majority), German, indigenous languages
Religion: Christian (majority), indigenous beliefs
Currency: Namibian dollar (N$) = 100 cents
National holiday: March 21, Independence Day
Embassy: 1605 New Hampshire Avenue, NW, Washington, DC 20009

Nauru (Republic of Nauru)
Location: Oceania, island in South Pacific Ocean south of Marshall Islands
Capital: No official capital; government in Yaren District
Nationality: Nauruan(s)
Language: Nauruan (official), English
Religion: Protestant (majority), Roman Catholic
Currency: Australian dollar ($A) = 100 cents
National holiday: January 31, Independence Day

Nepal (Kingdom of Nepal)
Location: Southern Asia, between China and India
Capital: Kathmandu
Nationality: Nepalese (sing. and pl.)
Language: Nepali (official), other
Religion: Hindu (majority), Buddhist, Muslim, other
Currency: Nepalese rupee (NR) = 100 paisa
National holiday: December 28, Birthday of His Majesty the King
Embassy: 2131 Leroy Place, NW, Washington, DC 20008
Website: http://www.info-nepal.com

Netherlands (Kingdom of the Netherlands)
Location: Western Europe, along North Sea between Belgium and Germany
Capital: Amsterdam (seat of government: The Hague)

Nationality: Dutchman(men), Dutchwoman(women)
Language: Dutch
Religion: Roman Catholic, Protestant, Muslim, other
Currency: euro (EUR); guilder (also called gulden or florin)
   (f.) = 100 cents
National holiday: April 30, Queen's Day
Embassy: 4200 Linnean Avenue, NW, Washington, DC 20008
Website: http://www.cbs.nl/enindex.htm

New Zealand
Location: Oceania, islands in South Pacific Ocean southeast of Australia
Capital: Wellington
Nationality: New Zealander(s)
Language: English (official), Maori
Religion: Anglican, Presbyterian, Roman Catholic, Methodist, Baptist, other
Currency: New Zealand dollar (NZ$) = 100 cents
National holiday: February 6, Waitangi Day
Embassy: 37 Observatory Circle, NW, Washington, DC 20008
Website: http://www.stats.govt.nz/statsweb.nsf

Nicaragua (Republic of Nicaragua)
Location: Middle America, along Caribbean Sea and North Pacific Ocean
   between Costa Rica and Honduras
Capital: Managua
Nationality: Nicaraguan(s)
Language: Spanish (official), English, Amerindian languages
Religion: Roman Catholic (majority), Protestant
Currency: gold cordoba (C$) = 100 centavos
National holiday: September 15, Independence Day
Embassy: 1627 New Hampshire Avenue, NW, Washington, DC 20009

Niger (Republic of Niger)
Location: Western Africa, southeast of Algeria
Capital: Niamey
Nationality: Nigerien(s)
Language: French (official), Hausa, Djerma
Religion: Muslim (majority), Christian, indigenous beliefs
Currency: Communaute Financiere Africaine franc (CFAF) = 100
   centimes
National holiday: December 18, Republic Day
Embassy: 2204 R Street, NW, Washington, DC 20008

Nigeria (Federal Republic of Nigeria)
Location: Western Africa, along Gulf of Guinea between Benin and
  Cameroon
Capital: Abuja
Nationality: Nigerian(s)
Language: English (official), Hausa, Yoruba, Ibo, Fulani
Religion: Muslim, Christian, indigenous beliefs
Currency: naira (N) = 100 kobo
National holiday: October 1, Independence Day
Embassy: 1333 16th Street, NW, Washington, DC 20036

Norway (Kingdom of Norway)
Location: Northern Europe, along North Sea and North Atlantic Ocean
  west of Sweden
Capital: Oslo
Nationality: Norwegian(s)
Language: Norwegian (official), Lappish, Finnish
Religion: Evangelical Lutheran (majority), other Protestant, Roman
  Catholic
Currency: Norwegian krone (NKr) = 100 oere
National holiday: May 17, Constitution Day
Embassy: 2720 34th Street, NW, Washington, DC 20008
Website: http://www.ssb.no/www-open/english

Oman (Sultanate of Oman)
Location: Middle East, along Arabian Sea, Gulf of Oman, and Persian Gulf
  between Yemen and United Arab Emirates
Capital: Muscat
Nationality: Omani(s)
Language: Arabic (official), English, Baluchi, Urdu, Indian dialects
Religion: Ibadhi Muslim (majority), Sunni Muslim, Shi'a Muslim,
  Hindu
Currency: Omani rial (RO) = 1,000 baiza
National holiday: November 18, National Day
Embassy: 2535 Belmont Road, NW, Washington, DC 20008

Pakistan (Islamic Republic of Pakistan)
Location: Southern Asia, along Arabian Sea between Afghanistan, China,
  and India
Capital: Islamabad
Nationality: Pakistani(s)

Language: Urdu and English (both official), Punjabi, Sindhi, Saraiki,
  Pashtu, Balochi, Hindko, Brahui, Burushaski, other
Religion: Sunni Muslim (majority), Shi'a Muslim, Christian, Hindu, other
Currency: Pakistani rupee (PRe) = 100 paisa
National holiday: March 23, Pakistan Day
Embassy: 2315 Massachusetts Avenue, NW, Washington, DC 20008
Website: http://www.pak.gov.pk

Palau (Republic of Palau)

Location: Oceania, islands in North Pacific Ocean southeast of Philippines
Capital: Koror
Nationality: Palauan(s)
Language: English and Sonsovolese (official in Sonsoral), Angaur and
  Japanese (official in Anguar), Tobi (official in Tobi), Palauan (official
  in other states)
Religion: Christian, Modekngei
Currency: U.S. dollar (US$) = 100 cents
National holiday: July 9, Constitution Day
Embassy: 1150 18th Street, NW, Washington, DC 20036
Website: http://www.visit-palau.com

Panama (Republic of Panama)

Location: Middle America along Caribbean Sea and North Pacific Ocean
  between Columbia and Costa Rica
Capital: Panama
Nationality: Panamanian(s)
Language: Spanish (official), English
Religion: Roman Catholic (majority), Protestant
Currency: balboa (B) = 100 centesimos
National holiday: November 3, Independence Day
Embassy: 2862 McGill Terrace, NW, Washington, DC 20008

Papua New Guinea (Independent State of Papua New Guinea)

Location: Southeastern Asia, islands between Coral Sea and South Pacific
  Ocean east of Indonesia
Capital: Port Moresby
Nationality: Papua New Guinean(s)
Language: pidgin English, English, Motu, over 700 other indigenous
  languages
Religion: Roman Catholic, Protestant, indigenous beliefs
Currency: kina (K) = 100 toea

National holiday: September 16, Independence Day
Embassy: 1615 New Hampshire Avenue, NW, Washington, DC 20009
Website: http://www.pngembassy.org

Paraguay (Republic of Paraguay)

Location: Central South America, northeast of Argentina
Capital: Asuncion
Nationality: Paraguayan(s)
Language: Spanish (official), Guarani
Religion: Roman Catholic (majority), Mennonite, other Protestant
Currency: guarani (G) = 100 centimos
National holiday: May 14-15, Independence Days
Embassy: 2400 Massachusetts Avenue, NW, Washington, DC 20008

Peru (Republic of Peru)

Location: Western South America, along South Pacific Ocean between
    Chile and Equador
Capital: Lima
Nationality: Peruvian(s)
Language: Spanish and Quechua (both official), Aymara
Religion: Roman Catholic
Currency: nuevo sol (S/.) = 100 centimos
National holiday: July 28, Independence Day
Embassy: 1700 Massachusetts Avenue, NW, Washington, DC 20036

Philippines (Republic of the Philippines)

Location: Southeastern Asia, archipelago between Philippine Sea and
    South China Sea east of Vietnam
Capital: Manila
Nationality: Filipino(s)
Language: Pilipino and English (both official)
Religion: Roman Catholic (majority), Protestant, Muslim, Buddhist, other
Currency: Philippine peso (P) = 100 centavos
National holiday: June 12, Independence Day
Embassy: 1600 Massachusetts Avenue, NW, Washington, DC 20036
Website: http://www.census.gov.ph

Poland (Republic of Poland)

Location: Central Europe, east of Germany
Capital: Warsaw
Nationality: Pole(s)

Language: Polish
Religion: Roman Catholic (majority), Eastern Orthodox, Protestant, other
Currency: zloty (Zl) = 100 groszy
National holiday: May 3, Constitution Day; November 11, Independence Day
Embassy: 2640 16th Street, NW, Washington, DC 20009
Website: http://www.polishworld.com

Portugal (Portuguese Republic)

Location: Southwestern Europe, along North Atlantic Ocean west of Spain
Capital: Lisbon
Nationality: Portuguese (sing. and pl.)
Language: Portuguese
Religion: Roman Catholic (majority), Protestant, other
Currency: euro (EUR); subdivision: Portuguese escudo (Esc) = 100 centavos
National holiday: June 10, Day of Portugal
Embassy: 2125 Kalorama Road, NW, Washington, DC 20008
Website: http://infoline.ine.pt/si/english/port.html

Qatar (State of Qatar)

Location: Middle East, peninsula along Persian Gulf north of Saudi Arabia
Capital: Doha
Nationality: Qatari(s)
Language: Arabic (official), English
Religion: Muslim
Currency: Qatari riyal (QR) = 100 dirhams
National holiday: September 3, Independence Day
Embassy: 4200 Wisconsin Avenue, NW, Washington, DC 20016
Website: http://www.mofa.gov.qa

Romania

Location: Southeastern Europe, along Black Sea between Bulgaria and Ukraine
Capital: Bucharest
Nationality: Romanian(s)
Language: Romanian, Hungarian, German
Religion: Romanian Orthodox (majority), Roman Catholic, Protestant
Currency: leu (L) = 100 bani
National holiday: December 1, National Day of Romania

Embassy: 1607 23ʳᵈ Street, NW, Washington, DC 20008
Website: http://www.embassy.org/romania

Russia (Russian Federation)

Location: Northern Asia, along Arctic Ocean between Europe and North
  Pacific Ocean
Capital: Moscow
Nationality: Russian(s)
Language: Russian, other
Religion: Russian Orthodox, Muslim, other
Currency: ruble (R) = 100 kopeks
National holiday: June 12, Independence Day
Embassy: 2650 Wisconsin Avenue, NW, Washington, DC 20007
Website: http://www.undp.org/missions/russianfed

Rwanda (Rwandese Republic)

Location: Central Africa, east of Democratic Republic of the Congo
Capital: Kigali
Nationality: Rwandan(s)
Language: Kinyarwanda, French, and English (all official), Kiswahili (Swahili)
Religion: Roman Catholic (majority), Protestant, Muslim, indigenous
  beliefs, other
Currency: Rwandan franc (RF) = 100 centimes
National holiday: July 1, Independence Day
Embassy: (temporary) 1814 New Hampshire Avenue, NW, Washington,
  DC 20007

Saint Kitts and Nevis (Federation of Saint Kitts and Nevis)

Location: Caribbean, islands in Caribbean Sea between Puerto Rico and
  Trinidad and Tobago
Capital: Basseterre
Nationality: Kittitian(s), Nevisian(s)
Language: English
Religion: Anglican, other Protestant sects, Roman Catholic
Currency: EC dollar (EC$) = 100 cents
National holiday: September 19, Independence Day
Embassy: 3216 New Mexico Avenue, NW, Washington, DC 20016

Saint Lucia

Location: Caribbean, island along Caribbean Sea and North Atlantic
  Ocean north of Trinidad and Tobago

Capital: Castries
Nationality: Saint Lucian(s)
Language: English (official), French patois
Religion: Roman Catholic (majority), Protestant, Anglican
Currency: EC dollar (EC$) = 100 cents
National holiday: February 22, Independence Day
Embassy: 3216 New Mexico Avenue, NW, Washington, DC 20016

Saint Vincent and the Grenadines
Location: Caribbean, islands in Caribbean Sea north of Trinidad and
    Tobago
Capital: Kingstown
Nationality: Saint Vincentian(s) or Vincentian(s)
Language: English, French patois
Religion: Anglican, Methodist, Roman Catholic, Seventh-Day Adventist,
    Hindu
Currency: EC dollar (EC$)= 100 cents
National holiday: October 27, Independence Day
Embassy: 3216 New Mexico Avenue, NW, Washington, DC 20016
Website: http://www.heraldsvg.com

Samoa (Independent State of Samoa)
Location: Oceania, islands in South Pacific Ocean between Hawaii and
    New Zealand
Capital: Apia
Nationality: Samoan(s)
Language: Samoan (Polynesian), English
Religion: Christian
Currency: tala (WS$) = 100 sene
National holiday: June 1, National Day
Embassy: 820 Second Avenue, New York, NY 10017

San Marino (Republic of San Marino)
Location: Southern Europe, enclave in central Italy
Capital: San Marino
Nationality: Sanmarinese (sing. and pl.)
Language: Italian
Religion: Roman Catholic
Currency: Italian lira (Lit) = 100 ccntcsimi
National holiday: September 3, Anniversary of the Foundation of the
    Republic

Sao Tome and Principe (Democratic Republic of Sao Tome and Principe)

Location: Western Africa, island in Gulf of Guinea on Equator west of Gabon

Capital: Sao Tome

Nationality: Sao Tomean(s)

Language: Portuguese (official)

Religion: Roman Catholic, Evangelical Protestant, Seventh-Day Adventist

Currency: dobra (Db) = 100 centimos

National holiday: July 12, Independence Day

Saudi Arabia (Kingdom of Saudi Arabia)

Location: Middle East, along Persian Gulf and Red Sea south of Iraq and Iran

Capital: Riyadh

Nationality: Saudi(s)

Language: Arabic

Religion: Muslim

Currency: Saudi riyal (SR) = 100 halalah

National holiday: September 23, Unification of the Kingdom

Embassy: 601 New Hampshire Avenue, NW, Washington, DC 20037

Senegal (Republic of Senegal)

Location: Western Africa, along North Atlantic Ocean between Guinea-Bissau and Mauritania

Capital: Dakar

Nationality: Senegalese (sing. and pl.)

Language: French (official), Wolof, Pulaar, Jola, Mandinka

Religion: Muslim (majority), indigenous beliefs, Christian

Currency: Communaute Financiere Africaine franc (CFAF) = 100 centimes

National holiday: April 4, Independence Day

Embassy: 2112 Wyoming Avenue, NW, Washington, DC 20008

Serbia and Montenegro. See Yugoslavia.

Seychelles (Republic of Seychelles)

Location: Eastern Africa, islands in Indian Ocean northeast of Madagascar

Capital: Victoria

Nationality: Seychellois (sing. and pl.)

Language: French and English (both official), Creole

Religion: Roman Catholic (majority), Anglican, other
Currency: Seychelles rupee (SRe) = 100 cents
National holiday: June 18, National Day
Embassy: 820 Second Avenue, New York, NY 10017

Sierra Leone (Republic of Sierra Leone)
Location: Western Africa, along North Atlantic Ocean between Guinea and
 Liberia
Capital: Freetown
Nationality: Sierra Leonean(s)
Language: English (official), Mende, Temne, Krio
Religion: Muslim (majority), indigenous beliefs, Christian
Currency: leone (Le) = 100 cents
National holiday: April 27, Republic Day
Embassy: 1701 19th Street, NW, Washington, DC 20009
Website: http://www.Sierra-Leone.org

Singapore (Republic of Singapore)
Location: Southeastern Asia, islands between Malaysia and Indonesia
Capital: Singapore
Nationality: Singaporean(s)
Language: Chinese, Malay, Tamil, and English (all official)
Religion: Buddhist (Chinese), Muslim (Malays), Christian, Hindu, Sikh,
 Taoist, Confucianist
Currency: Singapore dollar (S$) = 100 cents
National holiday: August 9, National Day
Embassy: 3501 International Place, NW, Washington, DC 20008
Website: http://www.singstat.gov.sg

Slovakia (Slovak Republic)
Location: Central Europe, south of Poland
Capital: Bratislava
Nationality: Slovak(s)
Language: Slovak (official), Hungarian
Religion: Roman Catholic (majority), atheist, Protestant, Orthodox,
 other
Currency: koruna (Sk) = 100 halierov
National holiday: September 1, Slovak Constitution Day; August 29,
 Anniversary of Slovak National Uprising
Embassy: 2201 Wisconsin Avenue, NW, Washington, DC 20007
Website: http://www.slovakemb.com/index.html

Slovenia (Republic of Slovenia)
Location: Southeastern Europe, along Adriatic Sea between Austria and
    Croatia
Capital: Ljubljana
Nationality: Slovene(s)
Language: Slovenian (majority), Serbo-Croatian, other
Religion: Roman Catholic (majority), Lutheran, Muslim,
    other
Currency: tolar (SIT) = 100 stotins
National holiday: June 25, National Statehood Day
Embassy: 1525 New Hampshire Avenue, NW, Washington, DC 20036

Solomon Islands
Location: Oceania, group of islands in South Pacific Ocean east of Papua
    New Guinea
Capital: Honiara
Nationality: Solomon Islander(s)
Language: Melanesian pidgin, English, numerous indigenous
    languages
Religion: Anglican, Roman Catholic, Baptist, United Methodist, United
    Presbyterian, Seventh-Day Adventist, other Protestant, indigenous
    beliefs
Currency: Solomon Islands dollar (SI$) = 100 cents
National holiday: July 7, Independence Day
Embassy: 820 Second Avenue, New York, NY 10017

Somalia
Location: Eastern Africa, along Gulf of Aden and Indian Ocean east of
    Ethiopia and Kenya
Capital: Mogadishu
Nationality: Somali(s)
Language: Somali (official), Arabic, Italian, English
Religion: Sunni Muslim
Currency: Somali shilling (So. Sh.) = 100 cents
Website: http://gala.info.usaid.gov/horn/somalia/somalia

South Africa (Republic of South Africa)
Location: Southern Africa, southernmost tip of Africa along South
    Atlantic and Indian oceans
Capital: Cape Town (legislative), Pretoria (administrative), Bloemfontein
    (judicial)
Nationality: South African(s)

Language: Afrikanns, English, Ndebele, Pedi, Sotho, Swazi, Tsonga,
  Tswana, Venda, Xhosa, and Zulu (all official)
Religion: Christian (majority), Muslim, Hindu, indigenous beliefs
Currency: rand (R) = 100 cents
National holiday: April 27, Freedom Day
Embassy: 3051 Massachusetts Avenue, NW, Washington, DC 20008
Website: http://www.statssa.gov.za

Spain (Kingdom of Spain)
Location: Southwestern Europe, along Bay of Biscay, Mediterranean Sea,
  and North Atlantic Ocean southwest of France and east of Portugal
Capital: Madrid
Nationality: Spaniard(s)
Language: Castilian Spanish (majority), Catalan, Galician, Basque
Religion: Roman Catholic (majority), other
Currency: euro (EUR); subdivision: peseta (Pta) = 100 centimos
National holiday: October 12, National Day
Embassy: 2375 Pennsylvania Avenue, NW, Washington, DC 20037
Website: http://www.DocuWeb.ca/SiSpain

Sri Lanka (Democratic Socialist Republic of Sri Lanka)
Location: Southern Asia, island in Indian Ocean south of India
Capital: Colombo
Nationality: Sri Lankan(s)
Language: Sinhala (official and national language), Tamil (national
  language), English
Religion: Buddhist (majority), Hindu, Christian, Muslim
Currency: Sri Lankan rupee (SLRe) = 100 cents
National holiday: February 4, Independence and National Day
Embassy: 2148 Wyoming Avenue, NW, Washington, DC 20008

Sudan (Republic of the Sudan)
Location: Northern Africa, along Red Sea between Egypt and Eritrea
Capital: Khartoum
Nationality: Sudanese (sing. and pl.)
Language: Arabic (official), Nubian; Ta Bedawie; Nilotic, Nilo-Hamitic,
  and Sudanic dialects; English
Religion: Sunni Muslim (majority), indigenous beliefs, Christian
Currency: Sudanese dinar (SD) = 100 piastres
National holiday: January 1, Independence Day
Embassy: 2210 Massachusetts Avenue, NW, Washington, DC 20008
Website: http://www.sudan.net

Suriname (Republic of Suriname)
Location: Northern South America, along North Atlantic Ocean between French Guiana and Guyana
Capital: Paramaribo
Nationality: Surinamer(s)
Language: Dutch (official), English, Sranang Tongo, Surinamese (Taki-Taki), Hindustani, Javanese
Religion: Hindu, Protestant, Roman Catholic, Muslim, indigenous beliefs
Currency: Surinamese guilder, gulden, or florin (Sf.) = 100 cents
National holiday: November 25, Independence Day
Embassy: 4301 Connecticut Avenue, NW, Washington, DC 20008

Swaziland (Kingdom of Swaziland)
Location: Southern Africa, between Mozambique and South Africa
Capital: Mbabane (administrative) and Lobamba (legislative)
Nationality: Swazi(s)
Language: English and siSwati (both official)
Religion: Christian (majority), indigenous beliefs
Currency: lilangeni (E) = 100 cents
National holiday: September 6, Somhlolo (Independence) Day
Embassy: 3400 International Drive, NW, Washington, DC 20008
Website: http://www.realnet.co.sz

Sweden (Kingdom of Sweden)
Location: Northern Europe, along Baltic Sea and Gulf of Bothnia between Finland and Norway
Capital: Stockholm
Nationality: Swede(s)
Language: Swedish (majority), Lapp, Finnish
Religion: Evangelical Lutheran (majority), Roman Catholic, Pentecostal, other
Currency: Swedish krona (SKr) = 100 oere
National holiday: June 6, Day of the Swedish Flag
Embassy: 1501 M Street, NW, Washington, DC 20005
Website: http://www.scb.se/scbeng/keyeng.htm

Switzerland (Swiss Confederation)
Location: Central Europe, east of France and north of Italy
Capital: Bern
Nationality: Swiss (sing. and pl.)
Language: German, French, Italian, Romansch, other
Religion: Roman Catholic, Protestant, other

Currency: Swiss franc, franken, or franco (SFR) = 100 centimes, rappen, or centesimi
National holiday: August 1, Anniversary of the Founding of the Swiss Confederation
Embassy: 2900 Cathedral Avenue, NW, Washington, DC 20008
Website: http://www.swissembassy.org.uk; http://www.admin.ch/bfs/eindex.htm

Syria (Syrian Arab Republic)
Location: Middle East, along Mediterranean Sea between Lebanon and Turkey
Capital: Damascus
Nationality: Syrian(s)
Language: Arabic (official), Kurdish, Armenian, Aramaic, Circassian, French, English
Religion: Sunni Muslim (majority), other Muslim sects, Christian, Jewish
Currency: Syrian pound (£S) = 100 piastres
National holiday: April 17, National Day
Embassy: 2215 Wyoming Avenue, NW, Washington, DC 20008

Taiwan
Location: Eastern Asia, islands along East China, South China, and Philippine seas and Taiwan Strait off southeastern coast of China north of Philippines
Capital: Taipei
Nationality: Chinese (sing. and pl.)
Language: Mandarin Chinese (official), Taiwanese (Min), Hakka dialects
Religion: Buddhist, Confucian, and Taoist mixture (majority); Christian; other
Currency: New Taiwan dollar (NT$) = 100 cents
National holiday: October 10, National Day (Anniversary of the Chinese Revolution)
Website: http:www.gio.gov.tw

Tajikistan (Republic of Tajikistan)
Location: Central Asia, west of China
Capital: Dushanbe
Nationality: Tajikistani(s)
Language: Tajik (official), Russian
Religion: Sunni Muslim (majority), Shi'a Muslim
Currency: Tajikistani ruble (TJR) = 100 tanga

National holiday: September 9, National Day
Website: http://www.soros.org/tajkstan.html

Tanzania (United Republic of Tanzania)

Location: Eastern Africa, along Indian Ocean between Kenya and
Mozambique
Capital: Dodma (old capital: Dar es Salaam)
Nationality: Tanzanian(s)
Language: Swahili (or Kiswahili) and English (both official), Arabic,
numerous local languages
Religion: Christian, Muslim, indigenous beliefs
Currency: Tanzanian shilling (TSh) = 100 cents
National holiday: April 26, Union Day
Embassy: 2139 R Street, NW, Washington, DC 20008

Thailand (Kingdom of Thailand)

Location: Southeastern Asia, along Andaman Sea and Gulf of Thailand
southeast of Myanmar (Burma)
Capital: Bangkok
Nationality: Thai (sing. and pl.)
Language: Thai, English, ethnic and regional dialects
Religion: Buddhism (majority), Muslim, Christian, Hindu, other
Currency: baht (B) = 100 satang
National holiday: December 5, Birthday of His Majesty the King
Embassy: 1024 Wisconsin Avenue, NW, Washington, DC 20007
Website: http://emailhost.ait.ac.th/Asia/info.html

Togo (Togolese Republic)

Location: Western Africa, along Bight of Benin between Benin and Ghana
Capital: Lome
Nationality: Togolese (sing. and pl.)
Language: French (official), Ewe, Mina, Kabye, Dagomba
Religion: Indigenous beliefs (majority), Christian, Muslim
Currency: Communaute Financiere Africaine franc (CFAF) = 100 centimes
National holiday: April 27, Independence Day
Embassy: 2208 Massachusetts Avenue, NW, Washington, DC 20008

Tonga (Kingdom of Tonga)

Location: Oceania archipelago in South Pacific Ocean between Hawaii and
New Zealand
Capital: Nuku'alofa

Nationality: Tongan(s)
Language: Tongan, English
Religion: Christian
Currency: pa'anga (T$) = 100 seniti
National holiday: June 4, Emancipation Day

Trinidad and Tobago (Republic of Trinidad and Tobago)
Location: Caribbean, islands along Caribbean Sea and North Atlantic
 Ocean northeast of Venezuela
Capital: Port-of-Spain
Nationality: Trinidadian(s), Tobagonian(s)
Language: English (official), Hindi, French, Spanish
Religion: Roman Catholic, Hindu, Anglican, other Protestant, Muslim
Currency: Trinidad and Tobago dollar (TT$) = 100 cents
National holiday: August 31, Independence Day
Embassy: 1708 Massachusetts Avenue, NW, Washington, DC 20036

Tunisia (Republic of Tunisia)
Location: Northern Africa, along Mediterranean Sea between Algeria and
 Libya
Capital: Tunis
Nationality: Tunisian(s)
Language: Arabic (official), French
Religion: Muslim (majority), Christian, Jewish
Currency: Tunisian dinar (TD) = 1,000 millimes
National holiday: March 20, National Day
Embassy: 1515 Massachusetts Avenue, NW, Washington, DC 20005
Website: http://www.tunisiaonline.com

Turkey (Republic of Turkey)
Location: Southwestern Asia, along Black, Aegean, and Mediterranean seas
 between Greece and Syria
Capital: Ankara
Nationality: Turk(s)
Language: Turkish (official), Kurdish, Arabic
Religion: Sunni Muslim (majority), other Muslim, Christian, Jewish
Currency: Turkish lira (TL)
National holiday: October 29, Anniversary of the Declaration of the
 Republic
Embassy: 1714 Massachusetts Avenue, NW, Washington, DC 20036
Website: http://www.turkey.org

Turkmenistan
Location: Central Asia, along Caspian Sea between Iran and Kazakhstan
Capital: Ashgabat
Nationality: Turkmen(s)
Language: Turkmen (majority), Russian, Uzbek, other
Religion: Muslim (majority), Eastern Orthodox
Currency: Tukmen manat (TMM) = 100 tenesi
National holiday: October 27, Independence Day
Embassy: 2207 Massachusetts Avenue, NW, Washington, DC 20008
Website: http://www.turkmenistan.com

Tuvalu
Location: Oceania, island atolls in South Pacific Ocean between Hawaii and Australia
Capital: Funafuti
Nationality: Tuvaluan(s)
Language: Tuvaluan, English
Religion: Church of Tuvalu (majority), Seventh-Day Adventist, Baha'i, other
Currency: Australian dollar ($A) or Tuvaluan dollar ($T) = 100 cents
National holiday: October 1, Independence Day
Website: http://www.emulateme.com/tuvalu.htm

Uganda (Republic of Uganda)
Location: Eastern Africa, west of Kenya
Capital: Kampala
Nationality: Ugandan(s)
Language: English (official), Ganda (Luganda), other Niger-Congo languages, Nilo-Saharan languages, Swahili, Arabic
Religion: Roman Catholic, Protestant, Muslim, indigenous beliefs
Currency: Uganda shilling (USh) = 100 cents
National holiday: October 9, Independence Day
Embassy: 5911 16th Street, NW, Washington, DC 20011
Website: http://www.nic.ug

Ukraine
Location: Eastern Europe, along Black Sea between Poland and Russia
Capital: Kiev (Kyyiv)
Nationality: Ukrainian(s)
Language: Ukrainian, Russian, Romanian, Polish, Hungarian

Religion: Ukrainian Orthodox, Ukrainian Autocephalous Orthodox,
   Ukrainian Catholic (Uniate), Protestant, Jewish
Currency: hryvnia = 100 kopiykash
National holiday: August 24, Independence Day
Embassy: 3350 M Street, NW, Washington, DC 20007
Website: http://www.rada.kiev.ua

United Arab Emirates
Location: Middle East, along Gulf of Oman and Persian Gulf between
   Oman and Saudi Arabia
Capital: Abu Dhabi
Nationality: Emirian(s)
Language: Arabic (official), Persian, English, Hindi, Urdu
Religion: Muslim, Christian, Hindu, other
Currency: Emirian dirham (Dh) = 100 fils
National holiday: December 2, National Day
Embassy: 1255 22nd Street, NW, Washington, DC 20037
Website: http://www.uae.org.ae; http://www.emirates.org

United Kingdom (United Kingdom of Great Britain and Northern Ireland)
Location: Western Europe, islands along North Atlantic Ocean and North
   Sea northwest of France and including northern part of island Ireland
Capital: London
Nationality: Briton(s), British (collective pl.)
Language: English, Welsh, Gaelic (Scottish form)
Religion: Anglican (majority), Roman Catholic, Muslim, Presbyterian,
   Methodist, Sikh, Hindu, Jewish
Currency: Pound sterling (£) = 100 pence
National holiday: Second Saturday in June, Celebration of the Birthday of
   the Queen
Embassy: 3100 Massachusetts Avenue, NW, Washington, DC 20008
Website: http://www.ons.gov.uk/ons-f.htm; http://www.genuki.org.uk

Uruguay (Oriental Republic of Uruguay)
Location: Southern South America, along South Atlantic Ocean between
   Argentina and Brazil
Capital: Montevideo
Nationality: Uruguayan(s)
Language: Spanish, Portunol, or Brazilero
Religion: Roman Catholic (majority), Protestant, Jewish, other
Currency: Uruguayan peso ($Ur) = 100 centesimos

National holiday: August 25, Independence Day
Embassy: 2715 M Street, NW, Washington, DC 20007
Website: http://www.embassy.org/uruguay

Uzbekistan (Republic of Uzbekistan)
Location: Central Asia, north of Afghanistan
Capital: Tashkent (Toshkent)
Nationality: Uzbekistani(s)
Language: Uzbek (majority), Russian, Tajik, other
Religion: Sunni Muslim (majority), other Muslim, Eastern Orthodox, other
Currency: sum = 100 tyyn
National holiday: September 1, Independence Day
Embassy: 1746 Massachusetts Avenue, NW, Washington, DC 20036
Website: http://www.gov.uz

Vanuatu (Republic of Vanuatu)
Location: Oceania, group of islands in South Pacific Ocean between Hawaii and Australia
Capital: Port-Vila
Nationality: Ni-Vanuatu (sing. and pl.)
Language: English and French (both official), pidgin
Religion: Presbyterian, Anglican, Roman Catholic, indigenous beliefs, Seventh-Day Adventists, Church of Christ, other
Currency: vatu (VT) = 100 centimes
National holiday: July 30, Independence Day

Vatican City (Holy See) (Vatican City State)
Location: Enclave within the city of Rome, Italy
Language: Italian, Latin
Religion: Roman Catholic
Currency: Vatican/Italian lira (L)
Website: http://www.vatican.va

Venezuela (Republic of Venezuela)
Location: Northern South America, along Caribbean Sea and North Atlantic Ocean between Columbia and Guyana
Capital: Caracas
Nationality: Venezuelan(s)
Language: Spanish (official), indigenous dialects
Religion: Roman Catholic (majority), Protestant

Currency: bolivar (Bs) = 100 centimos
National holiday: July 5, Independence Day
Embassy: 1099 30th Street, NW, Washington, DC 20007
Website: http://www.embassy.org/embassies/ve.html

Vietnam (Socialist Republic of Vietnam)
Location: Southeastern Asia, along Gulfs of Thailand and Tonkin and South China Sea between China and Laos and Cambodia
Capital: Hanoi
Nationality: Vietnamese (sing. and pl.)
Language: Vietnamese (official), Chinese, English, French, Khmer, ethnic languages
Religion: Buddhist, Taoist, Roman Catholic, indigenous beliefs, Muslim, Protestant, Cao Dai, Hoa Hao
Currency: new dong (D) = 100 xu
National holiday: September 2, Independence Day
Embassy: 1233 20th Street, NW, Washington, DC 20036
Website: http://www.batin.com.vn

Western Sahara
Location: Northern Africa, along North Atlantic Ocean between Mauritania and Morocco
Nationality: Sahrawi(s), Sahraoui(s)
Language: Hassaniya Arabic, Moroccan Arabic
Religion: Muslim
Currency: Moroccan dirham (DH) = 100 centimes

Western Samoa. See **Samoa.**

Yemen (Republic of Yemen)
Location: Middle East, along Arabian and Red seas and Gulf of Aden between Oman and Saudi Arabia
Capital: Sanaa
Nationality: Yemeni(s)
Language: Arabic
Religion: Muslim (majority), Jewish, Christian, Hindu
Currency: Yemen rial (YER) = 100 fils
National holiday: May 22, Proclamation of the Republic
Embassy: 2600 Virginia Avenue, NW, Washington, DC 20037
Website: http://www.nusacc.org/yemen

Yugoslavia (Federal Republic of Yugoslavia [not recognized by U.S.])

Location: Southeastern Europe, along Adriatic Sea between Albania and Bosnia and Herzegovina

Capital: Belgrade (Serbia), Podgorica (Montenegro)

Nationality: Serb(s) and Montenegrin(s)

Language: Serbo-Croatian (majority), Albanian

Religion: Orthodox (majority), Muslim, Roman Catholic, Protestant, other

Currency: Yugoslav new dinar (YD) = 100 paras

National holiday: June 28, St. Vitus Day

Embassy: 2410 California Street, NW, Washington, DC 20008

Website: http://www.gov.yu

Zaire. See Congo (Democratic Republic of the Congo).

Zambia (Republic of Zambia)

Location: Southern Africa, east of Angola

Capital: Lusaka

Nationality: Zambian(s)

Language: English (official); about 70 indigenous languages

Religion: Christian (majority), Muslim, Hindu, indigenous beliefs

Currency: Zambian kwacha (ZK) = 100 ngwee

National holiday: October 24, Independence Day

Embassy: 2419 Massachusetts Avenue, NW, Washington, DC 20008

Website: http://www.zamnet.zm

Zimbabwe (Republic of Zimbabwe)

Location: Southern Africa, northeast of Botswana

Capital: Harare

Nationality: Zimbabwean(s)

Language: English (official), Shona, Sindebele (Ndebele)

Religion: Syncretic, Christian, indigenous beliefs, Muslim

Currency: Zimbabwean dollar (Z$) = 100 cents

National holiday: April 18, Indpendence Day

Embassy: 1608 New Hampshire Avenue, NW, Washington, DC 20009

Accounting

The evolution of the practice of accounting as a means of enabling businesses to keep track of past events and provide them with useful information for making future decisions has been essential to business expansion. The most important advance has been the introduction of computer technology (see Chapter 1, "The Online Office," The Computer) to improve and vastly accelerate the handling of accounting and data-processing activities. For example, books of account can be maintained more efficiently with various accounting software, and tax returns can be prepared with far greater efficiency with tax-preparation software. Also, complex calculations can be made more rapidly and easily using spreadsheet software.

Every business must handle certain financial and tax matters and subsequently keep records of these transactions as well as report them to various persons and groups outside the organization, including government agencies. Office professionals often perform many of the daily tasks related to these types of financial transactions.

BASIC ACCOUNTING PRINCIPLES

Accounting is called the "language of business." The first step in using any language is to learn its rules and the meanings of its terms. Present-day accounting practice has produced a number of generally accepted principles that standardize both terminology and methods of recording the activities of a business. This standardization allows a company's accounting reports to be meaningful to managers, bankers, stockholders, creditors, government agencies, and others interested in its financial reports. These generally accepted principles provide the language of business that is understood by a diverse group of individuals.

Dual-Aspect Concept

Assets and liabilities. Business accounting deals with the relationship between two aspects of business ownership: assets and liabilities. The items of value that a company owns are called *assets*. A company's assets are entered into the records at their original cost to the company, indicating that the value of the assets is equal to their cost. Over time, certain items owned by a company increase or decrease in value. However, once an asset is recorded at its original, or historical, cost, it's almost never adjusted to a current market value. Such an adjustment could require continual revaluation to reflect the almost daily changes in the real or current market values of a company's numerous assets.

Assets owned by a company may include the following:

- Cash (in the bank as well as petty cash)
- Accounts receivable
- Marketable securities (stocks, bonds, certificates of deposit)
- Prepaid items (insurance, rent deposits)
- Property, plant, and equipment (land, buildings, equipment, furniture, fixtures)
- Inventory (raw materials, work in process, finished goods)

The money or funds used to acquire assets are provided either by the owners or the creditors of a company. *Creditors* are individuals or companies that lend money or extend credit to a business for a certain period. When this occurs, they acquire a claim of that amount against the business. Because a business will use its assets to pay off these claims, the claims are therefore claims against assets. If a business refuses to pay a claim, the person to whom it is due may sue the business in a court of equity. Thus all claims against assets are called *equities*. A court of equity will usually hold the business liable for the amount of the claim.

Basic accounting equation. An understanding of claims helps explain the accounting term for the equity of a creditor: *liability*. Any asset not claimed by a creditor will be claimed by the owners of the business. These claims are called *owners' equity*. The total of all claims may not exceed what there is to be claimed. This leads to a dual-aspect concept, also known as the *basic accounting equation:*

Assets = Liabilities + Owners' Equity

Monetary Concepts

An accounting system records only those events that can be expressed in terms of dollars, such as the purchase of land or equipment or the sale of inventory for cash or on account. The morale and health of company personnel can't be expressed in dollar terms, however, so the accounting system doesn't consider such factors. Thus a company's accounting records don't reveal all the facts, or even all the important facts, about a business.

The Business Entity

Accounting records in a business are maintained for the business entity, not for the persons who own, operate, or are otherwise associated with the business. Records reflect only what is happening to the company and not the personal transactions entered into by people related to the company. For example, if the owner of a business buys a home, this purchase has no bearing on what is happening to the business, since the owner is an entity separate and distinct from the business entity.

A business may be operated under any one of several legal forms, such as a *corporation* (owned by shareholders), a *partnership* (having two or more owners), or a *proprietorship* (having one owner). Regardless of legal status, the business-entity concept applies.

The Accrual Principle

The accrual principal is based on the fact that the net income of a business is related not to the flow of cash but rather to changes in the owners' equity resulting from the operations of a business. Revenue of a business adds to the owners' equity, and expenses decrease the owners' equity. The difference between revenue and expenses is the company's *net income.*

Two other generally accepted principles also relate to the accrual concept:

- The *realization concept* states that revenue is recognized when goods are delivered or when services are performed. It doesn't specifically relate to the specific date when cash is received for the sale of goods or services.

- The *matching concept* states that expenses of a period are costs associated with the revenues or activities of that period. The expenses don't relate to the actual cash disbursements for those expenses.

Most entities account for revenues and expenses as well as cash receipts and cash payments. Many individuals and some small businesses keep track only of cash receipts and cash payments. This type of accounting is called *cash accounting.* If you record your deposits, the checks you write, and your balance in a bank account, you're doing cash accounting.

To measure the income of a period, a company must measure revenues and expenses, and this requires the use of *accrual accounting.* Under this system, income and expenses are allocated to the periods to which they apply, not to the date when payment is made or income received. Accrual accounting is the only method that measures true changes in owners' equity.

ACCOUNTING REPORTS

Balance Sheet

Format. Accounting information is given to third parties outside the company on three main financial statements: balance sheet, income statement, and statement of cash flows. Those who set up such reports must follow the format required by their employers and store the format in their computers for subsequent use.

One of the reports, the *balance sheet,* shows a company's assets, liabilities, and owners' equity *at a given time.* It therefore presents the company's financial position at a specific moment, while recognizing that events may subsequently occur that will change certain aspects of the items of value that a company owns, as well as claims against those assets by creditors and owners.

The arrangement of information in the illustration Balance Sheet is fairly typical, although it's also common to find the assets listed on the left-hand side of a page and the liabilities on the right-hand side. In either case, the dual-aspect principle described earlier (see Dual-Aspect Concept) is followed, and the total dollar amount of assets will equal the total amount of liabilities and owners' equity. The totals, however, don't indicate the company's financial condition. Only after analysis of the various accounts listed on the balance sheet can you come to any conclusions about the financial health of a company.

Balance sheet accounts. A balance sheet showing a number of items becomes more useful when the items are classified into significant groups of assets and liabilities. It would be possible to list each individual account receivable, inventory item owned, piece of equipment, and account payable, but this usually provides much more detail than is needed for a balance sheet analysis. For the practical purpose of making the balance sheet more informative, items are grouped into classifications. There's no limit to the number of classifications, but the ones in the Balance Sheet illustration are common.
Current assets. The first balance sheet classification is current assets. This classification includes cash and other assets that can reasonably be expected to be realized in cash or sold or consumed during the normal operating period of the business, usually one year. Current assets may be subclassified as indicated in the following list:

- *Cash:* This includes all cash owned by a company, including cash in the bank (in a checking or savings account) and petty cash. The

ANDREWS MANUFACTURING COMPANY
Balance Sheet
December 31, 2001

ASSETS

Current Assets
Cash		$ 10,000
Marketable Securities		13,000
Accounts Receivable, net		72,000
Inventories		101,000
Prepaid Insurance		3,000
Total Current Assets		199,000

Fixed Assets
Land	$ 120,000	
Buildings	500,000	
Furniture and Fixtures	73,000	
Equipment	104,000	
	797,000	
Less: Accumulated Depreciation	407,000	
Total Fixed Assets		390,000

Other Assets
Long-Term Investments	93,000	
Long-Term Receivables	10,000	
Goodwill, net of Amortization	72,000	
Other Assets	17,000	
Total Other Assets		192,000

TOTAL ASSETS		$781,000

LIABILITIES & OWNERS' EQUITY

Current Liabilities
Accounts Payable		$ 53,000
Bank Loan Payable		100,000
Accrued Wages and Salaries Payable		7,000
Current Portion of Mortgage Payable		5,000
Taxes Payable		10,000
Total Current Liabilities		175,000

Long-Term Liabilities
Mortgage Payable	$200,000	
Bonds Payable	150,000	
Total Long-Term Liabilities		350,000

Total Liabilities		525,000

Shareholders' Equity
Capital Stock	100,000	
Retained Earnings	156,000	
Total Shareholders' Equity		256,000

TOTAL LIABILITIES AND SHAREHOLDERS' EQUITY		$781,000

Balance Sheet

amount of cash a company has will change through the receipt of cash for sales and the payment of bills with cash (or checks). An adequate amount of cash is vital to a company's survival, and sufficient amounts should be available to meet the immediate needs of the company's operations.

- *Marketable securities:* If a company has more cash on hand than it needs for the immediate future, it may use the excess cash to purchase short-term investments, such as certificates of deposit or stock or indebtedness of other companies. The investing company earns short-term returns, such as interest or dividends, just as an individual's savings account in a bank earns interest. These investments can be readily sold in the marketplace and converted back into cash on very short notice.

- *Accounts receivable:* This account often constitutes a large portion of a company's current assets and represents amounts of money owed to the company by its customers. It's generally collectible within the next 12 months. This account is reported as its *net value,* which means that the actual value of the receivables has been reduced by an amount equivalent to the company's expectations of receivables that will not be paid. A company maintains detailed records of accounts receivable by customers in a subsidiary accounts receivable ledger. This subsidiary record has a page devoted to each customer and lists all sales "on account" as well as cash collections related to these sales. The total of every page balance in the subsidiary ledger is shown as the amount owed to the company as total accounts receivable.

- *Inventories:* Inventories often represent the largest portion of current assets for a company. For manufacturing firms, inventories include raw materials to be converted into a finished product, work-in-process inventories that include partially completed products, and finished products ready for sale. Inventories generally can't be converted into cash as quickly as receivables, since it takes time for the goods to be sold (usually resulting in an account receivable) and for the cash to be collected.

- *Prepaid items:* This represents prepayments for resources such as rent, interest, insurance, and deposits that will be used up during the next 12 months. When they're *prepaid,* they haven't yet been used up or consumed, so they're still assets (items of value) to the company. They're rarely converted into cash (although conversion is possible) and are therefore listed last under current assets.

Fixed assets. The next major asset classification is fixed assets, which may also be called *plant assets; property, plant, and equipment;* or *tangible fixed assets.* Fixed assets are relatively long-lived assets that are held for use by the business in the production of goods, sale of goods, or services. They're not acquired for resale in the ordinary course of business but must have a useful life of at least one year. The reported value of fixed assets is based on the amount it cost the company to acquire them, called the *historical,* or *acquisition, cost.* Items in this category include the following:

- *Land:* On which the company may have already constructed buildings
- *Buildings:* Office or plant locations used in routine business operations
- *Furniture and fixtures:* Desks, chairs, and similar furnishings used by company personnel
- *Equipment:* Office or production machines used by the company

Fixed assets, other than land, are assumed to have limited lives because time, obsolescence, and normal use eventually reduce their benefit to the business. Those assets are therefore called *depreciable assets.* The process of allocating the cost of these assets ratably to the accounting periods in which they are consumed and benefit the company is called *depreciation.*

Depreciation expense is taken each accounting period as an expense on the income statement and results from an attempt to allocate systematically the asset's acquisition cost over its anticipated useful life. The depreciation accumulated from all previous periods appears on the balance sheet as a reduction of the related fixed asset account cost. This yields the *book value* to the company at the balance sheet date.

The useful life of an asset is an estimate and is subject to many uncontrollable external factors such as obsolescence, technological advancements, and unexpected wear and tear. Therefore, the balance sheet value of fixed assets doesn't necessarily represent the value a company would receive if the asset were to be sold at the balance sheet date.

Other assets. Other assets, if reported at all, refers to miscellaneous assets that are difficult to classify as either fixed or current assets. Investments, long-term receivables, and goodwill are examples of assets that the company intends to hold for more than one year. Investments may include securities of other companies that the business has invested in or that the employer owns or controls and which don't have a readily ascertainable market value. Long-term receivables may indicate the sale of expensive items for which payments are spread out over more than one year.

Goodwill is associated with the price paid by one company to purchase another and is often higher than the value of the net physical assets acquired. The excess amount paid is called *goodwill* and reflects the purchaser's belief in the company's potential to earn high profits.

Current liabilities. Claims of creditors against the assets of the business are known as *liabilities*. Current debts or obligations that must be paid or otherwise settled within one year or the normal operating cycle of a business are called *current liabilities*. The latter are the company's most immediate obligations, and cash or other current assets are necessary to liquidate them. These claims are usually not against a specific asset of the company. Within the classification of current liabilities there are several subclasses:

- *Accounts payable:* This represents amounts owed to ordinary business creditors for purchases of inventory and supplies. If the claim is evidenced by a note or other written document, it's usually segregated as a note payable.

- *Bank loan payable:* This represents money owed by the company to its bank. Because it's shown as a current liability, it implies that it's payable within one year.

- *Accrued wages and salaries payable:* This refers to amounts owed to employees of the business at the time the balance sheet was prepared. An example of this is when employees are paid on a weekly basis and the balance sheet has been prepared at a point during one of the pay periods. As a result, wages and salaries owed to employees but not yet paid to them are recorded as a liability.

- *Current portion of long-term debt:* This amount represents the portion of the long-term debt principal (not interest) payable within 12 months of the balance sheet date.

- *Taxes payable:* This amount is owed but not yet paid to the federal, state, or local government for taxes due on income, payroll, inventory, and so on.

- *Unearned revenues:* These are obligations to provide goods or services to customers who have made advance payments. For example, subscription receipts that have been received by a magazine publisher in advance of sending the magazine issues are unearned revenues. Rent that is received in advance by a landlord is another example of this type of liability.

Long-term liabilities. These claims against assets are due to be paid after the next 12 months. This category includes property mortgages payable, long-term loans payable, notes payable, and bonds or debentures payable.

Unlike accounts payable, these liabilities tend to be evidenced by formal documents indicating a definite obligation to pay at some future time. Often long-term liabilities are a guaranteed claim against some specific assets, known as a *lien*. Any portion of long-term payables becoming due within one year from the balance sheet date should be included in the current liabilities category. Any amount recorded here represents only the principal amount due.

These types of obligations usually have an interest payment associated with them. The interest due is not recorded on the balance sheet, however, because interest relates to the use of money or funds over time. Interest is not initially recorded until your company has had the use of someone else's funds for a certain period. Then the expense is recorded in the income statement and the payable is recorded separately as a current liability.

Owners' equity. The owners' equity section of the balance sheet represents claims made against the assets by the owners of the business and is simply the portion of the company not claimed by anyone else. It is also known as *book value* or *net worth*. The manner of reporting owners' equity on the balance sheet depends on the type of business for which the balance sheet is prepared and whether it is organized as, for example, a sole proprietorship, partnership, corporation, or limited liability company (LLC).

The owners' equity section of Andrews Manufacturing Company in the illustration Balance Sheet indicates that it's organized as a corporation. Corporations are created under, and regulated by, state and federal laws. These laws require that a distinction be made between the amount invested in the corporation by its owners (the original shareholders) and the increase or decrease in owners' equity due to daily operations.

The amount invested by the owners, called *capital stock*, is entered on the balance sheet at its stated value, which might be the price paid for the stock, its par value, or some other figure agreed upon at the time the stock was issued or sold. Subsequently, there is no relationship between the recorded value and the market value of the stock. The increase or decrease in owners' equity due to daily operations, called *retained earnings*, reflects the earnings of the company from daily operations in prior years that have been left in the business and have not been paid out to the owners in the form of dividends.

The word *surplus* was used in place of *retained earnings* in the past but is not in current use today. Retained earnings or accumulated amounts of net income belong to and are a claim of the company's owners, and they're always shown after capital stock in the owners' equity section of the balance sheet.

When a business is owned by one person, it's called a *sole proprietorship*, and the sole proprietor's equity may be reported on the balance sheet in either of the following two ways:

I. Ryan Andrews, capital	$256.000

2. Ryan Andrews, capital, January 1, 2001	$200,000
Net income for the year ended December 31, 2001	$323,000
Withdrawals	267,000
Excess of earnings over withdrawals	56,000
Ryan Andrews, capital, December 31, 2001	$256.000

When two or more persons own a business as partners, changes in their equities resulting from earnings and withdrawals are normally shown in a supplementary financial statement entitled the *statement of partners' equity*. Only the amount of each partner's equity and the total equities are shown on the balance sheet itself:

Partners' Equity

Ryan Andrews, capital	$128,000
Daniel Andrews, capital	128,000
	$256.000

Thus in the owners' equity section of the balance sheet, capital (cash or assets) contributed by the owners of the company, as well as earnings accumulated since the business began, are accumulated as claims against assets.

Income Statement

A second type of financial statement, the *income statement*, presents the results of a company's operations for a given period: a month, three months, or a year. The last day of that period will be the date of the balance sheet information that accompanies the income statement. The income statement is also known as the *profit and loss report, P&L,* or *statement of revenues and expenses.*

This statement presents sales, the cost of the specific goods or services sold, the other costs associated with selling the goods or services, and the resulting profit or loss (net income, bottom line, or net profit). Thus this statement shows all sources of revenue generated by the company's operations as well as all related expenses incurred to generate that revenue. The format and specific revenue and expense classifications will vary, but the Income Statement illustration is fairly typical.

ANDREWS MANUFACTURING COMPANY
Income Statement
for the Year Ending December 31, 2001

Gross Sales		$3,600,000
Less Sales Returns, Allowances, and Discounts		250,000
Net Sales		3,350,000
Less Cost of Goods Sold		1,650,000
Gross Profit		1,700,000
Less Operating Expenses		
Selling, General, and Administrative Expenses		
Insurance	$ 12,000	
Office Salaries	311,000	
Selling Expense	175,000	
Heat, Light, and Power	23,000	
Advertising	165,000	
Telephone	57,000	
Office Supplies	17,000	
Automobile Expense	30,000	
Bad Debt Expense	97,500	
Travel Expense	133,000	
Depreciation Expense	20,000	
Miscellaneous Expense	53,500	
Total Selling, General, and Administrative Expenses		1,094,000
Research and Development Costs		250,000
Other Operating Expenses		16,000
Total Operating Expenses		1,360,000
Operating Profit		340,000
Other Income and Expenses		
Interest Expense	100,000	
Interest Income	(73,000)	
Miscellaneous Income	(10,000)	
Total Other Income and Expenses		17,000
Profit Before Taxes		323,000
Provision for Corporate Income Taxes		147,000
Net Income		$ 176,000

Income Statement

Accounting Period

Income statement periods. For most businesses, the official accounting period is one year. However, income statements, considered *interim statements,* are usually prepared for shorter periods. For example, most companies have income statements prepared on a monthly basis to report the operation of the business during the past month. Thus the accounting period covered in a monthly income statement is one month. The report is prepared from information accumulated in the accounts of the business. Information often must be reported to various government agencies and banks on a monthly or quarterly basis, so income statements are often generated for these reasons as well.

Common accounting periods. For most companies, the accounting period is a *calendar year,* the year that ends on the last day of the calendar, December 31. Some companies, however, end their year at the end of their busy season. This is called a *fiscal year end.* Colleges and universities, for example, usually have a June 30 year end. Retailers often end their year at the end of January. Sports-related businesses end their year at the end of the month that their season ends. The accounting period for these businesses is a *natural business year,* not a calendar year.

The fact that accounting assigns events to a set period makes the problem of measuring revenue and expenses into that period one of the most difficult problems in accounting, but it doesn't affect the daily operations of the company. In rare instances, an accounting period may extend beyond one year if the business activities of the company extend beyond 12 months from the time the transaction is initiated until it is completed. This situation occurs in companies dealing with long-term contracts or in companies whose production processes are lengthy. Therefore, if your company falls into this category, the accounting period and the income statement covered by it may extend beyond 12 months.

Income Statement Accounts

Sales. The first entry on the income statement is sales for the period. It's customary to show gross sales revenue earned by the accrual method and then to deduct any returns; allowances, such as price reductions; and discounts given during the period to arrive at net sales. By showing sales returns and allowances separately, attention is called to any unusual amounts (increase) shown in this category.

Sales revenues are inflows of cash and other assets received from others for goods exchanged or services performed. The result is an increase in total assets, a decrease in total liabilities, or a combination thereof. Terms such as *income, revenue, earned,* and *received* preceded by a noun such as *rent, interest,* or *commissions* identify a revenue source. Revenues derived from sales to customers are often described as *sales revenue, fees earned,* or *commissions earned* in the income statement. Other revenues unrelated to customer sales include *commissions earned, dividends received, interest income,* and *rental revenue.*

Expenses. In accounting, *expenses* are the outflow of cash or other re-sources of a business during a specific period. The accrual principle is therefore followed. Expenses relate to the consumption of assets or the in-currence of debt for goods or services consumed by the company to pro-duce revenue. The common classifications of expenses are as follows:

Cost of goods sold. This represents the cost of purchasing goods for resale as well as the cost incurred in manufacturing products for sale to cus-tomers. This category should include, to the extent possible, only the costs associated with goods sold during the *current* accounting period. In a manufacturing company, such costs include raw materials, direct labor, and manufacturing overhead. Manufacturing overhead includes all allo-cated product-related costs other than raw materials and direct labor, in-cluding indirect labor, fringe benefits, supervision costs, plant rent, in-surance, freight, light and power, plant depreciation, quality assurance, and shipping. The cost of any goods remaining on hand at the end of the period is shown as inventory in the current assets section of the balance sheet.

Gross profit. This represents the amount of sales revenue realized in excess of the cost of goods sold. This amount must exceed the amount of all remain-ing expenses of operating the business if the business is to be profitable. Gross profit is also known as *gross margin.*

Operating expenses. Operating expenses are incurred in the normal opera-tions of the business. Operating expenses are not incurred in producing a product. Rather, they're considered costs of the period. They're often sub-classified by function, such as selling and distribution, research and devel-opment, and general and administration expenses.

- *Selling expenses* include all expenses incurred during the period to perform the sales activities of the firm, including salaries paid to sales people, commissions, rental of sales facilities, depreciation on sales equipment, and advertising costs.

- *General and administrative expenses* are those incurred during the year in administering overall company activities, including office supplies, officers' salaries, depreciation of the office building and equipment, rental of office space, property taxes, legal fees, account-ing fees, office employee salaries, and related fringe benefits.

- *Research and development (R&D) expenses* are incurred by the com-pany in pursuit of further improvement of existing products or development of new products and include salaries of R&D person-nel, facilities and equipment expense, and other expenses of research and development efforts.

Operating profit. This represents profit earned from the normal business operations of the firm. It represents sales revenues minus the cost of goods sold and operating expenses. Operating profit also may be called *income from operations* or *net operating revenue.*

Other income and expenses. This refers to *nonoperating sources of revenues or expenses* not resulting from the daily operations of the business. It includes items such as interest income from investments, interest expense on loans or other outstanding debts, profit or loss on the sale of fixed assets, and revenue from nonrelated business operations. These items are listed separately to highlight their difference from other revenue and expenses related to the business' primary operations.

Profit before taxes. This is the net difference between all revenues and expenses of the business and also may be called *income before taxes.*

Provision for corporate income taxes. Included in this classification are all federal corporate income taxes. Local and state income taxes are included here or are included with general and administrative expenses. If the company is a sole proprietorship or partnership, the business pays no taxes. Rather, the owners include their pro rata share of the business profit (or loss) on their personal tax returns and pay taxes on this profit individually.

Net income. Also known as *net profit* or *"the bottom line,"* net income represents the amount of profit the company has earned for the period covered by the income statement.

Statement of Cash Flows

A third type of financial statement is the *statement of cash flows.* Although this financial statement must be presented with the balance sheet and income statement under generally accepted accounting principles, it's not regularly used by management. The statement presents the sources and uses of cash and cash equivalents of a company for the same period covered by the income statement. This information helps inform its readers about events that have occurred within the company that affect cash balances but that are not reflected in the other two financial statements or are not related to the items a company owns at a specific time and not related to the results of operations for a certain period.

This financial statement is also known as the *source and application of funds statement* or the *"where got — where gone" statement.* See the illustration Statement of Cash Flows.

SYSTEMS AND PROCEDURES

Office professionals who are familiar with accounting as the language of business are better able to handle the many duties and functions they

ANDREWS MANUFACTURING COMPANY
Statement of Cash Flows
for the Year Ending December 31, 2001

Cash Balance, January 1, 2001			$ - 0 -

Cash Flows Generated (Used) from Operating Activities

Net Income for the Period		$176,000	
Adjustments to Reconcile Net Income to			
Net Cash Provided by Operations:			
Depreciation		20,000	
Decrease in Marketable Securities		10,000	
Increase in Accounts Receivable		(30,000)	
Decrease in Inventories		19,000	
Increase in Prepaid Insurance		(3,000)	
Decrease in Accounts Payable		(30,000)	
Decrease in Accrued Salaries Payable		(2,000)	
Decrease in Taxes Payable		(2,000)	
Cash Flows Generated from Operating Activities			$158,000

Cash Flows Generated (Used) from Financing Activities

Increase in Mortgage Payable, net of repayments		$ 75,000	
Decrease in Bonds Payable		(77,000)	
Sale of Common Stock		50,000	
Cash Flows Generated from Financing Activities			48,000

Cash Flows Generated (Used) from Investing Activities

Purchases of Fixed Assets		$(153,000)	
Purchases of Long-Term Investments		(43,000)	
Cash Flows (Used) from Investing Activities			(196,000)
Net Cash Generated (Used) for the Year Ending December 31, 2001			$ 10,000
Cash Balance, December 31, 2001			$ 10,000

Statement of Cash Flows

encounter. Included are activities related to handling cash, such as recording cash receipts and disbursements, controlling petty cash, and performing a bank reconciliation; recording investments in securities; and recording the acquisition of fixed assets.

An *accounting system* consists of all business papers, records, reports, and procedures used in recording and reporting transactions. With a computerized system, computers of varying sizes and sophistication are used to process information accurately and rapidly. This equipment has a large capacity to store data and the capability to manipulate and recall data with great speed. Computer processing involves the use of hardware (the central processing unit and related peripherals, described in Chapter 1, "The Online Office," The Computer), systems software (the computer programs that give instructions to the computer), applications software (such as a spreadsheet program), and other related items needed for system operations (such as training material).

Such equipment performs many functions that the accounting process requires. It can handle arithmetic procedures (add, subtract, multiply, and divide), memory storage (file maintenance, described in Chapter 10, "Information Management," Electronic Files), memory recall, comparison of information, repetition of the same set of instructions, yes-no decisions, and what-if analyses. See also Chapter 1, "The Online Office," The Computer, for a description of computer technology.

Computers process data with extraordinary speed and accuracy. Before they can do this, however, a human being must think through the procedures that the computer will use in processing data, anticipate every processing exception, and then instruct the computer in great detail how to do the job. Although computers are particularly helpful in the processing of accounting information, they are only as good as the people programming them and depend on the accuracy of the data being processed.

The Accounting Process

The basic accounting process is the same for all businesses, large and small. The purpose of an information processing system is to facilitate the accumulation of data needed to make decisions and to prepare financial statements. The basic components of that information processing system are the same. (See the illustration The Basic Accounting Record-Keeping System.) The components of the system include the following:

Component	Purpose
General journals and special journals	For formally recording the data obtained from the analysis of individual transactions.
General ledger	For accumulating and summarizing the data recorded in the journals in terms of the dual-aspect concept for the balance sheet and income statement accounts. There is a separate account page for each general ledger account. See the illustration General Ledger.
Subsidiary ledgers	To provide a detailed analysis of the balance recorded in a specific general ledger account (accounts receivable, notes receivable, marketable securities, inventories, fixed assets, and notes payable).

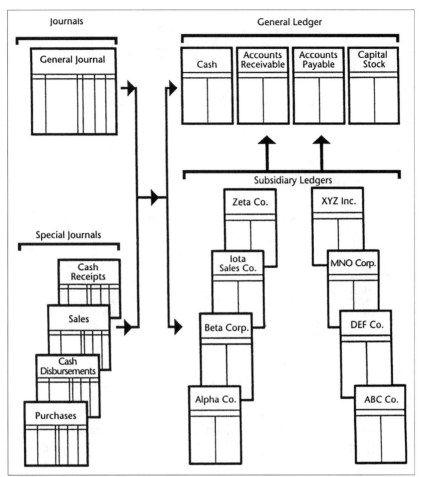

The Basic Accounting Record-Keeping System

When a company must record hundreds or thousands of similar transactions, such as credit sales or purchase of materials, the information-processing system must handle the transaction as efficiently as possible. This makes the use of special journals that record and summarize like transactions advantageous:

Transaction	Special Journal
Purchase of merchandise or raw materials on credit	Purchases journal
Cash payments	Cash disbursements journal
Credit (and sometimes cash) sales	Sales journal
Cash collections	Cash receipts journal

ANDREWS MANUFACTURING COMPANY
GENERAL LEDGER

AS OF 12/31/01   PAGE 1

ACCT NO.	ACCOUNT NAME	FOLIO		BALANCE FORWARD	CURRENT PERIOD	BALANCE
1000	CASH IN BANK			.00		
	INV REG SUMMARY	IR			.00	.00
1001	CASH IN BANK – CHECKING			.00		
	CHECKS FOR PERIOD	CD1			3,704.00-	
	RECEIPTS FOR PERIOD	CR1			9,191.00	
						5,487.00
1002	CASH IN BANK – SAVINGS			.00		
	CHECKS FOR PERIOD	CD2			.00	
	RECEIPTS FOR PERIOD	CR2			.00	
						.00
1100	ACCOUNTS RECEIVABLE –			.00		
	ALPHA COMPANY	CR1	12/04/01		730.00-	
	ZETON W.	CR1	12/20/01		1,000.00-	
	DELTA COMPANY	CR1	12/30/01		550.00-	
	INV REG SUMMARY	IR			.00	
	INV REG SUMMARY	IR			.00	
						2,280.00-
1200	MARKETABLE SECURITIES			.00		
	SALE OF MKT SEC	CR1	12/12/01		2,000.00-	
						2,000.00-
2000	ACCOUNTS PAYABLE - TR			.00		
	ABC COMPANY - NO. C370	CD1	#7031		1,313.00	
	MDSE PURCH SUMMARY	MP			.00	
	MDSE PURCH SUMMARY	MP			.00	
						1,313.00
2600	BANK LOAN PAYABLE			.00		
	BANK LOAN	CR1	12/21/01		4,500.00-	
						4,500.00-
3050	RETAINED EARNINGS			.00		
	PERIOD NET INCOME (CR) OR LOSS (DR)				1,980.00	
						1,980.00

General Ledger

The formats of special journals vary depending upon the needs of management. The two special journals discussed in detail are typical examples but may be modified to meet goals for cost and time savings.

Cash receipts journal. The *cash receipts journal* is used to record all cash receipts of the company. It's designed to handle not only payments of credit and cash sales but also other revenue sources. The procedures to follow in recording cash receipts are performed daily. (See the illustration Cash Receipts Journal.) In the journal illustration, the date and payer are entered first, followed by the general ledger account number and the subsidiary account number (if any). Following that is the amount as well as any discount amount, with the net amount recorded in the sixth column.

The columns in the cash receipts journal are totaled on a monthly basis, and the totals are recorded in the general ledger accounts. (The total of any miscellaneous account column would not be recorded in the general ledger since it would represent the sum of amounts already recorded in several different accounts.) Start a new page in the cash receipts journal each month and number each page sequentially.

ANDREWS MANUFACTURING COMPANY
CASH RECEIPTS
CASH IN BANK - CHECKING

AS OF 12/31/01   PAGE 1

DATE	PAYER	G/L ACCT	SUB ACCT	DETAIL	NET AMT
12/04/01	ALPHA CO	1100	C101	730.00	
		4010		7.00-	
					723.00
12/07/01	CASH SALE	4000			471.00
12/12/01	SALE OF MARKETABLE SECURITY	1200			2,000.00
12/20/01	ZETON W.	1100	C102	1,000.00	
		4010		27.00-	
					973.00
12/21/01	BANK LOAN	2600			4,500.00
12/30/01	DELTA CO	1100	C103	550.00	
		4010		26.00-	
					524.00
	BATCH TOTAL				9,191.00
	TOTAL				9,191.00

Cash Receipts Journal

Cash disbursements journal. The *cash disbursements journal* is used to list all checks written during the period. (See the illustration Cash Disbursements Journal.) In the disbursements illustration, the date, payee, and check number are entered first, followed by the general ledger account number and the subsidiary account number (if any). Following that is the amount as well as any discount amount, with the net recorded in the seventh column.

The columns in the cash disbursements journal are totaled on a monthly basis, and the totals are recorded in the general ledger accounts. (The total of any miscellaneous amount column would not be recorded in the general ledger since it would represent the sum of amounts already recorded to several different accounts.) Start a new page in the cash disbursements journal each month and number each page sequentially.

Both cash receipts and cash disbursements records may be simplified for a small company or greatly expanded for a larger, more sophisticated accounting system. The system should be designed to meet the needs of a particular company's managers and owners.

ANDREWS MANUFACTURING COMPANY
CASH DISBURSEMENTS
CASH IN BANK - CHECKING

AS OF 12/31/01   PAGE 1

DATE	PAYEE	CHECK NO.	G/L ACCT	SUB ACCT	DETAIL	NET AMOUNT
12/12/01	ABC CO - NO. C370	7031	2000			1,313.00
12/17/01	R.W. WALP	7032	6200			1,100.00
12/20/01	QRS CO – NO. 1107	7033	5000		750.00	
			5010		22.00-	
						728.00
12/21/01	BANK LOAN INTEREST	7034	6100			300.00
12/27/01	ACTON WATER DEPT	7035	6230			152.00
12/30/01	XYZ CO – NO. KBQ3	7036	5000		125.00	
			5010		14.00-	
						111.00
	BATCH TOTAL					3,704.00
	TOTAL					3,704.00

Cash Disbursements Journal

Petty Cash Fund

Many companies maintain small amounts of cash on their premises to cover small disbursements when it's impractical to write a check or when cash is needed immediately. These petty cash funds may cover the purchase of office supplies, postage, and so on. Also known as an *imprest fund,* the petty cash fund is normally established at an amount sufficient to cover two to four weeks of needs and is usually between $100 and $500. When a sufficient amount is determined, a check payable to "Petty Cash" is made out and cashed, and the cash is then placed in a locked box or drawer under the control of a designated employee who has sole responsibility for the fund.

Using petty cash vouchers. Only the designated employee may make payments from the petty cash fund, and this person must provide adequate documentation to support the payments. Often petty cash vouchers, purchased from any stationery or office-supply store, are used for such documentation. Each voucher shows the date, purpose of the expenditure, the department or account to be charged, the signature of the person receiving the cash, the signature of the person disbursing the funds, the amount disbursed, and a sequential voucher number. This information may be maintained on a separate disbursement sheet rather than on petty cash vouchers, but that practice is less common.

Replenishing the fund. At any time, the amount of cash on hand plus the amount of disbursements noted on the petty cash vouchers (or disbursement sheet) should equal the established amount of the petty cash fund. When the cash in the fund is low, it can be replenished by writing a check to "Petty Cash" for the amount needed to restore the fund to its authorized amount. The check is cashed, and the proceeds are placed in the petty cash box. The fund is then back at its original amount and is ready for use once again.

In some offices, the designated employee must prepare a list, or record, of transactions (as recorded on the vouchers) before a new check can be cashed. This record should contain (1) the amount in the fund at the beginning of the period; (2) an itemized list of each expenditure (date, voucher number, to whom paid, for what paid, amount); and (3) the balance in the fund at the end of the period (after deducting all the expenditures from the beginning amount in the fund).

Some people keep a handwritten or computer record during the period, recording each payment from the fund as it occurs, so that a final copy can be quickly prepared at the end of the period. For a handwritten record, use a columnar-style accounting sheet. For a computer record, set up columns like a table. In both cases, use the items listed in the previous paragraph as headings (date, voucher number, and so on), and fill in the appropriate information in the columns below each heading.

Investment Transactions

Many organizations invest in stocks, bonds, and other assets to earn a return on excess funds. It's important to record all information related to these transactions properly, not only for the company's financial records but also to comply with governmental agency requirements. When handling securities transactions, you should maintain the following documents or files:

- Keep a separate record for each security owned, and maintain the records in alphabetical order. Post all investment activity as it occurs. See the illustration Record of Securities Transactions.

ANDREWS MANUFACTURING COMPANY
Record of Securities Transactions

Security _____

Security Listed on [Exchange] _____

Broker _____

No. of Shares	Date	Purchase/ Sale	Price/Share	Broker's Commis.	Total Purch. Price Pd/Sales Price Rec'd

Cap. Gain (Loss) on Sale		Balance	
Short Term	Long Term	Shares Owned	Total Cost

Record of Securities Transactions

ANDREWS MANUFACTURING COMPANY
List of Securities Owned
December 31, 2001

Security	No. of Shares or Face Value	Securities Name and Description	Total Cost	Current Market Value
Stocks				
Bonds				
Investment Funds				
Other				
TOTALS				

List of Securities Owned

- Compile an alphabetical list of all investments in securities owned, and update it on a weekly, biweekly, or monthly basis, depending on the volume of investment activity. See the illustration List of Securities Owned.

- Keep a file of all brokers' confirmation notices. This is the basis for recording information in the individual securities records. A confirmation notice lists the purchase or sale of a specific investment, including the trade date, settlement date, purchase or sales price, broker's commission, and securities being purchased or sold.

- Keep a file of monthly brokers' statements that are verified by tracing to the individual securities records maintained by the company and noting agreement of month-end information.

- Keep a record of interest or dividend income received based on actual cash receipts and deposits into the cash account. See the illustration Record of Interest and Dividend Income.

- Keep securities certificates in a locked vault with access limited to a very few people. Access should never be permitted to fewer than two authorized persons accompanying each other.

ANDREWS MANUFACTURING COMPANY
Record of Interest and Dividend Income
Period Covered _____

Interest Income [grouped by security]

Security	Date Received	Amount	Annual Total

Dividend Income [grouped by security]

Security	Date Received	Amount	Annual Total
	qtr 1:		
	qtr 2:		
	qtr 3:		
	qtr 4:		
	qtr 1:		
	qtr 2:		
	qtr 3:		
	qtr 4:		

Record of Interest and Dividend Income

Fixed Assets Record

Records of plant assets having a productive or service life beyond one year must be maintained to insure the proper safeguarding of company-owned assets and to allocate properly the cost of the asset to the appropriate period the asset is benefiting (depreciation). Refer to the illustration Fixed Assets Record for an acceptable format.

The estimated life of a fixed asset is the period that the asset is used in producing or selling other assets or services. This period varies by type of asset

ANDREWS MANUFACTURING COMPANY
Fixed Assets Record

Asset Description:

Purchase Price [incl. freight & installation costs]:

Asset Location:

Asset Identification No.:

Estimated Life:

Depreciation Method:

Annual/Monthly Depreciation [if applicable]:

Estimated Salvage Value:

Disposition Date:

Sales Price When Sold:

Year	Original Cost	Depreciation Expense	Net Book Value	Sales Price	Gain (Loss) Upon Disposition

Fixed Assets Record

(buildings, equipment, furniture, or fixtures) but is usually standardized by company policy. *Salvage value* is that portion of the asset cost that is expected to be recovered at the end of the asset's productive life.

Allocating the cost of the asset over its service life (*depreciation*) can be done by many methods. Four methods traditionally used are the straight line, units of production, declining balance, and sum of years digits methods.

- When the *straight line method* is used, the cost of the asset minus the estimated salvage value is divided by the asset's productive life in years or months. This method allocates an equal share of the asset's cost to each accounting period.

- The *units of production method* divides the cost of an asset after deducting estimated salvage value by the estimated units of product that the asset will produce over its service life. This process gives depreciation per unit of product. Depreciation for the period is determined by multiplying the units produced in a period by the unit depreciation.

- Under the *declining balance method,* depreciation of up to twice the straight line rate, without considering salvage value, may be applied each year to the declining book value of a new plant asset having an estimated life of at least three years. If this method is followed and twice the straight line rate is used, the amount charged each year as depreciation expense is determined by (1) calculating a straight line depreciation rate (100 percent divided by the useful life in years) for the asset, (2) doubling this rate, and then (3) at the end of each year in the asset's life, applying the doubled rate to the asset's remaining book value.

- Under the *sum of years digits method (SYD),* the years in an asset's service life are added, and the sum is used as the denominator of a series of fractions used in allocating total depreciation to the periods in the asset's service life. The numerators of the fractions are the years in the asset's life in their reverse order. The following example shows the SYD method used to calculate the depreciation of an asset having a five-year life and a cost of $6,000 (Number of years for the denominator $= 1 + 2 + 3 + 4 + 5 = 15$):

Year	Annual Depreciation Calculation	Annual Depreciation Expense
1	5/15 × $6,000	$2,000
2	4/15 × $6,000	1,600
3	3/15 × $6,000	1,200
4	2/15 × $6,000	800
5	1/15 × $6,000	400
		$6,000

Business Law

Businesses must perform their activities in compliance with the laws and regulations that affect them. Office professionals, whether or not they work in a law office, will therefore benefit from an understanding of legal concepts and basic terminology. Also, those who are seeking certification, such as that of Certified Professional Secretary® (CPS®), may be tested on their knowledge in this area.

To deal with various documents and issues effectively and confidently, you need to be familiar with the general principles of contact law, agency, and corporate law. You also should be aware of a number of statutes and regulations that are generally applicable to the conduct of business. In particular, you need to recognize common legal documents, such as a contract, and be familiar with the terminology used in them.

CONTRACTS

The law of contracts is basic to business law, since the negotiation, preparation, execution, and performance of contracts are the foundation for much of the conduct of business. An understanding of the elements of a valid contract and its legal formalities will help you when your office is involved in producing and executing such documents.

An understanding of contracts may also be helpful in handling various aspects of office management. It's important, for example, in purchasing supplies or equipment and in dealing with human relations matters.

If your company executes a substantial number of similar contracts, such as an employment contract or an outside-services contract, you may have standard fill-in forms stored in your computer. In that case, you'll simply fill in the appropriate information in the required places. In other cases, an attorney may prepare a completely new document.

General Principles

A *contract* is an agreement that is legally enforceable. The essential components are (1) an offer, (2) an acceptance, and (3) consideration. A contract may be created by an oral promise or a written document, or it may be implied when the circumstances indicate. In any case, the object of the contract must not violate any public policy or statute.

It isn't always necessary to have a formal, written agreement for a contract to exist. The factors necessary to create an enforceable agreement include *parties* who are competent to contract, an expression of the *terms* of the agreement, and *consideration* for the agreement.

Consideration. The *consideration* for a contract most commonly consists of payment in exchange for services or goods or of a promise in exchange for another promise. Except in limited circumstances, if there is no consideration or if the consideration is regarded as inadequate, the contract will not be enforceable. The law considers that a promise not supported by consideration is a gift rather than a binding obligation, and the courts won't compel a party effectively to make a gift.

In spite of this rule, a contract under seal is considered enforceable without regard to consideration. (A contract *under seal* is a formal contract that either states that it is under seal, has an impression of a seal on it, or has the word *seal* or the letters *L.S.* printed on it.) Furthermore, the courts will rarely look behind a statement in a contract indicating that the parties believe the consideration is adequate.

Competency. Two issues are relevant in determining whether a party is competent to create a contract: whether the party has any legal disability, such as minority (not of legal age), mental incompetence, or intoxication, and whether the party has the proper authority to enter into the contract.

The issue of authority depends on the circumstances. An agreement made by an individual who is legally competent will be binding on that individual. Agreements made by corporations or other business entities will be binding if they are executed by officers, agents, or employees who have been authorized to bind the company, either under the rules of agency or by specific corporate action. For more about this, see the discussion in Agency.

Terms of agreement. No specific rules exist about the expression of the terms of an agreement, although it is often said that there must be a "meeting of the minds" to create a binding contract. Sufficient evidence therefore must exist to establish that the parties have reached an agreement even though all of the terms and conditions are not clearly defined.

Although the parties' failure to express the terms of their agreement adequately may result in a finding that no contract exists, a court will usually attempt to reconstruct what the parties intended *at the time they entered into the contract.* This is especially true when one of the parties has performed or partially performed its part of the agreement.

In certain instances, some of the terms of an agreement will be provided by statute if the parties have not expressed them. This is especially the case with regard to sales of goods under the Uniform Commercial Code. (See the discussion in Uniform Commercial Code.) It's generally more satisfactory, however, if the terms are clearly expressed by the parties.

Such a statement need not be extensive. A merchant's offer to provide a certain product for a specified price and a customer's acceptance of that offer by tendering payment or submitting a purchase order is a sufficient expression of the terms of the agreement. More extensive provisions, however, are necessary in more complicated relationships.

Formalities

A well-written agreement should follow certain rules of form, some of which relate to the elements described previously and some of which are simply good business practice. Many of the following suggestions about form can be varied to meet a particular situation or suit an individual's style and are intended to serve only as a general guide.

Introductory clause. The agreement should begin with an introductory clause that describes the agreement and identifies the parties. Some circumstances require inclusion of the full address of each of the parties. Even when such information is not required, it's good practice to include it.

The introductory clause provides an opportunity to assign a short, descriptive term to each of the parties, such as *Buyer* and *Seller,* as a means of easy reference throughout the agreement. The date should also be stated either in the introductory clause or in the testimonium clause. (See Testimonium.) The following example is a common form of introductory clause:

> This Agreement is made this third day of February 2001 between
> Hemingway Incorporated, a Delaware corporation with a usual place
> of business in Boston, Massachusetts, hereinafter called the
> "Company," and Peter F. Trombley, of 123 Park Street, Newton,
> Massachusetts, hereinafter called the "Consultant."

Individual or sole proprietor. The manner of identifying a party will vary depending on the legal status of the party. An individual should be identified by his or her name and, usually, residence address. If the individual is in business as a sole proprietor and the agreement relates to that business, the business address should be used.

Corporation. A corporation should be identified by its registered name, state of incorporation, and principal place of business. The name of the corporate officer who will be signing on behalf of the corporation should *not* appear in the introductory clause. The description of the corporation may be in the form indicated in the preceding example, or a more formal approach may be used:

> ... Hemingway Incorporated, a corporation duly organized and validly
> existing under the General Corporation Law of the State of Delaware
> and maintaining a usual place of business at 73 Tremont Street,
> Boston, Massachusetts ...

Sometimes a corporation is organized under one name but conducts its business under a different name. The phrase *doing business as* is often abbreviated as *dba* or *d/b/a.* If the information about the different name is available, it should be included as follows:

> ... Hemingway Incorporated, a Delaware corporation doing business
> in California as Hemingway Business Forms, Inc., and maintaining
> a usual place of business at 1999 Wilshire Boulevard, Los Angeles,
> California ...

Professional corporations should be identified by their corporate names in the same manner as business corporations.

Limited liability company. The limited liability company is an increasingly common form of business organization. Like corporations and partnerships, it's authorized by state statute. A limited liability company retains most of the simplicity of a partnership and limits liability for acts or omissions of the business.

A limited liability company (LLC) and a professional limited liability company (PLLC) should be identified by their registered names.

Partnership. In most jurisdictions, general partnerships are not considered legal entities apart from the individual partners, and for purposes of bringing a lawsuit, each of the general partners must be named. A general partnership usually conducts its business under a trade name, however, and is referred to by that name in most agreements, especially when there are a large number of general partners:

> ... Thayer & Crispin, attorneys at law, a general partnership engaged in
> the practice of law ...

It's also appropriate to identify each general partner by name in an agreement (more common when there aren't a large number of general partners):

> ... Jean G. Thayer and Sandra Crispin, general partners engaged in the practice of law under the name of Thayer & Crispin ...

A *limited partnership* consists of one or more general partners who manage the business and can bind the partnership and one or more limited partners who have no managerial authority. The partnership name must be registered, usually with the secretary of state.

A limited partnership should be identified by its registered name, and the state of registration should be stated.

Trust. A number of different types of trusts may be formed, including general trusts, business trusts, and realty trusts. Generally, a trust does not have a separate legal identity, and an agreement involving a trust should be made in the name of the trustee:

> ... James P. Overmeyer, as trustee of the Adam Thomas Family Trust and not individually ...

Other fiduciaries. When a contract is made by any other fiduciary, such as the guardian of a minor, the conservator of an incompetent, or the executor of a will, the fiduciary should be named as a party and clearly identified as acting in a fiduciary capacity.

Recitals. It's common practice to *recite* the background of an agreement, the relationship of the parties, or other facts that tend to clarify the basis on which each party enters into the agreement. In addition, a recitation of the *consideration* for the agreement is often made, either as part of the preliminary recitals or in the body of the agreement (or in both).

Recitals are generally stated in one of the following forms, the first being the more traditional style:

Traditional Style

WITNESSETH:

WHEREAS, Seller has developed and markets a software program relating to legal time and billing that has been adapted for uses on the XYZ personal computer; and

WHEREAS, Buyer is a law firm that has need for a legal time and billing program for use on its XYZ personal computer and desires to acquire a license to use Seller's program;

NOW, THEREFORE, in consideration of the payment of the licensee fee by the Buyer to the Seller and of the mutual covenants and promises set forth herein, the parties agree as follows: . . .

Contemporary Style

RECITALS

a. The Seller is in the business of manufacturing headsets for use with tape-recording equipment and has the capacity to produce in excess of 5,000 headsets per week.

b. The Buyer is in the business of marketing tape-recording equipment to the general public and has need for headsets that can be used with its equipment;

c. The Buyer desires to reserve the Seller's capacity to produce 5,000 headsets per week on the terms and conditions of this Agreement.

The Parties therefore agree as follows: . . .

Body. The body of the contract contains all provisions relating to the actual terms of the agreement. There are no rules about format or style other than general rules applicable to all business documents. For more about style and the preparation of documents, refer to Chapters 6, "Document Creation," and 7, "Business Style Guide."

Testimonium. The *testimonium* is the clause that appears at the end of the body of a contract and before the signatures of the parties. Such a clause, in its various forms, serves to affirm that the parties are aware that they are entering into an agreement and that they intend to be bound by the terms of the written document they are signing. The following are common forms of testimonium clauses:

> IN WITNESS WHEREOF, the parties have hereunto set their hands and seals to this Agreement the date and year first set out above.

> IN WITNESS WHEREOF, the parties have executed this Agreement in duplicate the 5th day of June 2001.

The following forms, used for business entities, clarify that the agreement has been signed by officers or other such individuals authorized to sign for the organization:

> IN WITNESS WHEREOF, the parties have caused this Agreement to be executed by their duly authorized officers on the 1st day of February 2001.

> Joseph P. Smith, as trustee of the Smithfield Realty Trust, and George A. Grey, as President of George A. Grey Associates, Inc., have signed this Agreement this 3rd day of April 2001.

Frequently, the testimonium clause will state that the parties have *set their hands and seals* or that the document is to have the effect of a *sealed* document. The concept of a sealed document derives from early common law, which provided that the presence of a seal eliminated the need to prove that there was consideration to support the contract.

The effect of a seal and its necessity under current law depend on the circumstances and the applicable law of the jurisdiction. A seal is generally used to prove corporate authority. Most jurisdictions provide by statute that a statement to the effect that a document is sealed is sufficient to give it the force of a sealed document, even if no seal is actually included.

Signatures. The agreement should be signed by an individual who is a party or who is authorized to bind a party. The signer's name should appear below the signature line, and except when an individual is signing on his or her own behalf, the authority of the person who is signing should be indicated. The following example is a proper form for the execution of a document:

> Hemingway Incorporated
>
> By _____
> James P. Jacobs, President

In general, an agreement on behalf of the following entities should be signed by a person who fills one of the indicated positions:

Entity	Permissible Signatory
Corporation (including professional corporations)	Corporate officer
Limited liability company	Officer
General partnerships	General partner
Limited partnerships	General partner
Trusts	All trustees, unless there is evidence of authority to act alone
Estates	Executor or administrator

If one person is a party to a contract in more than one capacity, the best practice is to have the person sign the document on separate lines for each capacity. The description under a single signature line should make it clear that the person is signing in more than one capacity.

Attestations. Although signatures are not always required, they're often attested by witnesses to the signing. This may be helpful if later some doubt exists about who actually signed or the circumstances under which the document was signed. An *attestation* may be the signature of the witness under the word *witness,* or an attestation clause may recite any information that is relevant, such as the following:

> Signed, sealed, and delivered by the above-named Peter Gregory, in my presence, at Boston, Massachusetts, this 3rd day of June 2001.

Signatures of corporate officers are often attested by the corporate clerk or corporate secretary to verify that the corporation has authorized the document to be signed. The attestation takes the following form, and the corporate seal is embossed over the attestation:

Attest: [*corporate seal*]

_____
Clerk/Secretary

Acknowledgment. Some documents, most notably affidavits and documents dealing with real property, must be *acknowledged* before a public official such as a notary public or judicial officer qualified to administer oaths. An acknowledgment executed by a public official has the effect of verifying the facts stated in the acknowledgment, without the necessity of proving them by testimony. The following are common forms of acknowledgment:

Example 1

December _____, 20 ____

State of _____
County of _____

Then personally appeared the above-named James P. Jacobs and acknowledged the foregoing to be his free act and deed, before me,

_____
Notary Public

Example 2

December _____, 20 ____

State of _____
County of _____

Then personally appeared the above-named James P. Jacobs, Vice President and General Manager of Hemingway Incorporated, and acknowledged the foregoing instrument to be the free act and deed of the corporation, before me, _____
Notary Public

The following is a common form of acknowledgment for an affidavit or other statement of facts:

State of _____
County of _____

The undersigned, Lynn F. Greene, known to me and known to be the person who executed the foregoing document, personally appeared before me this _____ day of _____, 20 __, and stated that the facts stated therein are true to the best of her knowledge and belief.

_____
Notary Public

If the affidavit includes a statement by the affiant that the statements contained therein are true to the best of his or her knowledge and belief, it's sufficient to add only the notary clause at the end of the document after the signature of the party offering the statement. This should include a statement of the venue (state and county) and the language "Subscribed and sworn to before me," as well as the notary's signature and seal.

AGENCY

Businesses are regularly involved in arrangements with people or organizations that act in the capacity of agent or agency. The law of agency is concerned with a number of issues that are raised when an individual acts on behalf of another party.

Contract law and business relationships, for example, raise a number of questions that involve issues of agency, such as who is able to bind a corporation contractually. For many purposes, an employee is considered to be an agent of the employer, and office professionals should be aware of the potential consequences of their actions, especially when they have administrative or managerial responsibilities.

Legal Principles

Agent-principal relationship. An *agent* is an individual authorized to act on behalf of another party, and the party on whose behalf the agent acts is called the *principal.* The principal may be either an individual or a business entity.

When a valid agency exists, the agent can bind the principal, and the principal will then be responsible for acts of the agent that are within the scope of the agency or that occur while the agent is fulfilling his or her duties as agent. For example, if an office manager is authorized to order supplies and submits a purchase order, the principal is responsible for payment of the vendor's invoice.

In some forms of agency, the principal's liability to third parties for the acts of an agent may extend to acts not directly related to the agency, such as when an employee is involved in an automobile accident while making a delivery for the employer. In other forms of agency, the principal's liability to third parties may extend to acts not expressly authorized by the principal, such as when a managerial employee refuses to hire an applicant because of the applicant's race.

Scope of authority. An agent's scope of authority depends on the terms of the agency. In some cases, the agent's authority is a legal consequence of the relationship of the parties. Corporate officers are therefore agents of the corporation, and general partners are agents of the other general partners and of the limited partners in a limited partnership. In each case, the agent's authority to act for and bind the principal exists only to the extent that the agent is acting within his or her role as corporate officer or general partner.

Unfortunately, it's not always clear whether the agent is acting within this role, and that issue often leads to serious disputes. In other principal-agent relationships, the scope of the agent's authority is created by an express agreement and is, consequently, more clearly defined. For example, a homeowner may retain a real estate broker to find a buyer for his or her house at a certain price. The broker is the agent of the homeowner only for that limited purpose and, otherwise, clearly is not authorized to act for the homeowner.

Authority to bind a principal. Generally, an agent is able to bind a principal contractually only to the extent that he or she acts within the scope of the agency. To some extent, third parties that deal with the agent do so at the risk that the agent is acting outside the scope of his or her agency.

When it isn't clear from principles of agency that the agent is authorized to act as a consequence of his or her relationship to the principal, or when there's any other question of authority, a third party may require evidence of authority. An example of such evidence would be a certificate signed and sealed by a corporate clerk confirming that the officer signing an agreement is either generally or specifically authorized to do so.

In some circumstances, an agent can bind a principal even without express authority. The authority to do related acts may be implied from the express authority given to the agent, such as when an office manager's authority to hire a receptionist also implies the authority to fire the receptionist.

An *apparent agency* may exist when the circumstances lead a third party reasonably to believe that the apparent agent has the authority to act for another person who could, but does not, do anything to deny the agency. In some situations, a person will ratify (approve) the acts of another who purported to be his or her agent and thereby create an agency by ratification. In each case, the determination of whether an agency exists depends on the particular facts.

Principal's liability. The extent of the principal's liability for acts of an agent that aren't within the scope of the agency largely depends on the degree of control that the principal exercises over the agent. The strictest agency relationship has been traditionally referred to as a *master-servant relationship.* It exists when the principal exercises significant control over the conduct of the agent, such as by setting hours of work, providing tools or equipment, and supervising the work performed. It generally applies to employer-employee relationships.

In a strict agency relationship, as a result of the high degree of control and close supervision, the employer is liable not only for authorized contractual commitments made by its employees on its behalf but also for accidents and personal injuries caused negligently or intentionally by them during their employment. The employee need not be actually performing work for the employer at the time he or she causes personal injuries or similar damage. As long as a reasonable link exists between the activity and the employment, the employer may be liable.

In other types of agency relationships, when the principal exercises a lesser degree of control over the actual performance by the agent, such as those involving independent contractors, the scope of the principal's liability is correspondingly smaller. Even when the principal is liable to third parties for injuries caused by an agent, however, the agent is primarily liable to the injured party. When the injured party recovers from the principal, the agent may be required to reimburse the principal.

Power of Attorney

Many agencies are created by the use of a *power of attorney*, a written document by which another person is specifically authorized to act for the person signing the document. When a person is authorized to act for a definite and specified purpose, he or she is often referred to as an *attorney in fact* for such purpose.

No particular form is required to create a power of attorney, although certain governmental entities — most notably, the Internal Revenue Service — have issued printed forms that they require one use for matters brought before them. Any document intended to serve as a power of attorney should contain a clear statement of the powers and duties of the attorney in fact.

In executing the power of attorney, the formalities required to complete the act effectively should be observed. For instance, if the attorney in fact is given the power to execute a deed, an act requiring an acknowledgment by an official, the power of attorney must likewise be acknowledged. It's always important to provide an attestation by witness, even though it may not be required legally, since it may avoid questions later about the signature of the principal granting the power of attorney.

Execution of Documents

Whenever an agent is acting for a principal in the execution of a document, whether under a power of attorney or other agency, it's important that the fact of the agency be expressed. If it's unclear whether the agent is acting for himself or herself or for a principal, the agent may be personally liable on the contract. It's also possible that the principal will not be liable at all, which may be to the detriment of both the agent and the third party. For more about the execution of contracts, refer to the previous discussion in Contracts.

UNIFORM COMMERCIAL CODE

The *Uniform Commercial Code (UCC)*, a collection of laws relating to commercial transactions, has been adopted in varying forms in all states. It's intended to provide for relatively consistent regulation of commercial transactions among the various jurisdictions. The discussion here focuses on two areas covered by the UCC: transactions involving the sale of goods and secured transactions. These areas are relevant in most business environments and hence are of the greatest interest to office professionals.

Sales

Article 2 of the UCC applies to transactions involving sales of goods and has two basic functions. Broadly, it establishes standards of fair dealing among buyers and sellers primarily by imposing an overriding obligation of good faith and commercial reasonableness in sales transactions. Article 2 also provides definitions of commonly used commercial terms that serve to clarify the expectations of the parties and standardize terminology in the commercial world.

In addition to its general role, Article 2 has a more practical application. Although the law gives the parties wide freedom to set the terms of their agreement, it also recognizes that parties occasionally fail to provide for all contingencies. Numerous situations may arise when the UCC will come into play unless the parties agree otherwise.

Article 2, for example, contains rules for determining, in the absence of an express agreement, the following:

- Whether an offer has been made and accepted
- Where the goods are to be delivered
- What warranties are given or implied
- The buyer's right to inspect and reject goods
- The seller's right to withhold shipment
- Remedies for breach by either party

Frequently, the parties will intentionally omit a provision in a contract knowing that the UCC will govern or will specifically refer to the relevant section of Article 2 and incorporate its provisions into the agreement.

Security Interests

When your business finances the purchase of office equipment or similar items, or if the company takes out a loan for other purposes, the lender will usually require a security interest in the items financed or in the assets of the corporation. Article 9 of the UCC governs the creation of security interests and provides for a filing procedure by which such interests are perfected.

Except in very limited circumstances, one *perfects* a security interest by filing a financing statement with the appropriate governmental agency. The proper place of filing varies from state to state and may also depend on the type of collateral covered by the security agreement. To ensure proper filing, therefore, one must check the statute in effect in the place where the collateral is located.

Security agreement. A security interest is created by the agreement of the parties. The agreement should be in writing and signed by the debtor. The parties are generally free to set the terms of the security agreement, although certain provisions of Article 9, primarily with respect to the rights of third parties, will override contradictory provisions in a written agreement.

Generally, a security interest gives the secured party the right to repossess the collateral if payments are not made or if the debtor is otherwise in default and to receive the proceeds if the collateral is sold. If the security interest is perfected, the secured party may repossess the collateral even if it has been sold or transferred to a third party. (A security interest is enforceable against third parties only when it has been perfected.)

Financing statement. Most states have adopted some version of a relatively standard financing statement called a *Form UCC-1*. Since variations exist among the states, businesses should check the particular requirements of their states to determine which form must be used. If your company is frequently involved in UCC filings, keep the appropriate form on file in your computer.

The debtor must sign a financing statement, unless the security agreement signed by the debtor is filed with the financing statement. Often it's necessary to file the financing statement with more than one office, and a duplicate designated as Form UCC-2 is designed for this purpose. In addition, a Form UCC-3 may be used to continue, terminate, release, assign, or amend a previously filed UCC-1 financing statement.

REGULATION OF BUSINESS

Office professionals, like all employees, are affected by the various statutes and regulations that govern the conduct of business in their companies.

Some of these statutes and regulations may affect the conduct of the business generally, and others may affect only specific aspects of operation.

Some statutes, for example, govern the creation of business corporations and provide rules for the basic structure and functioning of a corporation. Another set of laws and regulations affects the offering and issuance of securities, and still other statutes regulate certain relationships between businesses.

Every business that has employees is required to comply with a variety of laws and regulations relating to certain aspects of the employer-employee relationship, such as payment of wages, hours worked, discrimination, worker safety, and benefits for injured workers. In fact, two areas that are likely to be relevant in any business are corporate law and the employment relationship.

Some enterprises are subject to regulation because of the nature of their business. Historically, the most common examples of this specialized regulation are telephone and utility companies, insurance companies, and banks. However, changes in technology and in federal and state law have altered the monopoly and regulatory status of many public utility, insurance, and banking businesses. Businesses dealing with consumers are generally subject to consumer-protection statutes, and those involved in hazardous operations may be required by law to follow extraordinary safety precautions.

Corporate Law

Corporations exist only if created in accordance with state law, and every state has enacted a statute that sets forth the requirements for establishing a corporation and maintaining its corporate existence. Most states have adopted the Uniform Corporations Act, with or without variations. General rules relating to corporate functions, such as stock issues or annual stockholder meetings, are also found in the statute.

Often, the corporation's counsel does much of the paperwork relating to the creation and continued existence of a corporation. However, you may see certain forms and procedures in your work as well, and the following general explanation may help you understand such matters more fully.

Organizational structure. A corporation is organized in three tiers consisting of the stockholders, the board of directors, and the officers:

- The *stockholders* own the stock, elect the board of directors, and must approve certain corporate actions, such as authorization of additional stock, mergers, or sale of the corporate assets.

- The *board of directors* is responsible for overseeing the operation of the corporation at all levels and elects corporate officers to handle the day-to-day affairs of the corporation.
- The *officers*, who generally include a president, one or more vice presidents, a treasurer, and a secretary or clerk, have duties given to them by the bylaws or the board of directors.

A small company may have only one or a few individuals as stockholders, directors, and officers. Large corporations may have a very complex organization of officers and directors and, usually, a large number of stockholders not otherwise involved in the business.

Charter. The charter document for a corporation is often called a *certificate of incorporation, articles of incorporation,* or something similar. It usually contains the following information:

- Name of the corporation and its purpose
- Address of its principal place of business
- Type and number of shares of corporate stock authorized
- Any stock restrictions or special rules for governing the corporation
- Names of the initial officers and directors of the company

The charter document must be filed with the proper state official, usually the secretary of state, and becomes effective upon approval. Amendments may be made by vote of the stockholders of the corporation and also must be filed and approved to become effective.

Bylaws. The corporate *bylaws* are the rules by which the corporation conducts its internal affairs. The bylaws, which must be consistent with state law, generally describe the relative functions and powers of the corporate officers, board of directors, and stockholders. Bylaws do not need to be filed and are effective upon adoption by the stockholders. They also may be amended by the stockholders or in some instances by the board of directors.

Securities law. Although the corporate structure is established pursuant to state law, one important aspect of the corporation operation — the sale of securities — is regulated under two federal securities statutes, as well as under securities statutes known as *blue sky laws*. The latter are in effect in every state.

In general, the securities statutes require that stock either be registered with a regulating authority or specifically be exempt from registration under the statute. Under federal laws, stock that is not exempt must be registered with the Securities and Exchange Commission (SEC), and each state has identified a state agency that enforces its blue sky law.

Registration. Registration of stock involves the preparation and filing of a statement and prospectus that fully disclose pertinent facts about the history of the corporation, its financial and business affairs, and similar information. Once stock has been registered, the company must continually update the information provided in the statement filed at initial registration.

Properly registered stock may be traded publicly, which means that it may be offered for sale to the general public. All stock traded on the major stock exchanges or sold over the counter is registered stock.

Exemption. The federal securities law and most of the state blue sky laws exempt private offerings or limited offerings from the registration requirement, although a corporation must meet strict statutory requirements to qualify for this exemption. Most small corporations whose stock is owned by a few individuals and is not offered for sale to outside investors would qualify for it.

Employment Relationship

The rights of employers and employees and their obligations to each other are governed in part by the express agreement of the parties; in part by statutory regulation by federal, state, and local governments; and in part by the common law. Although the agreement of an employer and employee generally establishes the terms and conditions of the employment relationship, that agreement may intentionally or inadvertently fail to address many issues that arise during employment. It may also include provisions that are unenforceable because they violate public policy or a specific statute.

In some cases, an *independent contractor* may do the work for a business. The performing party may be an individual or a separate business engaged to accomplish a particular task or project, without direct supervision by the business that engages the party. The independent contractor commonly uses its own equipment and schedules its work in cooperation with, but not under the direction of, the principal business.

The relationship between a business and an independent contractor is governed by a contract rather than by an employment agreement. Therefore, laws relating to employment relationships don't apply.

Employment agreements. The agreement between an employer and employee, like any contract, may be oral or written, simple or complex. For the benefit of both parties, the agreement should be as specific as possible with respect to the basic issues:

- What work is to be performed by the employee?
- Is there a formal performance review and evaluation?
- Is there a probationary period?
- What is the salary and when is it paid?
- Are there benefits such as medical and dental insurance, profit sharing or pension plans, and life insurance?
- What provisions are made for overtime work?
- Is vacation and sick time provided?

Within the limits of certain regulatory statutes, the foregoing are all issues that are open for negotiation, and it's a good idea to raise them early. The oral and written agreement of the parties with respect to these and similar terms and conditions of employment constitute the employment contract. If the employer has written employee policies, they, too, will be considered part of the contract.

If you're interviewing or hiring new employees, you're considered an agent of your employer, and what you say will be binding on the company. For more about the agent's authority to bind a principal, see the previous discussion in Agency.

In most instances, the relationship between an employer and employee is considered a *contract at will*. This means that either party may terminate the contract for almost any reason or for no reason. The agreement may require one or two weeks' notice, but generally no reason is needed to justify or explain the termination. However, problems may arise upon termination by the employer, even in an at-will contract, when the reason for terminating is prohibited by law or public policy, such as when the employer terminates an employee to avoid paying a large commission that is about to become due.

Wages and hours. An employee may not waive the protections established by the federal wage and hour laws. The National Fair Labor Standards Act, applicable to most employers having 15 or more employees and engaged in interstate commerce, establishes minimum wages for regular and overtime work. The Wage and Hour Division of the Department of Labor enforces the statute.

In general, an employer must pay its employees not less than the minimum wage for the first 40 hours of work per week. The employee must be compensated at one and one-half times his or her regular hourly rate for all hours worked in excess of 40 hours for the week.

In addition to the federal statute, state and local laws may regulate the maximum number of hours a person can be required to work, whether work may be required on holidays or Sundays, under what conditions minors may work, and related issues.

Employment discrimination. A number of federal and state laws prohibit discrimination in employment. The following are examples of important federal laws:

- *Title VII of the Civil Rights Act of 1964* applies to most employers having at least 15 employees and makes it unlawful to base employment decisions on or to discriminate with respect to terms and conditions of employment because of an individual's race, color, religion, sex, or national origin.

- The *Age Discrimination in Employment Act (ADEA)* prohibits most employers with 20 or more employees from discriminating against employees between the ages of 40 and 70.

- The *Equal Pay Act* is part of the wage and hour law and makes it illegal to pay unequal wages to men and women who do substantially equal work.

- The *Americans with Disabilities Act of 1990* forbids businesses with 15 or more employees from discriminating on the basis of disability and requires that places of business provide access for disabled persons.

Like the federal government, many states have similar statutes prohibiting discrimination in employment.

Enforcement procedure. The federal Equal Employment Opportunity Commission (EEOC) monitors compliance with Title VII, ADEA, and the Equal Pay Act. Many states have local agencies or commissions responsible for enforcing the state discrimination statutes.

The procedure established under most discrimination statutes requires the employee to file a claim with the proper agency within a relatively short time of the incident claimed to constitute discrimination. Generally, the agency then has the option to investigate, attempt to conciliate, bring a legal action on behalf of the claimant, or authorize the individual to bring legal action. The filing of the claim within the period established by the applicable discrimination statute is almost always a prerequisite for later court action.

Employer liability. When a supervisory employee is responsible for a discriminatory decision, the employer will be liable. The employer also will be liable for discriminatory acts by employees who aren't in supervisory positions if the employer is or should be aware of the conduct and does nothing to correct the situation. An employer guilty of employment discrimination may be required to hire or reinstate the affected individual, to pay back wages, and in limited circumstances to pay compensatory damages.

Some forms of employment discrimination are more obvious than others. Also, a pattern or practice that tends to affect any of the identified classifications can constitute prohibited discrimination, even if there was no overt discrimination against an individual.

Sexual harassment is a form of sex discrimination and exists when there are sexual advances, requests for sexual favors, and other verbal or physical conduct of a sexual nature. It's illegal if it affects the terms and conditions of an individual's employment or if it creates a hostile or negative working environment. Refer to Sexual harassment in Chapter 3, "Human Relations," for guidelines on steps that an employee may take to deal with this problem.

Worker's compensation. Worker's compensation laws have been enacted in every state. Although the statutes vary from state to state with respect to what kinds of employees are covered, how claims are administered, and what benefits are payable, they generally require that every employer maintain worker's compensation insurance to cover compensable losses of covered employees or their dependents. *Compensable losses* may be broadly defined as injuries or death from accidents or diseases resulting from an individual's employment.

Worker's compensation insurance. Businesses are required to cover most employees by worker's compensation insurance, whether they are employed by a private business or by a public agency. A few statutes exempt businesses with fewer than three employees, and some permit corporate officers, working partners, and owners of the business to be excluded from coverage. An employer may face significant penalties for failing to provide worker's compensation insurance, including fines, imprisonment, inability to raise defenses to a claim, personal liability of owners or corporate officers, and increased levels of compensation.

If an employee is injured on the job or suffers injury or disease resulting from his or her employment, the employee is entitled to receive compensation for lost wages, medical expenses, and rehabilitation costs. With few and limited exceptions, a worker's exclusive remedy against an employer for work-related injury is the recovery of worker's compensation benefits.

This means that the employee may not bring a personal injury suit against the employer, even if the employer was negligent or otherwise at fault for the injury.

On the other hand, workers' compensation benefits are payable regardless of whether the employer was at fault. In this system, an employee is assured of a reasonable measure of compensation to be paid without delay, and an employer is relieved of the burden of defending personal injury suits in exchange for providing the insurance that pays the compensation benefits.

The amount of benefits payable under worker's compensation is established by statute and depends primarily on the wage level of the injured employee but also may involve other factors including the type of injury, whether the employee is totally or partially disabled, and whether the disability is temporary or permanent. Usually, there's a ceiling on the amount recoverable for a single injury.

Worker's compensation insurance is available from private insurance companies and, in a few states, from a public fund. In addition, many states permit self-insurance by large corporations or groups of smaller businesses.

Most state worker's compensation statutes are governed by a board or commission and, in a few cases, by the courts. The usual procedure is for an employee to file a claim with the employer and the employer to notify the insurance carrier. The administrative agency responsible for implementing the statute receives reports concerning claims and resolves disputes concerning the extent or duration of the injury and the amount of benefits payable.

Unemployment insurance. The unemployment insurance system is part of the Social Security Act of 1935. Through this system, unemployed persons are paid a weekly income for a specified period. All employers are required to contribute a certain portion of an employee's wages to this fund. The amount of money that an unemployed person can collect is determined by the amount that was paid into the person's account by the employer when the person was still employed.

Index